Teaching and Learning Innovations in Higher Education

Teaching and Learning Innovations in Higher Education

Kayoko Enomoto, Richard Warner and Claus Nygaard

THE INNOVATIONS IN HIGHER EDUCATION SERIES

First published in 2021 by Libri Publishing

Copyright © Libri Publishing

Authors retain copyright of individual chapters.

The right of Kayoko Enomoto, Richard Warner and Claus Nygaard to be identified as the editors of this work has been asserted in accordance with the Copyright, Designs and Patents Act, 1988.

ISBN 978-1-911450-73-3

All rights reserved. No part of this publication may be reproduced, stored in any retrieval system or transmitted in any form or by any means, electronic, mechanical, photocopying, recording or otherwise, without the prior written permission of the copyright holder for which application should be addressed in the first instance to the publishers. No liability shall be attached to the author, the copyright holder or the publishers for loss or damage of any nature suffered as a result of reliance on the reproduction of any of the contents of this publication or any errors or omissions in its contents.

A CIP catalogue record for this book is available from The British Library

Cover design by Helen Taylor

Design by Carnegie Publishing

Libri Publishing
Brunel House
Volunteer Way
Faringdon
Oxfordshire
SN7 7YR

Tel: +44 (0)845 873 3837

www.libripublishing.co.uk

Contents

Foreword ix
Paul Bartholomew

Chapter 1: What Drives Teaching and Learning Innovations in Higher Education? 1
Kayoko Enomoto, Richard Warner and Claus Nygaard

Chapter 2: A Learning-centred, Five-tier Model of Innovation in Higher Education 19
Eva Dobozy and Claus Nygaard

Chapter 3: Is Higher Education Ready for the Transformed Learner Coming from 9–12? A Case Study 47
Lennie Scott-Webber, Pam Loeffelman, Dennis Runyan and Marilyn Denison

Chapter 4: Flexible Classroom Design to Facilitate Learning, Engagement and Integration of Knowledge and Cultures 83
Elena Forasacco

Chapter 5: Emergency Remote Teaching in Interior Architecture: A Necessary Shift 109
Selin Ust

Chapter 6: Best Practices of Teaching Diverse Cohorts in a Webcam-enabled Virtual Environment 129
Kristina Rigden

Chapter 7: Impacts of Using Technology-Enhanced Language Learning in Second Language Academic Writing at a Vietnamese University 147
Henriette van Rensburg and Triet Thanh La

Chapter 8: Using Arts-based Instructional Strategies in E-learning to Increase Students' Social-emotional Learning Outcomes 173
Beth Perry and Margaret Edwards

Contents

Chapter 9: Using a Community of Inquiry Framework to Foster Students' Active Learning   195
Giovanna Carloni

Chapter 10: An Innovative Assessment Method to Evaluate Independent Learning and Academic Writing Skills   209
Richard Warner and Kayoko Enomoto

Chapter 11: Affirm–Apply–Advance: Transitioning Undergraduate Students through their Theory-into-practice Journey   233
Michelle Bissett and Melanie Roberts

Chapter 12: An Innovative Model for University-Industry Collaboration in Course Design and Delivery   257
Sami Heikkinen

Chapter 13: Project-Based Learning in a Japanese University: A Disruptive Innovation in Business Education   273
Sarah Louisa Birchley, Keiko Omura and Kayoko Yamauchi

Chapter 14: Facilitating Active Student Learning Using Innovative Approaches in Pre-Service Teacher Education   301
Lana YL Khong

Chapter 15:
Innovative Assessment in Higher Education: A Public Dissemination Assessment Model for Language Students   323
Rhiannon Evans

Chapter 16: Teaching from the Native American Circle: An Innovative Teaching Framework   339
Diana Schooling

Chapter 17: Discovering Professional Musician Identity through Reflective Narrative Writing: A Case Study of Pedagogic Proficiency   357
Jennifer Rowley

Chapter 18: Using Fiction and Non-fiction Literature to
Teach Sensitive Health Issues in Teacher Education 375
Brenda Kalyn, Beverley Brenna and Judy Jaunzems-Fernuk

Chapter 19: Collaborative Enquiry-based Learning in an
Oral Health Program 405
Hanna Olson

Chapter 20: Transformative Inquiry through the
Human Curriculum 425
Judy Jaunzems-Fernuk, Stephanie Martin and Brenda Kalyn

Chapter 21: Using Cross-disciplinary Object-based
Learning to Create Collaborative Learning Environments 451
Judy Willcocks and Silke Lange

Chapter 22: Building Employability Skills through
Collaborative Group Work 475
Sarah Swann

Foreword
Academic Innovation as a Strategic Act

Paul Bartholomew

I should first of all acknowledge that I have a long association with the LiHE series of books, having written about a dozen chapters in the past and have edited about half a dozen of the books. That of course means that I have attended a number of the symposia, which I have found to be immensely valuable for my own personal development.

For me, the value of the LiHE book-writing process is multifaceted. Firstly, it yields a book – a compendium of practice accounts that are reflective, articulated with theory and are practice-based; these accounts are useful to others and have the opportunity to multiply the impact of innovative academic practice through wide dissemination. Secondly, the process of reflecting on one's work and 'writing it up' in a format such as this adds new value for the innovator-author; indeed, I have found that part of the process to be transformative. Thirdly, the LiHE process gives an opportunity for the innovator-author to immerse themselves in a community of practice and to grow as a result.

Consequently, because of my association with LiHE, I was delighted to be asked to provide a foreword for this book, not least because the methods used to replicate the 'LiHE process' this year has had to be innovatively adapted to meet the needs of the contemporaneous Covid-19 context. The innovation-upon-innovation context is laudable and, as I discuss below, resonant with our sector's higher education strategic needs.

As the Vice-Chancellor of one of the United Kingdom's most complex large universities, I have a strategic interest in academic innovation. If ever there was a time when higher education teaching needed to adopt innovative approaches and bolster innovation capacity – it has been during this period of the global pandemic.

But more generally I would contend that we, as universities, need innovators – we need to grow them, nurture them and reward them. Modern higher education is characterised by its need to be cutting edge, agile, (necessarily) efficient and (most of all) demonstrably effective. That requires an institutional capacity for innovation – and where does that innovation come from? Our people.

Individual propensity for innovation leads to institutional capacity for innovation. An investment in personal/personnel development to bolster the propensity for innovation is an investment in future gains on the bottom line, future gains in our students' experiences and indeed future gains in the quality of the working lives of staff/faculty. It is a win-win scenario.

So, can innovation as an academic practice be taught and/or strategically supported? Yes it can. At two universities, over the course of more than a decade, I have run staff/faculty development courses teaching how to become an innovator in higher education. Those courses have had a significant impact to individuals' capability for innovation, and thus for their institution's capacity to respond to desirable change and by so doing enhance the experiences of students and faculty and deliver business success.

As manager/leader in higher education, I know only too well the responsibility I have to set a context that nurtures the innovative capabilities of our faculty and other staff. Broadly, innovators will thrive in environment where they are 'willing', 'able' and 'allowed' to innovate.

To bolster 'willing' we need to ensure innovation is not penalised – we have a management responsibility to ensure the risk-taking that goes hand-in-hand with doing things differently is not discouraged. Indeed, we might consider incentivising innovation by making reference to it within the criteria for promotion.

To bolster 'able', we have to invest in staff/faculty development and we need to acknowledge that this investment can be direct – through the provision of courses, and indirect as we invest in staff/faculty so that they can participate in their community of practice – for example by ensuring development time is included within any workload allocation consideration and that travel and subsistence funds are available for participation in events such as LiHE book writing symposia (for example).

To bolster 'allowed', we need to look to our management practices and take steps to ensure that the nurturing-of-innovation perspective is operationalised within the full depth of the management strata within the university. From experience, I know that this is the most critical thing to get right.

Succeed in supporting staff/faculty to be 'able', 'willing' and 'allowed' to innovate and step towards success as a university.

I have contended above that innovators in higher education add real business value to their universities – this becomes all too apparent as one looks at the foci of the chapters in this book: how to use learning spaces effectively; preparing a pipeline of potential students; coping with Covid-19; student motivation; effective use of technology; collaborative practice; curriculum design; creativity; assessment design; identity; and evaluating the efficacy of a range of pedagogical approaches. All vital things for a university to do well.

If you are university leader, these author-innovators (and those myriad of fellow pedagogic innovators around the world) are the R&D wing of your teaching business, the solvers of some of your academic operations problems and a vital part of the life -blood of your main strategic asset – your community of people. An investment in them is an investment in your business capability.

Sometimes being an innovator in higher education can feel lonely and unrewarding and although outlets such as an LiHE symposium are validating and engaging, all too often innovation is happening in higher education as an unconnected process – disconnected from strategic intent, oversight or even any management awareness at all. And although I appreciate that most innovators would not necessarily welcome strategic 'oversight' of their work, I would like to encourage staff/faculty to get their work on the corporate radar, for doing so can often yield recognition and the ability to secure the vital resources of time and funding.

The lived experience of running a university is often realised as a series of problems to be solved. Of course, in the traditional sense, we as researchers solve problems – it's one of our main academic activities; but in the management sense we have daily problems to solve that are as never-ending as they are myriad: How do we grow income? How we grow margin from that income? How can we enhance students' learning experiences? How can enhance the working lives of our staff/faculty? How can we make a civic contribution?... To name but a few.

Managers and leaders in higher education are tasked with finding solutions to such problems and pedagogical innovators hold most of a university's potential to address these challenges. When I was teaching courses in how to become an innovator in higher education, I encouraged the participants to understand the way their university worked, what were the strategies? Where was there discretionary funding? How were they accessed? Who were on the committees that decided things? How can I access those people? And then, having come to an understanding of how to navigate the institution, how can one utilise that infrastructure and resource-base to support one's innovative practice? From that perspective, the innovator can acquire institutional sponsorship for their activities and indeed be formally recognised for their work.

Through that way of working, academic innovation becomes a strategic act – the innovator acts strategically, articulating their work (and value) with the requirements of their institution and university leaders, through their sponsoring/supporting/nurturing of innovators, make a strategic investment decision in the future of its business.

Win-win.

About the Author

Paul Bartholomew is Vice-Chancellor of Ulster University, where he was also Deputy Vice-Chancellor (Academic) and Pro-Vice-Chancellor (Education). Paul has worked at four UK universities, both in the field of staff/faculty development and in the field of diagnostic radiography education. Paul won a UK National Teaching Fellowship in 2004 for his own innovative practice. He is a Principal Fellow of the Higher Education Academy and a Fellow of the Academy of Social Sciences.

Chapter 1
What Drives Teaching and Learning Innovations in Higher Education?

Kayoko Enomoto, Richard Warner and Claus Nygaard

Introduction

Education is an important requisite for society to both endure and grow. This means not standing still, rather, as Serdyukov (2017:4) points out: *"[education]…must continuously evolve to meet the challenges of the fast-changing and unpredictable globalized world"*. Education is intertwined with economic development, being both a driver of such changes whilst, at the same time, being dependent on the economy to be able to fund and mobilise these changes. Furthermore, we cannot afford to 'rest on our laurels', amid the myriad global changes that the continuing effects of the Covid-19 pandemic have only served to highlight. All of us involved in the higher education sector must take stock of this fast-evolving situation so that universities can remain relevant to the needs of today and tomorrow. These needs can take several forms, such as economic, health and social needs, and responding to these needs is paramount, if universities are to survive and function efficiently. Universities' relevance in broader society is diminished:

- if their research and development does not sufficiently value-add to the myriad requisites of the broader world;
- if teaching and learning practices experienced at university do not help graduates both to obtain jobs and function appropriately in their career pathway; and
- if their uptake of technologies and digital forms of communicative interactions lags behind the demands of society.

In this rapidly changing and interconnected world, to remain relevant, universities need to be innovative across a whole range of requirements.

However, innovation should not be for its own sake but rather a change which adds value. The scope of the famous quote *"necessity is the mother of invention"* attributed to Plato, is extended by Hørsted et al. (2017:3) who point out that *"innovation = invention + value"*. Only when an innovation does add value in higher education or any other field, can it be perceived as being beyond a change just for the sake of a change. Never has this need-to-innovate been as strong as it is today, with the growth of information economies worldwide, demanding that we, as educators, stay relevant to the changing needs of our students. Moreover, our innovations need to bear in mind the requirements of university graduate attributes: *"a range of skills beyond those that are discipline-specific, such as those described as life-long learning, generic, transferable or 'soft skills'"* (Oliver & Jorre de St Jorre, 2018:821). The theme of employability, an issue which is widely addressed in this book, has been a motivating factor for the development of graduate attributes and in itself has functioned as one amongst many drivers for teaching and learning innovations in higher education.

Yet, there is another abstract concept, which has been assumed thus far, that needs to be unpacked here – the notion of innovation itself. Amongst a plethora of definitions, the following one succinctly outlines innovation in a multi-disciplinary context thus: *"the multi-stage process whereby organizations [in our case in higher education] transform ideas into new/improved products, service or processes, in order to advance, compete and differentiate themselves successfully in their marketplace"* (Baregheh et al., 2009:1334). Innovation is a must in higher education if we are to maintain our role as a leader in broader society (Lašáková et al., 2017), rather than a follower thereof.

A multi-disciplinary definition of innovation still sells us short somewhat in the field of higher education. However, there are two distinctive types of innovation which pertain to this field. The two types are what Mykhailyshyn et al. (2018:9) term *"innovations in education"* and *"educational innovations"*. This former type, innovations in education, relates to a broader educational context and includes such variables as innovations in academic infrastructure, technological developments, organisation, educational and legal oversight (Mykhailyshyn et al., 2018) and responses to government social and economic philosophies and policies. On the other hand, educational innovations relate more to the micro-level and can be seen in changes in methodologies, such as the medium of delivery (such as from face-to-face to online) and pedagogical practices that have a significant variance from more recognised practices and function in this competitive educational marketplace environment (Mykhailyshyn et al., 2018). Such an environment, with its twin goals of growing both effectiveness and market share, is one in which so many of us – in higher education – find ourselves.

Indeed, if we find ourselves speaking the 'corporate speak' of management, which aligns with the increasing perceptions (in many societies) of higher education being a commodity, as opposed to a human right, we run the risk of our innovations being driven by analytics (so easily created in this age of information technology), as opposed to the intangibles of the student experience. Short-term endpoints, such as course grades or grade point averages have, as noted by Blouin et al. (2009), the predictable consequence of short-term thinking by all stakeholders associated with the educational institution(s). For students, this can mean a focus on grade and questions like: *"I need to pass this course to get my degree. 50% is a pass. A pass is a degree. So, how much work do you think I need to do to pass this course?"* (Enomoto & Warner, 2013:185), rather than the more cerebrally stimulating type of question: *"How will I be able to use this material once I am in practice?"* (Blouin et al., 2009:1). The latter question type both recognises the link with and feeds-forward to the world beyond formal academic studies. Promoting and rewarding this type of thinking, in our innovations, can help students move beyond being rewarded mostly for 'discipline memory' and have a closer intellectual connect with the demands of the world beyond, and in so doing, enhance their employability.

The world beyond, both in a narrower employment sense for our graduates and in a broader sense for societies as a whole, requires that we continually innovate for our betterment. Innovation relates to sustainability in our future, and if we look at the human condition, we can see that, as Hoffman and Holzhuter (2012:3) in Serdyukov (2017:5), state, innovation: *"resembles mutation, the biological process that keeps species evolving so they can better compete for survival"*. In short, innovation in any form, including that with an educational focus, can be seen as an evolutionary requisite for our long term sustainability and endurance- we ignore being innovative at our peril. Moreover, we need to remember that the drivers of innovation are multi-faceted, yet characterised by a common goal of growth and development.

Chapter 1

The linkage between higher education and other foundations of society serves to remind us that much of what drives innovations in growth and development society-wide, is equally applicable to the higher education sector. Such engines of growth include cooperation and dialogue, positive role-modelling and governance, which is participatory (Lašáková et al., 2017). Likewise, there are barriers to innovations and growth in both higher education and broader society, which include inflexible control structures, lack of cooperation and being opaque as opposed to transparent (Lašáková et al., 2017). Hence, the drivers for teaching and learning innovations in higher education are mainly a mirror of societal drivers for innovations. They are part of the bigger picture of growth and development in the broader context of sustainability.

Nonetheless, there are peculiarities inherent within higher education, impacting on our innovative capacity, which make comparisons between our sector and industry inexact. As Layne (2015) observes, there is a certain irony, in that whilst higher education institutions promote critical and innovative thinking on the part of their students, the pace of innovations in higher education can often be somewhat slower when compared to innovations in the corporate or industrial world. Even if a higher education institution seeks a competitive edge, she notes, there could well be constraints such as drawn-out discussions, a reluctance to commit financial and human capital and administrative configurations levelled by governing bodies at the state, national or private levels. The slow changes, often characteristic of the higher education world, may often be beneficial to some institutions, who as Layne (2015) indicates, adopt a wait and see approach in their observations of others who are being experimentally innovative. Notably, this often slow and measured approach mirrors what Layne (2015:27) calls the: *"…fundamental purpose of institutions of higher learning, a deliberate, measured and considered examination of the human condition and ways to improve it"*.

In an extensively interrogated study on the tension between accountability and innovation in higher education, Findlow (2008:313) explores the struggle between the different but interconnected agendas- what she terms *"audit-driven accountability"* and academic (focused) innovation. She outlines the extent to which currently predominant models of sector-based higher education which are economic and bureaucratic can be inhibitory to quality-related academic innovations. Findlow (2008:213) exemplifies this – in a British context at least – when she shows how academic innovation can often be unrealised, due to sectoral and institutional tensions pertinent to *"cultural capital, trust, risk avoidance, ambivalence and subversion"*. A reluctance to innovate can be, as Tierney and Lanford (2016) stress, the result of certain elements of the global academy, being resistant to change, perhaps with a fear of 'rocking the boat' in the face of their own existing sectoral or institutional success.

Indeed, when innovative sectoral and institutional change does take place in higher education, it can be driven by substantial reflection determining a need for sweeping change. Perhaps this is reflected, in the earlier part of the twenty-first century, in the wholesale adoption of digital technologies. Such innovations have been seen in administration, in learning management systems and online or blended learning, in a 'need to stay ahead', more market-driven neoliberal environment, characteristic of many higher education sectors around the world. Accordingly, when we focus on drivers for change in the higher education sector, we should bear in mind that tradition has often acted as a brake on innovation, albeit seemingly less so in the teaching and learning sphere. Yet, that is not to say that just because of the power of convention, we should withhold or dilute innovation, suffice to say we need to bear this tradition in mind, which could be a point of difference between higher education and industrial innovations.

Seven drivers for innovations in teaching and learning in higher education

There are several internal drivers of innovation in higher education, some of which relate to both the sector itself and more hands-on drivers applicable to the pragmatics of context-specific teaching and learning strategies and circumstantial constraints. Also, many drivers pertain to external forces, such as graduate employability, with impacts on how higher education institutions deal with such drivers, both organisationally and in the classroom or other learning spaces. As one way to visualise this, Figure 1 illustrates multi-faceted drivers of innovation that share a common goal of growth and development in teaching and learning in higher education. In this section, we will examine seven of the many regularly overlapping drivers, with our focus of concern being teaching and learning practice perspectives (see Figure 1).

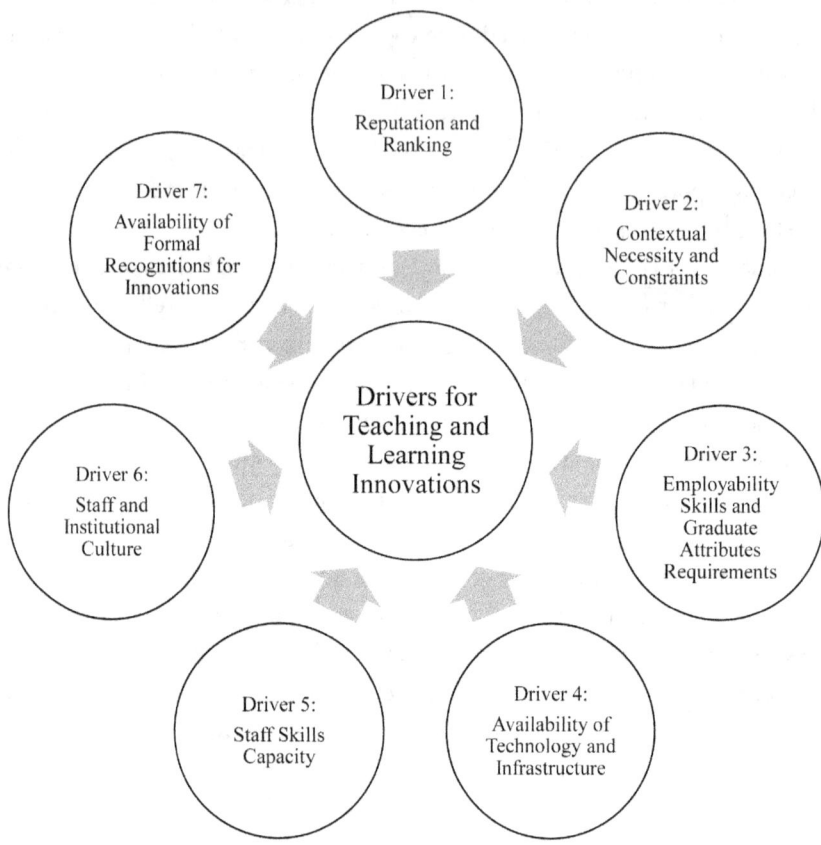

Figure 1: Seven drivers for teaching and learning innovations in higher education.

Driver 1: Reputation and ranking

The early part of the twenty-first century has seen for many of us, in different higher educational environments around the world, a significant shift towards higher education being viewed as a marketable commodity, which Lašáková et al. (2017:77) term an: *"education designated product"* and the student becomes a consumer thereof. One driver of teaching and learning-related innovations, emerging from this philosophical shift, is the growth in importance, both nationally and internationally, of higher institutional ranking indices. These international rankings, the best known of which is probably the Times Higher Education (THE) World University Rankings, use analytics across a range of categories to determine where the different higher education institutions rank against each other. THE publish their rankings yearly, and for teaching and learning related innovations, this can mean such indexed measures as student satisfaction that tends to derive from the quality of teaching that they experience. A reputation of having happy, satisfied students is often perceived as crucial in bringing about more excellent student recruitment opportunities both nationally and worldwide (and thus, bring in more university income). As innovators in the teaching and learning dimension, we are well poised to put into practice innovations to achieve high-quality teaching, that is not only pedagogically sound, but also correlates with increased student satisfaction ratings. They can make institutional administrators 'sit up', as they can boost institutional rankings in this sphere. Indeed, all of the innovations presented in this book can lead to the improvement of their own institution's reputation in various ways.

Driver 2: Contextual necessity and constraints

The pragmatics of circumstantial necessity and constraints can also drive teaching and learning innovations in higher education. As educators, we find ourselves at times forced to be innovative in adapting our curriculum designs and pedagogical approaches (in many cases without even intending to so). This happens when we face teaching and strategy-related necessities and/or context-specific constraints that are out of our control. Examples of such necessity and constraints include the accommodation of student disability-related issues, the inclusion of student diversity, a large class size, lack of staff resources and funding, and so forth. Nowhere is this more exemplified than in the Covid-19 'new normal' world. The pandemic has brought with it the need for universities worldwide to be adaptable like never before. Indeed, innovations in some chapters in this book (Chapter 5 by Ust; Chapter 9 by Carloni; Chapter 19 by Olsen; Chapter 21 by Willcocks & Lange) have been driven by the Covid-19 pandemic contextual constraints and the necessity to achieve the same level of student learning outcomes. These different authors express the face of innovative teaching and learning in this pandemic affected world.

Driver 3: Employability skills and graduate attributes requirements

Often overlapping with the above contextual necessity is the requirement for realising students' graduate attributes, publicly espoused by many universities and demanded by future employers. Of several commonly stipulated graduate attributes, one critical attribute -widely recognised and increasingly shared by universities worldwide- is employability skills that are deemed transferable beyond university studies into the twenty-first-century workplace. The value of employability skills, as a graduate attribute, has been increasingly evidenced through the growth of internships and work integrated learning (see Chapter 12 by Heikkinen), resulting in closer connections between higher education and the workplace. Employability skills typically include communication skills, teamwork skills, intercultural competence and digital capabilities (Enomoto & Warner, 2018). These employability related requirements necessitate employability skills development to be embedded within course curricula and to be also assessed as part of student learning outcomes, thus driving teaching and learning innovations in how we design our curricula and assess our students. In this book, further examples of this driver can be found in Chapter 11 by Bissett & Roberts, Chapter 17 by Rowley, Chapter 21 by Willcocks & Lange, and Chapter 22 by Swann.

Driver 4: Availability of technology and infrastructure

In the twenty-first century, the almost revolutionary driver of innovation worldwide, that is digital technology, has had dramatic impacts in higher education, in terms of the sector itself, the individual institutions, research and teaching. However, as Crisp (2018) observes, digitising what was previously an analogue experience, does not justify being called innovative in teaching and learning terms, if it only, for example, produces learning space or time efficiencies. Whilst such efficiencies might be desirable from an institutional perspective, and they might well be cheaper online, Crisp asserts that they are not pedagogically innovative, especially if the content, learning activities and assessment remain essentially unchanged. Nevertheless, there can be innovative shifts, if we replace the more traditional lecture-based format with scenario-based or problem-based formats, for example, using role plays, or students having inputs into assessment practices. Such shifts can manifest as disruptive innovations (Crisp, 2018; Tierney & Lanford, 2016; Chapter 5 by Ust; Chapter 9 by Carloni). Disruptive innovations can be characteristic of those innovations that challenge existing pedagogical practices, typically enacted, in the early part of the twenty-first century, through significant technological developments allowing online delivery of courses. Yet, the development of educational technology as a means to deliver pedagogical innovations hardly stands alone as a driver for innovations.

Driver 5: Staff skills capacity

To bring about innovations in teaching and learning, there must be a sufficient level of existing staff skills capacity. This includes teaching and learning skills, digital literacy and capabilities, motivation to innovate, adaptability and resilience, to name but a few. For instance, this book exemplifies such issues pertaining to staff skills capacity in Chapter 3 by Scott-Webber *et al.*, Chapter 10 by Warner & Enomoto, Chapter 16 by Schooling, Chapter 18 by Khong, and Chapter 21 by Willcocks & Lange. Bartholomew (2015) reports from a professional development program at Aston University in Birmingham, UK, which solely focused on empowering staff to engage in innovations in teaching and learning. A central message emerging from these publications is that innovative teaching and learning requires the empowerment of staff and distributed autonomy that allows staff to make decisions about curriculum innovations.

Driver 6: Staff and institutional culture

Similarly, for innovations to be encouraged in higher education institutions, every institution must invest in promoting and supporting both staff and institutional culture that openly values not only innovation itself, but also teaching and learning scholarship and higher education research. If staff and institutional culture values and supports innovative teaching and learning, teaching staff are more likely to become drivers of innovation themselves, representing the growth of the scholarship of teaching and learning. In this book, Chapter 13 by Birchley et al., Chapter 16 by Schooling and Chapter 18 by Khong reflect on the cultural elements of innovative teaching and learning.

Driver 7: Availability of Formal Recognitions for Innovations

Likewise, as a significant part of cultivating staff and institutional culture that values innovations, availability of 'formal' recognitions is crucial for encouraging teaching staff to innovate and creative to support student learning and experience. Such recognitions include their career or professional development opportunities, promotions, successful teaching and learning grant applications (e.g. Chapter 11 by Bissett & Roberts), and teaching excellence awards not only recognised within an institution, but also nationally and internationally. The UK AdvanceHE (formerly Higher Education Academy), for example, recognises the value of teaching and learning innovations that are evidenced by scholarship in higher education, in their award of prestigious fellowships for which innovative educators worldwide can apply.

---oOo---

Thus, the current reality in higher education is that there is overlap in these drivers, and no one single driver alone is driving teaching and learning innovations. In moving forward through the fast-evolving educational context, we would like to see higher education institutions invest more and more in cultivating and publicly showcasing their intuitional culture that not only values teaching and learning innovations but also recognises the scholarship that theoretically underpins innovations. Today, whilst higher education institutions overall, have come a long way towards increasingly valuing teaching and learning, it is also true that such changes in culture and attitude have been still relatively slow since the last century, especially compared with the private, corporate sector.

Innovations must always meet the demands of a particular context. In practice, this means we need to innovate, restricted by how our government and higher education institutions fund and run our higher education sector. In this book, chapter authors will show how they have been able to bring about their teaching and learning innovation to add value in their particular context, guided by learning theory to inform their teaching and learning practices. There is one common goal that motivated our innovations in this book – to help enrich our students' learning experiences and outcomes regardless of the wide range of discipline areas.

We have divided this book into five sections, and each section contains examples of innovative teaching and learning practices under a common theme. The five sections are:

- Section 1: Teaching and Learning Innovations Using Learning Space Design (Chapters 3–5);
- Section 2: Teaching and Learning Innovations Using e-learning (Chapters 6–9);
- Section 3: Teaching and Learning Innovations Using Case Methodology, Business Practice and Fieldwork (Chapters 10–13);
- Section 4: Teaching and Learning Innovations Using Creative Methodologies (Chapters 14–18);
- Section 5: Teaching and Learning Innovations Using Other Reflective Methodologies (Chapters 19–22).

In Chapter 2, *A Learning-centred, Five-tier Model of Innovation in Higher Education*, Dobozy and Nygaard present a learning-focused five-tier model of innovation in higher education, within which all of the following chapters situate themselves. This chapter serves to help educators in the sector to be sufficiently theory-informed to be able to engage in innovative pedagogical practices in the higher education sphere. The authors argue that any innovation in such pedagogical practices, without the backing of and comprehension of underlying theories in teaching and learning, would either be unworkable or be successful only by chance.

In Chapter 3, *Is Higher Education Ready for the Transformed Learner Coming from 9–12? A Case Study*, Scott-Webber, Loeffelman, Runyan and Denison take a constructivist approach to teaching and learning in their chapter, which presents a case study showcasing how innovations in both design and teaching in grades 9–12 can impact higher education. They show how reimagination became an innovative design solution, incorporating many elements of the five-tier model (Dobozy & Nygaard, 2021);

including process, services and a final product in the vision, building design, teaching and learning models and practice of a secondary school in Arizona, USA.

In Chapter 4, *Flexible Classroom Design to Facilitate Learning, Engagement and Integration of Knowledge and Cultures*, Forasacco takes a constructivist approach in a product innovation, showing how a flexible classroom design can support an active teaching style. She outlines what the students' perceptions are of a flexible classroom design and its effectiveness in facilitating active learning strategies. This preliminary study focuses on the degree to which classroom design as a 'teaching tool' in itself can determine learning and teaching strategies.

In Chapter 5, *Emergency Remote Teaching in Interior Architecture: A Necessary Shift*, Ust, in a process innovation, employs constructivist principles when outlining the teaching and learning strategies successfully impacting upon the experiences of interior architecture and environmental design students in their graduation project process. This graduation project, in a Turkish university, began in a traditional face-to-face mode but moved online, compelling students to complete their studies in an emergency, Covid-19 related, remote education mode.

In Chapter 6, *Best Practices of Teaching Diverse Cohorts in a Webcam-enabled Virtual Environment*, Rugden takes an instructivist perspective, when showcasing a product-based innovation, which focuses on best practices incorporated in teaching diverse student cohorts in a synchronous, webcam-enabled learning environment. The author presents an innovative, pragmatic use of the Adobe Connect platform, out of a US university, which enables educators to deliver synchronous classes via webcam technology.

In Chapter 7, *Impacts of Using Technology-Enhanced Language Learning in Second Language Academic Writing at a Vietnamese University*, van Rensburg and La Thanh, in a process innovation, show how, in an academic study, they used constructivist principles to inform Technology-Enhanced Language Learning (TELL) in English academic writing classes to help motivate Vietnamese university students. Utilising TELL for teaching practice is innovative in its own right in a developing country, such as Vietnam, where the use of information and communication technologies remains limited.

In Chapter 8, *Using Arts-based Instructional Strategies in E-learning to*

Increase Students' Social-emotional Learning Outcomes, in a product innovation, informed by a constructivist perspective, Perry and Edwards outline arts-based instructional strategies, namely photovoice, parallel poetry, poetweet, word sculptures, and my music moments, they created and evaluated in an e-learning environment. The authors illustrate that these types of instructional strategies (pertinent to those arts that encompass elements of creativity and human emotion) helped learners to increase digital caring and achieve positive social-emotional learning outcomes.

In Chapter 9, *Using a Community of Inquiry Framework to Foster Students' Active Learning*, Carloni presents an innovation, which is aligned with constructivist principles, outlining the implementation of digitally-enhanced activities targeted at propagating active learning during emergency remote education. This product innovation, which came into being in as a response to the Covid-19 lockdown in the 2020 spring semester, was designed within the Community of Inquiry (CoI) framework.

In Chapter 10, *An innovative Assessment Method to Evaluate Independent Learning and Academic Writing Skills*, Warner & Enomoto follow a constructivist approach in their innovative assessment method of evaluating the independent learning skills and academic writing skills of English as an additional language (EAL) students. The authors explain how a collaborative four-stage panel assessment process by English for Academic Purposes instructors and faculty-based academics, provides both academic rigor and equity for EAL students studying in a pre-university academic pathway program run at an Australian university.

In Chapter 11, *Affirm–Apply–Advance: Transitioning Undergraduate Students through their theory-into-practice journey*, Bissett and Roberts follow the constructivist tradition in their process innovation within a four-year undergraduate health program at an Australian university. The authors designed and enacted four annual transition workshops to help support students in the transition from theory to practice, both within the program and beyond into the workplace.

In Chapter 12, *An Innovative Model for University-industry Collaboration in Course Design and Delivery*, Heikkinen takes a constructivist approach to teaching and learning, outlining an innovative model for university and industry collaboration. The author shows how the collaborative model has been used successfully at a Finnish university to provide more up-to-date knowledge within the course itself. Moreover, the collaborative industry partner, with its corporate presence visible and image improved in the eyes of the students, could lead to it seeing an increasing number of possible recruits.

In Chapter 13, *Project-based Learning in a Japanese University: A Disruptive Innovation in Business Education*, Birchley, Omura and Yamauchi, through a constructivist lens, illustrate how they implemented Project-Based Learning (PBL) as a disruptive product innovation in both curriculum design and delivery at a Japanese university. This bottom-up product innovation helps students to develop requisite language skills, business content knowledge, and 21st-century skills for their future employability.

In Chapter 14, *Facilitating Active Student Learning Using Innovative Approaches in Pre-service Teacher Education*, Khong takes a constructivist approach to teaching and learning in a process (teacher-training related) innovation in Singapore. The author reveals how, in a core education course, an innovative and authentic lesson design is utilised, in the facilitation of active learning opportunities for novice student teachers, through the design of interactive seminars for their peers.

In Chapter 15, *Innovative Assessment in Higher Education: A Public Dissemination Assessment Model for Language Students*, Evans presents a constructivist, process aligned public dissemination assessment model for language students at an Australian university. The model provides a format for communication of research and knowledge that is understandable and accessible for the general reader. The author also outlines the transferability of this authentic assessment which promote the development of communication skills within virtually all disciplines.

In Chapter 16, *Teaching from the Native American Circle: An Innovative Teaching Framework*, Schooling presents a highly original process innovation, informed by a constructivist perception of learning, based on the Native American Circle. This Circle is unpacked and used by the author as a foundation for high impact teaching and learning in the context of Native American Indian education. Its success is such that The Circle is now utilised in schools which are beyond the original context, of the original large Bureau of Indian Education school, in which it had its first iterations.

In Chapter 17, *Discovering Professional Musician Identity through Reflective Narrative Writing: A Case Study of Pedagogic Proficiency*, Rowley offers a constructivist process innovation as a method to encourage Australian undergraduate music students in their transition to professional practice, by way of an intensive work-integrated learning experience. The innovation draws upon the Rowley & Munday's (2020) Arts-based Learning Model as a framework for the analysis of student reflexive narratives for capturing their transition.

In Chapter 18, *Using Fiction and Non-fiction Literature to Teach Sensitive Health Issues in Teacher Education*, Kalyn, Brenna and Jaunzems-Fernuk, showcase the integration of literary texts with post-secondary Health Education curricula for teacher candidates (TCs) in a Bachelor of Education Program. Crucial to the authors' constructivist and original innovation was a process invitation for TCs to attain knowledge via stories, and respond to literature in ways that could parallel the responses of their future students to textbooks with non-traditional content coverage.

In Chapter 19, *Collaborative Enquiry-based Learning in an Oral Health Program*, Olson draws upon constructivist principals in showing how collaborative enquiry-based learning is used, in an innovative process method to engage students in both student-directed learning (SDL) and self-reflection. This innovative method was successfully implemented for final year undergraduate Oral Health students in a semester-long course, 'Community Oral Health & Oral Health Promotion' at a university in New Zealand.

In Chapter 20, *Transformative Inquiry through the Human Curriculum*, Jaunzems-Fernuk, Martin and Kalyn showcase a process innovation, informed by constructivism, in a fourth-year undergraduate course that introduced 'The Human Curriculum' to a student cohort, in a Canadian College of Education. The innovation provided an opportunity for teacher candidates (TCs) to learn through the prism of 'the human curriculum', based on the humanistic and relational elements of teaching and learning processes.

In Chapter 21, *Using Cross-disciplinary Object-based Learning to Create Collaborative Learning Environments*, Willcocks and Lange outline a process innovation that, following constructivist principles was implemented in the discipline of museological teaching in higher education at a university in London. The authors' innovation draws upon pedagogy and curriculum development and places object-based learning in a collaborative learning environment; in so doing, it fosters cross-disciplinary explorations and exchanges.

In Chapter 22, *Building Employability Skills through Collaborative Group Work*, Swann's process innovation demonstrates how collaborative group work to build undergraduate employability skills was actioned at a UK university, as part of the BA (Hons) Childhood Studies degree, called The Legacy Projects. This collaborative group work, based on constructivism, can make university education more relevant and meaningful; furnish students with the experience, skills and qualities that employers' value; and meet needs and 'real world' demands such as accountability, taking responsibility and solving problems.

---oOo---

We hope that reading these inspirational accounts of teaching and learning innovations in higher education will, in turn, inspire you to continue developing your own innovations – for the improvement of student engagement, student learning and student employability.

About the Authors

Kayoko Enomoto is a Senior Lecturer, Head of Asian Studies and Director, Student Experience in the Faculty of Arts at the University of Adelaide, Australia. She can be contacted at this e-mail: kayoko.enomoto@adelaide.edu.au

Richard Warner is an Adjunct Lecturer in the School of Education in the Faculty of Arts at the University of Adelaide, Australia. He can be contacted at this e-mail: richard.warner@adelaide.edu.au

Claus Nygaard is Professor and Executive Director of The Institute for Learning in Higher Education. He can be contacted at this e-mail: info@lihe.info

Bibliography

Baregheh, A., Rowley, J. & Sambrook, S. (2009). Towards a multidisciplinary definition of innovation. *Management Decision*. 47(8), pp. 1323–1339.

Bartholomew, P. (2015). Learning through auto-ethnographic casestudy research. In Guerin, C., Bartholomew, P. & Nygaard, C. (Eds.), *Learning to Research – Researching to Learn*, pp. 241–255. Oxfordshire, UK: Libri Publishing Ltd.

Beverley O. & Jorre de St Jorre, T. (2018). Graduate attributes for 2020 and beyond: recommendations for Australian higher education providers. *Higher Education Research & Development*, 37(4), pp. 821–836.

Blouin, R. A., Riffee, W. H., Robinson, E. T., Beck, D. E., Green, C., Joyner, P. U., Persky, A. M. & Pollack, G. M. (2009). Roles of innovation in education delivery. *American Journal of Pharmaceutical Education*, 73(8), 154, pp. 1–12.

Crisp, G. (2018). Foreword. In Enomoto, K., Warner, R. & Nygaard, C. (Eds.) *Innovative Teaching and Learning Practices in Higher Education*, pp. vii–ix. Oxfordshire, UK: Libri Publishing Ltd.

Enomoto, K. & Warner, R. (2013). Building student capacity for reflective learning. In C. Nygaard, J. Branch & C. Holtham (Eds.), *Learning in Higher Education – Contemporary Standpoints*, pp. 183–201. Oxfordshire, UK: Libri Publishing Ltd.

Enomoto, K. & Warner, R. (2018). Developing undergraduate students' transferable generic skills through an innovative group drama project. In Enomoto, K., Warner, R. & Nygaard, C. (Eds.), *Innovative Teaching and Learning Practices in Higher Education*, pp. 115–140. Oxfordshire, UK: Libri Publishing Ltd.

Findlow, S. (2008). Accountability and innovation in higher education: a disabling tension? *Studies in Higher Education*, 33(3), pp. 313–329.

Hoffman, A. and Holzhuter, J. (2012). In Serdyukov, P. (2017). Innovation in education: what works, what doesn't, and what to do about it? *Journal of Research in Innovative Teaching & Learning*, 10(1), pp. 4–33.

Hørsted, A., Branch, J., Bartholomew, P. & Nygaard, C. (2018). A possible conceptualisation of innovative teaching and learning in higher education. In Hørsted, A., Branch, J., Bartholomew, P. & Nygaard, C. (Eds.), *New Innovations in Teaching and Learning in Higher Education*, pp. 1–22. Oxfordshire, UK: Libri Publishing Ltd.

Lašáková, A., Bajzíková, Ľ. & Dedze, I. (2017). Barriers and drivers of innovation in higher education: case study-based evidence across ten European universities. *International Journal of Educational Development*, 55, pp. 69–79.

Layne, P. C. (2015). Transforming higher education institutions. In Layne, P. C. & Lake P. (Eds.), *Global Innovation of Teaching and Learning in Higher Education. Transgressing Boundaries*, pp. 27–45. New York: Springer.

Layne, P. C. & Lake P. (2015). Introduction: teaching and learning at the crossroads. In Layne, P. C. & Lake P. (Eds.), *Global Innovation of Teaching and Learning in Higher Education. Transgressing Boundaries*, pp. 1–10. New York: Springer.

Mykhailyshyn, H., Kondur, O. & Serman, L. (2015). Innovation of education and educational innovations in conditions of modern higher education institution. *Journal of Vasyl Stefanyk Precarpathian National University*, 5(1), pp. 9–16.

Oliver, B. & Jorre de St Jorre, T. (2018). Graduate attributes for 2020 and beyond: Recommendations for Australian higher education providers. *Higher Education Research & Development*, 37(4), pp. 821–836.

Serdyukov, P. (2017). Innovation in education: what works, what doesn't, and what to do about it? *Journal of Research in Innovative Teaching & Learning*, 10(1), pp. 4–33.

Tierney, W. G. & Lanford, M. (2016) Conceptualizing innovation in higher education. In Paulsen, M.B. (Ed.), *Higher Education: Handbook of Theory and Research*, Higher Education: Handbook of Theory and Research 31, pp. 1–40. Switzerland: Springer Publishing.

Wisdom, J. (2015) Foreword. In Layne, P. C. & Lake P. (Eds.), *Global Innovation of Teaching and Learning in Higher Education. Transgressing Boundaries*, pp. v–vi. New York: Springer.

Chapter 2

A Learning-centred, Five-tier Model of Innovation in Higher Education

Eva Dobozy and Claus Nygaard

Introduction

With this chapter, we contribute to the book, *Teaching and Learning Innovations in Higher Education*, with a learning-centred, five-tier model of innovation in higher education (HE). We designed this model, to assist educators to engage in theory-informed innovations in HE. In this particular context, 'theory-informed' explicitly points to learning theory, as there is nothing as practical as applied theory. We believe that without an explicit understanding of key principles underpinning major theories of teaching and learning, any HE innovation would be impractical or randomly successful.

The focus on innovation in HE is essential to enable the timely reporting, testing and dissemination of new products, processes or services. The education industry needs to respond to current geopolitical challenges with decisive action, sensitivity and above all, research-informed innovative practices. We argue, following Waller *et al.* (2019:74), that there is a need for staying future facing in HE and engaging in perpetual innovation, because *"increasingly, the only sustainable competitive advantage in global higher education is continuous innovation"*. For this chapter, and based on research by Skillicorn (2016), we define innovation as the systematic and often evidence-based practice of successfully translating an idea into a tangible product, process or service to create value for one or multiple stakeholder groups. This definition – along with the learning-centred, five-tier model of innovation in higher education – becomes the guideline for the chapters of this book. Authors of the different chapters all reflect their innovations in relation hereto. We argue that all innovations in HE ought to be informed by learning theory, no matter what type of innovations they may be. Therefore, we find it imperative that innovators in HE engage deeply with, and articulate, their perception of learning when they engage in innovation processes.

The learning-centred, five-tier model has, as its starting point, the theory of learning, which guides and influences the way in which a particular problem is identified and innovative solutions are conceptualised. Even when innovators conceptualisations of teaching and learning are implicit, that is, they are not aware of, and not accustomed to articulating their deep-seated assumptions about teaching and learning, the intrinsic values and beliefs they hold still inform how they teach and innovate. Therefore, we open the chapter with a presentation of three broad theoretical orientations to teaching and learning to highlight in more detail, how innovators' own philosophical ideas inform how they teach and think about innovations in HE. The model we developed supports innovators in becoming aware of the learning theories they ascribe to and to better understand the theoretical underpinnings of their practices.

Overview of main sections

In Section 1, we firstly introduce the theory of learning that is guiding the innovation, before outlining the individual reflection points of the five-tier innovation and implementation process. Each tier holds a central question, which an innovator should be able to confidently answer. This part of the model, as explained in Section 2, serves both as a guideline and a checklist of essential aspects, which we argue, should be considered when developing any kind of innovation in relation to teaching and learning in HE. In Section 2, we further provide brief examples of innovative products, processes and services in HE, underpinned by the three different learning theories outlined in Section 1. In particular, we focus on role changes as an outcome of the innovation. These are changes in the role of curriculum, educators, and students.

Section 1: Learning theory

This section is devoted to what is generally called learning theory. More precisely, we examine commonly shared beliefs about the nature of teaching and learning among proponents of specific theories, and the different roles ascribed to: (a) the curriculum, (b) the educators, and (c) the students. Our aim is, as noted above, to make apparent the importance of theory-informed innovation in teaching and learning. For this to happen, it is imperative that innovators are able to align themselves, in principle, with particular belief claims to better articulate the significance and viability of their innovation. There are three broad theoretical orientations to teaching and learning that have developed over the past century. These include theories of (i) instructivism, (ii) cognitivism and (iii) constructivism. We discuss each learning theory in detail below, briefly outlining the key principles and historical grounding of each theory before posing a question to innovators to self-check their theoretical alignment with the theory.

(i) Instructivism

This theory of learning views learning much as a process of 'information in and knowledge out' model of instruction. In instructivist philosophical thought, one would argue that a person learns best through being directly and explicitly instructed what to do through structured and sequences lessons, or trained what to do through guidance and instruction. Instructivism is also known as objectivism or behaviourism.

This idea of learning as a behavioural response to a given stimulus dates back to scholars, such as Thorndike (1898) and Skinner (1936, 1968) who studied animal behaviour. Thorndike published his theory of *Law of Effect* based on his studies of cats; Skinner published his theory of *Operant Conditioning* based on his studies of rats and pigeons. The animals they studied had to solve different puzzles to receive a reward. By reinforcing rules, repeating practices, and the application of reward and punishment, the animals would be trained in quite complex behaviours. Although human behaviours are more complex, reinforcement of desired behaviour in learning situations can be easily achieved through immediate feedback and getting praised for the correct answer on a test or reprimanded for a wrong answer on a test. In light of these studies and scientific arguments about behaviour, these pioneers of educational theory were linking empirical research to philosophical thinking. Their aim was to explain all social and cultural phenomena in both biological and scientific terms, enabling instructivism to pay close attention to observable and measurable variables in learning.

In contemporary higher education, we see many examples of instructivist practices, which are grounded in the belief that students learn best through guidelines, rules, and direct instruction. Educators who adhere to an instructivist orientation to teaching and learning are motivated by the ideas of objectivity as an attribution of fairness through a one-size-fits-all approach. They believe in input education, transmitting information via lectures and direct instruction. The distinguishing characteristic of direct instruction is the active and directive role assumed by the educator and the passive and receptive role taken by students. Students are expected to learn through activities, such as listening to lectures, watching instructional videos, and practice exercises of prepared materials. Educators believing in the effectiveness of instructivist approaches see learning itself as an object, which can be objectively observed and measured.

The key to success is to take one step at the time. The purpose of instructivist approaches to teaching and learning is substantial 'just-in-case' knowledge and skills development. A traditional lecture-style interaction pattern is valued, with the primary focus on new knowledge development and content mastery. Student collaboration is not encouraged but instead seen as a distraction and inefficient use of time. The lecturer is in charge of content and process decisions, with little flexibility and agency afforded to students. Assessments are very traditional, exclusively summative and mainly high stakes.

(ii) Cognitivism

This theory of learning got its name because it focuses on the role of cognitive (mental) processes for learning. It was developed by cognitive psychologists who paid close attention to both observable and unobservable aspects of learning. They were interested in studying how the human mind/brain worked while people learn. Cognitivism dates back to Piaget (1936), who developed a stage theory of child cognitive development. He saw the mind/brain to be in a dynamic relationship with the environment, where the mind/brain was the subject and the environment was the object. Where instructivists see the person as an object being governed by another object (the environment), cognitivists see the person as a subject, an actor with free will and purpose, whose mind/brain is responsible for processing, organising and interpreting information (objects). Our mind/

brain is subjectively responsible for our learning. Cognitivism, therefore, focuses on students' ability to think through their actions and control their impulses. It emphasises the role of cognition (including metacognition) in learning.

The main focus of cognitivist educators is on helping students become better learners. Key variables are attention, information processing (working memory), and metacognition. Cognitivism claims that students are active agents, able to learn and process information to act consciously upon the world and influence the environment to help them achieve their goals. Self-efficacy beliefs are key to success in learning as they affect whether students think optimistically or pessimistically, or act in ways beneficial or detrimental to achieving goals, approach or avoid tasks. The purpose of cognitivist approaches to teaching and learning is substantial 'just-in-case' knowledge and skills development. The pedagogy used is a mix of teacher-centric and learner-centric approaches, focusing on skills development and basic content knowledge. The interaction pattern is a mix of lecturer-to-student and student-to-student engagement, ensuring the lecturer is in control of the classroom and content decisions, but students may have input into process decisions. Hence, cognitivist educators may provide some degree of flexibility to students. Individual excellence and mastery of learning content are highly valued. The application of new knowledge and skills, as well as more effective learning skills, are encouraged. Unsurprisingly, summative assessments are highly valued, and authentic assessment tasks are also encouraged.

(iii) Constructivism

Constructivist learning theory pays close attention to the ways in which people construct knowledge, linking new information to prior knowledge and experience. Common for both instructivism and cognitivism is that knowledge is considered to be external to the learner, and thus the learning process is a process of internalising knowledge. With constructivism, knowledge is seen as a process of individual and collective construction. Knowledge is not external information waiting to be internalised through instruction (instructivism) or dynamic information processing, and accommodation (cognitivism). Knowledge is an internal construct based on the learners' perception of the world, the learners' individual and/or collective experiences, and the learners' existing knowledge. Instructivists argue that the learner (object) is governed by the environment (object). Cognitivists argue that the learner (subject) processes, organises and interprets information (objects). Constructivists, however, argue that the learner (subject) constructs her or his version of reality and has the ability to act upon the environment (intersubject).

Constructivism dates back to Dewey (1896) who argued that learning is a social activity, and that the learner takes both individual (subjective) and sociocultural (intersubjective) dimensions of her or his construction of knowledge into account when learning. In *The Reflex Arc Concept in Psychology* (Dewey, 1896), he argued that the profession of psychology needs to reconsider the relationship between person and environment, as it has far too long treated the person as being detached from the environment. Vygotsky (1978) studied how children construct knowledge, arguing that the child best learns through social interaction with a more knowledgeable other. He focused on the 'Zone of Proximal Development,' to explain the importance of guided and self-regulated learning and collective knowledge construction through collaborative dialogue. His research pointed towards the effect of learning environments and social relations on knowledge construction.

Educators following a constructivist orientation to learning mainly focus on student self-conception, self-esteem, self-efficacy beliefs, autonomy, agency and relatedness. Learning as knowledge sharing and meaning-making through experience and exchange is emphasised. Attention is given to authenticity, intentionality, diversity and open-mindedness. Learning is highly personalised. Constructivist theory claims that students will be highly motivated to learn when the learning material is personally meaningful, when students understand the reason for their behaviour, and when they perceive the learning environment to be supportive of their efforts to learn. The primary pedagogical approaches are learner-centric and situated. The interaction pattern is primarily student-to-student, encouraging collaborative problem solving, analysis, synthesis and reflection, cumulatively referred to as higher-order thinking skills. Unsurprisingly, educators believing in the effectiveness of constructivist approaches, value student agency, and focus on students' learning skills development. They see the syllabus as a means to an end. Students are given much choice and a high degree of flexibility in how and when to engage with the curriculum. Assessments are constructed to be authentic and meaningful, and the emphasis is put on 'assessment for learning.'

The importance of learning theory

The brief elaborations may provide innovators in teaching and learning with an insight into the importance of reflecting upon, and articulating, their philosophical beliefs and assumptions about learning and learners, when engaging in innovation in teaching and learning in HE. For example, if an innovator wishes to implement digital badges, intuitively, she or he may think that using such a tool will be innovative, because it is something she or he may not have used before, although others may already have had considerable experience with it. So, what is the problem the educator may wish to address with the innovative practice (in this case designing and implementing the digital badges in the course)? Some considerations are:

- What do the innovators believe should be their role when using the new tool?
- How will the innovative practice, in their professional opinion, affect the delivery of the curriculum?
- What is the anticipated reaction of students based on the implementation of the digital badge (in this case) in their course?
- What is the anticipated learning gain / learning outcome?

Table 1 provides a synthesis of key similarities and differences of roles of the curriculum, the educator and students, depending on underlying assumptions of the nature of teaching and learning. It was designed to assist innovators answer specific questions related to the relevance of the innovation for specific stakeholder groups, enabling them to be confident that their innovation is theory-informed and grounded in evidence.

	(i) **Instructivism**	(ii) **Cognitivism**	(iii) **Constructivism**
(a) Role of Curriculum	Predominantly content/syllabus focused	Content/syllabus & process-focused	Predominantly process focused (syllabus as a means to an end)
(b) Role of Educator	Knowledge teller	Mentor & knowledge teller	Facilitator, coach, mentor & knowledge curator
(c) Role of Student	Tabula rasa (clean slate, empty vessel or blank paper), consumer of pre-packaged curriculum information	Some prior knowledge acknowledged and misconceptions expected, consumer of pre-packaged curriculum information & increased reflection about & improvement of learning-to-learn skills expected	Producer & sharer of dynamic knowledge, building on collective prior knowledge of the team, challenging and displacing individual misconceptions & active building of 21st century competencies

Table 1: Three theories of learning and their possible implications for teaching.

Section 2: The five-tier innovation in higher education model

We developed the five-tier innovation in higher education model to assist educators in understanding the importance of, and to have a practical tool to engage in, theory-informed innovations in HE teaching and learning. This model is intended to be used as a structured reflection tool, deliberately avoiding abstract conceptualisation and instead specifically addressing innovation in HE teaching and learning (Inkermann *et al.*, 2020).

For the benefit of the innovation, its value and implementation success, we suggest that innovators will use the model together with their colleagues to map, evaluate and align their personal teaching philosophies, which underpin their daily practices. In this way, the model is able to serve as a guideline, reflection tool and a checklist for essential aspects of the innovation. We outline the five separate but interrelated tiers of the model in Table 2.

Tier	Focus	Question to be answered by the innovator
Tier 1	Innovation Type	What type of innovation is it (product, process or service)?
Tier 2	21st Century Graduate Capabilities	What are the highly desirable and necessary 21st century graduate capabilities enabled through the innovation?
Tier 3	Challenging Status Quo	How is the innovation challenging the status quo, conventional wisdom and mindsets?
Tier 4	Usability & Value	How is the innovation able to articulate the intricate balance of its desirability, feasibility and validity?
Tier 5	Implementation Fidelity	What evidence is provided to ensure an implementation fidelity assessment has been carried out?

Table 2: The five-tier innovation process.

Below, we outline each of the tiers individually, and we give examples of ways in which the tier may be approached by educators with differing teaching philosophies.

Tier 1: Innovation type – What type of innovation is it (product, process or service)?

In innovation theory (Keupp et al., 2012; Meissner & Kotsemir, 2016) scholars distinguish between three types of innovation: (1) product innovation, (2) process innovation, and (3) service innovation. This distinction is important, because these three types of innovation are different in nature and they solve different problems. Below we examine some examples of these and how they may link to learning theory and your personal teaching philosophy.

(1) Product innovation

A product innovation in HE is an innovation of a product designed to help students succeed. Being a product means that it is tangible and concrete. It is something that we can see, touch, and use. It can be implemented and its use can be evaluated. Importantly, we can also assess students' development when using the product.

An example of a product innovation in HE is a MOOC (a massive open online course) aimed at unlimited participation and open online access. Universities like Harvard, Massachusetts Institute of Technology, Australian National University, London School of Economics, University of Oxford and University of Hong Kong are all important contributors to this new type of product innovation in HE. In fact, almost every major university today is present in the educational online market and most of them deliver MOOCs.

MOOCs can be instructivist product innovations. They offer students a pre-designed course structure containing course materials, such as filmed lectures, readings and problem sets. During the course, students follow a curriculum with pre-designed activities planned in time. All students receive the same instructions and go through the same teaching and learning activities. Because learning is seen as a behavioural response to a given stimulus, the educational practice focuses on what academic content to deliver to students as a stimulus for learning. Here the educator is seen to be responsible for both the teaching and for student learning, as we think that students learn when they become familiar with the pre-designed content and activities. In this view, product innovation is to choose the right online learning platform for the MOOC – it could be EdX, Coursera or Udemy – and design the curriculum including the content, activities, tests, and assessment tools. Once that is done the project is considered ready for deployment. The MOOC can run itself once the technology is in place.

Other MOOCs are cognitive product innovations. These MOOCs also use a curriculum with pre-designed activities planned in time, and they follow a given structure. Yet because learning is seen as a dynamic interaction between the student and the environment where the mind/brain is subjectively responsible for learning, these MOOCs provide interactive features, such as user forums or social media communities to support interaction between students and faculty. They also include more personal and tailored assignment feedback and learning activities to help students learn. Here, the educator is also seen to have a major responsibility for both the teaching and for student learning, because students are perceived to learn from the planned interactions with content, students and faculty. In this perspective, product innovation focuses on the design of the curriculum, including the content, activities, tests, assessment tools, user forums, social media communities and feedback methods. An important consideration is that the MOOC cannot run itself with the aid of technology alone. The interrelationship between the student and the learning environment is very important, hence, the presence of faculty and fellow students is vital for success.

Yet, other MOOCs are constructivist product innovations. Because learning is seen as a subjective construction of knowledge, stemming from the students' individual and collective activities, the centerpiece of the MOOC is the virtual arena for learning. It could be the social community group designed as a meeting place, where the students take both individual and sociocultural dimensions of their construction of knowledge into account when learning. They engage in academic debates and collaborate to construct knowledge. Therewith, they are grappling with, and building a collective mentality. The curriculum also contains pre-designed online lectures, readings, and problem sets. Whereas the instructivist and cognitivist version of the MOOC would see students follow a curriculum with pre-designed activities planned in time, the constructivist MOOC sees these kinds of materials as learning resources, which the student may or may not consult. Here, students are required to take responsibility for their learning. In this view, product innovation focuses on the design of the environment, providing a space for networking, individual and collective learning, where students and faculty can interact and inspire each other to construct knowledge. This MOOC cannot run itself once the technology is in place, because the arena for learning needs to be fueled with activities, active dialogue, and feedback, to support students in their individual and collective construction of knowledge.

As can be seen from these three examples, the innovation management of a MOOC does not simply entail the development of a MOOC as a product to be used. The MOOC designers will need to be explicitly aware of their teaching philosophy, perception of learning, the roles of the curriculum, educator, and student, because the underpinning assumptions have significant implications for the MOOC product to be developed.

Another instructivist product innovation was that of Perumalla *et al.* (2017), who designed two online courses in the Faculty of Medicine at the University of Toronto, using the Blackboard Learning Management system. Blackboard allowed the instructors to create a robust 'virtual learning environment' where they were able to manage the course content flexibly, including posting videos and other learning modules, administer online assessments (quizzes), submit assignments and also to manage Grade Books where students could access their respective grades. For the students, it provided a 'one-stop-shop', where they accessed course material, created a community of learners through chat and discussion boards, and could easily and conveniently access bulk announcements.

Koç (2017) engaged in a constructivist product innovation, as he designed an online environment to stimulate self-regulated and self-directed learning. This innovation allowed freedom for learners to create their learning path using the software Webspirationpro with feedback from educators in the form of a concept map. As the learners did choose their path, they could access the necessary resources from videos uploaded by the educator. Also, the freedom of learners was extended to create evaluation schemes by negotiating with the educator and peers in line with self-directed learning principles. Both Moodle and YouTube were used for assignment and resource sharing.

As we have demonstrated, product innovations come in various forms. The above examples are designed to inspire innovators to think of their own product innovation, in accordance with their teaching and learning paradigm and perception of learning. Now, we examine the second type of innovation, namely process innovations.

(2) Process innovations

A process innovation in HE is an innovation of an educational process, a new pedagogical practice, a new curriculum design process, or the like, designed to help students succeed. It can also be new technology-supported pedagogies or the introduction of staff upskilling, or competencies, approaches, models and frameworks to support an existing or a new education product or service. Being a process means that it is intangible. Nevertheless, it is important when innovating new processes that they are described and explained so they can be implemented and assessed. As was the case with product innovations, process innovations are also shaped by the innovator's teaching philosophy.

An illustrative example of a constructivist process innovation in HE is the development and widespread implementation of formal learning design and learning analytics models in recent years (Dobozy & Cameron, 2018; Ifenthaler et al., 2018). Learning Design and Learning Analytics are two separate, but interrelated fields of educational research and practice. They are generally grounded in constructivist perspectives and firmly focused on helping educators be more effective practitioners. They help educators gain better insights into the teaching and learning process through visual learning design representation and actual granulated student engagement data. Learning Design researchers have developed visual tools and frameworks to (a) guide novice teachers through the learning design process, and (b) more effectively share, adapt and reuse theory-informed teaching ideas and learning design sequences (Dalziel et al., 2016). The explicit, theory-informed learning design process allows educators to track, measure and report on desired and actual learning engagement and outcomes of students through the implementation of learning analytics. Hence, learning analytics and learning design are able, through the employment of an iterative loop, to make explicit, by way of visual representation, lesson sequencing on the one hand, and intentional data collection and measurement on the other hand, intended and actual impact of learning design decisions on specific contexts and student groups.

Meier and Nygaard (2009) developed a constructivist process innovation, as they designed a process model for problem-oriented project work, based on a constructivist perception of learning. Their model could be implemented by eductors who wanted to support the development of learning-centered HE. Focusing on process innovation based on constructivist principles, they also discussed the implications for teachers, students, study boards, and curriculum designers in adopting this process model. They did so, because they were aware that HE process design often has wide implications on the teaching and learning context, because when processes are changed so are the activities, educator and student roles and interrelations in the educational context.

Bartholomew (2015) made a constructivist process innovation as he designed and implemented a new process for professional development of researchers at Aston University in Birmingham, UK. He introduced auto-ethnographic case study research and educators were encouraged to draw on their own experiences of research in order to advance their understanding of what research can achieve. The insights developed through these processes of self-understanding and self-reflection led to a new typology of case study research among the faculty.

Hager (2016) made a constructivist process innovation as she worked on a long-term project to innovate a new self-assessment process, which could be used in graduate education. She worked from a constructivist perception of learning and introduced a self-assessment process based on ePortfolios, which allowed for students to integrate, apply, and make their learning visible across courses and in complementary learning activities. In her work she focused on how ePortfolios fostered and harnessed student-centered learning and self-assessment, and how this informed their learning practices. The process once implemented and tested was so well described that it could act as a product in future educations.

As can be seen from these examples, processes can be very different. Some regard what students do, and others what teachers do. Others again have an effect on the curriculum. One thing is important, though, namely the perception of learning underlying the process innovation. Because Hager (2016) had a constructivist perspective on learning, she centered her innovation on student self-assessment and on students making their learning visible across contexts. As a result, she was forced to choose a technology which supported these processes, and it became ePortfolios. If she had worked from an instructivist perception of learning, she could have chosen an online quiz as the assessment method. And she probably would not have focused on making learning visible across contexts, because once students had been positively assessed within one course/module, they had fulfilled the needs and passed the course/module. Having explored process innovations we will now examine the third type of innovation, namely service innovations.

(3) Service innovations

A service innovation in higher education is an innovation of a service designed to help students succeed. It can be student services that help new students navigate their way around the virtual and physical university spaces. In recent years, HE institutions have focused on breaking down silos and/or working outside conventional boundaries to help students better develop transferable skills. Service innovations can often stimulate positive change and better access to HE services for minority students and population groups traditionally excluded from tertiary studies. Strategic, private-public partnerships and vocational and tertiary education partnerships (Rodan, 2016) are also examples of service innovations. Another type of service innovation links to extra-curricular activities, such as community service, which includes volunteer work. A service innovation can also be the policy or strategy of a university to support a certain type of teaching and learning activity. Service innovations, similar to product and process innovations require clarity about the link to underpinning learning theory and your personal teaching philosophy, because deep seated assumptions about effective teaching and learning will influence the perception of certain problems and the search for possible solutions.

McCormack and Scanlon (2017) described an instructivist service innovation at La Trobe University in Melbourne, Australia. The university developed a strategy to make entrepreneurial education accessible to every undergraduate student as a standard part of the coursework. The design and implementation of this service innovation was driven by a number of interrelated factors: (a) enhancing student employability in a highly competitive labour market, (b) changing patterns of employment, and (c) the demands of national economic competitiveness. They argued that the success of the innovation was due to students developing the knowledge, skills and mindset needed to be innovative and entrepreneurial, either for themselves in developing a start-up or working for an employer.

Another instructivist service innovation was reported by Branch and Alyssa (2013) in their advocacy for universal design for learning as a service to support students with learning impairments. Their service innovation was put forward as a plea for HE to follow a universal design for learning model where HE was: accessible, flexible, comprising simple and intuitive instruction, with perceptible information, a tolerance for error, and a low physical effort to contribute. This type of service innovation was important, they argued, as the number of students with learning impairments is rapidly increasing.

Copenhagen Business School made an instructivist service innovation as they established Student Affairs as a one-stop-shop contact point for enrolled, as well as potential full-time degree students, offering a multitude of student-facing services (Copenhagen Business School, 2019). Student Affairs provide students with information about university, course and assessment deadlines, dispensations, credit transfer, state grands, and offer general as well as specific guidance about special needs education support. Almost every university provides similar services, but they are often dispersed and hard to navigate.

As can be seen, service innovations are different from product innovations, because they explicitly focus on the service provided.

To sum up tier 1, we invite you to distinguish between product-, process-, and service innovations, and to work with the innovation, based on your perception of learning.

Tier 2: 21st century graduate capabilities – What are the highly desirable and necessary 21st century graduate capabilities enabled through the innovation?

The next tier invites innovators to reflect upon the anticipated high-level and holistic learning outcomes that measure students' learning success as they engage with an innovation. What is it that the innovation is expected to provide to students, in terms of non-discipline specific learning outcomes? It is important to develop a clear statement of what students are expected to be able to do (capabilities) and what they need to know (knowledge) following their deep engagement with the innovation.

High-level and holistic learning outcomes combine discipline-specific and generic knowledge, skills, and personal attitudes, which are often referred to as 21st century (21C) graduate capabilities and allow a person to utilise their capacity to realise specific outcomes (Stevens, 2012). Hence, it is vital to distinguish *capability* from *competency*, precisely because a capability is the realisation of a person's capacity effectively and sustainably.

Knowledge workers are characterised as individuals with both highly specialised knowledge and skills along and more generic, high level cognitive, social and ethical capabilities, which are transferable across contexts and disciplinary domains. The contemporary and increasingly global employment market requires a combination of these highly specialised technical and generic capabilities. The high level generic or transferable skills and positive personality traits have been variously referred to as soft skills, graduate attributes, general capabilities, employability skills, professional skills or 21C to point to their portable and flexible nature (Dobozy & Dalziel, 2016). Indeed, employers worldwide expect HE graduates to demonstrate a range of relevant professional and interpersonal skills, not only narrowly defined technical and/or discipline knowledge. Consequently, HE graduates will need to be able to demonstrate strong core competencies that can be assessed and compared on an international stage.

Linking 21C graduate capabilities, such as creative problem solving, effective verbal and written communication, cultural awareness, entrepreneurship, ethical decision making, to the three theories of learning, enables us to show how different perceptions would lead to different outcomes and emphasise the importance of the development of these graduate capabilities. Typically, instructivist philosophy would put a limited focus on any of the 21C graduate capabilities, as the concern is with the imparting of specific and discrete content knowledge and skills that can be quickly and accurately tested. Typically, cognitivist philosophy would focus on the development of creative problem solving. Typically, constructivist philosophy would focus on the development of the all 21C graduate capabilities, but priority is given to effective communication, self-management, teamwork, self-reflection and self-awareness.

Torrisi-Steele (2020) engaged in a constructivist process innovation by implementing design thinking principles (Plattner *et al.*, 2011) to facilitate a shift from teaching-centred to learning-centred learning. The result of the deeply human-centric learning processes that students are immersed in is the development of a number of 21C graduate capabilities. Torrisi-Steele (2020) sees her innovation as constructivist and argues this to be a shift away from instructive approaches.

Yang and McKenzie (2018) designed a cognitivist process innovation as they developed a method of career development learning in two undergraduate courses. They defined their learning outcome in the 21st century to cultivate students as whole persons, not just professionals. They argued that it was not enough for their students to obtain an academic qualification (standard credentials). In their teaching, they used career development learning processes to improve student career-associated self-efficacy. They reported that 91.3% of the students experienced significantly more self-efficacy: self-appraisal, became better at career goal selection, finding occupational information and at planning their career.

The above are some examples of how 21C graduate capabilities can be integrated in learning outcomes that are aligned with the innovators teaching philosophy. Learning outcomes could be designed and worked with in alternative ways. Educators could set the key attributes of an innovative mindset to be their expected learning outcomes. Scholars with an innovative mindset agree that such outcomes would be creativity, a willingness to challenge conventional wisdom, and highly developed critical thinking abilities, requiring a mental readiness to (a) work with ambiguity, and (b) fail, learn from failure; make strategic changes based on insight and experience (Sweeney & Imaretska, 2016; Kurato et al., 2019). The relationship is well established between these attributes and increasing expectations that knowledge workers show strong soft skills and innovative capabilities, solve ill-described problems, work in transdisciplinary and international teams, show cultural sensitivities and effective communication skills (Dalziel, 2015). Alternatively, learning outcomes could be designed and worked upon in the light of Bloom's Taxonomy (Dobozy, 2011) or Higher Order Thinking Skills (Brookhart, 2010) as defined learning outcomes. Clearly stating expected learning outcomes is important, because they allow an educator to focus on the anticipated student learning impact of the innovation.

Tier 3: Challenging the status quo — How is the innovation challenging the status quo, conventional wisdom and/or mindsets?

Tier 3 of the innovation reflection model is concerned with gaining conceptual clarity. Innovation is situated in creativity and strives to go beyond improvement and evolutionary thought and practice: *"any new piece of work must be statistically novel as well as non-trivially valuable to some group of people if it is to be considered creative*" Harrington (2018:118). Therefore, an innovative and creative mindset requires openness to, and an active search for, new mental models and schemas, with a defining goal: to create new realities, and pathways to the development and testing of new products, processes and services. These creative processes are based on a deep understanding of the status quo and some perceived or real misalignment of what is available, required and value-adding (Anderson et al., 2014).

Given the need for evidence-based argumentation of the move beyond improvement mindsets and a willingness and ability to challenge conventional wisdom, it is essential to a) identify specific innovation indicators, enabling more precise classification of activities as 'innovative,' and b) to link innovation with best practice principles. Often, innovation in education is perceived as disruptive and technology-focused. Although changes in education have been constant in an endeavour to grow access and improve the learning outcomes of diverse students (Darling-Hammond et al., 2020), innovation is more than gradual change. It is the widespread adoption of change. Innovation has a great potential to be disruptive in the sense that it unsettles the status quo, and breaks down societal, economic and political boundaries to provide quality education through online and remote learning (Anderson & McGreal, 2012). Taking into account the three theories of learning that we present here, they too have an impact on how educators perceive innovations. Typically, educators with an instructivist theory of learning would focus attention on innovating discrete elements of the curriculum that can easily be observed, measured and replicated.

Cygman (2015) used mobile telephone technology in a disruptive instructivist product innovation to assess the performance of student pilots. Mobile phone technology disrupted the traditional pilot education, as usually instructors were faced by the general problem of being unable to assess students, as a result of the limited interaction inherent in field education. The innovation was a technological solution, implemented in flight education. Cygman's findings illustrate how the implementation of this technology supported meaningful dialogue, strengthened the learning outcomes, and enhanced student engagement.

Cognitivist philosophy generally focuses attention on intrapersonal cognition and essential advancements in interdisciplinary research in neuroscience and education. By contrast, constructivist philosophy typically focuses attention on interpersonal knowledge construction processes that enable unique product and service development. There is also an increased awareness of group differences and the need for personalisation of education. Meier and Nygaard (2019) compared different collaborative technologies to be used in HE from a constructivist process innovation perspective. They were interested in evaluating collaborative technologies that best support students in their process of co-construction of new knowledge. They found that such processes could be supported by technologies, such as GoogleDocs, Padlet, and Realtimeboard, whereas educational technologies, such as Kahoot and Canvas LMS did suit an instructivist process better.

Tier 4: Usability and value – How is the innovation able to articulate the intricate balance of its desirability, feasibility and validity?

The fourth tier of the model offers a discussion of the intricate balance between an innovation's key characteristics to assess and document the perceived value-adding nature of the innovation. Innovation in any field requires a careful analysis of three criteria: desirability, feasibility, and viability, which need to be explicitly understood, articulated and working in harmony (Leavy, 2010). That is also the case with HE innovation.

Starting with an evaluation of 'desirability', requires thinking of the desire of the stakeholders for an innovation. In HE, students probably make up the most important stakeholder group, and we need to account for students' desire to use the innovation. In terms of making a product innovation, why should students wish to use the product? Is it because they have to, as the product innovation is a part of the curriculum? Is it because they want to, as they experience better learning outcomes when using the product innovation? Questions to be answered are: What stakeholder group or groups are the targets of the innovation? What evidence is there that the targeted user groups want, or express a particular need for, the product, service or process? What evidence is there that the innovation makes sense to them? Answers to such questions are affected by the educator's theory of learning.

Typically, educators engaged in instructivist product innovations would argue for desirability based on aspects that would provide students with easy access to information and learning materials. Because students learn through instruction, having easy access to a variety of learning materials would be considered as desirable.

The next criteria to be considered is a 'feasibility' analysis of innovation, looking at the practicality, workability and sustainability of an innovation. Questions to be answered are: Is technology needed to implement the innovation available? Are the users' technical skills and capabilities sufficiently developed or is upskilling required? What evidence is there that users will adapt to, and make use of, the new product, service or process? What are the resource implications of implementing the innovation? What is the evidence that it is cost and/or time effective? How scalable and sustainable is the innovation?

The last of the three criteria to be considered is the 'validity' of the innovation, investigating the overall soundness of the innovation and its alignment with the university's mission, vision and values. Questions to be answered are: What evidence is there that the innovation aligns with the stated organisational goals? What are the anticipated outcomes and benefits for the organisation? What will the return on investment in the innovation look like? How important is the innovation for the organisation, its operation and its stakeholders?

Validity considerations are also affected by the theory of learning underlying the innovation. If it was an instructivist process innovation of a new assessment design, a key concern would be quality assurance through rigorous testing and validating of high-stakes automated tests that are context-independent. If the assessment design was seen as a cognitivist process innovation, the cognitivist philosophy would focus attention on observable meaning-making and information processing. A key concern would be to design assessment tasks that are sufficiently complex to enable the students to demonstrate their problem-solving abilities and application of specific learning content in differing contexts. By constrast, would the assessment design be seen as a constructivist process innovation, the focus of attention would lie on social and cultural factors to ensure all students have an equal chance to succeed in their studies. A key concern would be the ethics of high stakes testing and alleviating cultural test bias. Providing specific and explicit responses to some of the questions posed above enables a systematic quality analysis of the innovation through the support of *"cross-functional and cross-boundary coordination"* (Boer & Boer, 2019:438). Articulating the relevant and intertwined considerations of an innovation provides legitimacy and quality assurance to enhance systematic effectiveness, efficiency and relevance through targeted analysis, which is related to Tier 2 of the innovation process.

Tier 5: Implementation fidelity – What evidence is provided to ensure an implementation fidelity assessment has been carried out?

The fifth tier of the model is concerned with knowledge transfer and implementation fidelity, with suggestions of how to ensure that innovation is implemented in the way it was intended. Evidence-based practice is generally understood as the integration of the best available theoretical or practical research evidence with clinical expertise. It is scientifically-based knowledge translation, making use of research processes, programs or interventions that have been established to produce desired or intended results (Grimshaw *et al.*, 2012). However, the implementation of an innovation in a specific context will need to demonstrate implementation fidelity, to ensure that the innovation was implemented as intended, adhering to scientific methodologies and implementation protocols to be effective and replicable.

Typically, instructivist philosophy would focus attention on objective measures and correct processes in the implementation of the innovation, being concerned with demonstrating that proper procedures were followed in the generation of high-level quantitative data to enable generalisability of findings. If required, extrinsic motivational tools would be applied in the form of rewards.

Cognitivist philosophy would focus attention on mastery of novel tools, processes and services, ensuring that stakeholders understand the aim of the innovation as well as the implementation procedures. Stakeholders may require specialist training and upskilling to enable a successful implementation of the innovation. Attention would be given to cognitive load and personal motivation to ensure successful implementation. Care would be taken to demonstrate that proper procedures were followed in the generation of mixed data sets (quantitative and qualitative) to enable some level of generalisability of findings.

Characteristically, constructivist philosophy would focus attention on contextual factors and diversity needs in the implementation of innovation. Specialist training and upskilling of diverse stakeholders would be seen as a priority to ensure high-level transfer of knowledge. Value would be placed on democratic buy-in from stakeholders to ensure the implementation of the innovation is successful. However, suggestions for adaptation to suit different contexts or clientele would be encouraged. Mastery of novel tools, processes and services, ensuring that stakeholders understand the aim of the innovation as well as the implementation procedures.

A precise measure of the fidelity of a learning and teaching innovation is learning impact. Moreover, learning impact measures delivered through rich data, i.e. learning analytics, provide evidence that the innovation in a given education setting has a definite positive and measurable impact on access, affordability, engagement, retention, student and/or teacher wellbeing, and/or quality that is sustainable (Vincent-Lancrin et al., 2019). An ability to implement teaching and learning innovations as intended, with fidelity and in a sustainable and scalable manner, is essential to achieve long-term learning impact. Therefore, any learning and teaching innovation implementation should be accompanied by a performance fidelity assessment (Stains & Vickrey, 2017), because the measurement of fidelity allows the attribution of positive intervention outcomes to the original innovation. As Walton et al. (2020:39) explain:

> "Without understanding whether interventions are delivered as planned and engaged with, it is difficult to fully understand whether or not an intervention is effective. Therefore, measuring fidelity and engagement as part of a process evaluation is essential for understanding how and whether an intervention works."

It is vital to focus on fidelity measures to ensure that the benefits of innovations can successfully be implemented not only in one specific context but can be sustained and scaled (Dearing & Cox, 2018; Simpson & Clifton, 2017). Researchers have argued that, too often, a failure of effective knowledge transfer occurs for the community to benefit from research findings. To aid the closing of the innovation implementation gap, innovation fidelity implementation assessments must be carried out (Stains & Vickrey, 2017).

Similar to other research practices, fidelity assessment will need to collect and report on specific data, such as the aim of the fidelity assessment, sampling and context, inter-rater agreement, consistency of results, participant attitudes towards the innovation implementation, practicality of innovation and measure. To determine similarities and differences in implementation patterns of innovations, it is imperative to address implementation fidelity concerning teaching and learning innovation to support evidence-based practice and the sustainability and scalability of an innovation.

Conclusion

In this chapter, we commenced in Section 1 by presenting three broad and idiosyncratic theoretical orientations to teaching and learning in HE. We then introduced, in Section 2, our learning-centred, five-tier model of innovation in higher education, which we believe can fruitfully guide educators as they engage in innovation development and implementation in HE. In Section 3, we argued for the importance of considering the possible role changes for curriculum, educators and students stemming from the innovation. We argue that our learning-centred, five-tier model of innovation offers specific advantages in working with innovations in HE. It invites innovators to reflect upon, and articulate, their personal teaching philosophy, and to seek to understand the impact of their deeply held beliefs and assumptions on their teaching and innovation practice. In this way, the model serves as a guideline and a checklist of essential aspects to help innovators focus on and prioritise the successful implementation of their innovation.

About the Authors

Eva Dobozy, PhD is the former Deputy Dean, Learning and Teaching and Director, Quality Assurance, for the Faculty of Business and Law at Curtin University in Western Australia and Adjunct Professor at Curtin Malaysia. She can be contacted at this e-mail: eva.dobozy@curtin.edu.au

Claus Nygaard is Professor and Executive Director of The Institute for Learning in Higher Education. He can be contacted at this e-mail: info@lihe.info

Bibliography

Anderson, T. & McGreal, R. (2012). Disruptive pedagogies and technologies in universities. *Educational Technology & Society*, 15(4), pp. 380–389.

Anderson, N., Potočnik, K. & Zhou, J. (2014). Innovation and creativity in organisations: A state of-the-science review, prospective commentary, and guiding framework. *Journal of Management*, 40(5), pp. 1297–1333.

Bartholomew, P. (2015). Learning through auto-ethnographic casestudy research. In Guerin, C., Bartholomew, P. & Nygaard, C. (Eds.), *Learning to Research – Researching to Learn*, pp. 241–263. Oxfordshire, UK: Libri Publishing Ltd.

Boer, H. & Boer, H. (2019). Design-for-variety and operational performance: The mediating role of internal, supplier and customer integration. *Journal of Manufacturing Technology Management*, 30(2), pp. 438–461.

Branch, J. & Alyssa M. (2013). Universal Design for Learning in Higher Education. In Nygaard, C., Branch, J. & Holtham, C. (Eds.), *Learning in Higher Education — Contemporary Standpoints*, pp. 111–126, Oxfordshire, UK: Libri Publishing Ltd.

Brookhart, S. M. (2010). *How to assess higher-order thinking skills in your classroom*. Alexandria, Va.: ASCD.

Copenhagen Business School (2019). Student Affairs. https://www.cbs.dk/en/about-cbs/organisation/programme-administration/programme-administration-services/student-affairs

Custovic, E. (2020). 20 books to ignite the innovator in you. *The Nest*. LaTrobe University.

Cygman, L. (2015). Using mobile technology to enhance field education: a blended learning model. In Branch, J., Bartholomew, P. & Nygaard, C. (Eds.), *Technology-Enhanced Learning in Higher Education*, pp. 233–253. Oxfordshire, UK: Libri Publishing Ltd.

Czerniewicz, L. (2018). Unbundling and Rebundling Higher Education in an Age of Inequality. *Educause Review*. https://er.educause.edu/articles/2018/10/unbundling-and-rebundling-higher-education-in-an-age-of-inequality

Dalziel, J. (2015). *Learning design: Conceptualising a framework for teaching and learning online*. New York, N.Y.: Routledge.

Darling-Hammond, L., Flook, L., Cook-Harvey, C., Barrow, B. & Osher, D. (2020). Implications for educational practice of the science of learning and development. *Applied Developmental Science*, 24(2), pp. 97–140.

Dearing, J. & Cox, J. (2018). Diffusion of innovation theory, principles and practice. *Health Affairs*, 37(2), pp. 183–190.

De May, N. (2020). *7 top-notch books on innovation*. https://www.boardofinnovation.com/blog/7-top-notch-books-on-innovation/

Dobozy, E. (2011). Structured dialogue design in LAMS through interactive lecture podcasting. In Chris Alexander, James Dalziel, Jaroslaw Krajka & Richard Kiely (Eds.), *LAMS and Learning Design*. Nicosia, Cyprus: University of Nicosia Press.

Dobozy, E. & Cameron, L. (2018). Editorial: Special issue on learning design research: Mapping the terrain. *Australasian Journal of Educational Technology*, 34(2), pp. i–v.

Gerber, J. (2020). *How to Prototype a New Business*. IDEO U. https://www.ideou.com/blogs/inspiration/how-to-prototype-a-new-business

Grimshaw, J., Eccles, M., Lavis, J., Hill, S. & Squires, J. (2012). Knowledge translation of research findings. *Implementation Science*, 7, Article 50.

Gross, P., Sonnemann, J. & Griffiths, K. (2017). *Engaging students: Creating classrooms that engage learning*. Melbourne, Vic: Grattan Institute.

Hager, L. (2016). Student Self-assessment: ePortfolios and Learning in Higher Education. In Bartholomew, P., Branch, J. & Nygaard, C. *Assessing Learning in Higher Education*, pp. 133–150. Oxfordshire, UK: Libri Publishing Ltd.

Harrington, D. (2018). On the usefulness of 'value' in the definition of creativity: A commentary. *Creativity Research Journal*, 30(1), pp. 118–121.

Ifenthaler, D., Gibson, D. & Dobozy, E. (2018). Informing learning design through analytics: Applying network graph analysis. *Australasian Journal of Educational Technology*, 34(2), pp. 117–132.

Inkermann, D., Gurtler, M. & Seegrun, A. (2020). *RECAP – A framework to support structured reflection in engineering projects*. International Design Conference – DESIGN 2020.

Keupp, M., Palmié, M. & Gassmann, O. (2012). The strategic management of innovation: A systematic review and paths for future research. *International Journal of Management Review*, 14(3), pp. 367–390.

Koc, D. K. (2017). Promoting Self-Regulated Language Learning through a Technology Enhanced Content-based Classroom. In Branch, J., Hayes, S., Hørsted, A. & Nygaard, C. (Eds.), *Innovative Teaching and Learning in Higher Education*, pp. 351–362. Oxfordshire, UK: Libri Publishing Ltd.

Kuratko, D. F., Goldsby, M. G. & Hornsby, J. S. (2019). Understanding the innovative mindset. In Kuratko, D. F., Goldsby, M. G. & Hornsby, J. S. (Eds.), *Corporate Innovation. Disruptive Thinking in Organizations*. London, UK: Routledge.

Leavy, B. (2010), Design thinking – a new mental model of value innovation. *Strategy & Leadership*, 38(3), pp. 5–14.

McCormack, S. & Scanlon, C. (2017). Integrating Innovation and Entrepreneurship into All Undergraduate Courses: The Case of La Trobe University in Australia. In Branch, J., Hørsted, A. & Nygaard, C. (Eds.), *Teaching and Learning Entrepreneurship in Higher Education*, pp. 101–126. Oxfordshire, UK: Libri Publishing Ltd.

Meier, F. & Nygaard, C. (2009). Problem Oriented Project Work in Higher Education. In Nygaard, C. & Holtham, C. (Eds.), *Understanding Learning-Centred Higher Education*. Copenhagen: Copenhagen Business School Press.

Meier, F. & Nygaard, C. (2019). Ten e-learning technologies to support problem based work. In Evans, R. & Nygaard, C. (Eds.), *E-learning 1.0, 2.0, and 3.0 in Higher Education*, pp. 189–210. Oxfordshire, UK: Libri Publishing Ltd.

Meissner, D. & Kotsemir, M. (2016). Conceptualising the innovation process towards the 'active innovation paradigm' – trends and outlook. *Journal of Innovation and Entrepreneurship*, (5), Article 14.

O'Bryan, M. (2013). Innovation: The Most Important and Overused Word in America. Wired, November issue. https://www.wired.com/insights/2013/11/innovation-the-most-important-and-overused-word-in-america/

O'Donnell, A., Dobozy, E., Bartlett, B., Nagel, M., Youssef-Shalala, A., Reeve, J. & Smith, J. (2019). *Educational Psychology* (3rd ed). Australia: John Wiley & Sons.

Perumalla, C., Kee, N., Andreopoulos, R. & Patterson, S. (2017). Impact of eLearning: Looking past the hype. The impact of two Life Science courses on global learners. In Branch, J., Hayes, S., Hørsted, A. & Nygaard, C. (Eds.), *Innovative Teaching and Learning in Higher Education*, pp. 375–386. Oxfordshire, UK: Libri Publishing Ltd.

Piaget, J. (1936). *Origins of intelligence in the child*. London: Routledge & Kegan Paul.

Plattner, H., Meinel, C., & Leifer, L. (Eds.) (2015). *Design Thinking Research: Building Innovators*, Cham, Switzerland: Springer.

Rodan, P. (2016). Public-private partnership in higher education. *Australian Universities' Review*, 58(1), pp. 5–12.

Serdyukov, P. (2017). Innovation in education: What works, what doesn't, and what to do about it. *Journal of Research in Innovative Teaching and Learning*, 10(1), pp. 4–33.

Skillicorn, N. (2016). Infographic: 15 Experts on What Innovation Actually Means. Inc.com. https://www.inc.com/nick-skillicorn/9-defining-characteristics-of-successful-innovation.html

Skinner, B. (1968). *The Technology of Teaching*. New York: Appleton-Century-Crofts.

Simpson, G. & Clifton, J. (2017). Testing diffusion of innovation theory with data. Financial incentives, early adopters, and distributed solar energy in Australia. *Energy Research & Social Science, 29*(1), pp. 12–22.

Stains, M. & Vickrey, T. (2017). Fidelity of implementation: An overlooked yet critical construct to establish effectiveness of evidence-based instructional practice. *CBE – Life Science Education, 16*(1).

Stensaker, B. (2018). Quality assurance and the battle for legitimacy – discourses, disputes and dependencies. *Higher Education Evaluation and Development, 12*(2), pp. 54–62.

Stevens, R. (2012). Identifying 21st century capabilities. *International Journal of Learning and Change,* 6 (3/4), pp. 123–137.

Sweeney, J. & Imaretska, E. (2016). *The Innovative Mindset. 5 Behaviours for Accelerating Breakthroughs.* Hoboken, New Jersey: John Wiley & Sons, Inc.

Thorndike, E. L. (1898). Animal intelligence: An experimental study of the associative processes in animals. *Psychological Monographs: General and Applied, 2*(4), pp. i–109.

Torrisi-Steele, G. (2020). Facilitating the Shift from Teacher Centred to Student Centred University Teaching: Design Thinking and the Power of Empathy. *International Journal of Adult Education and Technology, 11*(3), Article 2, pp. 22–35.

Vincent-Lancrin, S., Urgel, J., Kar, S. & Jacotin, G. (2019). Measuring Innovation in Education 2019: What Has Changed in the Classroom? *Educational Research and Innovation.* Paris: OECD Publishing.

Vygotsky, L. (1978): *Mind in Society. The Development of Higher Psychological Processes.* Cambridge, MA: Harvard University Press.

Waller, R., Lemoine, P., Mense, E., Garretson, C. & Richardson, M. (2019). Global higher education in a VUCA world: Concerns and projections. *Journal of Education and Development, 3*(2), pp. 73–83.

Walton, H., Spector, A., Williamson, M., Tombor, I. & Michie, S. (2020). Developing quality fidelity and engagement measures for complex health interventions. *British Journal of Health Psychology, 25*(1), pp. 39–60.

Yang, J.-L. & McKenzie, S. (2018). Using Career Development Learning in Science and Information Technology Courses to Build 21st-Century Learners. *The Journal of Continuing Higher Education,* (66)3, pp. 137–145.

Chapter 3
Is Higher Education Ready for the Transformed Learner Coming from 9–12? A Case Study

Lennie Scott-Webber, Pam Loeffelman, Dennis Runyan and Marilyn Denison

Introduction

With our chapter, we contribute to this book, *Teaching and Learning Innovations in Higher Education*, as we tell the story of the transformation of the Canyon View High School (CVHS) in the Agua Fria Union High School District #216 in the State of Arizona, USA. The transformation stems from a thorough learning space redesign process used at CVHS. This redesign process led to innovations in design and teaching practices, increased student academic engagement performances, and resulted in the creation of an innovative learning place with a strong community of learning. Figure 1 shows images from the redesigned campus.

Figure 1. No cells, no bells, just a community of learners (with permission of DLR Group, 2019a).

As it appears from the pictures above, the learning space redesign process has enabled CVHS to increase active learning. We recognise that active learning has been practiced in higher education (Scott-Webber *et al.*, 2013; deJong, 2019; Peshterliev *et al.*, 2018; Rai *et al.*, n.d.), and that we may see higher education start to more intentionally incorporate active learning models, although through a different lens and set of parameters. For higher education, one sees the major areas of teaching models moving to active learning primarily in the sciences. Examples include: SCALE-UP (Beichner, 2002), TEAL (Dori & Belcher, 2005), TILE (Fisher-Ingram *et al.*, 2013), and LearnLab (Steelcase, 2012). Our case study of CVHS illustrates how learning space redesign has led to authentic, active learning expectations of high school students. Building on Dobozy and Nygaard (2021, Chapter 2 in this book), the learning theory used in this example is constructivist.

The innovation process at CVHS followed the school district's vision, and used the architect's design-thinking process to realise a full implementation of professional development to modify teaching practices and mindsets. In many ways, this innovation process was disruptive (Christiensen, 1997; Christensen & Raynor, 2003; Kelley & Littman, 2001). Disruptors can be both positive and negative, but in this case, they are all positive. The learning space redesign process at CVHS was led by Dr. Dennis Runyan (current Superintendent of Agua Fria Union High School District of 8,500 students, in Arizona, USA). He had to make some difficult choices in response to the future learning strategies the district would want to pursue, in terms of how the planned learning objectives, and learner experiences would be actualised into a built place. To be effective, he knew from years of experience, he must turn an opportunity to build an 'innovative high school' into a positive disruptor for all. He recognised innovations would need to be holistic and systemic: no small challenge. What transpired reflects the goals of having learning experiences become more real, transformative, systematic, and measurable. Linking back to the five-tier model of innovations in higher education (Dobozy & Nygaard, 2021, Chapter 2 in this book), the learning space redesign process at CVHS became an innovative design solution implementing process, service, and product innovations.

Reading this chapter, you will:
- see the connection between innovation and disruption, and the challenges faced during the change process at CVHS;
- be provided with a rich set of specific examples of design processes and protocols from using this one exemplary school; and
- know 'it takes a village' of experts to realise: (a) a vision, and (b) a plan for sustaining the vision across time in a built place for all users, and (c) the effort incorporating research evidence for:
  - professional development;
  - architectural design; and
  - evaluation of student academic engagement as important indicators of success.

Overview of main sections

Our chapter has 4 sections. In Section 1, we give the background for the learning space redesign process at CVHS and contextualise the ambition to develop a learning space which supports active learning. In Section 2, we show how active learning calls for a paradigm shift. In Section 3, we document the outcomes of the learning space redesign process at CVHS as we share survey results and documented changes in teaching and learning practices. Section 4 holds some reflections on how to move forward with active learning activities now that the learning space has been redesigned.

Section 1: The background

It all started with the educational vision for CVHS as expressed by Dr. Runyan's team:
- "*The divorce between historically traditional classroom learning structures and the emerging potential of clearly dynamic instructional spaces will be evident at Canyon View High School. The lines between individual learning and group dynamics will become softened and enriched through a constant daily drumbeat of collaboration and collective planning*" (conversation with Dr Runyan).

His educational vision is in line with the push of the alpha generation and the pull of industry – to develop future-centred educations by making teaching and learning more practice-based and by putting students' learning experiences first (Ruffo, 2008; Flynn & Vredevoogd, 2010). The process at CVHS evolved from the development of a holistic vision encompassing: (a) deep learning experience expectations, (b) supportive design solutions, (c) professional development, and (d) measuring student engagement outcomes. The challenges were many, but the vision was strong. Using a new build opportunity, the aim was for the design of the built space to provide the visual and physical connecting means to actualise the district's vision. To support this vision, four important changes were made at CVHS. The changes included:

1. defining a clear vision for the curriculum and teaching expectations using evidence-based knowledge about learning;

2. developing a visionary architectural design supporting how these goals would be actualised in a built place;

3. providing professional development sessions expanding on the educators' ability to see how these new methods and new setting designs compliment/support what they will do; and

4. measuring student academic engagement levels through post-occupancy evaluation surveys. It illustrates how this visionary approach (i.e., teaching model, design and teaching preparation) is bridging opportunities for a continuum of education among 9–12 and higher education communities.

In this process, CVHS teamed up with DLR Group, the architectural firm hired to design the new school. DLR Group had a specific process and led a series of collaboratory, ideation (Co-Labs) community sessions generating a vision accommodating a shift – to become fully focused on the students' learning experiences; to create a new architecture for education (as the learning place). Ideation collaboratories are brainstorming sessions (Kelly & Littman, 2001) where all participants contribute in a 'hands-on' process. During these Co-Lab sessions it also became clear that educators, as professional learners, teaching the new curricula while establishing student-centred learning experiences, might benefit from professional development of a different nature. Dr. Runyan and his team used this opportunity to collaborate with DLR Group again having them provide the professional development service – Bridging Organization Learning & Design (BOLD™) (Denison, 2018).

Lines are blurred between ages and abilities with a focus on authentic learning and curricular exploration by expanding the definition of what a 'place-based' high school may become. These changes affect the situational culture's premise, teaching practices, mind-sets, scheduling, and the physical designs of the formal and informal areas of buildings on learning campuses at the micro and macro levels (Scott-Webber *et al.*, 2000). Expectations of how one is allowed to learn is more personal, by employing inquiry-based methods, and allowing students to 'own their own knowledge-gathering processes.' Learners become college and/or career ready with the expectations that these learning experiences will continue through to higher education. If the systems are significantly different (i.e. high school vs. higher education), how might this model translate? Many questions for connecting the two arise and are not fully tackled in this chapter. What the evidence is saying however, is that this new 'norm' is raising the levels of student engagement as seen by both students and their educators – significantly statistically ($P < 0.001$) (Scott-Webber *et al.*, 2017; 2018; 2019b).

The district's vision-to-realisation was challenging. It required leadership to bring an entire community, and an architectural practice to 'see it', and then to generate it into a new reality; since the 'thing' had never before been realized. This chapter focuses on:

1. articulating the district's vision and how it was meant to change learning and teaching experiences, and the challenges faced;

2. recognising how designing to support articulated functions gave way to opportunities to 'think outside the box' and deliver an innovative, award-winning solution;

3. remembering that teaching methods and practices would need to rely on the design of the built place, and thus professional development was provided to support the 'divorce;' and

4. measuring these efforts from both the students' and educators' perspectives post-occupancy was important.

This chapter documents the continuum from vision-to-measurement efforts.

Chapter 3

Section 2: The practice – paradigm shift / generating the vision

For hundreds of years, higher education has been built on teaching – the delivery of information by content experts. Higher education has an issue of how to stack 'em deep to teach them cheap, or efficiencies vs. efficacies (Scott-Webber, 2004; 2012; 2014; 2017; 2019a); the Henry Ford factory model – Instructivist Theory. Hence many new buildings and campuses continue to build large lecture halls (with 10 square feet or .93 meters per person allowance). This design solution perpetuates a passive learning model, even though this format for teaching may more easily, and perhaps more effectively be placed online using a FLIP/Blended learning strategy (Kintu *et al.*, 2017).

Active learning needs space (24/27 square feet or 2.2/2.7 meters per person). Learners must physically be encouraged to move to learn (Kilbourne *et al.*, 2017). Active, authentic learning is learning at a deep level, and means one must experience learning with the employment of all of the senses to keep the 'data' coming into the brain, have emotional and social connections to that data, and then process it into patterns for later retention. Benjamin Franklin is believed to have said, *"Tell me and I forget. Teach me and I remember. Involve me and I learn."* Jean Piaget (Lefa, 2014) the Swiss child psychologist echoed Franklin's thinking by saying, *"Children learn by doing."* All education must transform from the process of educating to a systemic transformation into the involvement in meaningful learning. Today's educational framework is increasingly focusing on 'authentic' learning (Nicaise *et al.*, 2000) allowing students of all levels to understand via context (preferably one of their passion), and thereby better assimilate the information as real.

The Agua Fria Union High School District recognised that holistic changes were needed to support this major paradigm shift. It would impact everything, including curricula, professional development/teacher mind-sets, as well as, the new building's design; including interiors and furnishings. Dr. Runyan explains these changes further:

- *"The access portal that drives the delivery of curriculum at Canyon View High School is centered on technology use interfacing with student grouping variations. In almost 60 percent (60%) of these engagement structures, the teacher interacts as a facilitator rather than as a content expert. In this learning environment, the teacher is metaphorically similar to an artist painting a colourful, almost endless mural rather than planning a linear focus on 'content.' Both the subject matter and materials utilized are jointly selected through ownership of the student. Since the school opened, we have seen a clear intrinsic motivation for students to use the overwhelming abundance of technology tools available. In turn, it is also natural that we have seen intentional space utilization become dynamic rather than static"* (conversation with Dr. Runyan).

A major challenge was not just realising how models and practices for teaching and learning would change, but how the design of these learning places reimagined would need to support these innovative practices. Behaviours for educators and students would be different (Barker, 1968). This change meant a move away from a traditional situational culture of 'ME'/'MY' (i.e., 'my classroom', 'my space') to a 'WE' culture of team-teaching and co-teaching and collaboration. The situational culture had to morph to not just supporting active learning but also supporting active collaboration. The micro area of the built environment gives the cues.

Traditional classrooms (left) are designed in static rows and force students to sit and listen passively. Active learning classrooms (right) promote more interaction between students and instructors. Learning outcomes improve as students become more engaged.

Figure 2: Traditional Passive to New Active (with permission of Steelcase, 2019:5).

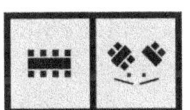

Similarly, the design of traditional conference rooms (left) can cause people to tune out and disengage. Active collaboration settings (right) promote movement, equal participation and deeper engagement.

Figure 3: Traditional Communicating to New Collaborating (with permission of Steelcase, 2019:5).

Visualising the architecture for CVHS is used here as a means to connect the reader with how the paradigm shift's changes manifested themselves in the built form. As architects learn and understand more about how these active learning/collaboration needs function, it means the design of the built place must now be purposeful and offer cues for what types of behaviours are encouraged – designing intentionally aligns expected behaviours (refer back to Figures 2 & 3). The formal and informal places for learning blur as people move from one area of a space, or building, to another focusing on the 'tools' that people need to generate a solution for a specific problem. The learner has choice and control over where and how to get the job of learning done, therefore, learners are given agency; not necessarily orchestrated by the educator or a system.

2a. Design supports an innovative practice

CVHS has been up and running since fall 2018. The divorce between historically traditional classroom learning structures and the emerging potential of clearly dynamic, active, instructional spaces is complete. Specifically, the age-old factory-model design of the formal learning place (row-by-column seating) (Scott-Webber, 2004), or the lecture hall/'classroom' where passive behaviour (refer back to Figure 2) is the norm, is no longer acceptable in the new. In fact, even the word 'classroom' now yields to 'fort', 'maker place', 'nook', learning studio/lab, etc., in an effort to provide behavioural cues that something different is expected here; it will not be passive for either the student or the educator. This chapter uses the process of designing this new building to show the innovative paradigm shift by sharing the premise, the process, and the curricula changes. The authors also share how professional development helped redirect teacher mind-shifts, teacher engagement and collaboration opportunities, and provided spatial orientation connected to content delivery. Finally, it shares research measuring how the design of the built space impacted student engagement levels post-occupancy; a vision-to-measurement effort.

2b: Overview of wholesale changes and how the design process facilitated them

A series of collaboratory, or Co-Lab ideation sessions were facilitated by the architectural firm focused upon:
   1. developing guiding principles based on the school's vision premise;

2. discovering the key pillars for learning, curricula and delivery styles;

3. understanding how technology, both analogue and digital will be infused;

4. knowing that the design of the building will intentionally support these identified and intentional needs; and

5. using a post-occupancy, online survey tool to measure student academic engagement levels as a measure of student success.

2c: Organization of the innovation

To maximise the design firms' series of Co-Lab's collaborative and ideation activities, the district harnessed the creative capacity of its community: students, teachers, administrators, board members, higher education leadership, businesses and design professionals. It wanted multiple perspectives in order to drive the idea to transform CVHS to new levels of creativity and innovation in application; where the continuum through to higher education and industry represented the duality of college and/or career foci. The community visioning helped define a continuum of teaching and learning, and was developed to understand the current circumstance in contrast to a desired future. Students shared that a merger of personal passions into curriculum would be critical to engage them deeply and broaden opportunities for understanding. Rigor, relevance and relationships were to work collectively to support student engagement and success. Each step of the Co-Lab process (Platter *et al.*, 2011) built upon the last, providing greater clarity as the team collectively cemented the programmatic (what will actually get built) variables into a final master plan version for design and construction.

CVHS developed its own premise. It is, "*Blurring the lines between ages and abilities, we will foster authentic learning and curricular exploration by expanding the definition of what a 'place-based' high school may become*" (conversation with Dr. Runyan). Key pillars for learning included common intentional language around supportive terminology, the collective for all stakeholders in planning, and high levels of peer-student collaboration; which lead to the ownership of learning together. What is different? The access portal to drive the delivery of curriculum at CVHS is centred on:

- technology interfacing with student or teacher grouping variations;
- combinations of one-to-one personal interactions (i.e., peer-to-peer, peer-to-teacher, teacher-to-teacher, and person-to-technology);
- the subject matter and materials utilised are being jointly selected through ownership of the student; and
- teacher interactions as a facilitator rather than as a content expert.

The guiding design principles resulting from this collective planning are seen in Figure 4.

Teaching and Learning Provide spaces and places that allow teachers to advance their professional skills, students to examine coursework more deeply and develop collaborative opportunity with peers globally as they do on campus.

Community The school will be a focal point for the community, allowing access to amenities and opportunities for social and intergenerational engagement. These enhanced environments will not only benefit the students with a better education, but the community as a whole.

Partnerships Partnerships between higher education institutions and businesses will provide students with the exposure, experience and opportunities necessary for success.

Healthy Learning Environment Learning will be enhanced through a healthy, sustainable, performance-driven environment that includes the following: natural day-lighting, views to the surrounding community, shade and protection from natural elements, comfortable furniture and a flexible, safe, and sustainable space with a light footprint on the environment.

Technology Technology should be integral to the learning environment and provide students with the skills and experience to be prepared for the future. The school will support project-based learning, the latest science, engineering and creative arts for STEM learning and connections with applied learning and workforce development, all the while adapting to future needs.

Figure 4: Canyon View High School / Schematic Design Book: Guiding Principles for Agua Fria Union High School District (with permission of DLR Group, 2017:14).

Since the school opened, a clear intrinsic motivation for students to use the overwhelming abundance of resources (such as people and technology) is seen. In turn, it is also natural that intentional space utilisation became dynamic rather than static. Thus, *"The lines between individual learning and group dynamics become softened and enriched through a constant daily drumbeat of collaboration and collective planning"* (conversation with Dr Runyan).

It is hot in the state of Arizona, USA, so due to this state's intense climate, a range of place experiences both indoor and outdoor were provided; as the importance grows for time out-of-doors no matter the weather or climate (Bjorge *et al.*, 2017). A variety of places supported the spectrum from the individual, to small-group, to whole-group/gathering, and spaces with different thermal situations. Connections were provided to connect to content and to each other – a setting for what might become a new 'benchmark' for education and educational design.

All aspects of curriculum planning reflect the knowledge that connecting and using sensory experiences is critical for knowledge retention and deep learning. The curricula are focused on the learners' experiences. Curricula were set up to shift learning experiences throughout the day, the hour, and the week; not just physically by moving to different locations, but also by being supported through different educational experts, and 'real world' content. Where curricula meet teaching strategies, and then meets physical designs is shared. The CVHS's vision for curricula became, "*We will maximize content mastery through hands-on exploration, develop skills for success in college/career/life, and allow students to apply their learning in real time in the real world*" (conversation with Dr Runyan). Now that students were set up for success, it was time to prepare educators to navigate in this fully realized Constructivist Theory world.

The design vision for the educator was 'operationalised' using the Bridging Organization Learning & Design (BOLD™) (Denison, 2018) process with the eventual users. Curricula, teaching practices, and the professional development to change mind-sets in a codified fashion where expectations are clear was provided. The intentionality focused on how the spatial design could influence the new practice ideas for learning, and also recognised the need for career readiness whether through the route of higher education or a career/technical path. The building's design was to offer the opportunity to strengthen relationships, foster multiple teaching strategies (such as individual, team-, and co-teaching; within disciplines, and across disciplines) in order to better individualise learning opportunities and nurture a culture of transformational practices that were student-focused, faculty-guided and/or self-guided.

Behavioural changes were expected. To facilitate new behaviours a new vocabulary was introduced to define settings including: Accelerator, fort, learning lab, and agora. A provision of fluid 'in-the-moment' space shifting with 'no closed spaces' was the design norm. A note from the new principal when interviewing for new faculty, "*If you think you're going to come here, go into your classroom and teach for eight hours, that is not going to happen here*" (conversation with Principal, Phillip Nowlan (https://www.aguafria.org/cvhs).

2c: Organization of the innovative practice

Visions do not develop in darkness. Dr. Runyan and his team provided thoughtful consideration of learning theories, instructional models, pedagogical strategies, classroom ownership, schedules, spatial diversity, movement and time. They realised all were necessary considerations in the development of CVHS as an innovative model for the future of engaged learning.

To fully understand how the vision would function in the 'real world', DLR Group used an activity with the stakeholders – 'A Day in the Life.' This activity was conducted and cast in a future context of 2026 through three stakeholder lenses: student, teacher and community member. This activity was then compared to the district exercise that included the present 2016 day as well as the future 2026 day. The present 2016 student day was chronicled, through in-person classroom observations, where the architectural experts spent two days at district schools, attending classes as student shadows. During this time on campus, team members noted activities taking place, time in any one configuration (whole class, small group, individual work, etc.) as well as any spaces used. Recognising that the 16+ classes attended could not capture the depth and breadth of learning activities, the team also asked faculty to outline the same factors for courses in each department to gain a broader perspective. All of the observations and input collected were then charted for comparison (see Figures 5 & 6). The 2026 future state was also outlined in a narrative schedule format in Co-Lab sessions complete with: (a) structure (academic organizational model), (b) focus (central idea), and (c) key attributes (critical element for each stakeholder type) were captured.

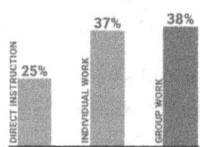

Current Instruction
The bar charts depict current observations and input collected during our "Day in the Life" activities in 2016 as a District exercise, as well as the data collected from Agua Fria High School teachers in 2017 for the masterplan.

Activities tend to lean towards a historically traditional instructional model with most teachers owning classrooms and utilizing lecture and direct instruction collectively.

Figure 5: Canyon View High School / Schematic Design Book – Current State Planning (with permission of DLR Group, 2017:66).

Future Planning

These charts quantify both the percentage of time modality and anticipated location-based needs for curriculum and instruction projected in the future at the high school and the district. The charts on the right indicate small group instruction is anticipated to be the dominant learning modality.

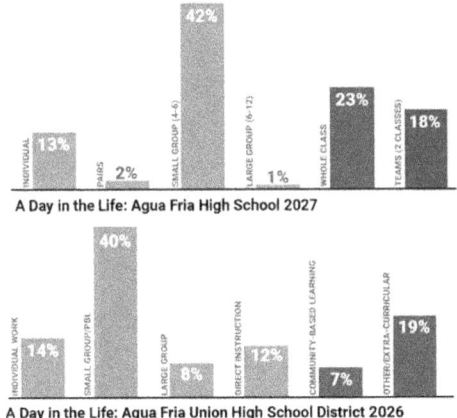

Below, the host locations for the modalities appear to be highly varied and uniformly distributed across the facility, again validating a collective ownership model for the campus.

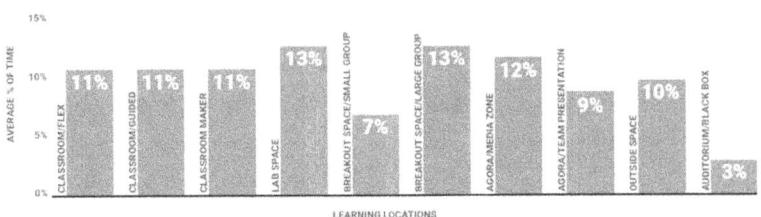

Figure 6: Canyon View High School / Schematic Design Book – Future State Planning (with permission of DLR Group, 2017:73).

The 'Day in the Life' exercises provided insights to move to the next planning step – utilisation.

2d: Preparation for the innovation practice – utilisation

As mentioned, thoughtful consideration of instructional models, pedagogical strategies, classroom ownership, schedules, spatial diversity, movement and time were deemed necessary in the development of CVHS. As each step of the Co-Lab process sessions built upon the last, each provided greater clarity as the team collectively cemented the programmatic variables into this final master plan version for design and construction. Synergy existed among the stakeholders on specific ideas related to the structure, foci, and key attributes. Collective ownership of space, in stark contrast to the teacher-owned classrooms today, provided movement and freedom to explore curriculum and became critical in the design and function of spaces for the school. The design firm's program modelling tool accounts for student enrolment at the individual class level, ensuring that spatial typologies are supportive of the curricular needs on a course by course basis. It also accounts for the fact that classrooms rotate on a weekly basis to maximise the variety in experiences by both teacher and student. Those patterns are then translated into space needs and square footages (square meters). Any future courses not offered today were also entered, so that the high school would be ready as growth occurs.

2e: What was learned?

There were four main learnings and these are shared next. Firstly, learning must be inspiring. Student input was critical to the success of the project. Obtaining first-hand accounts of current needs, as well as what students wanted for those who would follow them, was profound. While the process was centred around this new campus, the feedback would be considered district-wide. It was heard that tutoring, access to materials and resources, curricular choice, multiple ways of learning topics, the ability to find passion in and relevance for the coursework would drive students towards success faster. In some cases, students expressed that relevance of the coursework could also help them choose a career or college major that suited their skills, or at least show them what they might not be adept at, sooner rather than later, when it was costing time and money after high school.

Secondly, learning requires a positive culture; the teacher must play a variety of roles as the shift towards a student-centred learning environment occurs. As the curriculum changes, collaboration between teachers becomes more important than ever. Interdisciplinary and project-based learning, for example, requires creativity, constant iteration and critical feedback from peers, and processes and protocols that clearly define expectations. Working this way requires great spaces for teachers beyond the classroom including ranges of space alternatives, from working alone in an isolated space to large whole class gathering areas (Scott-Webber, 2020).

Thirdly, teachers should not be left behind. Spaces should be built where teachers are encouraged to actively collaborate and co-create, as well as concentrate, assess, and prepare (Scott-Webber, 2020). At the same time, spaces must foster a professional community throughout the school. The informal spaces, in-between, from classroom portals to corridors, are just as important to collaboration as formal spaces. Given the challenging nature of the work, teachers require ample downtime, with spaces for them to get away, relax and recharge.

Fourthly, learning happens in the community. Involving the community in the design and learning process adds an important context and connection. This process provides the time to embrace elements of a larger culture (such as safety, health, engagement, challenge, support). It also requires thinking about a return to 24-hour community use, every day of the year where the total environment is considered a collaborative space. The learning culture is more than the school facility itself – the collective relationship is what will develop this culture.

Utilisation variables ultimately controlled the design master plan program's size. The core team discussed the effect that adjusting the variables would have on the final design solution based upon the forecasted instructional approach, flexibility, movement and student choice (scheduling). "Those variables are further defined as follows:

1. *Student Population* was the planned enrolment or the ideal number of students that the facility would be designed to accommodate in an educationally adequate manner in keeping with design parameters described;

2. *Planned Room Utilisation* was a measurement of time. With six school periods per day, the agreed upon 83% utilization signified that every room would be available, at least one period per day, outside of planned or assigned uses. As a global program factor, the significance of this was twofold, as it afforded future flexibility in master scheduling, as well as the ability to adjust course offerings overtime; and

3. *Scheduling / Course Offering Factor* was a measurement of a single room's occupancy rate. The closer the number was to 1.0, the program model anticipated that each seat was full, leaving less freedom for students to enrol in electives like art, music or CTE

courses" (DLR Group, *Canyon View High School – A4LE James D. MacConnell Award Dossier, 2019b:28*). The typical schedule block was developed for 90 minutes.

Figure 7 depicts the CVHS's design class sizes input into the program model. Each class size was then applied to a space type, and then to a course type. Courses may be divided, on a percentage of time basis, into multiple sizes to simulate class activities, along with both student and teacher movement throughout the day. For this purpose, a wide variety of space sizes are input.

Class Size / Students	
38	General Instruction: Max Enrolment
12	Large Group
6	Small Group
76	Teams (2x General Instruction)
50	PE / Wellness Section Size
18	Special Services

Figure 7: Canyon View High School / Class size variables (with permission of DLR Group, A4LE James D. MacConnell Award Dossier, 2019b:28).

Through these visioning and design efforts, the school works to maximise content mastery through hands-on exploration, develop skills for success in college/career/life, and allow students to apply their learning in real time, and in the real world.

Section 3: The outcomes; no stone left unturned

CVHS is different, and the differences were intentional. The traditional boundaries of teaching and learning were expanded to create the best possible learning experience for students and teachers attending CVHS. To support the district's vision of a new school, a team of educators, designers, engineers, community members, and researchers set out to turn the traditional collaborative process into an experimental, co-creative journey. A journey that began in 2015 continues to influence how we might re-invent a new way of 'doing school' for the future of teaching and learning. Particular initiatives enabled innovative change: (1) courage to experiment, (2) catalyst for change, (3) spatial agility, (4) allied partnerships and community, (5) small learning communities, (6) the Accelerator, and (7) flexible learning suites. These intentional, innovative initiatives enabled change. They were deemed important enough to do primary research as a case study. The next segments share the research protocols, an explanation of these initiatives, and a demonstration of user perceptions in reference to their experiences, in the new building's design.

3a: Research protocols

A research initiative was launched to use post-occupancy evaluations by an independent researcher (Scott-Webber *et al.*, 2019b). Both the students' and the teachers' perspectives were measured. This research used a Human-centred Research Design (HcRD) protocol (Scott-Webber *et al.*, 2019b; 2000), with mixed-methods, and an online survey tool questioning both students and educators. These surveys were done to garner findings from both students and educators, in a post-occupancy situation. In the USA, the average in-class time is 7 hours per day for approximately 180 days = 1,260 hours per year. Research over multiple years has indicated from both the students' and the educators' perspectives that the design of the school makes a significant difference relative to student academic engagement performance (Nissim *et al.*, 2016; Scott-Webber, 2012, 2014, 2019a; Scott-Webber *et al.*, 2008; 2013; 2014; 2018; 2019b).

Engagement does matter – online or onsite. Engagement performance is a high predictor of student success across multiple domains and learning/work experiences (NSSE, 2010), and this research's focus. The research question was, '*Can we demonstrate that the design of the built environment for grades 9–12 impacts student academic engagement levels post-occupancy?*' The teachers' survey was submitted online to all teachers in a pre-condition, and then to all students and educators who voluntarily, self-reported perceptions three months post-occupancy.

A Post-Occupancy Evaluation (POE) studies the impact of design on its users (Preiser & Rabinovits, 1988). It also provides the opportunity to: (a) understand the level of academic engagement as perceived by both students, and educators about their students, (b) understand where design is supporting educational efforts relative to teaching models and practices, and then (c) how this knowledge may be used to impact the design of the next learning spaces. Two indexes have been developed specifically for DLR Group's K-12 Education Practice and tested for reliability and validity to measure the research question. The resulting survey instruments are the Student Engagement Index™ (SEI) and Teacher Engagement Index™ (TEI).

Each question analysed different aspects of engagement from the ability to move about freely, to simple items as being able to hear, see, connect with others and be comfortable (Scott-Webber et al., 2000). The two surveys had some differences. The students (SEI) had them sharing their perceptions of his/her engagement. The teachers (TEI) were asked his/her impressions of his/her students' engagement levels using the same questions used for the students. This approach allowed for a direct comparison between the two sets of perceptions. However, the teachers were also asked several questions relative to their own individual levels of engagement, and how the design supported pedagogy and workplace culture.

Environmental qualities were also asked about along with teaching strategies. Q3 and Q5 are particularly telling in that the first provides insight on whether the student perceived a relation between the design of space and their individual motivation to do better, get higher grades – in other words stay actively engaged in their learning process. The latter has become the index identifier. And design does matter to the student ($P > 0.001$), and their perceptions match previous work done on this age cohort (Scott-Webber et al., 2017; 2018; 2019b). An explanation about the initiatives is next, along with pertinent research findings.

3b: Design initiatives and research findings

The overall design is like a community learning marketplace, as seen in Figure 8. *"We solicited feedback from community members as to what a high school might look like, not from a design standpoint but from a substantive performance point of view. The questions that drove the discussion were, 'What and who is the 2019 student? How does he/she learn? How should this student be taught, and what kind of a teacher will team them. How will these same questions be answered a decade from now? Will our project still be relevant?' The answers to our questions became Canyon View High School"* (Ron T., community member).

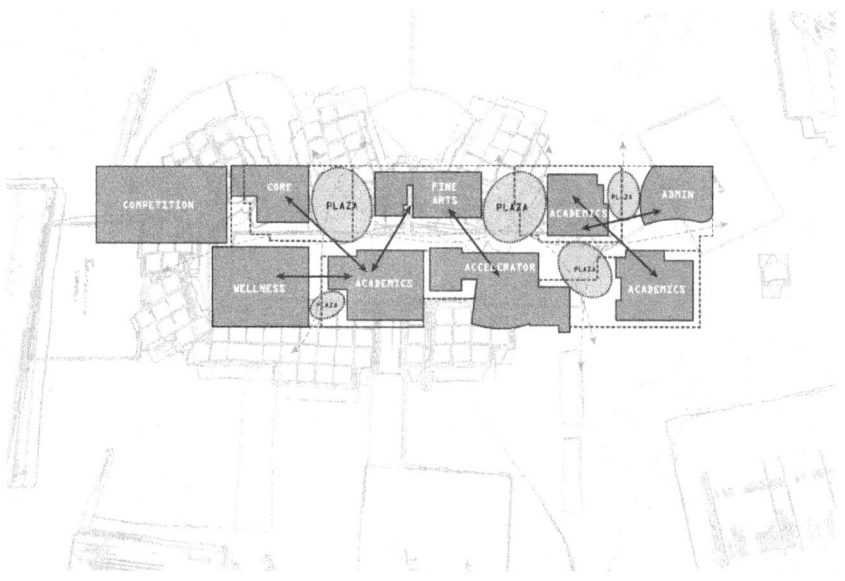

Figure 8: Canyon View High School / A Learning Marketplace (with permission of DLR Group, A4LE James D. MacConnell Award Dossier, 2019b:11).

Each of the seven initiatives are explained and relevant research findings shared.

Initiative 1: Courage to experiment

Throughout the planning, design, construction, and professional development process – and now at the conclusion of year two – this school district has been pursuing an iterative process of experimentation to develop a new innovative model – using a process, a service and a product (Dobozy & Nygaard, 2021, Chapter 2 in this book) for a high school that engages each student with their own personal road map for success. Rather than leaving solutions up to conventional assumptions, an engaging holistic ethnographic approach was used to see more thoroughly into the world of teaching and learning; a reimagined active learning constructivist model.

Chapter 3

Questions 3 and 5, in Figures 9 and 10, capture the overall perspectives in terms of its impact on students from both users, along with the comparative pre / or 'before' (previous / before condition was not at this school) / post teacher analysis.

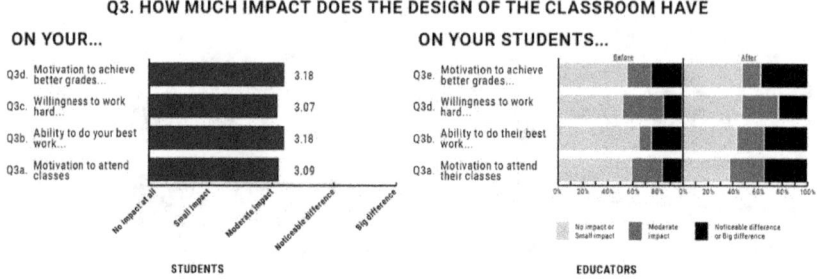

Figure 9: Q.3. How much impact does the design of the classroom have on your students...(students' and teachers' comparative data).

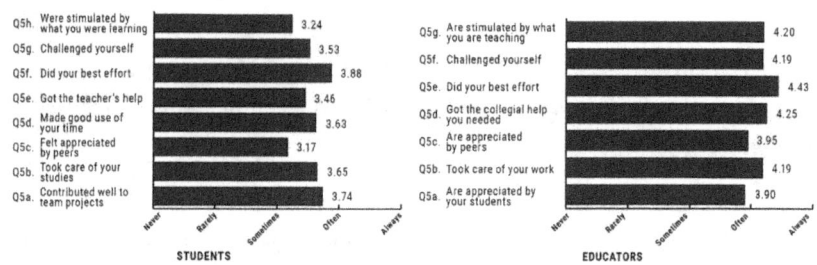

Figure 10: Q5. At the end of a school day, how often do you feel that you... (students' and teachers' comparative data).

Initiative 2: Catalyst for change

As expressed by the district, and supported by the community from day one, "This is the time to be bold. This is when we unite around a common set of goals that are on the horizon," as per Board Member. The outcome has been far reaching, with a solution for Canyon View High School as a substantial investment that will transform the community and continuum of learners for decades. Several questions provide a telling summary of transformations. The same question 9 is analysed in multiple ways. The graphs below for question 9 are worth studying. Clearly, students and educators have some differences of opinions (see Figure 11).

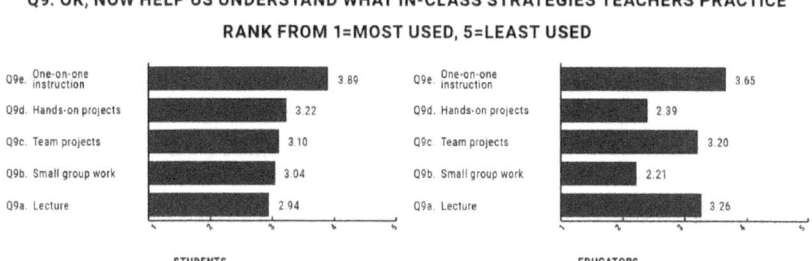

Figure 11: In-class teaching strategies (students' and teachers' comparative data).

While the educator sample size was too small for statistical inference, this next teaching practice runs from the before situation (teaching in a different school) to the current (teaching at CVHS). It clearly shows some attempt to change teaching practices in the new setting (see Figure 12).

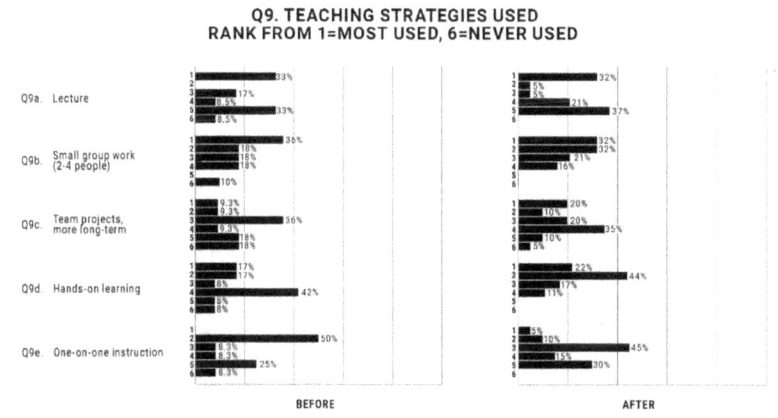

Figure 12: Q9. OK, now help us understand what in-class strategies you practice.

Chapter 3

A follow up question #10 was only for educators and is shown in Figure 13.

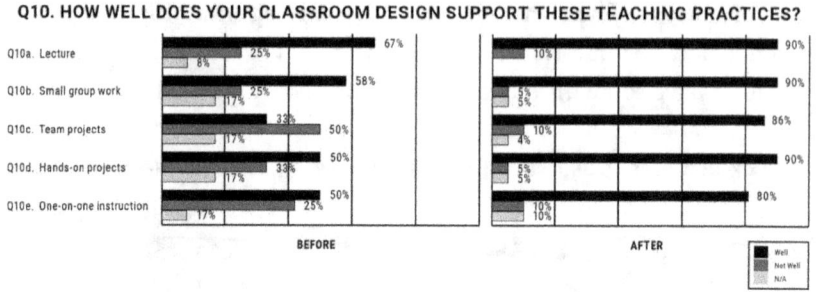

Figure 13: Q.10. How well does your classroom design support these teaching practices?

Initiative 3: Spatial agility

Flexible, agile spaces help students prepare for their higher education or workforce-ready futures. Open, democratic use of space allows the whole facility to be used by different groups in a variety of different ways: (a) from students-to-staff, and (b) to a community of lifelong learners, and (c) community partners throughout the region. Spaces are easily reconfigured school year to school year, but also hour-by-hour throughout the day. Every inch of every space is versatile enough to constantly be in use. Question 2, in Figure 14 shares the data on responses to this new model supporting moving to learn – active learning.

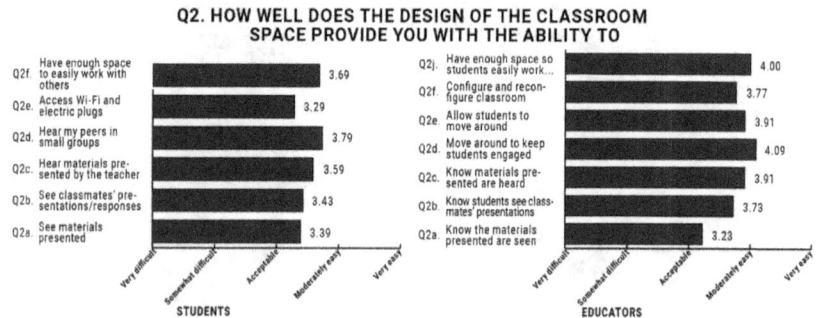

Figure 14: Q.2. How well does the design of the classroom spaces provide you with the ability to…(students' and teachers' comparative data).

Initiative 4: Allied partnerships & community

Community partnership added context and voice for this constituents' concerns. It was recognised that it was time to embrace elements of a larger culture, like: safety, health, engagement and well-being, challenge and holistic support. There was agreement to return to a 24-hour community use, every day of the year, whereby the whole campus is considered to be collaborative space; where the learning culture is more than the school facility itself. The collective relationships developed a vital presence for the community to play in the eventual success of CVHS. The sense of 'belonging' is necessary for people to excel. These next sets of findings (see Figures 15 and 16) suggest user success in connecting to the school as a community.

Figure 15: Q.6. Design features often tell a story. Based on the overall design of your school's physical spaces, what do you think your school values? (students' and teachers' comparative data).

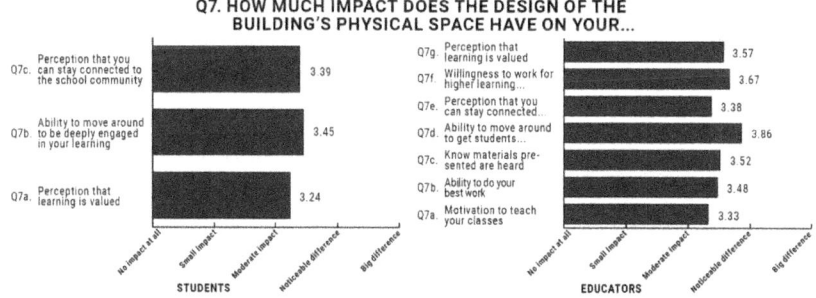

Figure 16: Q.7. How much impact does the design of the building's physical spaces have on your…(students' and teachers' comparative data).

Chapter 3

The design of the learning marketplace consisted of small learning communities, a central spine, purpose-built spaces and the combining factor, or heart as the Accelerator, and Flexible Learning Suites. Descriptions of the major spatial types are next along with data from the findings.

Initiative 5: Small learning communities

The design is the culmination of engineering a local climatic response for indoor-outdoor learning, alongside the charge to create small flexible learning communities for a student population of 1,800. Arranged as a linear series of opposing building forms along an exterior central spine, called the Agora, four small learning communities, called Academic Forts, are woven together by interior/exterior navigation pathways along the north. To the South of the Academic Forts, a series of building forms house public functions like the Auxiliary Gym, Music Suite, White Box Auditorium, and the Accelerator – a cluster of complimentary learning environments that promote exploration and experimentation into the future of teaching and learning. The campus plan was designed then to support small learning communities (e.g., academy model), where all students have to declare a passion, and there is a transdisciplinary interaction expected between content areas (see Figure 17).

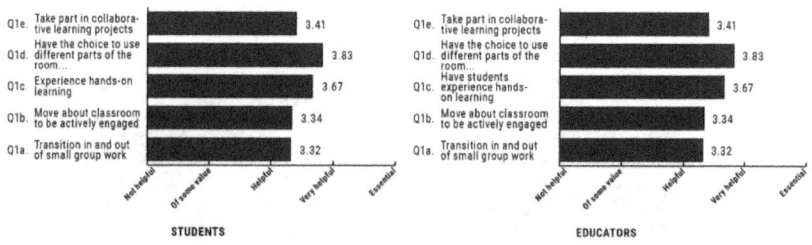

Figure 17: Q1. For you to be actively engaged in your learning, how important is it for you to be able to…(students' and teachers' comparative data).

A separate question asked the educators only how well the design performed (see Table 1).

Q1. How well does the design of the space support that activity?	N	Mean	Standard deviation
Q1a2. Transition in and out of small group work – Design supports	22.00	1.86	0.35
Q1b2. Move about classroom to be actively engaged – Design supports	22.00	1.91	0.29
Q1c2. Experience hands-on learning – Design supports	22.00	1.86	0.35
Q1d2. Have the choice to use different parts of the room to do work with others – Design supports	22.00	1.91	0.29
Q1e2. Take part in collaborative learning projects – Design supports	22.00	1.95	0.21

Table 1: How well does the design support pedagogical practices?

An overall question asked each to respond to how the indoor environmental qualities affected their learning and/or teaching (see Figure 18). Environmental factors often contribute to whether or not 'learning shuts down' (Scott-Webber *et al.*, 2000). The following figure 18 about the classroom and the building overall are particularly telling relative to the 'culture,' or climate of the environment.

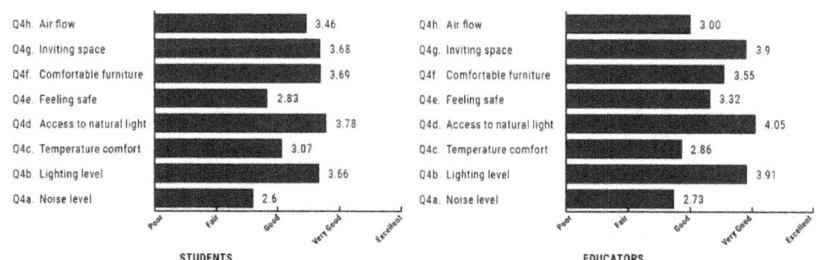

Figure 18: Environmental qualities compared (students' and teachers' comparative data).

Chapter 3

Initiative 6: The accelerator

"*The reshaping of space for multiple use design played a significant role in planning common use areas such as the Accelerator. The pivot from professional development, community use, and functional learning spaces was seamlessly available*" (Dr. Runyan). As the heart of the campus, the Accelerator infuses experimentation into everyday innovation with the Multi-Use Creative Lab, Maker Space, as well as providing a focal point for student and teacher professional development. It is here, at the heart, that ongoing invention and reinvention into the art of teaching and learning will occur – sustaining a creativity engine for decades to come. Primary to the Accelerator is the Theatre, equipped with traditional fixed seating in the lower bowl and a retractable flat floor seating system at the back of the bowl. The provision of flexible arrangements allows for a wide range of activities including functional testing or medium-to-large scale rapid prototyping. The adjacent complementary space, nicknamed the White Box – eluding to its theatrical and professional collaboration purposes – is designed to work independently or in tandem with the Theatre. Special features like glass airplane hangar doors enable the Agora, Accelerator, and Theatre to open to the Learning Stair which allows the aggregate settings to support the 137+ activities identified as district priorities; ranging from symposia, expositions, theatrical and lecture events – to hands-on project work and special guest events. There were no specific data points collected for the Accelerator.

Initiative 7: Flexible learning suites

- "*The collaboration options for grouping students becomes paramount and driven by teachers and students in a direct weekly design together which varies frequently. This situation would be in direct contrast to a more traditional model in many higher education environments which tend to look more like a traditional lecture format*" (Dr. Runyan).

The Academic Forts house learning suites as a series of connected settings that can flexibly merge with one another in support of 'pedagogy of the moment.' A blend of six primary Learning Studios are positioned around the perimeter of each suite with two labs and connections in-between.

Individual studio ownership is transferred to the collective community, affording students the freedom to explore curriculum that best aligns with their personal, academic, or professional interests. Each suite provides a variety of spaces that can flex in size and configuration throughout the day depending on the type of group activities scheduled or emerging – furniture as a resource and affordance aids in fostering a place that welcomes how students learn best – anytime, anywhere. Anchoring each Fort is a Faculty Collaboration Hub on the ground level adjacent to the Agora and learning studios as varied as Art & Graphic Design, Life Skills, and Career & Technical Education. What is important to know here is that both students and educators change learning spaces on a weekly basis. Due to these changes, "*A number of teachers, after their first year at CVHS, expressed their vision that the profession grew, or was positively restored*" (Dr Runyan). Several data findings share information on how students and teachers navigated these new learning environments.

In total, the building's forms and functional adjacencies blur the boundaries between inside and outside, teaching and learning, and public and private, giving rise to the deep need for flexibility as a context for relevant learning in the 21st century. The result of this experimental approach to design and education, begun in 2015, is clear: CVHS is a school with neither 'cells nor bells,' a school that is centred around the learner, and a place that is safe for failure and one that fosters success. This school's design and the holistic process to get there won the coveted MacConnell Award for Architecture – 2019 (see Figures 19 & 20) (Loeffelman, 2019).

Figure 19: Canyon View High School / Layouts CVHS (with permission of DLR Group, A4LE James D. MacConnell Award Dossier, 2019b:13)

Chapter 3

Figure 20: Canyon View High School, Agua Fria Union High School District (with permission of DLR Group, 2019b).

One student sums up his experience: *"It's the small details. The colours of the forts increase the creativity and your mindset of thinking,"* says Tony A., Freshman student. The information from the students at CVHS revealed that they clearly understand how the design of the built space impacts how well they perceived they were engaged academically. It also appeared to motivate them to achieve higher outcomes (the equivalent of higher grades).

We saw some pre- and post-comparisons from teachers and some 'telling' differences. The 'pre' examined teachers in their previous condition prior to coming to CVHS, the 'post' was held at the end of the second term in the new building. Once again, teachers indicated the design of the learning places has important factors encouraging the development of higher levels of student engagement. What this research continues to reveal is that although teachers appreciate that the design of the built space impacts their engagement levels, the 'cultural climate' in which they work is even more important to them (Scott-Webber et al., 2017, 2018, 2019b). Clearly, teachers were feeling that their students were more academically engaged, based on the new marriage of pedagogy and place; in part due to the design of the built space, both at the micro and macro levels. They also commented on how different it was to work in this new setting and how well they were supported.

3c: Innovative services for teacher professional development

Without an active teacher, active learning does not happen. Professional development to learn how to use new spatial designs is critical (Nissim et al., 2016). Therefore, another aspect of the transformational change provided was professional development. Here the leadership and teachers experienced a service-add, to potentially increase the understanding of how to operationalize the design vision, and a spatial orientation of how to use these new types of spatial solutions as 'learning tools.' The service used here was BOLD™.

The BOLD service (Loeffelman, 2019; Denison, 2018) is a robust change process that supports campus leadership and teachers in successfully implementing change and empowering teachers to leverage their new facilities fully – as 'tools for learning.' Technological advancements have driven massive changes in education. In the past, school systems invested heavily in technology hardware, but soon learned that investing in tools without training teachers to use them had varied results. Likewise building engineers and maintenance staff are trained to properly manage new, advanced building systems to improve efficiency. Staff are required to develop new behaviours and daily tasks to truly leverage the potential of the new systems provided. Furthermore, emerging research shows innovative learning environments are consistently tied to high levels of students' deep learning, but only when teachers also report high teacher mind frames. When investing in new innovative learning places, including physical space, furniture and technology, it is important to also invest in developing organisational systems to sustainably support changes in curricula and provide professional development to ensure new learning behaviours are optimised. Teachers at CVHS went through this professional development training process. Several structural changes were made:

- classroom ownership was transferred to the collective school, allowing students greater freedom to explore curriculum, wherever it may physically take them;
- educational experiences would take place both inside and outside of the building, have the flexibility to be held in spaces designed to suit the learning of the moment and adjust when necessary;

- communication and respect were core principles underpinning the success of this scheduling arrangement; and
- behavioural expectations for learning and teaching changed.
- "The design has made a big impact. I chose to go to this school. I could have gone anywhere. I am super excited and want to learn every day! Not only does the environment make us light up, it also makes the teachers light up. And the students can see that in the teachers, and it makes us want to do more" (Jade, Freshman student, recorded from the Principal's Advisory Group).

Section 4: Moving forward

CVHS and the Agua Fria Union High School District are models for the future and how higher education might benefit from its learnings – from vision-to-measurement efforts. Results include:

- 11% increase in the district's graduation rate; and a
- 200% increase in the number of students taking course work at advanced levels, reflecting college level preparation.

Clearly, more knowledgeable voices must be present early on in the pre-design and visioning sessions. Those voices ideally include teachers, students, community members and other disciplines such as interior design and research. There is so much knowledge, from so many domains, relative to the learner, the learning process, and the learning place, that all must be leveraged moving forward. These authors argue we have to start the design of the educational place with the understanding of: (a) what the learning behaviours look like, feel like, and need, (b) how to use this knowledge from CVHS to understand how teaching strategies, adoptions of learning theories will differ, (c) begin to develop intentionally designed, behaviour-supportive interior solutions, and (d) when to build the overarching structure to house them. Nevertheless, the community, teachers and students must understand how this vision will be realised in 'bricks and mortar,' and the essential roles they all play in the stewardship of realising the potential of that shared vision.

Conclusion

It can be done; it is being done. Active learning and active collaboration do not happen just by chance. Systematic, community-wide transformational processes are necessary in order for learning outcomes to advance; whether online or onsite. Empirical evidence shows the positive impact when these items are intentionally connected. That impact articulates that students are more highly engaged in their own learning processes when they are given agency over it, and the design of the built space is designed to support those activities. There are some important applications for higher education to consider based on this case study:

- professional development programs specific to teaching strategies should study the relationship between collaboration/learning space, technology usage, and student ownership of learning (i.e., the BOLD™ program);

- student engagement is expected. It must be cultivated and enriched through trust and collaboration to reach deep learning; and

- the architectural design of space is directly influencing learning, offering behavioural cues, and should be studied for equity, efficacy of learning, and faculty professional support.

Currently, the learnings from CVHS are influencing renovations of a 58-year-old high school, as it is reimagining itself with the principles set out by this architectural firm and the BOLD re-training of teachers; transitioning the teachers' creativity into these dynamic space types – all based on the Agua Fria, CVHS's experience.

Nevertheless, how might this model translate to a higher educational experience if the systems are significantly different? Many questions for connecting the two arise and are not fully tackled in this chapter. What evidence is saying however, is that this new 'norm' is raising the levels of student engagement, as student agency, as seen by both students and their teachers, and is statistically significant ($P < 0.001$).

- *"It is one thing to develop superior spaces that enable teachers to prepare students for the 21st century. We reached a whole new level when DLR Group facilitated our staff to allow space to support learning approaches. Through the team's superior professional development,*

> *our staff grew into the mission and acquired the necessary mindset and skills to use the building environments as designed. There is total alignment between the intent of the building design and instructional delivery to support teaching and learning. Well done and thank you!"* (Mary K., Governing Board Member Agua Fria School District).

Acknowledgement

This research was funded by DLR Group's K-12 Education Practice. We encourage readers to reach out to the authors for the full study.

About the Authors

Lennie Scott-Webber, Ph.D., is Owner / Principal at INSYNC: Education Research + Design. She can be contacted at this e-mail: lenniesw.insync@yahoo.com

Pam Loeffelman is K-12 Education Leader and Principal at DLR Group. She can be contacted at this e-mail: ploeffelman@dlrgroup.com

Dennis Runyan, Ph.D., is Superintendent at Agua Fria Union High School District #216. He can be contacted at this e-mail: drunyan@aguafria.org

Marilyn Denison, Ed.D., is K-12 Education Planner and Senior Associate at DLR Group. She can be contacted at this e-mail: mdenison@dlrgroup.com

Bibliography

Barker, R. G. (1968). Concepts and methods for studying the environment of human behavior. *Ecological Psychology*. Stanford, CA: Stanford University Press.

Beichner, R. J. (2002). SCALE-UP: Student-centered active learning environment for undergraduate programs. North Carolina State University. Retrieved from: https://www.compadre.org/per/items/detail.cfm?ID=585

Bjorge, S., Hannah, R., Rekstad, P. & Pauly, T. (2017). The behavioural effects of learning outdoors. Retrieved from. *SOPHIA. The St. Catherine University Masters of Arts in Education action research papers repository website*: https://sophia.stkate.edu/maed/232

Christensen, C. M. (1997). *The innovator's dilemma: When new technologies cause great firms to fail*. Boston, MA: Harvard Business School Press.

Christensen, C. M. & Raynor, M. (2003). *The innovator's solution: Creating and sustaining successful growth*. Boston: Harvard Business School Press.

deJong, T. (2019). Moving towards engaged learning in STEM domains; There is no simple answer, but clearly a road ahead. *Journal of Computer Assisted Learning*, 35, pp. 153–167.

Denison, M. (2018). DLR Group & Denison, M. BOLD™. *Bridging organizational change and design*. Retrieved from: https://www.dlrgroup.com/media/736347/bold-dlr-group-bridging-organizational-learning-and-design.pdf

DLR Group. (2017). Canyon View High School / Current state planning – schematic design book. DLR Group.

DLR Group. (2019a). Canyon View High School / Design development timeline. DLR Group.

DLR Group. (2019b). Canyon View High School / A4LE James D. MacConnell Award of Excellence. DLR Group.

Dobozy, E. & Nygaard, C. (2021). A learning-centered, five-tier model of innovation in higher education. In Enomoto, K., Warner, R. & Nygaard, C (Eds.), *Teaching and Learning Innovations in Higher Education*, pp. 19–46. Oxfordshire, UK: Libri Publishing Ltd.

Dori, Y. J. & Belcher, J. (2005). How does technology-enabled active learning affect undergraduate students' understanding of electromagnetism concepts? *The Journal of the Learning Sciences*, 14(2), pp. 243–279.

Fisher-Ingram, B., Jesse, M. & Van Horne, S. (2013). Transform, interact, learn, engage (TILE): Creating learning spaces that transform undergraduate education. In Carpenter, R. G. (Ed.), *Cases on higher education spaces: Innovation, collaboration, and technology*. IGI Global, pp. 165–185.

Flynn, W. J. & Vredevoogd, J. (2010), The future of learning: 12 views on emerging trends in higher education, *Planning for Higher Education*, 38(2), pp. 5–10.

Kelley, T. & Littman, J. (2001). *The art of innovation: Lessons in creativity from Ideo, America's leading design firm*. New York: Currency/Doubleday.

Kilbourne, J., Scott-Webber, L. & Kapitula, L. R. (2017). An activity-permissible classroom: Impacts of an evidence-based design solution on student engagement and movement in an elementary school classroom. *Children, Youth and Environments*, 27(1), pp. 112–134.

Kintu, M. J., Zhu, C. & Kagambe, E. (2017). Blended learning effectiveness: The relationship between student characteristics, design features and outcomes. In *Journal of Educational Technologies in Higher Education*, 14(7).

Lefa, B. (2014). The Piaget theory of cognitive development, and educational implications. *Educational Psychology* 1(1), pp. 1–8.

Loeffelman, P. (2019a). Retrieved from: https://www.dlrgroup.com/work/agua-fria-high-school/ https://www.aguafria.org/cvhs

Loeffelman, P. (2019b). Canyon View High School – A4LE James D. MacConnell Award Dossier. https://macconnell.a4le.org/

Loeffelman, P. (2017). *Canyon View High School schematic design book*. DLR Group.

Nicaise, M., Gibney, T. & Crane, M. (2000). Toward an understanding of authentic learning: student perceptions of an authentic classroom. *Journal of Science Education and Technology*, 9, pp. 79–94.

Nissim, Y., Weissblueth, E., Scott-Webber, L. & Amar, S. (2016). The effect of a new stimulating learning environment on pre-service teachers' motivation and 21st century skills. *Journal of Education and Learning*, 5(3), pp. 29–39.

NSSE. (2010). *Working with NSSE-data: A facilitator's guide*. National Survey of Student Engagement, 2. Retrieved from: https://nsse.indiana.edu/nsse/working-with-nsse-data/nsse-data-users-guide-with-worksheets/index.html

Peshterliev, S., Kearnery, J., Jagannatha, A., Kiss, I. & Matsoukas, S. (2018). Active learning for new domains in natural language understanding. *Computer Science / Computation and Language*. Cornell University.

Platter, H., Meinel, C. & Leifer, L. (Eds.) (2011). *Design thinking: Understand-improve-apply (understanding innovation)*. Berlin: Springer.

Preiser, W. F. E., White, E. & Rabinovitz, H. (1988). *Post occupancy evaluation*. New York: Van Nostrand Reinhold.

Rai, P., Saha, A., Daume, H. & Venkatasubramanian, S. (n.d.). *Domain adaptation meets active learning*. University of Utah.

Ruffo, J. A. (2008). Millennial or net generation students and their impact on the development of student-centered facilities, *Planning for Higher Education*, 37(1), pp. 5–6.

Scott-Webber, L. (2020). What design forgot. What happens when 'my classroom' goes away? EdSpaces Conference, EDsession: ES20THC2.

Scott-Webber, L., Konyndyk, R. & Denison, M. (2019a). POE: Understanding innovative learning places and their impact on student academic engagement – index 6–8 'alpha' survey developments. *Canadian Center of Science and Education*, 8(5), pp. 31–56.

Scott-Webber, L., Konyndyk, R. & French, R. (2019b). Developing instruments: Student academic engagement levels and satisfaction with school design. *European Scientific Journal, 15*(1), pp. 325–347.

Scott-Webber, L. (2019). Rethinking spatial designs to support learning. Cracking the cover: The school campus as a 3D textbook. WI: *Green Schools Catalyst Quarterly*, pp. 28–39.

Scott-Webber, L., Konyndyk, R., French, R. & French, J. (2018). Significant results: Space makes a difference for student academic engagement levels. *European Scientific Journal. 14*(16), pp. 1857–1874.

Scott-Webber, L., Branch, J., Bartholomew, P. & Nygaard, C. (Eds). (2014a). *Learning Space Design in Higher Education*. Oxfordshire, UK: Libri Publishing Ltd.

Scott-Webber, L., (2014b). The perfect storm: Education's immediate challenges. In Scott-Webber, L., Branch, J., Bartholomew, P. & Nygaard, C. (Eds.), *Learning Space Design in Higher education*. pp. 151–168. Oxfordshire, UK: Libri Publishing Ltd.

Scott-Webber, L., Strickland, A. & Kapitula, L. (2013). Built environments impact behaviours | Results of an AL-POE. *Planning for Higher Education Journal, 31*(2), pp. 16–34.

Scott-Webber, L. (2012). Institutions, educators and designers wake up! Current teaching and learning places along with teaching strategies are obsolete – teaching styles and learning spaces must change for 21st century needs. *Planning for Higher Education Journal, 41*(1), pp. 1–12.

Scott-Webber, L., Marini, M. & Abraham, J. (2008). Higher education classrooms fail to meet needs of faculty and students. *Journal of Interior Design, 26*(1), pp. 16–34.

Scott-Webber, L. (2004). *In-sync—Environmental behaviour research and the design of learning spaces*. MI: The Society for College and University Planning.

Steelcase (2019). Exploring innovations at work. The science of collaboration, *Steelcase 360, 16*. Steelcase, Inc.

Steelcase (2012). Richland College adds Steelcase LearnLab. Steelcase. https://www.steelcase.com/research/articles/topics/active-learning/steelcase-learnlab-at-richland-college/

Chapter 4

Flexible Classroom Design to Facilitate Learning, Engagement and Integration of Knowledge and Cultures

Elena Forasacco

Introduction

This chapter contributes to this book, *Teaching and Learning Innovations in Higher Education*, by demonstrating how a flexible classroom design supports an active teaching style, and what the students' perceptions of a flexible classroom design are and its effectiveness in facilitating active learning strategies. In this chapter, I define a flexible classroom design as a 'teaching tool' that enhances both inclusivity in the classroom and student experience and learning. This preliminary study focuses on the extent to which classroom design defines learning and teaching strategies. The educational strategy of the teacher should be reflected in the classroom design (Poellhuber *et al.*, 2018; Sommer, 1977; Berker *et al.*, 1973). Furthermore, because active learning is at the heart of my teaching philosophy, I explore which classroom design facilitates learning-related activities and interactions among students.

My innovation is a product innovation; the innovation lies in the design of a flexible classroom to facilitate an active teaching style and active learning strategies. I implemented the innovation in workshops related to research communication for doctoral students, offered by the Graduate School at Imperial College London. Referring to the learning-centred five-tier model of innovation in higher education (Dobozy & Nygaard, 2021, Chapter 2 in this book), my product innovation draws on a constructivist perception of learning. Perceiving learning as a constructivist, I primarily view my product innovation as a means to increase students' engagement, inclusivity and integration of knowledge. Doctoral students are adult learners who bring with them different experiences and cultural backgrounds; they are a reservoir of knowledge. In each workshop, this innovation facilitates the exchange of personal knowledge to construct new knowledge within the group. Implementing and using a constructivist product innovation has implications for both students and teachers.

Projects focusing on the evaluation of the efficacy of the Active Learning Classroom (ALC) in higher education contexts have emerged in the last 20 years (Talbert & Mor-Avi, 2018); examples include classroom seating consideration (Harvey & Kenyon, 2013); the TEAL project (Dori & Belcher, 2005); and the SCALE-UP project (Beichner & Saul, 2003). However, little consideration has been given to active learning pedagogical settings at postgraduate level. Therefore, this preliminary study aims to contribute to the literature, building upon previous studies that show how a flexible classroom design facilitates the use of multiple active learning strategies and how removing physical barriers (e.g. tables) leads to the development of a community of practice (e.g. Sawers et al., 2016; Dori & Belcher, 2005; Jamieson et al., 2000).

The theoretical framework underpinning this study is social constructivism, as defined by Vygotsky (Cole et al., 1978), whereby learning is socially constructed and developed, based on social interactions. Adams (2006) emphasises that the individual construction of learning is not an individual process; instead, it involves engaging interactions with other learners and teachers. This belief influenced the selection of phenomenology as my epistemological position. As Dowling (2007) highlights, phenomenology allows us to separately analyse different viewpoints, giving the same importance to all of them independent of their frequency. Phenomenology allowed me to gather multiple students' perceptions and to include, in my analysis, any infrequent results to support my research question. Specifically, embodied phenomenology resulted in the best approach because, as shown by Merleau-Ponty (1945, translation 1962; Davidson, 2000), space (or environment) and memories (or lived experiences) are crucial factors in understandings of the current experience of participants (Cibangu & Hepworth, 2016). Accordingly, I collected students' views on active learning strategies, experienced during their life as students, from primary school to university, to better understand the impact of their lived experiences on their current experiences. The variability of students' cultural backgrounds and lived experiences led me to collect a wide range of answers and to explain my findings exhaustively. Thus, with this chapter, readers can find practical advice in the application of a flexible classroom design in an active learning context, alongside some logistical and pedagogical issues teachers may face, and possible solutions thereof.

Reading this chapter, you will gain the following three insights:
1. how classroom designs influence teaching strategies;
2. how to overcome teaching and learning barriers, when moving from traditional lecture formats to active learning sessions; and
3. how students perceive a flexible classroom design.

Overview of main sections

This chapter has four main sections. In Section 1, I describe the rationale of the flexible learning environment I apply, explaining my teaching context and how the students' perceptions motivated this study. Section 2 contains the description of the flexible classroom design, from its planning to its application, and Section 3 includes the outcomes considering both students and teachers perspectives. More specifically, in Section 3a, I describe students' reflection on using the innovation, and in Section 3b, I describe my reflections on using the innovation. Section 4 describes potential new implementations to the flexible classroom design I apply to enhance additional competencies in students.

Section 1: The background

In 2017, Imperial College London adopted a new learning and teaching strategy, aiming to promote active learning strategies, to bring innovation into teaching, to apply a student-centred approach and to create an inclusive environment. As a senior teaching fellow in the Graduate School, active learning was already the cornerstone of my practice, because it is the most suitable tool to enhance students' competencies and professional identity, along with a deep understanding of their subject (Khong, 2021, Chapter 14 in this book; Waldrop, 2015; Wieman, 2014). Active learning strategies, such as group discussions, problem-solving group activities and simulations of real-life situations, are among the most effective active learning strategies (Ambrose et al., 2010; Kermis & Kermis, 2010; Gleason et al., 2011); they promote the exchange of knowledge and experiences and encourage the provision of reciprocal support, as explained in Smith et al. (2015). Exchanges are important to increase the individuals' knowledge, as delineated by Ambrose et al. (2010), the cognitive sphere of each individual rather than being a *tabula rasa* (empty folder) contains existing knowledge derived from their past experiences that increases through the acquisition of new concepts socially exchanged. In this context, I am the facilitator of learning and exchanges, not the donor of knowledge.

These strategies are suitable for my teaching context, composed of adult learners who can self-direct their learning and use their experiences and competencies during ground learning on real-life issues. During activities, they collaboratively use those experiences to co-create knowledge, as explained by Knowles (1990), and Bonk and Kim (1998). Blended learning (Rowley, 2014; Bonk & Cunningham, 2012) is used to support these activities. To this end, I use apps that act as mediators between students and myself, such as Padlet and Mentimeter, to help in the facilitation of group activities, collaboration and interactions.

Although my practice was already well-received and aligned with the College's Strategy, I developed a project to understand better the perceptions of students about activities used in workshops. As previously identified by Rands and Gansemer-Topf (2017), among the factors affecting students' engagement, classroom design was cited by all my interviewees and stimulated my interest. This led me to increase my knowledge of the subject and apply different classroom designs to facilitate activities. Figure 1 contains three examples of a physical learning environment. There are tables to facilitate group work and group discussion, on a line (Figure 1–1), or as a semi-circle (Figure 1–2), or tables with a U-shape to facilitate peer-discussion in pairs (Figure 1–3). Students in my workshops perceived the physical learning environment as a factor affecting their engagement in activities, as highlighted by Student C (in Figure 1–1): *"[The] learning environment was helpful, especially since the learning method was reliant on the group's work. [...] The set-up of the classroom was not very strict [...]. It was set up in a very relaxed manner, which I think was conducive to the group work"*. Interestingly, student D (in Figure

1–2), on the other hand, commented: *"even though we were put into groups, it was the table that puts us into those groups"*, perceiving tables as the factor that creates groups. In contrast, Student S (in Figure 1–3) shared their idea on the classroom set-up, commenting that: *"[…] tables make more feeling like a school. A desk-chair does make it feel more like a chat. […] When you enter a room, you just accept what is there"*, linking tables to a school classroom. These comments clearly underline the importance of the physical environment as conducive to activities.

Indeed, the two aspects (the classroom design affects the engagement, and tables make students feel like they are back at school) identified by these students are related to the concept expressed by Barker (1968), who argues that the classroom design influences the student's behaviours. On reflection, any classroom's design, in my context, should support students to operate in a Higher Education context where they can freely discuss and create groups and should not create barriers to such communication. I believe that in a classroom, its design should be adaptable to facilitate different activities, as expressed by Bartholomew and Bartholomew (2014). Despite the surge of studies highlighting the importance of physical factors affecting the learning in a classroom (such as temperature, lighting, movable furniture), the classroom layout is a factor usually neglected, also due to the impossibility of moving desks and chairs in lecture theatres (Poellhuber *et al.*, 2018; Scott-Webber, 2014; Harvey & Kenyon, 2013; Salter *et al.*, 2013). As Yang *et al.* (2013) state, there are no classrooms suitable for all activities at one time, but classrooms can be ideal for one activity at a time. Thus, following another comment expressed by Student C, I used the idea of a flexible classroom design: *"To move things around [tables and chairs], and not always have it in the same way, it shows plasticity, which is what learning is all about, at the end of the day, right?"*

Chapter 4

Figure 1–1: Horseshoe, not aligned due to the small physical classroom size

Figure 1–2: Horseshoe

Figure 1–3: U-shape

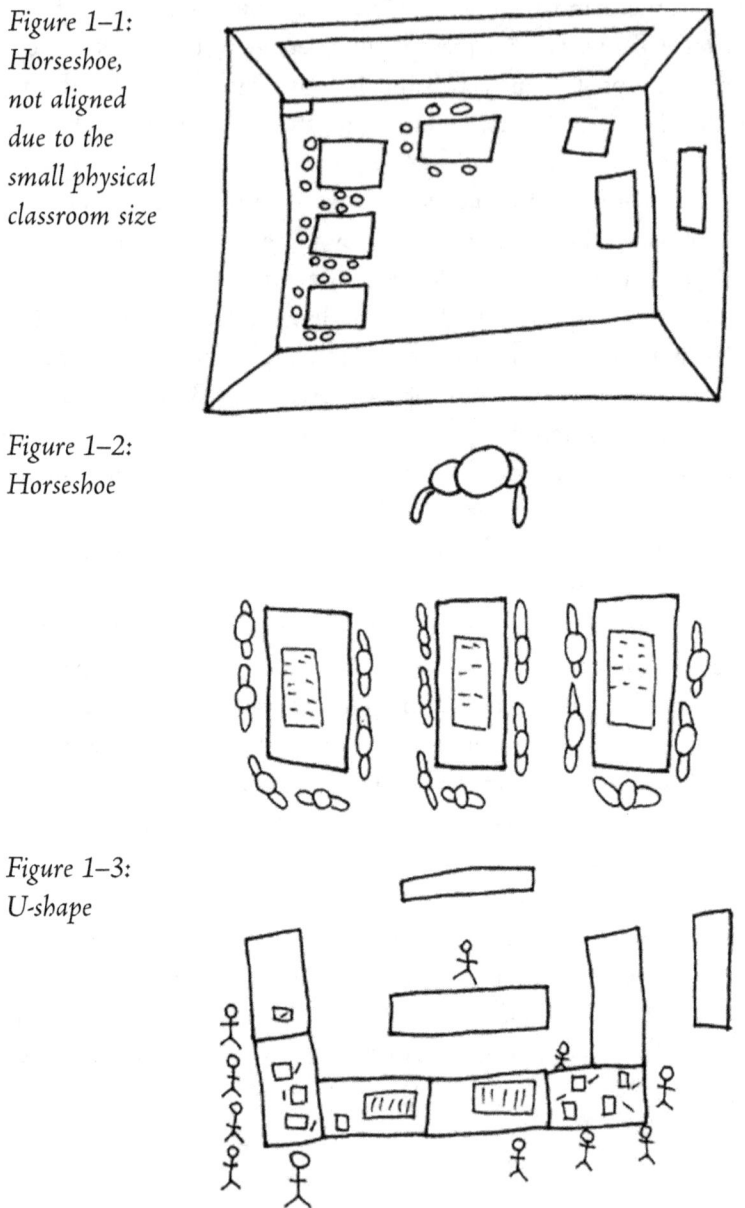

Figure 1: Representations of classroom set-up experienced during graduate school workshops: 1) horseshoe groups, not aligned due to the small physical classroom size (Student C); 2) horseshoe groups (Student D); 3) U-shape (Student S).

Section 2: The practice

'*Panta rei*' – everything flows (Heraclitus) – philosophically describes the flexible classroom design. Student learning is in continuous evolution, and the classroom's flexibility should support this evolution. Within a student-centred teaching pedagogy grounded in social constructivism, the students' growth is based on the sharing of knowledge, the *"social context matters to student learning"* (Walker & Baepler, 2018:8). The flexible classroom design presented in this chapter facilitates interactions. Modifications to the classroom include: removing physical barriers (such as tables) to remove metaphorical barriers and creating an inclusive and open environment, where students feel comfortable to share knowledge. Students and teachers are reservoirs of knowledge, and layouts that facilitate a non-formal sharing of experiences have considerable learning potential, as demonstrated by Parsons (2018) and Dobozy (2014).

Due to the variety of activities performed in each workshop, managing the physical space is critical. On the one hand, the creation of a barrier-free environment is essential. On the other hand, tables with laptops are useful for some activities. To solve this issue, a flexible classroom design can include different sub-environments in the same classroom, as indicated in *"Principle 1: Design space for multiple uses concurrently and consecutively"* and *"Principle 2: Design to maximise the inherent flexibility within each space"*, by Jamieson *et al.* (2000:226–227). The innovation presented in this chapter is about capitalising on the flexibility of the classroom design to maximise the learning potential, which is not only about an increase of knowledge, but also the development of skills and competencies (such as critical thinking and problem-solving; Dobozy, 2014). A flexible classroom design physically represents the concept that Savin-Baden *et al.* (2008:221) express: *"smooth curricular spaces which are open, flexible and contested spaces in which both learning and learners are always on the move"*.

Examples of flexible classroom designs with sub-environments in the same classroom are very few and are under-developed in modules for undergraduate students. Rae and Sands (2013) successfully introduced a double classroom set-up with tables for groups and tables for individual students, to decrease the apprehension students may have about not understanding and communicating in English. Quinn *et al.* (2011) experimented with a flexible classroom design: session by session students migrate between sub-environments. Both approaches stimulate the openness and flexibility in the students' mindsets. These designs work well in their specific contexts, but my workshops are not part of a module, each workshop has different groups of students and the use of (and migrations among) learning spaces happens in the same session.

Despite this difference, these case studies show the potentiality of my innovation, a flexible classroom design, with sub-environments where students exchange their knowledge to socially construct new knowledge while engaging with activities without restrictions. Considering the rising importance of active learning, this product innovation can be applied to other learning contexts, such as tutorials and small classes, with the adaptations explained in Sections 2c, 2d, and 3b.

2a: An introduction to the innovative practice

The workshops I design and deliver are based on the principles of maximising student engagement and sharing of knowledge, facilitated through the use of technology. This concept implies changes in the learning design and the design of the learning space. Classrooms have movable tables and chairs, but despite their suitability for different designs, the addition of laptops in the classroom created a logistical issue: the classroom design only with groups was no longer suitable, and there was no physical space for additional tables with laptops (Figure 2–1).

Facing this practical issue led me to re-evaluate the physical learning space to align it with my teaching pedagogy better and to maximise the engagement. Students in *"action seats"* (in the front row of the classroom, central position, Totusek and Staton-Spicer, 1982:159) and in the *"golden zone"* (central zone of the classroom, Park & Choi, 2014:749) are the most engaged in discussions and interactions, due to fewer distractions than in the *"shadow zone"* (back rows in the classroom, Park & Choi, 2014:749). In a classroom with rows of tables, usually, the teacher interacts only with students in the first couple of rows, while other students may feel out of the discussion (Parsons, 2018; Park & Choi, 2014). Students perceive the golden zone with action seats as beneficial because communication and participation are maximised (Park & Choi, 2014). The creation of only a golden zone -with action seats- makes the classroom an inclusive environment for all students, independently of their choice of seat.

Based on the concept that a classroom design is dependent on how the classroom will be used to facilitate collaborative learning (Morieson et al., 2018; Salter et al., 2103), I defined two distinct sub-environments in the classroom: a table-free area with a semi-circle of chairs for discussions, which represents the golden zone with action seats, and tables with laptops for group activities in the peripheral part of the classroom (Figure 2–2). During workshops, with students, we move around the sub-environments depending on activities, following Student C's suggestion (outlined in Section 1).

Similar designs have already been applied at the primary school level (Imms & Byers, 2017; Byers & Imms, 2016). In a higher education context, Walker (2017) outlined a small-scale study case, applied in computing laboratories with a central space for group discussion and a peripheral space with workstations. Salter et al. (2013) developed a classroom design with three vertical zones separated by steps, suitable for collaborative learning in the context of professional development for teaching staff in Higher Education. This design enhances discussions and engagement among participants, by increasing the visibility of participants and teachers and reducing the background noise.

The table-free area could be associated with the roundtable layout described by Parsons (2018), which facilitates discussions among students and teachers. Students like roundtable layout because they perceive its utility: it is conducive to discussion, it facilitates verbal communication, feedback and sharing knowledge, and it enhances their writing skills, presentation skills and critical thinking (Poellhuber et al., 2018).

The idea of having a separate sub-environment with laptops is aligned with the findings of Parsons (2018), who observed that students prefer learning environments where apps and media platforms are support tools. Technology should not distract students and limit visibility. Having specific areas with laptops in the peripheral part of the classroom, or *"laptop circles"* (Parson, 2018:29) allows and supports face-to-face discussions.

Chapter 4

Figure 2–1

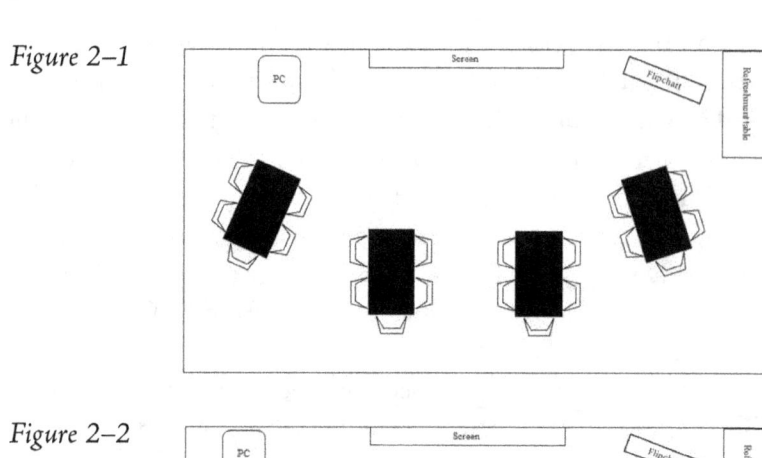

Figure 2–2

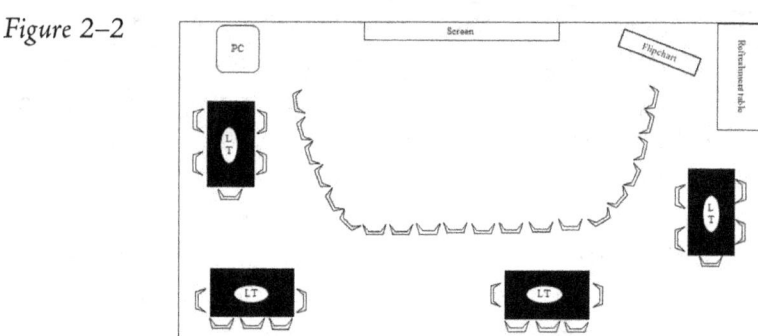

Figure 2–3

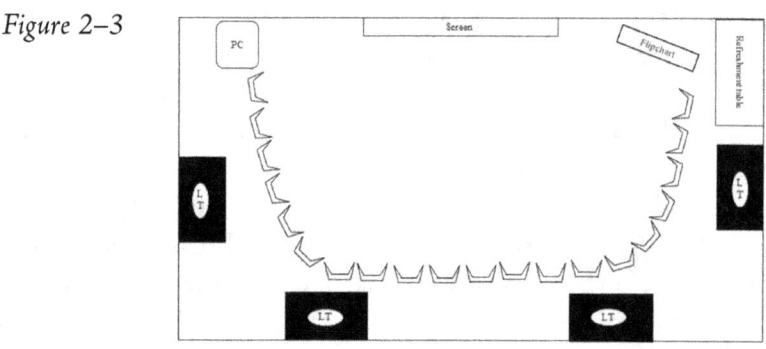

Figure 2: Representations of the classroom designs I use in my workshops: 1) original horseshoe set-up; 2) flexible classroom design with table-free area, and peripheral tables with laptops for group activities; 3) flexible classroom design when the classroom size is small, table-free area, and peripheral tables with laptops ready to be moved for group activities (LT = Laptops).

The flexibility and adaptability of this classroom design are conducive to active learning and reflect the adaptability of my provision, meet the students' needs and enhance the learning derived from active learning strategies. Du *et al.* (2017) developed a project in a higher education context, where active learning is the teaching pedagogy, and their findings support those of my project. They identified a clear view of the whiteboard, eye contact among participants and tutor, mobility around the classroom and good individual working space as the main factors affecting the students' engagement. Importantly, when students are busy moving for activities around sub-environments, they do not have time to get distracted and keep their focus on the session, as also observed by Walker (2017), and Yang *et al.* (2013).

2b: A brief overview of the curriculum

As a Senior Teaching Fellow in the Graduate School, my role is to create, design and deliver workshops, webinars and retreats to facilitate the professional development of doctoral students (class size: between 25 and 40 students in each workshop, retreat and webinar). I support doctoral students to enhance their communication competencies to effectively write and present their research projects in their thesis, journal articles, and conferences.

The Graduate School workshops stand alone. We do not have modules and courses, and we may meet students only once. As a consequence, engaging students might be challenging, because we do not know them and their experiences, the knowledge they bring to the classroom varies from basic to high. Tailoring workshops to this broad audience, to satisfy all students is difficult, but the flexible classroom design helps to support it. I recognise that my teaching context is quite distinctive because I support the professional development of experienced adult learners. However, this approach is suitable for all types of teaching contexts thanks to its flexibility and adaptability. It requires only additional planning from the teacher's side during the design of the workshop/course/module (Section 2d).

Chapter 4

2c: Organisation of the innovation

In this section, I explain how I organise the classroom and workshop on the day. Before the workshop, the classroom set-up has the two sub-environments described above, table-free environment for discussion, tables with laptops for group activities, and a table with material (e.g. papers, pens, markers), water and biscuits for: *"[…] improving classroom functionality-layout and the sensation of cosy-pleasant"* (Castilla et al., 2017:78) and create a relaxed environment far from the usual lecture-style classrooms. The functionality and quality of the physical environment affect the quality of students' experiences and learning, and are also reflected in the students' satisfaction; furniture (modern design, comfortable) and ambient conditions (daylight-good artificial lighting, air quality, humidity and noise level) mediate the learning and affect the evaluation and assessment of courses (Heesup et al., 2018; Poellhuber et al., 2018; Castilla et al., 2017; Scott-Webber et al., 2014; Yang et al., 2013).

During the workshop, together with students, we move around the sub-environments depending on activities: the multi-functionality and flexibility of this design maximise the students' learning and saves time as already identified by Kepez and Ust (2020). When there is space only for a sub-environment, to avoid limiting interactions and activities, the classroom design has first the table-free sub-environment with tables in the peripheral zone of the room (Figures 2–3). During the workshop, with the help of students, we create a second sub-environment suitable for activities (e.g. group work, Figure 2–1). When this situation occurs, a more detailed introduction of the workshop and classroom design is essential to prepare students, and they are always supportive in moving chairs and tables when they understand the benefits of it (See Section 2d, 'readiness for active learning').

2d: Preparation of the innovation

In this section, based on my growing experience, I explain the development of a workshop to include a flexible classroom design and the preparation of the classroom and students for a flexible classroom design.

As Morieson et al. (2018) suggest, the design of a workshop and its activities needs to be integrated with the classroom design, due to the difficulty of fitting learning activities within the existing classroom layout. Planning together a workshop and its classroom designs (how to make it flexible and how to prepare it, Section 2c), facilitates the parallel creation of activities and a suitable flexible layout. In practice, when designing workshops, I follow the steps below:

1. definition of the learning outcomes;

2. creation of a framework for the workshop, dividing the workshop into sections aligned with the learning outcomes and creating suitable activities;

3. identification of needed teaching tools and material for each activity;

4. definition of the most suitable environment(s) for activities;

5. survey of the classroom to evaluate the space available and how to allocate all the sub-environments needed for activities;

6. analyse the workshop design and modify it, if required. For example, when the classroom size is a limiting factor because it cannot fit all the sub-environments, either activities can be redefined to fit in the available space, or plan breaks between sections to have time to move tables and chairs.

When the classroom is spacious, I incorporate a practical suggestion from Student D to make the set-up suitable to share ideas: *"I always find that works better where there is a standing flip chart and people stand up and write"*. Each student has a marker to give a voice to all of them, they all can write and express their ideas. When only one student takes notes on the flipchart, there might be unconscious misinterpretations. This little modification positively changes group discussions by making inclusive the micro-environment around flipcharts, as previously observed by Rands and Gansemer-Topf (2017).

Likewise, students need to be prepared for this atypical classroom design experience. They might feel uncomfortable in a classroom with only chairs in the central area and tables in peripheral positions, since they are mainly used to lecture theatres with a fixed spatial configuration and tables providing a sheltering effect. Therefore, I have been working on two scaffolding strategies to prepare students for a flexible classroom design, i.e., 'readiness for active learning'. Before the workshop, students receive a reminder email to provide them with a framework of the workshop (topics and types of activities); to introduce the importance of engagement in activities; to explain that the workshop represents a safe, collaborative and open environment; and give them a short piece of 'homework'. Sending in-person reminders helps to make me, the teacher, a person. As a consequence, students come ready to engage and with their 'homework' done.

At the beginning of the workshop, when students arrive, I direct them to the sub-environment we will use first. Then, using a slide with the intended learning outcomes as a visual aid to increase the students' understanding, I explain the classroom design: its alignment with activities, learning outcomes and framework; its benefits on the learning; the use of sub-environments in relation to activities; and how we will move around the classroom. With these explanations, students realise that the classroom set-up is as flexible as their learning capability, and they may feel as safe as in a lecture theatre. Salter *et al.* (2013) experienced similar difficulties (to those I faced) when they introduced the collaborative vertical zones and identified a similar solution, as students need to be guided throughout the new layout to understand its rationale and benefits. In my context, composed of adult learners, explanations are also essential to engage them. According to the principle of *"orientation to learning"* (Knowles, 1990:47), they need to understand how their knowledge increases during this 'training' to engage them (for example the importance of activities and why they must move around the classroom).

Despite the above strategies, I am still learning how to tailor this introduction to each group of students, due to their high variability in scientific discipline and cultural background.

Section 3: The outcome

This chapter contains findings from my preliminary research project, based on six interviews with doctoral students who are at different stages of their doctoral research and have different cultural and scientific discipline backgrounds. The findings from these interviews led me to develop, apply and understand the suitability of a flexible classroom design. Students' perceptions of learning spaces were assessed, applying the embodied phenomenology approach (Merleau-Ponty, 1945, translation 1962; Davidson, 2000), which supports the understanding of the participants' lived experiences. I analysed data using the Interpretative Phenomenological Analysis (IPA) (Biggerstaff & Thompson, 2008) because it allows the analysis of complex topics through the description of individual themes and their combinations (Dowling, 2007).

3a: Student perspective

From the students' perspective, despite being adult learners, not having tables seemed initially shocking to them, because they are not used to being in an open environment, without the shelter provided by tables. For example, when sometimes not in use, tables are along the walls, I see some students moving chairs to sit at those tables facing the wall. To them, facing the wall, but being behind a table might seem more familiar than sitting facing the screen without tables. Similarly, Park and Choi (2014) noticed that some students felt uncomfortable when they cannot hide in the corner of the room, or when they cannot just listen to a lecturer and absorb knowledge from them.

Therefore, explaining to students the classroom design, and its alignment with the learning outcomes, is essential to make them comfortable even with no tables (Section 2d). Following the explanation, the majority of students feel comfortable in a few minutes. More reluctant or reserved students adapt little by little, but importantly all participants work together in an inclusive environment by the end of each workshop (and the presence/absence of tables is not a limiting factor anymore).

Considering the higher education context, Parsons (2018) observed temporary closure towards a flexible classroom design in some students and explained it with the diversity of students' behaviours, attitudes and past experiences as learners. Salter et al. (2014:817), observed *"students feeling somewhat disoriented"*, and attributed it to their Confucian cultural background. Similarly, I expected to find diverse reactions linked to the students' cultural background. But my interviews induced me to change my view. The past experiences my participants had as young learners are more likely to be the factor affecting the students' temporary closure, as also hypothesized by Kepez and Ust (2020). I call it 'the imprinting of the first teacher.' Most participants described similar learning experiences independently from their origins, mainly lecture-style teaching as represented in the following quotes:

- "We only had the lectures. It's not like engaging with students and tutors. We don't have like workshops, freely talks, engaged. So it was more lecture-based." (Student Ne);

- "The teaching style was quite like old fashion I would say. [...] Face-to-face, but occasionally we were able to work in small groups" (Student Cl);

- "[...] we were 373 people in a lecture theatre, learning about catenation and de-catenation of DNA. [...] it was simply someone lecturing at you, this was not particularly as stimulating as someone who was lecturing with you, or if you were being taught in a more interactive format" (Student D);

- "So for most time you came, you just seat in the classroom and no many interesting activities to prove what we have learnt in classes. [...] Sometimes we learn books by ourselves, you can imagine, and the lecturer stays there just like… when finishes teaching work every day" (Student N);

- "[...] it was always lectures in the morning. So that was like just being taught by one person for 3 hours" (Student S).

This idea is also represented in Student's N drawing, which clearly shows the teacher-centred lecture style (Figure 3).

Figure 3: Representation of the lecture-style teaching experienced by Student N in their past education.

Past experiences with active learning were contextualized as art lessons for Student Cl "*I think it was mainly face to face, but occasionally for, I don't know drawing or things like that, we were able to work in small groups. But it was fairly rare doing that, a bit, but not definitely not that much. [...] The class was already organised differently, in small groups like in a U*" and a few practical laboratory lessons for science classes by most students:

- "*I remember from a very young age being introduced to Bunsen burners, doing chemistry type experiments*" (Student D);
- "*We had like practical lessons for specific like courses like chemistry and physics*" (Student N);
- "*I just always remember my science lessons because they have been for me the most active and I will never forget my year seven teacher: he did experiments*" (Student S);
- "*We had some practicals at university, actually, which was more engaging. But that was it. [...] The first time I could know actually how working in a lab looks like is when I started in UCL* [referring to a master programme]" (Student Ne).

All active learning courses happened in a fixed classroom context, with benches and laboratory instruments in determined positions, like a lecture-style context (Figures 4–1 & 4–2). Only Student C experienced a flexible classroom design and was comfortable with it. "*I remember when I was either in primary school or secondary school, there were always moments 'Ok, cool, let's get rid of the desks and chairs, but we are still going to learn'. It just gives another aspect to learning, it takes away the seriousness of it [learning], that I think is important too, but it leaves especially the motivation to that [learning]*". Student C's comment (outlined in Section 1) was actually what prompted me to apply a flexible classroom design.

Chapter 4

Figure 4–1: Practical lessons in Biology

Figure 4–2: Practical lessons in Chemistry

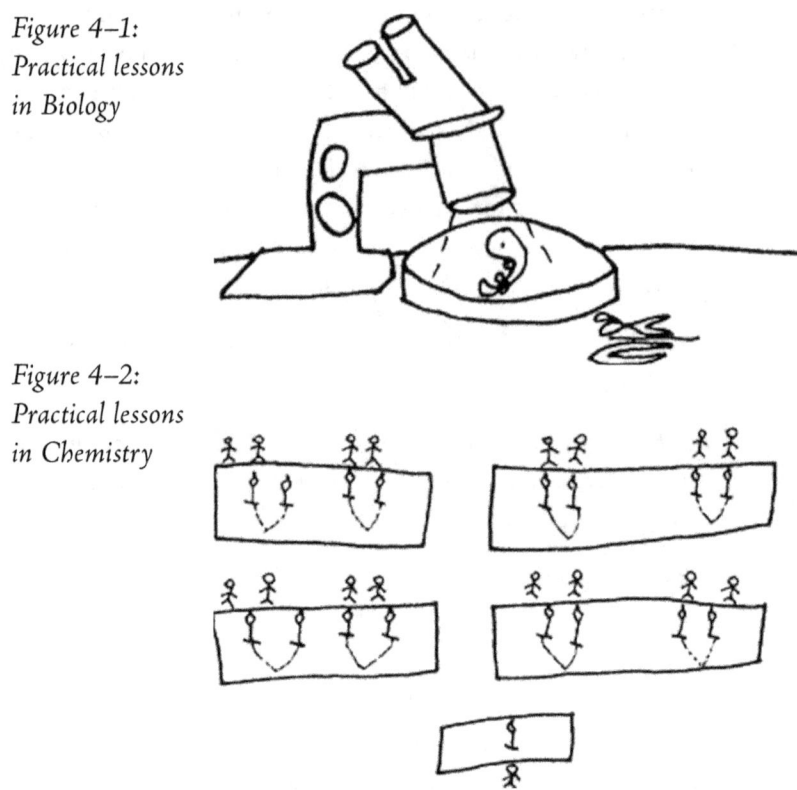

Figure 4: Representations of past experiences with active learning: practical lessons in 1) Biology for Student Ne, and 2) Chemistry for Student S.

The increased awareness of the primary cause of any temporary closure towards a flexible classroom design supported the development of my concept of, and strategies for, 'readiness for active learning' (outlined in Section 2d).

3b: Teacher perspective – my reflections

When I developed my flexible classroom design based on the literature (such as Holtham & Cancienne, 2014; Jamieson et al., 2000), I could see only benefits and I underestimated possible drawbacks. At the first workshop with a flexible classroom design, the students' reaction was astonishing: when entering the classroom, they looked for tables, and they waited for me to show them where to sit. I suddenly realised that the application of a flexible classroom design is not as easy as expected. Identifying the causes of the students' reactions (Section 3a) to define how to support students in their transition towards an active learning context where the classroom design is flexible is essential (Section 2d). As explained in Section 3a, the students' behaviour depends on their past experiences as learners. However, there might be concurrent causes maybe due to the students' high diversity (this aspect is still under analysis).

From my perspective, the first time I removed tables, I did not feel comfortable. My perception of students changed because the table no longer acted as a barrier, the teaching position was different, and I felt exposed, exactly as students felt. We were all out of our comfort zone. But, as soon as students' behaviours and engagement positively changed, I overcame my anxiety, and the flexible classroom design is in use in all my workshops. Removing my anxiety further increased the engagement, students see me relaxed and open, and they become more relaxed and open accordingly.

Moving (and removing) tables not only decreases the power distance between myself and the students, because I am physically part of the semi-circle of participants, but also increases the mobility around the classroom during activities. Results from Walker and Beapler (2018) and Rands and Gansemer-Topf (2017) align with my findings. They showed how a reduced distance between students and teachers creates a sense of community and different relationships in the classroom. From my perspective and my experience, all relationships change – at least temporarily – when a new classroom design is adopted, due to the novelty of it. All new relationships balance each other and, when the equilibrium is reached, students' learning is maximised. This case study provides additional evidence that a flexible design increases the socialisation and has not a negative effect on the students' learning. Still, it needs to be well planned and tailored to the specific case considering both students' and teachers' perspectives.

The creation of a sub-environment for laptops supports socialisation because it does not limit the visibility of students (Parson, 2018), and it facilitates interactions. Current students are accustomed to multimedia content. The use of mobile apps to share knowledge and promote reciprocal learning is natural for them. Importantly, in my flexible classroom design, the use of technology only in a sub-environment limits distraction, and supports the enhancement of students' verbal communication skills, as explored by other authors (e.g. Parsons, 2018; Yang *et al.*, 2013).

Section 4: Moving forward

The flexible classroom design applied in this innovative case study increases the students' engagement, meets the students' needs, and enhances the learning derived from active learning strategies, as already observed by other authors in comparable studies (e.g. Poellhuber *et al.*, 2018; Salter *et al.*, 2013). A flexible classroom design also meets the principles of the theoretical framework used to develop this case study. Aubrey and Riley (2015) highlighted how Vygotsky's original social constructivist concept already conceived learning as an adaptable social process always in evolution. Bonk and Cunningham (2012:35) synthesized and refreshed the Vygotskian concept: "[…] *learner-centred instructional practices are transforming learning from silent, solitary acts to lively, meaning-making events rich in discussion and interchange*". Accordingly, the adaptability of learning led me to apply the concept of a flexible classroom design: adaptable learning in an adaptable environment.

On reflection, I am confident that a flexible classroom design brings only benefits to learners. It supports the student-centred approach and increases inclusivity. Students are as equally important as the teacher; they feel valued for their knowledge and are actively involved in the teaching and learning process. They teach each other (including me) by sharing experiences and expertise, they learn from each other's knowledge and culture, differences are minimised, and the engagement is high. This study represents an application of the manifesto developed by Holtham and Cancienne (2014). However, it is still at a preliminary stage and, moving forward, it needs to be also tried by other teachers in my context. I am planning other interviews to collect students' perceptions and feedback for further improvement (study currently on hold due to the Covid-19 pandemic).

Due to the success of this atypical but effective classroom design, a step forward, which might push the classroom flexibility even further, is the addition of an unusual sub-environment to support the use of creativity. My teaching context is STEMM focussed, and students hardly ever use their creativity to become more efficient and/or solve problems. By working in an unusual sub-environment, students might start to think outside of the box. A sub-environment with yoga mats might free the students' minds from formulae and theories, and they might develop a useful but nonconformist solution to their problems. This new creative sub-environment could give good results on the students' learning. Still, I am aware that its success depends on the 'students' readiness for creativity', obtained with a suitable and robust scaffold for students, to be developed based on additional interviews and analyses.

Conclusion

Since the innovation of my flexible classroom design, I have observed an increased engagement and satisfaction in students. I associate these factors with the open and inclusive social context where workshops are delivered, a welcoming and relaxed environment, with comfortable chairs, movable tables, coloured features and refreshments, as shown by Poellhuber *et al.* (2018) and Castilla *et al.* (2017). All interactions among participants (including me) are entirely different from what participants were used to, as also found by Walker and Beapler (2018) in other active learning contexts. It takes time to accept these changes, depending on the students' character and the strength of the 'imprinting of the first teacher'.

Despite all challenges, I have faced in the application of a flexible classroom design, according to my experience as a teacher in higher education, a flexible approach to learning and teaching is suitable for all types of subjects and pedagogies. On the one hand, it requires planning and preparation from the teacher's side (Section 2b). On the other hand, the benefits of such an innovation are tangible and make the long preparation only a remote memory.

About the Author

Elena Forasacco is Senior Teaching Fellow in the Graduate School at Imperial College London, UK. She can be contacted at this e-mail: e.forasacco@imperial.ac.uk

Bibliography

Adams, P. (2006). Exploring social constructivism: Theories and practicalities. *Education*, 34(3), pp. 243–257.

Ambrose, S. A., Bridges, M. W., Di Pietro, M., Lovet, M. C. & Norman, M. K. (2010). *How learning works. 7 Research-Based Principles for Smart Teaching.* New Jersey: Jossey-Bass. A Wiley Imprint.

Aubrey, K. & Riley, A. (2015). Lev Vygotsky. An early social constructivist viewpoint. In *Understanding & using educational theories.* London: SAGE Publishing. pp. 47–58.

Barker, R. (1968). *Ecological Psychology: Concepts and Methods for Studying the Environment of Human Behavior.* Stanford, California: Stanford University Press

Bartholomew, N. & Bartholomew, P. (2014). Social and cognitive affordance of physical and virtual learning spaces. In Scott-Webber, L., Branch, J., Bartholomew, P. & Nygaard, C. (Eds.), *Learning Space Design in Higher Education*, pp. 69–88. Oxfordshire, UK: Libri Publishing Ltd.

Becker, F. D., Sommer, R., Bee, J. & Oxley, B. (1973). College classroom ecology. *Sociometry*, 36(4), pp. 514–525.

Beichner, R. J. & Saul, J. M. (2003). Introduction to the SCALE-UP (Student-Centered Activities for Large Enrolment Undergraduate Programs) Project. Retrieved from: http://www.ncsu.edu/per/Articles/Varenna_SCALEUP_Paper.pdf

Biggerstaff, D. L. & Thompson, A. R. (2008). Interpretative Phenomenological Analysis (IPA): a qualitative methodology of choice in healthcare research. *Qualitative Research in Psychology*, 5, pp. 173–183.

Bonk, C. J. & Kim, K. A. (1998). Extending Sociocultural Theory to Adult Learning. In Smith, M. C. & Pourchot, T. (Eds.), *Adult Learning and Development: Perspectives Form Educational Psychology.* pp. 67–88. New York: Routledge.

Bonk, C. J. & Cunningham, D. J. (2012). Searching for Learner-Centred, Constructivist, and Sociocultural Components of Collaborative Educational Learning Tools. In *Electronic Collaborators. Learner-centred Technologies for Literacy, Apprenticeship, and Discourse*, pp. 25–50. eBook edition Routledge.

Byers, T. & Imms, W. (2016). Evaluating the change in space in a technology-enabled primary year setting. In Fisher, K. (Ed.), *The Translational Design of Schools: an evidence-based approach to aligning pedagogy and learning environment design*, pp. 199–220. Rotterdam: Sense Publishers.

Castilla, N., Llinares, C., Bravo, M. J. & Blanca, V. (2017). Subjective assessment of the university classroom environment. *Building and Environment*, 122, pp. 72–81.

Cibangu, S. K. & Hepworth, M. (2016). The uses of phenomenology and phenomenography: A critical review. *Library & Information Science Research*, 38, pp. 148–160.

Cole M., John-Steiner V., Scribner S. & Souberman E. (Eds.) (1978). *L. S. Vygotsky: Mind in society: The development of higher psychological processes*. MA: Harvard University Press.

Davidson, J. (2000). A phenomenology of fear: Merleau-Ponty and agoraphobic life-worlds. *Sociology of Health & Illness*, 22, pp. 640–681.

Dobozy, E. (2014). Using the Theory of Practice of 'Built pedagogy' to inform learning space design. In Scott-Webber, L., Branch, J., Bartholomew, P. & Nygaard, C. (Eds.), *Learning Space Design in Higher Education*, pp. 263–282. Oxfordshire, UK: Libri Publishing Ltd.

Dobozy, E. & Nygaard, C. (2021). A learning-centred, five-tier model of innovation in higher education. In Enomoto, K., Warner, R. & Nygaard, C. (Eds.), *Teaching and Learning Innovations in Higher Education*, pp. 19–46. Oxfordshire, UK: Libri Publishing Ltd.

Dori, Y. J. & Belcher, J. (2005). How Does Technology-Enabled Active Learning Affect Undergraduate Students' Understanding of Electromagnetism Concepts? *Journal of the Learning Sciences*, 14(2), pp. 243–279.

Dowling, M. (2007). From Husserl to van Manen. A review of different phenomenological approaches. *International Journal of Nursing Studies*, 44, pp. 131–142.

Du, J., Wang, X., Geng, M. & Huang, R. (2017). Manage learning space to improve learning experience: Case study in Beijing normal university on classroom layout. *17th Conference on Advanced Learning Technologies*, Timisoara (Romania).

Gleason, B. L., Peeters, M. J., Resman-Targoff, B. H., Karr, S., McBane, S., Kelley, K., Thomas, T. & Denetclaw, T. H. (2011). An Active-Learning Strategies Primer for Achieving Ability-Based Educational Outcomes. *American Journal of Pharmaceutical Education*, 75(9), pp. 1–12.

Harvey E. J. & Kenyon M. C. (2013). Classroom Setting Considerations for 21st-century students and faculty. *Journal of Learning Spaces*, 2(1), pp. 1–13.

Heesup H., Kiattipoom K., Wansoo K. & Ju H. H. (2018). Physical classroom environment and student satisfaction with courses. *Assessment & Evaluation in Higher Education*, 43(1), pp. 110–125.

Holtham, C. & Cancienne, A. (2014). Collective learning spaces: constraints on pedagogic excellence. In Scott-Webber, L., Branch, J., Bartholomew, P. & Nygaard, C. (Eds.), *Learning Space Design in Higher Education*, pp. 225–240. Oxfordshire, UK: Libri Publishing Ltd.

Imms, W. & Byers, T. (2017). Impact of classroom design on teacher pedagogy and student engagement and performance in mathematics. *Learning Environments Research*, 20(1), pp. 139–152.

Jamieson, P., Fisher, K., Gilding, T., Taylor, P. G. & Trevitt, A.F.C. (2000). Place and space in the design of new learning environments. *Higher Education Research & Development*, 19(2), pp. 221-236.

Kepez, O. & Ust, S. (2020). Collaborative design of an active learning classroom with high school students and teachers. *International Journal of Architectural Research*, 14(3), pp. 525–541.

Kermis, G. & Kermis, M. (2010). Professional Presence and Soft Skills: A Role for Accounting Education. *Journal of Instructional Pedagogies*, 2, pp. 1–10.

Khong, L. (2021). Facilitating active student learning using innovative approaches in pre-service teacher education. In Enomoto, K., Warner, R. & Nygaard, C. (Eds.), *Teaching and Learning Innovations in Higher Education*, pp. 301–321. Oxfordshire, UK: Libri Publishing Ltd.

Knowles, M. (1990). *The adult learner: a neglected species*. Houston, Texas: Gulf Publishing Company, 4th edition.

Merleau-Ponty, M. (1945). *Phenomenology of Perception*. (Phénoménologie de la perception, original French edition 1945 published by Gallimard, Paris. English edition first published 1962 by Routledge and Kegan Paul). Abingdon, Oxfordshire: Routledge Classic 2002.

Morieson, L. Murray, G., Wilson, R., Clarke, B. & Lukas, K. (2018). Belonging in space: informal learning spaces and the student experience. *Journal of Learning Spaces*, 7(2), pp. 12–22.

Park, E.L. & Choi, B. K. (2014). Transformation of classroom spaces: traditional versus active learning classroom in colleges. *Higher Education*, 68, pp. 749–771.

Parsons, C. S. (2018). Learning spaces: the influence of roundtable classroom design on socialization. *Journal of Learning Spaces*, 7(2), pp. 23–34.

Poellhuber, B., Fournier Saint-Laurent, S. & Roy, N. (2018). Using the TAM and functional analysis to predict the most used functions of an active learning classroom (ALC). *Frontiers in ICT* 5 (8) pp. 1–11.

Quinn, D., Smith, E. J. & Aziz, S. M. (2011). First-Year Engineering Learning Space: Enhancing the Student Experience. *2011 ASEE Annual Conference & Exposition (Vancouver, BC)*.

Rae, K. & Sands, J. (2013). Using classroom layout to help reduce students' apprehension and increase communication. *Accounting Education: An International Journal*, 22(5), pp. 489–491.

Rands, M. L. & Gansemer-Topf, A. M. (2017). The room itself is active: How classroom design impacts student engagement. *Journal of learning Spaces*, 6(1), pp. 26–33.

Rowley, J. (2014). Enhancing student learning through the management of technology-rich physical learning spaces for flexible teaching. In Scott-Webber, L., Branch, J., Bartholomew, P. & Nygaard, C. (Eds.), *Learning Space Design in Higher Education*, pp. 53–68. Oxfordshire, UK: Libri Publishing Ltd.

Salter, D., Thomson, D. L., Fox, B. & Lam, J. (2013). Use and evaluation of a technology-rich experimental collaborative classroom. *Higher Education Research and Development*, 32(5), pp. 805–819.

Savin-Baden, M., McFarland, L. & Savin-Baden, J. (2008). Learning spaces, agency and notions of improvement: What influences thinking and practices about teaching and learning in higher education? An interpretive metaethnography. *London Review of Education*, 6(3), pp. 211–37.

Sawers, K.M., Wicks, D., Mvududu, N., Seeley, L. & Copleand., R. (2016). What drives students engagement: is it learning space, instructor behavior, or teaching philosophy? *Journal of Learning Spaces*, 5(2), pp. 26–38.

Scott-Webber, L. (2014). The perfect storm: Education's immediate challenges. In Scott-Webber, L., Branch, J., Bartholomew, P. & Nygaard, C. (Eds.), *Learning Space Design in Higher Education*, pp. 151–168. Oxfordshire, UK: Libri Publishing Ltd.

Smith, K. A., Sheppard, S. D., Johnson, D. W. & Johnson, R. T. (2015). Pedagogies of Engagement: Classroom-based practices. *Journal of Engineering Education*, 94(1), pp. 87–101.

Sommer, R. (1977). Classroom Layout. *Theory Into Practice*, 16(3), pp. 174–175.

Talbert, R. & Mor-Avi, A. (2018). A Space for learning: A review of research on active learning spaces. *SocArXiv*. Retrieved from: https://doi.org/10.31235/off.it/vg2mx

Totusek, P. F. & Staton-Spicer, A. Q. (1982). Classroom seating preference as a function of student personality. *The Journal of Experimental Education*, 50(3), pp. 159–163.

Waldrop, M. M. (2015). The science of teaching science. *Nature*, 523, pp. 272–274.

Walker, H. M. (2017). Lab layouts. *ACM Inroads*, 8(3), pp. 17–19.

Walker, J. D. & Beapler, P. (2018). Social context matters: Predicting outcomes in formal learning environments. *Journal of Learning Spaces*, 7(2), pp. 1–11.

Wieman, CE. (2014). Large-scale comparison of science teaching methods sends a clear message. *Proceeding of the National Academy of Science, 111*(23), pp. 8319–8320.

Yang, Z., Becerik-Berger, B. & Mino, L. (2013). A study on student perceptions of higher education classrooms: Impact of classroom attributes on student satisfaction and performance. *Building and Environment, 70,* pp. 181–188.

Chapter 5

Emergency Remote Teaching in Interior Architecture: A Necessary Shift

Selin Ust

Introduction

This chapter contributes to this book, *Teaching and Learning Innovations in Higher Education*, by outlining the experiences of interior architecture and environmental design students in their graduation project process. The graduation project began in a traditional face-to-face mode, but moved to an online mode, forcing students to complete their studies as emergency remote education. The most important issue to be underscored is that the experience was one of 'Emergency Remote Education', rather than 'Distance Education'. The reason was that, as instructors, we did not plan for this type of learning scenario from the beginning. As a result of Covid-19, when the declaration of a worldwide pandemic (by World Health Organization) required university closures around the globe, campus operations were redirected to prevent the spread of the virus. All teaching activities were moved online, and as instructors, we had to decide overnight how to continue teaching interior architecture without face-to-face interactions. The move to online learning as a result of emergency measures brought forth important questions and key considerations for the interior architecture education program. As the graduation project works to prepare students to merge into their professional lives, the timing of these emergency measures was not ideal. Many obstacles had to be overcome, as students were culminating their educational experiences and staging towards graduation. This meant that the studio education was needed to continue, with a new design to be adapted to this unexpected situation.

The studio is not a classroom; the project is not a lesson. Studio education is based on a unique, versatile, and layered network which the students concentrate on, by solving problems that simulate real-world scenarios related to their work. In this manner, students cover new ways of understanding and reflect what they sense into applicable knowledge (Schön, 1983; Schön, 1985; Schön & Wiggins, 1992; Salama, 1995; 2015). Studio education can be best explained by constructivist learning theory, in which knowledge is made by learners through their own experience. In constructivism, knowledge cannot simply transfer from one person to another, because it is not a copy of the external information (Jonassen et al., 1999; Phillips, 2000; Dobozy & Nygaard, 2021, Chapter 2 in this book). In design education, instructors give the same problem to their students and expect them to come up with different solutions by finding their own ways. Thus, it is a complex process of knowledge sharing; in other words, social interactions among peers and between students and instructors is encouraged. Because of a great deal of uncertainty, limited time, and increasing stress levels, as we were living through a pandemic, I did not have ideal conditions to design a well-planned online graduation studio. Therefore, I simply tried to move a face-to-face studio to a distance learning environment temporarily. Shifting to this alternate mode was solely in response to a global crisis.

In my chapter, I present a process innovation as an extraordinary solution, generated in a crisis situation. The solution required creative problem solving and quick thinking to meet the needs of senior interior architecture students. The innovation was implemented in a graduation project offered by the Interior Architecture and Environmental Design Department, at Ozyegin University, in Turkey. Referring to the learning-centred five-tier model of innovation in higher education (Dobozy & Nygaard, 2021, Chapter 2 in this book) – which serves as a model for coherence in this book – my process innovation draws on a constructivist perception of learning. Perceiving learning as constructivist, I primarily see my process innovation as a means to construct a new course design for the interior architecture graduation studio, which could be defined as a process that allows multiple solutions to help the learner to find 'the' correct one, as expressed by Duffy & Jonassen (1992). Implementing and using a constructivist process innovation has implications for both students and teachers in that it opens up possibilities in different ways.

In this chapter, innovation is defined as an extraordinary solution which is generated in a crisis situation, requiring creative problem solving to meet the needs of interior architecture students. Thus, I would like to share a new organisation constructed for a graduation studio that does not have any compromised curriculum or textbooks.

Reading this chapter, you will gain the following insights:
1. the way that Covid-19 is changing the face of interior architecture education;
2. a comparison of the traditional studio education with the distance studio education;
3. the advantages and disadvantages of distance education in the discipline of interior architecture; and
4. how changes to learning tools can be successfully incorporated into the interior architecture program.

Overview of main sections

This chapter has four main sections. In Section 1, I provide the background to what precipitated the innovation. Section 2 provides a more detailed analysis of what exactly the innovative practice was and how it was implemented. Section 3 is divided into two sub-sections, in sub-section 3a, I describe students' reflections on using the innovation, whereas in sub-section 3b, I describe my own reflections on using the innovation. In Section 4, I round the chapter off by examining how the experience gained from the implemented practice could be used to inform future iterations of the remote education studio.

Section I: The Background

The global crisis of our time, the Covid-19 pandemic, has become the greatest worldwide challenge we have faced in the twenty-first century (WHO, 2020; UNESCO, 2020). Similar to other countries in the world, Turkish authorities decided that all universities in the country would be closed in order to reduce the spread of the virus. This was implemented following the first official coronavirus case in Turkey, which was reported in March 2020. During this period, the capacities of universities for distance education were determined. The nature of design education, which has changed little over centuries, even with all the technological changes, and the culture it has produced, has meant most of the instructors being resistant to considerations of an online design studio. Since Ozyegin University embraced emergency remote education, due to the unpredicted case on 23 March 2020, the syllabus of the 'Interior Architecture and Environmental Design Graduation Project' had to be revised. The revision rather than being a planned activity was implemented as a survival strategy in a time of crisis, as Carloni (2021, Chapter 9 in this book) also points out, it was emergency remote education that was applied (Bozkurt & Sharma, 2020; Hodges *et al.*, 2020). Considering the fundamentals of an online course as a well-planned syllabus, audio and video teaching materials and a technology support system (Bao, 2020), I did not have any previous online teaching experience, early preparation, or support from educational technology teams.

Section 2: The practice

When the new architecture faculty building of Ozyegin University opened its doors to our students for the 2019–2020 Spring semester, students seemed excited about the realisation of their graduation project in the new building full of the latest technologies. Instead, they found themselves forced to remain at home to work on their projects. The students, who had completed the first five weeks of the graduation project in the real studio of the new building, were transferred to a virtual studio. The teaching staff also unexpectedly found themselves working remotely and using a distance education platform. Thus, we had to rapidly put into place our innovative process of transformation from traditional face-to-face education to emergency remote studio education during this contextual situation – our innovation came about as a result of trying to solve an unprecedented problem.

2a: An introduction to the innovative practice

Design education is a studio-based education type that requires time and continuity. Indeed, Cuff (1991) points out that the design studio approach, which is a combination of domestic and workspace, extends back into 18th century Europe. Every semester, interior architecture students have to deal with a new design problem, starting from a basic and elemental one in the first studio, to a much more complex project in the graduation studio. Interior architecture education is built upon modelling a 'real world' interior architecture studio. Thus, students and instructors meet twice a week in our studio to discuss the development of their work. All of the students are expected to participate in Monday and Thursday meetings and use the studio space as a learning environment. The design studios are crucial spaces where students spend not only class hours but also a great deal of their time. Thus, the studio has to support individual and group work, creativity by motivating working for long periods, and communication among students and between students and instructors.

With the pandemic lockdown, studio meetings had to be cancelled, having a negative impact on the communication generated by these meetings. Students who experienced Covid-19 related anxiety started to flounder and did not meet project milestones, perhaps because of a lack of motivation. This situation made me become an intermittent student coach, besides being the course instructor. Concurring with the role expectations of being a student coach (Whitworth *et al.*, 2008; Baron & Morin, 2009; Starr, 2016), I started to support my students, not only in planning each stage of the project, but also when focusing on their priorities, planning a route to success, and identification of and overcoming barriers to their success. Coaching is a collaborative process that brings about a transition in students' understanding and learning by developing their self-awareness and self-confidence (Whitworth *et al.*, 2008). I saw a need to motivate students by ensuring that they were not alone, although without any face-to-face contact with me. It was helpful for students to create additional time intervals, as online office hours, so that they could easily contact me, and I could thus try to keep them motivated. In addition to the studio hours, I wanted to have the capacity to meet the students in smaller groups out of class hours- to remain in touch with them, to address their anxiety in a timely manner and to keep them focused on their projects.

2b: A brief overview of the curriculum

In the final year, all interior architecture students take a 'Graduation Project' to show their ability in designing interiors through the integration of their undergraduate knowledge. As the graduation project is the last step before professional life, the students have to utilise their knowledge of spatial organisation, construction, detail, material, colour and lighting that they have learnt throughout their education and apply such knowledge in their projects.

For the 2019–2020 spring semester graduation project, 17 students were asked to renovate and refunction the old flour factory in Istanbul as a performance hall, where theatre, music and events would meet in the same place. Students had to propose a unique solution for the given design problem under their instructor's guidance. The course syllabus consists of three main phases. In phase one, the students analyse the site, collect data, do research on precedents, standards, specifications and trends, and then develop a design idea built upon solid research. In the second phase, they propose a holistic solution of the interior space and the environment with the existing structure and historical pattern. Also, they propose a solution for the constructional system within the interior architecture, solve security issues and combine the interior space with building service systems. In the last phase, they work on the atmosphere of the interior space using the techniques of material, lighting and colour.

At the end of the first phase, we had to stay off-campus and at home, owing to the lockdown. This was the turning point where our revamped practice was put into place.

2c: Organisation of the innovation

We had the very short timeframe of a one-week 'holiday' to prepare for emergency remote education. Comparable to other institutions, our university started to use digital communication platforms and programs it has kept on the sidelines for some years. Researching an online studio was the first step of my teaching innovation. After finding new learning tools to use to communicate with my students, I tried to get used to the software applications (Moodle Learning Management System, Microsoft Teams and Microsoft Stream), which our university expected us to use in distance education.

I collected, evaluated and analysed publications about distance education. Teaching and learning from a distance can be conducted in two different ways: asynchronously and synchronously. Synchronous communication in online learning involves real-time transmission between instructors and students, in other words, the participants all interact in a specific virtual learning environment, through a specific online medium, at a specific time for more direct social interaction and feedback. Asynchronous communication, whereby students can log on and access the provided materials and satisfy the requirements within a flexible time frame, supports student interactions and interactions with instructors, even if the participants cannot interact synchronously (Hrastinski, 2008; Giesbers *et al.*, 2014).

Our studio started off with asynchronous communication for the first two weeks. In an asynchronised studio model, students uploaded their assignments onto the Moodle Learning Management System (LMS) for every studio class, and I forwarded my comments and sent them back to the students individually. During this period, LMS submissions were essential. Students were expected to upload not only their projects but also an audio file, reflecting upon their own work, as it was a very important requirement for them to explain themselves verbally. To answer the students' questions, the LMS Discussion Forum feature was used, so that all students were able to benefit from the answers. In addition, informative lectures about the main contents of the weeks were recorded and uploaded to the LMS.

Beginning in the ninth week, we made the switch to the synchronised studio model, in which the instructor and the students were online twice a week, during a designated time period (Mondays 13:30–16:30, Thursdays 09:00–12:00). The reason for this move, away from asynchronous communication, was the feedback that was received from the students. Although they had the ability to access the course materials in their own time, shape their learning experience based on their needs and satisfy the requirements within a flexible time frame; most of the students complained about the asynchronous studio. Such complaints included being lonely, feeling less engaged and having lower levels of comprehension. In the synchronous studio model, the students were divided into four groups of four or five students per group. Each group was assigned an appointment for real-time interaction with me within these hours. Students uploaded their drawings a day beforehand, so that I could examine the drawings and make notes. The following day, during the synchronised studio hour (see Figure 1), I preferred to share my screen (desktop sharing) with the students who were in the same group, to show each student's work and discuss issues arising in a more efficient way than through asynchronous feedback. This screen-sharing also allowed all the students to be able to become familiar with their classmates' projects. Since we chose a particular time to meet with all participants, it was an effective way to manage student-instructor and student-student communications. As Rigden (2021, Chapter 6 in this book) also points out; synchronous communication enables students to develop, not only professionally, but also socially.

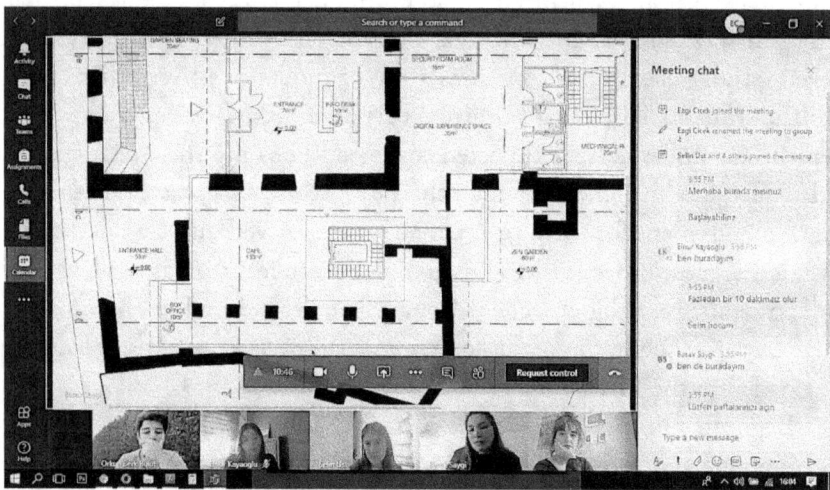

Figure 1: Photo taken by the research assistant during a synchronised studio hour.

With the implementation of emergency remote education, we also had to make revisions to the rules of the assessment system. The design jury, a traditional architectural learning assessment tool, plays an important role in interior architecture graduation projects. In a traditional graduation studio, students display their work on the wall and explain what their project is trying to accomplish, one by one in front of their classmates and all the instructors in the department. All faculty members and guests are welcome to attend the jury and give critiques to help the students develop their projects. However, grades are given by the jury members, who are the instructors that are predetermined and declared at the beginning of the term. Interior architects, as a requirement of the profession, must improve their verbal communication skills, so that they can effectively communicate with customers and other professionals. In the graduation project, students are expected to prepare their drawings and mock-up models, attend two interim juries, and a final jury to present their works. While interim juries can be thought of as learning experiences, from which the students receive formative feedback and determine how to improve their works, the final jury is the summative last step, when the jury members decide if the project is successful or not.

Since it was not an ordinary semester, I did not want to increase the tension and the stress of the students who were nervous enough under these unexpected circumstances. I decided to cancel the first jury execution in which the students would normally present their works in front of the jury members. Instead of conducting a synchronous jury, I asked my students to submit the final version of their projects on the LMS. I thought that it would be too early for a synchronous jury experience because some of the students would not have the ability to access either a personal computer or the internet or have a quiet workspace where they could work away from other family members. In the draft submission, the students submitted their presentation sheets with a video explanation – through the LMS – two days prior to the jury examinations. After jury members examined the projects, jury reports/evaluations were uploaded on the LMS. My aim was to make the format result in learning for adjustment and fine-tuning of concepts.

The second interim jury and the final jury was held online, as the design juries form the foundation of the interior architecture graduation studio. The students uploaded their presentation sheets two days prior to the jury meeting, hence the jury members were able to examine the presentations in detail. Then, each of the students was assigned a time period to be synchronously online the next day, including the jury members and their classmates. The students could hear the jury comments online and reply to them in the time period given.

Section 3: The outcome

To understand the student perspective of the innovative practices, forced upon us by the global pandemic, I asked my students give written evaluative feedback about their graduation studio education experience, which they had received that semester. The written evaluations were collected after assigning the final grades. A total of 10 (9 female, 1 male) out of 17 students in the graduation project 2019–2020 spring class, took part in the evaluation.

3a: Student perspective

The student comments were classified into two main groups: (a) opportunities of the distant studio, and (b) the challenges they faced during the distant studio.

Opportunities

Since the university campus was located outside the city centre, transportation was a major problem for students. Students stated that they saved time and money thanks to the shift to online learning. One student stated: *"When I compare the traditional studio with the online studio, the notion of time is the most important thing that comes to my mind. Because I was spending too much time while going to the university and coming back home."* Likewise, the students also mentioned that while engaged in emergency remote learning, they did not have to spend time and money to physically plot their work, because they were not expected to print out the sheets. One student stated that: *"It was tiring and stressful to print out my drawings early in the morning and reach the studio in time."*

As they could not go outside to get materials for model making, they had to express their ideas in three-dimensional drawings and renderings instead of physical models and mock-ups. It became an opportunity for them to improve 3-D representation skills. One student wrote: *"In the studio, I would make models in different scales to fully perceive the design that I proposed with two-dimensional drawings. Due to the sudden lockdown, it was impossible to find materials to make models. This situation pushed me to improve my ability of creating designs with 3d modelling software."* Another student stated that: *"I have started to use 3d modelling programs which I preferred only for visualization before…It is much more time and money-saving than physical model making."*

Some of the students commented that their workspace changed from the noisy studio to their quiet rooms in their houses (e.g. Figure 2,4).

The change in the workplace enabled the students to concentrate on their projects more easily and work more effectively. They also emphasised that their anxiety during critique and jury sessions was reduced due to the pre-recorded audios and videos about their projects. One student made a comparison between face-to-face and online juries: *"The atmosphere of traditional design juries was even more tense. This made me stressed, and it was getting harder to explain my project…In online juries, the instructors examined the submissions, watched the videos that we uploaded before the synchronous meeting. So we were just expected to make a short explanation of the main points of our projects."* (See Figure 3).

All of the students commented on the permanent and continuously accessible communication with the instructor. They stated that it was much more efficient than the traditional design studio to communicate with instructors. One student wrote: *"The instructor, whom we could only interact, communicate and debate in the studio during class hours before, became much more accessible in the online studio. She was ready to help whenever we needed."* In addition, they mentioned uploading the submission one day before the critique helps them to get more detailed and constructive feedback as the instructor had more time to examine the projects.

Figure 2: Photos taken by my students showing their workplaces during the lockdown.

Chapter 5

Challenges

When I examined the texts, the most common challenge that the students considered was the lack of face-to-face interaction. Although we communicated via the LMS forum, e-mail and Microsoft Teams chat, students commented that they were not as effective as face-to-face communication. They wrote that being at the studio makes them not only communicate more often and effectively with the instructor but also their peers. Most significantly, students commented on the importance of peer-to-peer learning. One student stated that: *"Being in the studio environment makes me more productive because we, as the students, talk about our projects, share our ideas, give feedback, help and learn from each other. The limited social interaction with my friends during the online studio had a negative impact on my performance."* Another student reported that: *"While we were all working in the same studio, I could easily ask a question to my classmates that I hesitated to ask the instructor or I could find the answer of my question by looking at my friends' projects."*

Another problem highlighted by the students was technological issues, such as limited access to the internet, disruptions in internet speed, insufficient memory of the computer, and lack of software. As it was an unexpected situation, the students had no additional preparation time for online education. In the traditional studio, they were expected to plot the presentation sheets, hang them on the wall and present their projects. Therefore, it was students' task to transform the digital sheets they produced for their projects into hard copies. In online juries, they had to submit the digital versions of their sheets on the LMS, so that the jury members could examine them before. At this point, most of the students were faced with problems relating to the resolution of their files, affecting the readability and quality of their sheets. While some students uploaded very poor quality files which were too hard to examine; there were also some students' submissions with very high resolution, so that the jury members could not even open the files because of low on memory warnings of their computers.

Emergency Remote Teaching in Interior Architecture

Figure 3: Photos taken by one of my students during the final jury session.

The last challenge that the students mentioned was the lack of productivity in the new working environment. One student stated, *"If you do not have a separation of going to and from the university, it becomes easy to get carried away thinking of the other tasks that need to be done at home."* Another student said, *"I do not have a proper working area at home. It made me demotivated, and also, my productivity decreased."* One of the students who struggled with self-regulation mentioned, *"Whenever I sat down in front of the computer to draw for my project, I found myself either eating something or watching TV series."*

Figure 4: Photos taken by students showing their working spaces during the lockdown.

3b: Teacher perspective – my reflections

The most important part that helped me to handle the transformation of the graduation studio was the first five "face-to-face interaction" weeks of the semester, where we were together in the studio. During these five weeks, I started getting to know my students and their personalities, which helped me coach students during the emergency remote teaching period. Considering that many students could not complete the term, because of their increased anxiety and depression levels in the other design studios, only two of my students could not meet the requirements of the class. I was very satisfied with the graduation projects that the students completed, which demonstrated the knowledge acquired and the skills developed throughout the educational program. Witnessing students' success is truly a joyous event for an instructor. Staying at home limited the access to the modelling and drawing materials, thus, making a model gave way to 3D modelling. Not only did the 3D modelling skills of the students improve considerably, but the quality of their presentations also increased greatly.

A studio is a learning environment supporting communication among students and between students and instructors (Salama, 1995; Kepez & Ust, 2017). During the spring semester in 2020, my students were much more proficient in technology than I was. Thus, I have learnt from them as much as they have learnt from me. It was a collaborative learning experience, which involved all of us working together to solve a problem. Unlike a traditional, instructivist higher education environment, in which the teacher/instructor is the transmitter of the knowledge, everyone in the studio had tried to act in an enabling capacity to the best of their ability. On a more personal note, my stress level increased, not only due to the lack of experience in online learning but also because of the difficulty of working from home. Since Covid-19 changed my workspace, I struggled with both in terms of creating a quiet environment away from other family members and attaining self-regulation. This is an ongoing challenge that many educators worldwide would share.

Section 4: Moving forward

I outlined 'Interior Architecture Graduation Project' as the innovative practice of this chapter. This practice was based on the evaluation of the students' feedback on their graduation studio experience, which started as a traditional, face-to-face studio learning event and turned into an online studio learning event.

I found myself in a different experience from my 12 years of face-to-face studio instructor expertise. Although it has been very stressful for me, as the only instructor in the graduation studio, I remained as a problem solver. The survey that Digital Promise and Langer Research Associates developed to reveal the experiences of undergraduate students taking their courses online due to Covid-19 also reported that the biggest challenge of the term was difficulty maintaining motivation (Means & Neisler, 2020). As I thought that motivation was an important issue, I worked hard, as a student coach, to mitigate the stress for my students by assuming roles outside of my academic role.

When I evaluated the situation at the end of the term, I realised that students have become competitively ready for professional life. I was very pleased to observe my students' dedication to their projects. This experience has provided clear directions to move forward through to the next iteration of the remote education studio. First of all, I realised that communication is the key to success. During the process, we did not experience any difficulties in instructor-student communication. However, the main problem I encountered, in the written comments, was the lack of peer-peer relation emphasised by most of the students. In order to provide an opportunity for communication between students, online courses have to be designed to create trusting or safe environments. If students do not know each other and they do not 'trust' each other, they prefer to limit their interactions in the group (Richardson *et al.*, 2012; Swan & Shih, 2005, Tu & McIsaac, 2002). Considering the fact that distance studio education will continue for some more time, I am planning to organise an informal networking event- for the students who do not have the opportunity to meet face-to-face. With the help of this ice-breaking event, which encourages the development of trust between students, they can get to know each other in a non-judgmental environment. In addition to that, I will frequently switch students in each of the workgroups to increase students' interaction with their friends. Thus, critiquing each other's work enables students to see their designs through the eyes of the others.

Yet technology also creates problems, when it cannot be used adequately. For example, creating a point detail that I could draw on a student's paper in two minutes, took much more time in a computer environment. Therefore, for the next academic year, I will improve my digital skills through the use of software that supports sketching. Adapting the digital techniques I learnt this semester, to the other classes will improve the communication with and engagement of my new generation students who were born into a world of vast technological innovations. This emergency innovation, though inevitably detrimental for some, has the potential to increase the motivation and the learning experience of the students. In addition, the pedagogical approach I followed, combined with technological facilities, bonded students to one other, to their projects and ultimately to their professions.

Conclusion

We have varying degrees of familiarity with the history of distance and automated educational technologies predating the digital revolution and research concerned with switching to online education in this field, including design education. Yet, one of the issues that is not surprising, but thought-provoking, is the foundation of design education, which has changed little for centuries, despite all the technological changes.

At the start of the transition to the online studio, I wondered how I would complete the term without knowing anything about distance education. Having come a full circle, I am very interested in experiencing the methods and the learning tools further. I learned, during this very sudden transition to emergency remote education, that traditional design studios can be adapted utilising the latest technology. Adapting the program in an emergency situation, though not ideal, helped us to explore new ways of thinking for design education.

In light of the likelihood that distance studio education will continue for some time, to some extent (perhaps permanently), the graduate programs must determine how to develop strategies that strengthen, stratify, and increase studio communication. The hybrid studio approach, where face-to-face communication is blended with technological facilities, opens up the possibility of a new concept emerging of 'how studio education will transform' to improve both student engagement and the quality of student learning. The use of innovative learning tools in traditional studios should be explored further as each can help students to create connections and interactions not previously considered between instructor and student, in design education.

Acknowledgement

I would like to thank the students and the instructors of our department for their valuable support and participation in this study. I would also like to extend my gratitude to Res. Asst. Ezgi Cicek for sharing my passion and helping me as the reporter of the graduation project course.

About the Author

Selin Ust, PhD, is an Assistant Professor in the Department of Interior Architecture and Environmental Design in Faculty of Architecture and Design at Ozyegin University, Istanbul, Turkey. She can be contacted at this e-mail: selin.ust@ozyegin.edu.tr

Bibliography

Bao, W. (2020). Covid-19 and online teaching in higher education: A case study of Peking University. *Human Behavior and Emerging Technologies*, 2(2), pp. 113–115.

Baron, L. & Morin, L. (2009). The coach-coachee relationship in executive coaching: A field study. *Human Resource Development Quarterly*, 20(1), pp. 85–106.

Bozkurt, A. & Sharma, R. C. (2020). Emergency remote teaching in a time of global crisis due to CoronaVirus pandemic. *Asian Journal of Distance Education*, 15(1), pp. i-vi.

Carloni, G. (2021). Using a community of inquiry framework to foster students' active learning. In Enomoto, K., Warner, R. & Nygaard, C. (Eds.), *Teaching and Learning Innovations in Higher Education*, pp. 195–208. Oxfordshire, UK: Libri Publishing Ltd.

Cuff, D. (1991). *Architecture: The Story of Practice*. Cambridge: MIT Press.

Dobozy, E. & Nygaard, C. (2021). A learning-centred, five-tier model of innovation in higher education. In Enomoto, K., Warner, R. & Nygaard, C. (Eds.), *Teaching and Learning Innovations in Higher Education*, pp. 19–46. Oxfordshire, UK: Libri Publishing Ltd.

Duffy, T. M. & Jonassen, D. H. (1992). Constructivism: New implications for instructional technology. *Educational Technology, 31(5)*, pp. 7–12.

Giesbers, B., Rienties, B., Tempelaar, D. & Gijselaers, W. (2014). A dynamic analysis of the interplay between asynchronous and synchronous communication in online learning: The impact of motivation. *Journal of Computer Assisted Learning, 30(1)*, pp. 30–50.

Hodges, C., Moore, S., Lockee, B., Trust, T. & Bond, A. (2020). The difference between emergency remote teaching and online learning. *Educause Review, 27*.

Hrastinski, S. (2008). Asynchronous and synchronous e-learning. *Educause quarterly, 31(4)*, pp. 51–55.

Jonassen, D. H., Peck, K. & Wilson, B. G. (1999). *Learning WITH technology: A constructivist perspective*. Columbus, OH: Merrill.

Kepez, O. & Ust, S. (2017). Post occupancy evaluation of a transformed design studio. *A| Z ITU Journal of the Faculty of Architecture, 14(3)*, pp. 41–52.

Means, B. & Neisler, J. (2020). *Suddenly online: a national survey of undergraduates during the Covid-19 pandemic*. Digital Promise.

Phillips, D. C. (2000). *Constructivism in Education: Opinions and Second Opinions on Controversial Issues*. Ninety-Ninth Yearbook of the National Society for the Study of Education. Chicago, IL: University of Chicago Press.

Richardson, J. C., Arbaugh, J. B., Cleveland-Innes, M., Ice, P., Swan, K. P. & Garrison, D. R. (2012). Using the community of inquiry framework to inform effective instructional design. In Moller, L. & Huett, J. B. (Eds.), *The next generation of distance education*, pp. 97–125. Boston, MA.: Springer.

Rigden, K. (2021). Best practices of teaching diverse cohorts in a webcam-enabled virtual environment. In Enomoto, K., Warner, R. & Nygaard, C. (Eds.), *Teaching and Learning Innovations in Higher Education*, pp. 129–146. Oxfordshire, UK: Libri Publishing Ltd,

Salama, A. M. A. (1995). *New trends in architectural education: designing the design studio*. Raleigh, NC, USA: Tailored Text Publishers.

Salama, A. M. A. (2015). *Spatial design education: new directions for pedagogy in architecture and beyond*. Farnham, Surrey, England : Burlington Ashgate.

Schön, D. A. (1983). *The reflective practitioner: How professionals think in action*. New York: Basic Books.

Schön, D. A. (1985). *The design studio: An exploration of its traditions and potentials*. London: RIBA Publications.

Schön, D. A. & Wiggins, G. (1992). Kinds of seeing and their functions in designing. *Design Studies, 13*(2), pp. 135– 156.

Starr, J. (2016). *The coaching manual: The definitive guide to the process, principles, and skills of personal coaching.* Edinburgh: Pearson Education.

Swan, K. & Shih, L. F. (2005). On the nature and development of social presence in online course discussions. *Journal of Asynchronous Learning Networks, 9*(3), pp. 115–136.

Tu, C. H. & McIsaac, M. (2002). The relationship of social presence and interaction in online classes. *The American Journal of Distance Education 16*(3), pp. 131–150.

UNESCO (2020). Covid-19 Educational disruption and response. Retrieved from: https://en.unesco.org/themes/educationemergencies/coronavirus-school-closure

Whitworth, L., Kimsey-House, K., Kimsey-House, H. & Sandahl, P. (2008). *Co-Active Coaching.* California: Davies-Black Publishing.

WHO (2020). *Coronavirus disease 2019 (Covid-19) situation report – 96.* World Health Organisation.

Chapter 6

Best Practices of Teaching Diverse Cohorts in a Webcam-enabled Virtual Environment

Kristina Rigden

Introduction

This chapter contributes to this book, *Teaching and Learning Innovations in Higher Education*, by showcasing best practices of teaching diverse student cohorts in a synchronous, webcam-enabled learning environment. The chapter presents innovative, practical use of the Adobe Connect platform that enables educators to deliver synchronous classes via webcam technology. In this chapter, synchronous webcam-enabled learning is defined as virtual learning that requires students to log in at a specific time and have real-time interactions with text, audio, and/or a video chat (Malik *et al.*, 2017). When I discuss synchronous webcam-enabled learning, I specifically focus on a virtual classroom environment where students log in at a specific time and have a class with their educator and classmates through video and text chat – same time/same 'place'. Synchronous, webcam-enabled learning is one type of e-learning. When students are not in a face-to-face learning environment, e-learning is a form of learning that can bridge the gap technologically. E-learning has transformed learning concepts and is an innovative method to facilitate a learning environment by utilising digital technologies to make learning more interactive (Afifi & Alamri, 2014; Khan, 2005; Fischer *et al.*, 2014). E-learning is becoming more popular among colleges and universities around the world. In the United States, over 6.6 million students were enrolled at higher education institutions that utilised e-learning in 2017 (National Center for Education Statistics, 2018). To bring about effective e-learning, it is imperative to understand the different technological components of synchronous, webcam-enabled learning and best practices using this medium in order to reach all students in one's classroom.

Chapter 6

Referring to the learning-centred five-tier model of innovation in higher education (Dobozy & Nygaard, 2021, Chapter 2 in this book), my product innovation draws on an instructivist perception of learning. Perceiving learning as instructivist, I primarily see my product innovation as a means to effectively teach courses in real-time using chat, audio and video features. This product innovation builds upon Korucu-Kis and Ozmen's (2018) framework of Instructional Technological Competence which views that distance learning courses must be designed and integrated with students' technological beliefs, knowledge and skills, in order to address their technological awareness. There is a need to keep the synergy between these three components for clear technological integration in distance learning courses. Within distance learning courses, synchronous environments allow for a social context in which students can collaborate with each other in real-time, which closely resembles traditional classroom interactions (Viola *et al.*, 2020). Synchronous learning provides real-time interaction between the educator and students, which recognises a better evaluation of student performance (Moser & Smith, 2015). Thus, this chapter outlines my innovative practice of using synchronous, webcam-based instructional technology.

Reading this chapter, one will gain the following three insights:

1. practice of using synchronous, webcam-enabled class delivery;

2. evidence-based teaching strategies for synchronous, webcam-enabled learning; and

3. best practices for using synchronous, webcam-based instructional technology.

Overview of main sections

This chapter has three main sections. In Section 1, I describe my background in e-learning and discuss the unique advantages of delivering online courses in a fully synchronous format. Section 2 explains the practice of using synchronous, webcam-enabled learning with evidence-based teaching strategies, whilst presenting figures to help illustrate the layout of the platform. In Section 3, I discuss students', educators' and my own reflection on this innovative practice.

Best Practices of Teaching Diverse Cohorts in a Webcam-enabled Virtual Environment

Section 1: The background in e-learning

This chapter explores synchronous, webcam-enabled learning on the Adobe Connect platform. I implemented this innovative teaching and learning practice during my Master's studies with my Teaching English to Speakers of Other Languages (TESOL) students. My passion for e-learning started many years ago when I discovered that the University of Southern California had recently launched a fully-online Master's degree program in 2010. Due to living in a remote town, I immediately enrolled in this program. The program used the Adobe Connect platform to deliver synchronous, virtual learning. The Adobe Connect virtual classroom is accessible anywhere, on any device, and delivers immersive virtual classroom experiences (Adobe, 2020). This platform mimics a physical classroom experience virtually. The class happened at a specific time period online, and students in this program were completing the same rigorous curriculum and achieving the same learning outcomes as their peers on-campus (USC Rossier, 2020).

Such practice of using synchronous, webcam-enabled learning is innovative since very few universities have a fully synchronous format for online courses. Most universities offer asynchronous (different time/different 'place') classes for the convenience of students completing the coursework on their own time (Brown University, 2020). Synchronous courses allow the students to meet regularly with their classmates and educator via webcam and engage in discourse in a cohort format. This cohort format enables social presence in online learning environments, as illustrated by Carloni (2021, Chapter 9 in this book). Students who participate in a cohort format are more effective at developing their voice, thinking critically, and engaging professionally with others (Opacich, 2019). Synchronous webcam-enabled learning can build upon the cohort model to develop students academically, socially, and professionally. Ust (2021, Chapter 5 in this book) moved from an asynchronous to synchronous model of teaching and learning, because the students felt asynchronous was lonely, and they were less engaged and had lower levels of comprehension. Ust (*ibid.*) reports that in the synchronous model, students felt there was greater interaction between the educator and the student.

Section 2: The practice of using synchronous, webcam-enabled learning

2a: An introduction to the innovative practice

The need for rules, structure, and procedure is needed in a virtual learning environment (Hofstede, 2011). This is utilised in the Adobe Connect classroom, which has a good deal of functionality besides synchronous webcam video and audio footage. For example, there are buttons that students can click to send a message to the educator and other features like a synchronous chat box and a note pod. Two buttons of interest in the classroom are the turtle image button and the rabbit image button. If a student clicks the turtle image, it signifies to the educator to slow down their lecture/instructions. The rabbit image button indicates to the educator to speed up the level of instruction. Once a student clicks either of those two buttons, the button will illuminate for 10 seconds on the educator's screen. If students are constantly clicking both buttons, I would recommend conducting an anonymous poll (a feature available through Adobe Connect) with the students about the pace of one's lecture to get a group consensus. Another button is the "raise hand" button. When a student clicks this button, a notification is sent to the educator to verbally call on this student so the student can participate in the discussion without being interrupted by another student. This orderly fashion is greatly appreciated in a virtual classroom, so each student has their turn to contribute to the discussion.

Using the learning model of instructional technology for synchronous webcam-enabled learning, there are certain tools within the Adobe Connect platform to enhance student learning. These specific tools, like the synchronous chat and the note pod, establish structure in the virtual classroom (Hofstede, 2011) to assist students in their learning.

The synchronous chat is a small box, within the virtual classroom, that the students and educator can use. The students and educator can send messages individually or to the whole class. The educator can verbally ask a question and have students respond in the chat, or use the chat for students to ask questions about the lecture or assignment. The synchronous chat is a way for more of the quiet students to express their thoughts in a crowded virtual classroom (Rigden, 2017). The educator can always read some student responses aloud, answer a student's question, or verbally call on a student to explain their comment further. In Li's (2016) study, 79% of students post text chat messages in the synchronous web conferencing classroom to their educator, so they can have synchronous and ongoing conversations. The written chat enables clarification during class for all students and the educator to ensure there is no misunderstanding of the class content.

The note pod is an excellent resource for the educator to utilise. Only the educator can type in the note pod, but the students can see what the educator is typing. The educator can choose how big or small to make the note pod, as seen in Figure 1, and change the font size, color and style. Figure 1 shows the layout of the Adobe Connect Classroom and the chat, note pod, and file boxes are adjustable. The note pod can be used for the educator to take notes on the class discussion, type information or questions for the students, keep a class agenda, or list the order of speakers during a discussion or for short presentations. How the educator chooses to implement the structure of the note pod enables an interface design to accommodate the needs of the students (Khan, 2005). By using the note pod in the same style in every class section, it permits continuity during the virtual class sessions.

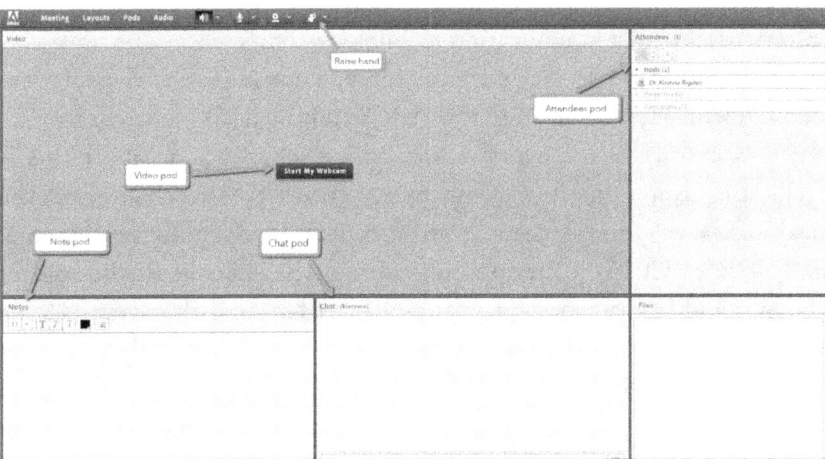

Figure 1: The Adobe Connect classroom layout.

An acknowledgement of group dynamics and classroom culture manifests itself in different student groupings. This can be achieved by using the break-out group option on Adobe Connect. The educator can assign students to smaller break-out groups, so the students can participate in small group discussion outside the larger virtual classroom environment. Small groups allow the students more interaction with each other (Wang, 2011), and allows for a student-centred discussion. When grouping students in the small break-out groups, it is important to group students heterogeneously and homogeneously to capture students' similarities and differences in experiences, ethnicities and languages (Rigden, 2017). It is also important to make sure that the same students are never in the same break-out group together throughout the semester; otherwise, a degree of monotony may be the result (Rigden, 2019).

2b: Organisation of the innovative practice using evidence-based teaching strategies

Before beginning synchronous webcam-enabled learning, it is imperative to have a basic competence of information and communication technology. Hampel and Stickler's (2005) skills pyramid, an adaptation of which is shown in Figure 2, outlines the necessary skills for successful synchronous online teaching. The bottom of the pyramid contains basic information and communication technology competence. The next level of the pyramid is specific technical competence regarding the software or platform used. The middle of the pyramid deals with constraints and possibilities of the medium and online socialisation. Above this is facilitating communicative competence, creativity and choice and the peak of the pyramid is the educator's own style. According to Hampel and Stickler (2005), educators must attain the skills at the bottom of the pyramid before moving to the skills at the top of the pyramid. The researchers understand that with technology changing rapidly, educators that teach virtually must develop their skills to move through all levels of the pyramid. By understanding this competence, then one can engage in synchronous webcam-enabled learning.

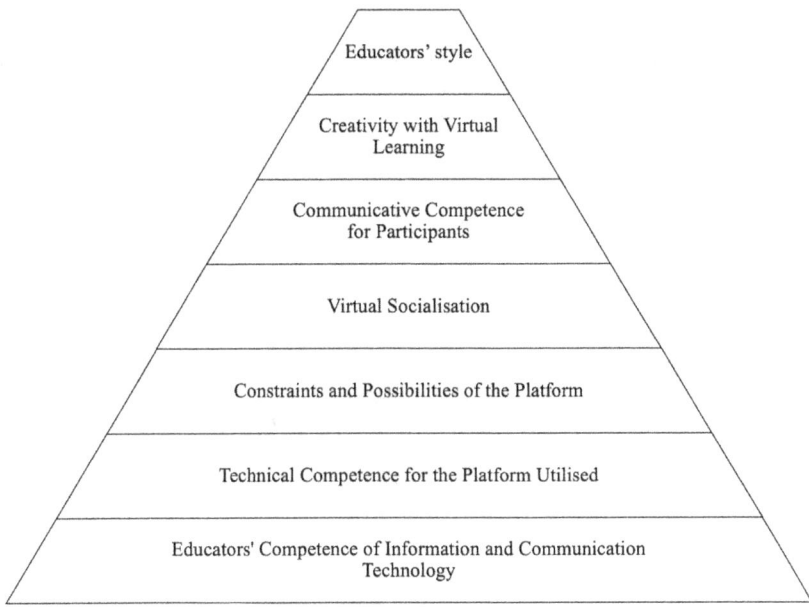

Figure 2: Skills pyramid for successful virtual teaching, adapted from Hampel and Stickler's (2005) skills pyramid.

Before getting started with any utilisation of the technological platform, it is important to participate in an introductory lesson on the platform. With Adobe Connect, there are many available webinars from the company and (perhaps) one's own institution if they implement Adobe Connect. The introductory lesson covers how to set up the virtual classroom and the tools and resources available. Figure 3 represents an active layout of a synchronous, webcam-enabled classroom. According to Germain-Rutherford and Ernest (2015), technical competence is imperative for an educator to be successful in a virtual learning environment. In addition, well-designed learning activities need to take place in order for students to succeed (Afifi & Alamri, 2014). These well-designed learning activities consist of games, simulations, and activities that allow students to apply their new skills to their learning environment.

Chapter 6

Figure 3: The Adobe Connect synchronous classroom session.

2c: Preparation of the innovative practice

The educator needs to give students the necessary resources for learning on this technological platform. By doing this, the learning system becomes learner-centred (Afifi & Alamri, 2014). Prior to the first class session, students should watch the informational webinar, so they understand how Adobe Connect works and know how to login to the virtual classroom. In the first class session, using synchronous webcam-enabled learning, it is important to orient students to the functionality of the virtual classroom. The educator must show the students all of the different button features, how to mute their audio when they are not speaking, how to download the files they will need for class, and how to use the chat box.

The synchronous chat feature is useful for use when the class is beginning and students are logging in. The educator can have a question of the day focused on the class content and have students write their response in the chat box. If utilising the chat feature for student responses, it is vital to allow sufficient time for students to type out their response and to read other student responses. The significance of this time consideration was borne out by Li's (2016) study, whereby 21% of the student cohort reported that the educator continued with the course content before the students can finish typing their answers in the chat box. It is also important to set student expectations of how and when to use the chat box (Hofstede, 2011). Using the chat box to supplement student learning is best in a synchronous webcam-enabled classroom.

There are several ways an educator can implement the note pod feature in the virtual classroom. The educator can take notes on the class discussion, type information or questions for the students, or use it to keep a class agenda. It is important to utilise the note pod in the same way, during every class session for the duration of the semester, so students have consistency and procedures around their learning (Holmes & Abington-Cooper, 2000). If the agenda is posted in the note pod every class session, then students know what to expect when they are in the virtual classroom. Having the agenda in a written form and the educator reading through the agenda at the beginning of class helps present the information in a verbal and written manner to students which assist with the student's discourse language (Tabrizi et al., 2014). Within the agenda, the educator can post the topic of the structured discussion (if there is one), and the list of student names as the order of speakers during the discussion. This procedure is very helpful to students who may feel shy, are non-native speakers, or students who want to prepare their discussion points at the beginning of class. If students prepare discussion points early, this will lessen student anxiety in the virtual classroom, and students will be more inclined to participate (Rigden, 2017). In addition, the note pod can also be utilised in the break-out sessions to list the discussion topic and questions for the students.

When utilising break-out groups within the larger construct of the virtual classroom, it is of value to spend sufficient time on assigning the break-out groupings before class begins. It is important for the educator to spend time in the planning phase, especially when teaching through instructional technologies (Smith & Ayers, 2006). By planning ahead of time, the educator makes sure that the same students are never in the same grouping, and they have the opportunity to virtually interact with all classmates. The groupings can also fluctuate between ability, heterogeneous and homogeneous student populations based on the task or classroom discussion topic (Wang, 2011). The different grouping also allows for cross-cultural collaboration.

Lastly, it is important to establish a social presence online and to have eye contact with students in a synchronous, webcam-enabled virtual learning environment. According to Vu and Fadde (2013) and Martin *et al.* (2012), observing facial expressions and body language – the paralinguistics – through a webcam can make the learning environment more personal. This method can help in the development of a community of virtual learners.

Section 3: The study

In order to evaluate best practices for teaching diverse students in a synchronous, webcam-enabled learning environment, an in-depth qualitative study was conducted with five educators and ten post-secondary students. The study consisted of classroom observations, interviews with the educators, and open-ended surveys for the students in the observed classroom. First, three virtual classroom observations of one hour each were conducted in three different courses. The courses were all master's-level courses with students majoring in Teaching or TESOL. Students from around the world were enrolled in this online program. I observed the educators in the virtual classroom and how they used the technological components as a teaching asset in the Adobe Connect classroom. Next, audio-recorded and transcribed interviews with five educators commenced. Each interview was conducted over the phone and lasted 25 to 45 minutes. The interviews took place following the classroom observations. Member checks were conducted in writing via email within two weeks of interviews with the five educators to make sure their interview responses were captured accurately.

A survey concerning learning in a synchronous virtual learning environment was given to ten post-secondary students. The students were all international students not from the United States; non-native English speakers who were enrolled in this online master's program. The survey had three open-ended questions about their interaction with the Adobe Connect platform, when learning in a synchronous virtual learning environment, in comparison to a face-to-face classroom.

The data was analysed qualitatively using a case study method (Merriam, 2009) to identify best practices for teaching in a synchronous, webcam-enabled learning environment. Analysis of qualitative data includes open, axial, and selective coding of all qualitative information. The observation notes, interview transcripts with five educators, and survey results were printed out and coded. All of the words or phrases about e-learning, synchronous learning, teaching and tools were typed into an Excel document with a definition and a page number to refer to the raw data. These words or phrases became the 75 open codes. Colour-coding the open codes that were similar resulted in 9 axial codes of categories. From the 9 axial codes, similar codes were combined to result in one selective code, and this code was used to identify evidence-based teaching strategies and best practices for teaching in a synchronous virtual learning environment. General results showed that students liked attending class online since they did not have to commute to campus. Synchronous learning enabled students to be responsible for their own learning by creating a schedule to log into class at the same time every week and build a sense of community with their peers (Flaherty, 2020). Many students appreciated having the same educators and curriculum that their on-campus peers had.

The outcome

This study builds on the work of my doctoral dissertation (Rigden, 2017). Results from the in-depth qualitative study determined that utilisation of the specific technological features of the Adobe Connect platform made for a more successful virtual learning environment for the students. Having a procedure for students (Holmes & Abington-Cooper, 2000), and employing the tools, such as a note pod and chat box, led to clarification during the discussion and more varying forms of participation among the students (Afifi & Alamri, 2014). While this study was conducted with ten post-secondary international students completing a graduate degree in the United States in a Western education context, the results indicate that the evidence-based teaching strategies can be applied to all populations of students using this technological platform. Further discussion follows below, from both the student and educator perspectives, for learning and teaching in a synchronous, webcam-enabled virtual learning environment.

3a. Student perspective

The ten post-secondary students in the study partook in an open-ended survey about learning in a synchronous virtual learning environment. Several of the comments on the survey focused on the note pod and break-out groups.

Students remarked that many of the class sessions focused on a discussion of the course readings. Before the discussion started, many educators in the observation had the discussion questions posted on the note pod. They gave the students a few minutes to gather their notes from the readings before the discussion started. This note collection was observed via the webcam, as many students had their head down, and it appeared that they were gathering and reviewing their notes. On the survey, one student remarked that he likes getting the discussion questions ahead of time, so he feels he can write down a thorough response that incorporates the reading material for that week of class. With the educator utilising Hampel and Stickler's (2005) skills pyramid of facilitating communicative competence, the educator was able to facilitate students' learning by giving them preparation through the note pod. The students were given the necessary resources to learn.

One virtual tool that was used frequently in the classroom was the "raise hand" button. Almost all of the students in the cohort used this feature, and in one classroom observation, the students used this button exclusively during the class discussion. Utilising this button can encourage class participation by shy or non-native speakers, so each student has the opportunity to contribute to the discussion.

In almost every observation, interview and survey, break-out sessions were mentioned. In the survey, one student stated that he likes the small group discussion because I can give "*...my opinion and perspective.*" Another student remarked that she likes having different classmates in each break-out session, so she is able to meet all of her classmates in a smaller virtual environment. Since the virtual classrooms observed were master's-level courses, much of the class content is focused on readings and discussion, as opposed to a lecture. On the survey, one student stated about the break-out groups: "*I'm so glad you [the educator] do that because we're so frustrated and we have so many questions coming from all different backgrounds around the country and around the world, that if you just lecture, we don't get a chance to express our opinions.*"

All of these reactions to the break-out groups solidified that learning is an act of constructing in a community of learners (Jitka *et al.*, 2018). All of the students used their peers to process the content through small group learning in this virtual platform.

Synchronous, webcam-enabled learning supported students through a variety of audio and visual mechanisms. Students were able to acquire information in a variety of ways (Smith & Ayers, 2006). With students mastering this online technology, they were able to take control of their own learning and engage, not only in the virtual platform but also in the content. This content, along with high impact practices, empowered students to fully participate in synchronous learning.

3b. Educator perspective

The teaching perspectives of the educators emerged through observations and interviews. In one observation, the educator had the question of the day in the note pod and asked all students to respond via the chat box. This question of the day was conducted at the start of class when students were logging into the virtual classroom, and starting their webcam and checking their audio. It is important to have expectations set for the students so that they know what to expect from the educator. As Holmes and Abington-Cooper (2000) assert, students need procedures around their learning in order to be successful.

During another observation before class started, when students were logging in, one student asked a question in the chat box about the due date for the upcoming assignment. Nobody responded in the chat box. The educator then verbally said *"Can anybody answer that question?"* and two students typed the answer in the chat box. The educator was acknowledging that not only does the educator have the answer, but students may have the answer too. This teaching method is rooted in constructivism, whereby students construct their knowledge in a community of learners (Jitka *et al.*, 2018). In the last observation that was conducted, the educator used the note pod to take notes during the large class discussion. This was at the beginning of the semester, so one student had asked the educator if he would receive a copy of the notes in the note pod after class and the educator said that all students would receive a copy of his notes via email.

During the interview, one educator mentioned how she uses the break-out groups to have student-centred discussions. Students reflect on their ideas and opinions with their peers. By utilising break-out groups, one educator said students *"co-construct the curriculum to meet their needs of understanding..."* in the small group discussion. Students are able to learn from one another in this context of a synchronous, webcam-enabled learning environment.

Lastly, one educator mentioned the training she had received to learn how to teach online using the Adobe Connect platform. She was given a remote training session and learned how to set up her virtual classroom and use the available tools. She said she was "scared to death" and she spent the whole summer practicing with the platform before teaching her online classes in the fall. She credits her training with learning how to bring her pedagogy from a face-to-face classroom to an online environment.

3c. My reflections

While an educator might have best practices for teaching in a face-to-face classroom or in a blended- or hybrid learning environment, teaching in a synchronous, webcam-enabled virtual classroom is different, providing a variety of components to give students the best possible learning experience. Synchronous virtual learning:*"...is not just about putting traditional content on a web site, it is also about a new mix of sources and interactivity supporting the performance of students and well-designed learning activities, that all depend on the instructional design of the distance E-courses"* (Afifi & Alamri, 2014:129). It is important to utilise all of the technological tools within the platform to adjust to each student's learning style.

The impact of the Covid-19 pandemic and many universities switching to distance learning, instead of face-to-face learning, have brought about an increase in awareness with regard to e-learning. Many universities have adopted both asynchronous and synchronous e-learning methods to address issues of student learning. With the product innovation discussed in this chapter, the instructivist perception of learning addressed best practices for teaching – in a synchronous, webcam-enabled virtual learning environment – which educators can implement.

Section 4: Moving forward

My experience moving forward with synchronous, webcam-enabled learning is to continue to use the technology with post-secondary students and develop specific teaching and learning strategies based on this virtual learning environment. It is also important to see and evaluate what other platforms are available that use synchronous, webcam-enabled learning, besides Adobe Connect. Although the findings in this chapter are specific to the Adobe Connect platform, the results can be applied with other synchronous learning platforms. In addition, more research can be conducted in terms of webcam-enabled learning in other academic disciplines and also in relation to possibilities for blended learning environments, in order to help facilitate best practice in developing student learning. The applicability of this technology can result in academic flexibility for both students and educators.

Conclusion

In order to be successful in this environment, an educator must be trained in the instructional design of synchronous learning (Hampel & Stickler, 2005) or have the assistance of an instructional design expert, so they know how to utilise the tools provided. Accessing webinars and training material on the platform that one will be using is a requisite. Once one is comfortable with the technological platform, it is important to make full use of the available resources like the note pod, chat box and indicator buttons. There is significant value in providing students with a written and verbal orientation, prior to or during the first class, so students know the expectation of learning in a synchronous virtual learning environment. Educators must set forth the expectations so students can be successful (Holmes & Abington-Cooper, 2000). Once students have the necessary skills to learn in this virtual environment, the likelihood of their success through this medium is enhanced.

Chapter 6

About the Author

Kristina Rigden, EdD, is the Director of Outreach Programs and Women in Engineering for the College of Engineering at California State Polytechnic University, Pomona, USA. She can be contacted at this e-mail: karigden@cpp.edu

Bibliography

Adobe (2020). *Adobe Connect for Learning.* https://www.adobe.com/products/adobeconnect.html

Afifi, M. K. & Alamri, S. S. (2014). Effective principles in designing e-course in light of learning technologies. *Turkish Online Journal of Distance Education,* 15(1), pp. 128–142.

Brown University. (2020). Asynchronous strategies for inclusive teaching. *The Harriet W. Sheridan Center for Teaching and Learning.* Retrieved November 4, 2020 from https://www.brown.edu/sheridan/asynchronous-strategies-inclusive-teaching

Carloni, G. (2021). Using a community of enquiry framework to foster students' active learning. In Enomoto, K., Warner, R. & Nygaard, C. (Eds.), *Teaching and Learning Innovations in Higher Education,* pp. 195–208. Oxfordshire, UK: Libri Publishing Ltd.

Dobozy, E. & Nygaard, C. (2021). A learning-centred, five-tier model of innovation in higher education. In Enomoto, K., Warner, R. & Nygaard, C. (Eds.), *Teaching and Learning Innovations in Higher Education,* pp. 19–46. Oxfordshire, UK: Libri Publishing Ltd.

Fischer, H., Heise, L., Heinz, M., Moebius, K. & Koehler, T. (2014, July). E-Learning trends and hypes in academic teaching. Methodology and findings of a trend study. Paper presented at the International Conference e-Learning, Lisbon, Portugal.

Flaherty, C. (2020). Zoom boom. *Inside Higher Ed.* Retrieved November 4, 2020 from https://www.insidehighered.com/news/2020/04/29/synchronous-instruction-hot-right-now-it-sustainable

Germain-Rutherford, A. & Ernest, P. (2015). Theoretical approaches and research-based pedagogies for online teaching. In Hampel, R. & Stickler, U. (Eds.), *Developing online language teaching: Research-based pedagogies and reflective practices,* pp. 12–27. The Open University UK: Palgrave Macmillian.

Hampel, R. & Stickler, U. (2005). New skills for new classrooms: Training tutors to teach languages online. *Computer Assisted Language Learning*, 18(4), pp. 311–326.

Hofstede, G. (2011). Dimensionalizing Cultures: The Hofstede Model in Context. *Online Readings in Psychology and Culture*, 2(1), Article 8, pp. 1–26.

Holmes, G. & Abington-Cooper, M. (2000). Pedagogy vs Andragogy: A false Dichotomy? *The Journal of Technology Studies*, 26(2).

Jitka, N., Jitka, P. & Pavlna, K. (2018). Teacher's concept of constructivism in real conditions of school teaching. *Journal of Education and Training Studies*, 6(11a), pp. 133–138.

Khan, B. H. (2005). *Managing E-learning: Design, delivery, implementation and evaluation*. London, Hershey, PA: Information Science Publishing.

Korucu-Kis, S. & Ozmen, K. (2018). Toward an integrated technology integration framework for teacher preparation: Instructional Technological Competence. *i-manager's Journal on School Educational Technology*, 14(2), pp. 31–50.

Li, C. (2016). A survey on Chinese students' online English language learning experience through synchronous web conferencing classrooms. In S. Papadima-Sophocleous, L. Bradley & S. Thouësny (Eds.), *CALL communities and culture – short papers from EUROCALL 2016*, pp. 265–270. Research-publishing.net.

Malik, M., Fatima, G., Ch, A. H. & Sarwar, A. (2017). E-learning: Students perspectives about asynchronous and synchronous resources at higher education level. *Bulletin of Education and Research*, 39(2), pp. 183–195.

Martin, F., Parker, M. A. & Deale, D. F. (2012). Examining interactivity in synchronous virtual classrooms. *International Review of Research in Open and Distance Learning*, 13(3), pp. 227–261.

Merriam, S. B. (2009). *Qualitative research: A guide to design and implementation*. San Francisco, CA: Jossey-Bass.

Moser, S. & Smith, P. (2015). Benefits of Synchronous Online Courses. Retrieved November 4, 2020 from https://files.eric.ed.gov/fulltext/ED571270.pdf

National Center for Education Statistics (2018). *Distance learning: Table 311.15*. Retrieved November 4, 2020 from https://nces.ed.gov/fastfacts/display.asp?id=80

Opacich, K. J. (2019). A cohort model and high impact practices in undergraduate public health education. *Frontiers in Public Health*, 7(132), pp. 1–10.

Rigden, K. (2019). Teaching soft skills to secondary students through internships. *International Journal of Education, Culture and Society*, 1(4), pp. 28–35.

Rigden, K. A. (2017). *Culturally responsive andragogy in a synchronous virtual learning environment*. [Doctoral dissertation, University of Southern California]. ProQuest Dissertations Publishing.

Smith, D. R. & Ayers, D. F. (2006). Culturally responsive pedagogy and online learning: Implications for the globalized community college. *Community College Journal of Research and Practice, 30*, pp. 401–415.

Tabrizi, A. R. N., Gupta, D., and Saxena, M. (2014). Discourse analysis in the ESL classroom. *Beyond Words, 2*(1), pp. 73–89.

USC Rossier (2020). *Curriculum*. Retrieved November 4, 2020 from https://rossieronline.usc.edu/masters/online-master-of-arts-in-teaching-program

Ust, S. (2021). Emergency remote teaching in interior architecture: a necessary shift. In Enomoto, K., Warner, R. & Nygaard, C. (Eds.), *Teaching and Learning Innovations in Higher Education*, pp. 109–127. Oxfordshire, UK: Libri Publishing Ltd.

Viola, S., Hendricker, E. & Saeki, E. (2020). Instructional technology in graduate psychology distance education: Trends and student Preferences. *Journal of Educators Online, 17*(1), n1.

Vu, Phu & Fadde, P. J. (2013). When to talk, when to chat: Student interaction in live virtual classrooms. *Journal of Interactive Online Learning, 12*(2), pp. 41–52.

Wang, C-M. (2011). Instructional design for cross-cultural online collaboration: Grouping strategies and assessment design. *Australasian Journal of Educational Technology, 27*(2), pp. 243–258.

Chapter 7

Impacts of Using Technology-Enhanced Language Learning in Second Language Academic Writing at a Vietnamese University

Henriette van Rensburg and Triet Thanh La

Introduction

With our chapter, we contribute to this book, *Teaching and Learning Innovations in Higher Education*, as we show how we have used Technology-Enhanced Language Learning (TELL) in English academic writing classes at the University of Foreign Languages (UFL), Ho Chi Minh City, in order to motivate Vietnamese university students. The utilisation of TELL for teaching practice is innovative in its own right in a developing country, such as Vietnam, where the use of Information and Communication Technologies (ICT) is limited. The internet, in 1994, was undoubtedly known to only a dozen people in the country (Hoang-Giang, 1999). Since then, there has been slow and limited integration of both ICT and TELL into teaching practice, mainly due to ICT infrastructure shortage, lack of technical support, absence of digital confidence and educators' negative attitudes towards ICT (Peeraer & Van Petegem, 2010). In Vietnam, teachers and students tended not to be adequately trained as to how to integrate the use of digital technologies for effective teaching and learning. As Nguyen and van Rensburg (2016:156) state, the: *"Vietnamese educational philosophy regarding English learning is traditionally associated with memorising and that Vietnamese learners lack English language skills due to ineffective teaching methods"*.

Significant differences exist between different higher education institutions in Vietnam. UFL is one of the most prestigious private universities in the south of Vietnam, offering a wide range of undergraduate and graduate second language courses such as English, Japanese, Korean, and Chinese. Unlike other universities in Vietnam, that use Vietnamese as a medium of instruction, in UFL, students in all majors from their first year, must participate in courses which are taught in English. Therefore, teaching first-year students English attracts the attention of many educational stakeholders, including the University Academic Board.

Although advancing proficiency in the four core English language skills (writing, reading, speaking and listening) is compulsory, reading and writing are essential for all students at UFL, because most learning resources and materials, reference books and assessments are written in English. Recognising the importance of the reading and writing skills, academic writing classes are specifically made available to the students. However, despite the significant need for academic writing skills in the UFL context, many students dislike the academic writing classes. In comparison with other core skills, the attendance records in the writing classes show that only 70% of students regularly participate in the writing classes; this number is the lowest of the four core skills. In addition, according to an unofficial (internal) survey, although more than 60% of students assume that academic writing is the most important skill, academic writing is not their priority. Surprisingly, however, most students at UFL tend to gain very high scores in the vocabulary and grammar sections, which are two main factors determining students' academic writing success.

Referring to the learning-centred five-tier model of innovation in higher education (Dobozy & Nygaard, 2021, Chapter 2 in this book), our process innovation – the integration of TELL into academic writing classes – draws on a cognitivist perception of learning. Perceiving learning as a cognitivist, we primarily see our process innovation as a way to increase student motivation in academic writing though utilising TELL.

Reading this chapter, you will gain the following three insights:

1. the initial difficulties first-year students encounter in English academic writing at UFL;

2. the practice of using computers and digital devices, and the benefits of integrating TELL into academic writing skills development; and

3. the impact of TELL on the motivation of first-year students in academic writing.

Overview of main sections

This chapter focuses specifically on TELL in second language learning practice, learners' attitude towards TELL, the advantages of TELL in teaching and learning practice (listening, speaking, reading and writing), the role of motivation in second language learning, and the effect of TELL on learning motivation in a South East Asian developing country – Vietnam.

The chapter has three main sections. In Section 1, we review the literature on the use of TELL in language teaching, that has informed our integration of TELL in to academic writing in English in the Vietnamese university. This is followed by Section 2, that outlines how we examined the effectiveness of using TELL in English academic writing classes. In Section 3, we discuss our findings referring back to the three insights above.

Section 1: The background

In general, studies have indicated that students tend to have a positive attitude toward using technology for second language learning, and their positive attitude toward computer-enhanced learning encourages them to approve of learning and teaching strategies, and therefore achieving better results (Teo, 2006). Smith (2011) examined the students' positive or negative response to using TELL as a part of language learning approaches. He concluded that there was a solid relationship between students' attitude towards the type of teaching and learning and their positive attitude toward certain TELL activities. It is crucial to determine students' attitudes towards TELL at different stages of their development. Attitude is regarded as the effective variable in implementing technology in the second language learning process and is a significant factor promoting success in initiative implementation. Ayres (2002) research on students' attitudes toward TELL showed that a significant majority of the students believed that TELL was applicable to their needs, provided beneficial sources of learning information, and a majority thought that TELL should be exploited much more in the language learning contexts. Lasagabaster and Sierra (2003) and Sangeetha (2016) investigated university students' attitude towards the effectiveness of TELL programs, also suggesting that the students regarded TELL programs as supporting tools in their learning. These researchers also assumed that TELL programs created an enjoyable and relaxed learning environment; learners had a positive attitude toward using TELL.

It has been argued that applying technology in second language learning has proven valuable. Smith (2011) claimed that computers both assist students' language learning and al help develop students' self-study ability, such as information analysis, critical thinking, and problem-solving skills; which have positive impacts on language learning skills. TELL has coined a direct bond with teaching methodology and their mutual relationship, especially by recognising benefits and taking advantage of TELL, which can determine learning success or failure inside the technology-enhanced language classrooms (Joshi, 2010). Levy (2009) defined TELL as the study and application of the computer in language teaching and learning practice (listening, speaking, reading and writing). According to Sangeetha (2016), TELL is not restricted to the area within the classroom setting. Students can learn at home and in class.

The focus of TELL research aimed to discover appropriate methods to use computers in language teaching and learning efficiently. Beatty (2003) suggested that TELL includes any process where a language learner uses a computer and, therefore, improves their language learning outcome. In other words, multimedia files, word processing, simulation or presentation-supported software, electronic guided drill and practice and World Wide Web applications, such as blogs, social networking sites, and e-mail are used for language learning purposes. Computer-based materials include computer courses, learning programs, computer games, SMS, YouTube, recording and translation tools, assessment tools, and software for teaching and learning, while Web-based materials include online teaching and learning materials (Sangeetha, 2016; Serdiukov, 2001; Tafazoli et al., 2018; Tsai, 2020). TELL software, online discussion boards and online conference tools such as text chat, whiteboard, audio, and video, offer opportunities for comprehensible input and output, and meaning negotiation (Chapelle, 2001). A: *"TELL activity has processes, products, and actions that can be assessed. …in a way that matches the activity objectives and approach"* (Sangeetha, 2016:1). Aikyo et al. (2018:14) summarise technology and computer applications, stating that: *"Technology can be used for teaching and learning in a variety of settings and for multiple purposes"*. Yet only at the start of the 21st century, did lecturers at tertiary institutions in Vietnam begin to pay attention to the important advantages of TELL, in teaching and learning practice in assisting language learning activities with different definitions and approaches.

Listening comprehension can improve when the target language is simulated in authentic language contexts. Jones (2002) claimed that, through visual, aural or written input, computers could enhance language learners' listening skills. Jones (2008) argued that the existence of visual and aural material is indispensable to improving listening skills. Moreover, through websites, a great amount of authentic material, readily updated and applicable, could be used for improving language listening skills. Mosquera (2001) concluded that teachers and learners can use authentic listening internet resources for listening, teaching and learning. O'Bryan and Hegelheimer (2007) also claimed that podcasts could be exploited to enable listening instruction and result in positive attitudes of both teachers and learners towards computer-based multimedia. Podcasts, accessed through digital devices, could create more opportunities, sharpen learners' listening skills and encourage them to participate dynamically in the learning process.

TELL materials, well-developed software in discourse genres and topical areas, could increase accuracy and fluency in mechanical aspects of speech (Kataoka, 2000). In a TELL classroom, learners could experience and take risks in simulated conversations without feeling uncomfortable when making mistakes. Many learners can feel more self-confident and comfortable to speak without feeling embarrassed by their pronunciation errors when practising with computers providing visual aids, than in a face-to-face context (Delmonte, 2000). Other: *"applications of computer aided language learning in the development of speaking skills include an electronic dictionary, verbal command recognition, the use of speech recognition and analysis for assessment purposes, and the integration of speaking with other language skills"* (Hubbard & Siskin, 2004:450). The use of digital technology in second language classrooms creates opportunities which encourage learners' interest, allows discussion and conversation, improves creativity, nurtures a sense of personal confidence, enables learners' collaboration in group or pair work, reinforces communication skills and creates profound second language learning experiences (Cameron, 1999).

TELL can help to increase learners' reading skills by multimodal programs that have embedded text, graphics, sound, video, or animation. Studies of computer-assisted reading instruction reported that students' comprehension and speed have increased significantly (Al Abdel Halim, 2009). According to Nomass (2013), using installed reading passages which are designed and arranged from a simplified 'version' to a complicated one, computers can encourage the learners' interest in reading. Ybarra and Green (2003) suggested that reading-based computer programs enable language learners to increase interaction with texts and improve their reading capacities through paying attention to individual needs. Digital technologies can execute many reading focused learning tasks simultaneously and can check learners' exercises submitted to evaluate learners' progress and recommend the next passage suitable for learner ability. In addition, the internet can enhance learners' second language reading comprehension. Newspapers, magazines, journals, electronic libraries, dictionaries, encyclopaedias and newsletters are also valuable learning resources (Kenworthy, 2004). Exploiting such learning resources can effectively boost reading ability.

The use of digital technology for writing classes includes software programs and word processing-oriented writing processes, supporting students' writing skills development, especially in more challenging tasks such as writing statements, paragraphs, and essays. An early study, Lichtenstein (1996) found an important difference between students who write their essays on computers and students who used paper and pen. Students using a computer in the writing process tended to write for longer periods of time with added detail; their scores were consequently higher than students using pen and paper. Ybarra and Green (2003) found that using computers with graphic-enhanced programs could make the writing more enjoyable, helping learners to express their ideas more clearly. In addition, with typing processors, the spelling and grammar can be checked automatically. TELL provides additional flexibility and caters to more learning styles in language learning compared to traditional styles of teaching (Sangeetha, 2016).

Technology provides learners with: *"automatic detection of grammatical errors, such as spell check among other auto corrections when writing in a foreign language"* (Vurdien, 2013:130) and when learners write in any format, can peer review writing and give feedback individually and together.

Technology used in writing classes provided opportunities allowing learners to collaborate at a higher level than before (Hoopingarner, 2009). When language learners used computer-assisted-communication to post target language writing, peer interaction promoted productive skills and encouraged peer correction (Zha, 2006). Writing on blogs or social sites, complemented by peer feedback, can be an interactive format, improving learner's motivation (Vurdien, 2013). Fellner and Apple (2006) implemented blog writing, in a computer assisted language learning program for low-proficiency and low-motivation university language students during a short course, and included computer-based tasks and traditional classroom tasks. Student writing outcomes were significantly different, in terms of both the word count and the proficiency levels in the students' blogs, at the start and at the end of the program.

A cross-cultural writing project, involving second language instructors in Ukraine, Russia and Saudi Arabia and their undergraduate students (Al-Jarf, 2006) found that when writing with computer network support, learners developed their ability to communicate and interact with students from other cultures- through the awareness of local and global cultural issues. Although the interaction between those instructors and students, who belonged to completely different cultures, political, linguistic and educational backgrounds, the students reported that they developed a wider cultural view, as well as their writing skills.

Motivation can be seen to play a crucial role in second language learning. Gardner's classic definition of motivation is a: *"complex of characteristics which may or may not be related to any particular orientation and these characteristics are attitudes toward learning the language, desire to learn the language, and motivational intensity"* (1985:10). He also described motivation as the most independent and influential factor in language learning practice. A motivated learner is always enthusiastic in language learning, eager to participate in any relevant learning activity, and has long term ability to maintain this status. Indeed, Gardner (1985) concluded that learner motivation, or the devoted nature of the motivated learners' participation, play an indispensable role and orientate both formal and informal contexts. Motivation is considered to be a mental process, starting with a need or requirement, leading to behaviours pushing a person towards attempting to achieve a goal (Melendy, 2008). In second language learning, motivation refers to a desire to learn a second language and a positive attitude toward this learning, and has a central impact on a learner's behaviour in the learning process (Dornyei, 2011; Erev & Barron, 2005; Barron & Harackiewicz, 2001; Nihan & Hüseyin, 2018; Busse & Walter, 2013). Sangeetha (2016:12) echoes this thus: *"TELL improves motivation and develops better attitudes in students towards learning"*.

Motivation can be divided into two categories, intrinsic and extrinsic (Li & Tsai, 2017). Based on competence and autonomy, intrinsic motivation is where students are engaged with learning materials and it creates inside interest, enjoyment, and satisfaction. A typical example of this kind of motivation is that students enjoy language learning because there is the satisfaction that they felt when new knowledge is acquired or because of the happiness and natural interest involved in the learning process. Extrinsic motivation can help a student achieve goals separate from the activity in and of itself. For instance, a person who wants to master a second language if they believe that bilingualism is a competitive advantage in the labour market or this new language will make their journey or business more enjoyable. Activities: *"can be initiated extrinsically and later be internalised to become intrinsically motivated, or they can begin out of intrinsic interest"* (La Guardia, 2009:100) and be maintained in order to obtain other positive outcomes. Moreover, motivation creates successful second language communicators by letting students feel more confident (Ebata, 2008).

The expansion of TELL has positive impacts on learners' motivation in various aspects. The use of computers and the combination of multimedia, such as soundtrack, graphics or video can promote learners' interaction, and stimulate learning attitudes which influence motivation (Tsou et al., 2002). Hartoyo (2010) found computers to be indispensable, and integrating computers into second language classrooms can be an effective solution for individualising learning. Ayres (2002) showed that learners appreciated and valued the learning involving technology and saw TELL as a vital part of the course and suitable for their needs. Moreover, using pre-writing activities, supported by graphic-enhanced software such as flow-charting tools or search engines, students are motivated to work with pictures, video, audio, and voice recordings to brainstorm ideas on the topic (Castellani & Jeffs, 2001).

Internet connectivity can also be beneficial to increase students' learning motivation. For example, in a Japanese second language learning context, teachers established an email exchange program between learners in English classes to improve their knowledge and skills in writing and encourage the engagement in learning activities. Based on the data collected from this program, Fedderholdt (2001) found that such electronic mail exchange programs could inspire students in learning writing. Similarly, studies have investigated the effect of a computer supported collaborative learning environment on students' writing performance. In such studies, the experimental group was supported by word processor software, search engines, and internet connections, and the control group used only pen and paper. Many such studies found that the experimental group had substantial gains and were more motivated than the control group (Preacher & Hayes, 2008; Truax, 2017; Teng & Zhang, 2018). This issue of motivation is further explored, along with other variables, in the study which follows.

Section 2: The Study

Sixty first-year students majoring in English language, enrolled in the 10-week period academic writing course at UFL participated in this study. Most of the students were unfamiliar with writing and studying writing skills with the use of digital technologies, especially taking advantage of the features and functions of the software. They were in two separate classes (experimental and control group) and instructed by the same lecturer, following the same basic teaching and learning methodologies, and were using the same prescribed course book. In the experimental group, the students used a digital device of their choice, such as laptops, desktop computers, tablets and smartphones, and were encouraged to use learning software and other applications of their choice, such as the online Cambridge or Oxford Advanced Learner's Dictionary, word processing software (e.g. Microsoft Word and Add-on Grammarly Premium supporting spelling, grammar and word choices), and social media (e.g. Facebook). The students were required to write their paragraphs and essays on their digital devices and to check the language components, by way of fully utilising the spelling and grammar check functions prior to submision.

There was more scope for self-determining learning strategies and learner autonomy in the experimental group. On the other hand, the control group just followed the normal study schedule using only the course book, without assistance of technology-based devices, such as laptops or mobile phones. The mainly urban students in this study were nineteen or twenty years of age, with a 30:70 male to female ratio. Each student (in both classes) completed an anonymous, paper-based questionnaire, using pseudonyms at the beginning and end of the course; the educator was also interviewed at the end of the course. It took students about 30 minutes to complete each questionnaire. Data was collected over 10 weeks (this included the course duration, 30 sessions, 3 times a week) in 2017 as part of the practice to help validation of the outcome. The questionnaires were completed at the beginning (week 1), and the end of the course after the final marks of the students had been released. The final mark was also regarded as important information for this study. The students and educator could respond in either Vietnamese or English. One author is a native Vietnamese speaker and translated questionnaires as needed.

Section 3: The findings

3a: Data analysis

We used a mixed methods approach. The quantitative element incorporated counting and synthesising the students' responses; Nvivo and Microsoft Excel 2010 were used for the synthesis process. The qualitative element included evaluating, comparing, and making implications from the data collected. The data was also coded, categorised and grouped as patterns emerged. In addition, the recorded interview with the educator was transcribed and used as qualitative data. The 20 questions in the questionnaire were generated to collect the data in order to answer the three questions (relevant to the three insights regarding the first-year students at UFL as mentioned earlier in the Introduction).

The first group of questions intentionally confirmed whether the UFL first-year students encountered academic writing as difficult, as well as the levels of difficulty. Around 75% of students studied writing at high school and writing was not new to the majority of them. A similar number stated that writing was 'difficult; approximately 10 % thought that it was 'very difficult', around 13% did not think that writing was a difficult language skill. Nearly half of students stated that a lack of vocabulary was the main reason for their poor writing skills, and just over a third said that a lack of grammar caused writing difficulties. Although there were various other ways (45%), reading books (31%) and learning vocabulary and grammar (24%) were two methods students used for improving their writing performance.

The second group of questions attempted to collect the data for evaluating students' familiarity with using digital technologies in their personal life and language learning. In the Vietnamese educational context, receiving a computer proficiency certificate, evidencing their study is vital, yet most students had not attempted to get a computer proficiency certificate. Over 90% of students use devices such as smartphones, laptops or desktops daily, yet the data collected revealed that only 24% used them for study or educational purposes.

The quantitative questions aimed to examine the benefits of digital technologies on learning English academic writing. The questionnaires were delivered to both the control and experimental groups at the end of the course when the final marks were released. In the UFL context, all students in the Department of Foreign Languages have to write the compulsory final examination in all courses. Slightly under half of control group students agreed that digital technologies can support their learning in general, whereas over 90% in the experimental group confirmed the assistance of digital technologies in language learning. However, there was a noticeable difference in the reasons between the two groups. While experimental group students indicated that their reasons were looking up words, brainstorming for ideas, and writing samples (35%) and using the dictionary (33%); control group students confirmed that using the dictionary (37%) was the main single benefit of an internet connection. Without teachers' instruction in applying the internet for learning, the power of the internet appeared fairly limited to students' learning.

Regarding the students' attitude towards the usefulness of installed software on the digital technologies, over 27% in the control group answered 'Yes', as opposed to 65% in the experimental group. The collected data also revealed that the reasons behind this were noticeably different. While control group students mainly focused on dictionary use (59%) and the necessity to type and write (24%), the experimental group students paid attention to the search engine and Wikipedia (38%), and dictionary use (33%). Data input choices and writing options were not even mentioned by the experimental group students. While 81% of the control group students stated that Microsoft Word was the most preferred software, the experimental group students stated that Microsoft Word (22%), the dictionary (20%), and Internet Explorer (22%) were popular. This difference partly demonstrated the potential of using software for writing with teachers' facilitating and teaching the writing process.

The students' final mark at the end of the writing course was considered as particularly important quantitative data, directly demonstrating the impact of TELL on the process of English teaching and learning at UFL. According to the collected data, the average Grade Point Average (GPA) of control group students was 6.00, while experimental group students averaged a GPA of 7.04 in the final writing paper test. In detail, it could be seen that in the marking/grading scale, the students who gained 9 (8%), 8 (24%), or 7 (39%) in the experimental group, were higher than those in the control group. In brief, the performance of the students in the experimental group was higher than in the control group.

The final and last group of questions in the questionnaire, collected after the course, was designed to collect data for examining whether TELL had an influence on the students' motivation when studying academic writing skills at UFL. There was a prominent contrast between two groups. While 35% of control group students studied academic writing after class, over 62% of experimental group students spent time improving their writing skills. The main reason for this was completing their assignments (48% in the experimental group and 18% in the control group). The students' interest in academic writing in the experimental group was higher (77%) than in the control group (56%). The experimental group was interested in 'spelling correction' (17%), a popular feature of Microsoft Word.

The data collected stated that over 74% of experimental group students preferred using digital technologies such as desktops or laptops for writing activities. Both groups stated that improving their writing skills and obtaining higher marks were the main expectations. The control group asked for 'more interesting' classes, while the students in the experimental group required more time for studying academic writing.

3b: Discussion of our findings

In this sub-section, we discuss the three insights stated in the Introduction, based on our analyses of the collected data. In so doing, we refer to relevant theories and practice of teaching and learning English academic writing in other educational contexts.

The initial difficulties first-year students encounter in an English academic writing course

The collected quantitative data based on questions 1 – 6 in the questionnaire have provided an overview on the first-year students' main difficulties in an English academic writing course context at UFL. Although there was not a direct question in the questionnaire confirming students' difficulties in academic writing, it seemed noticeable that the first-year students' difficulties in English academic writing correlated with current teaching practices at UFL. It is clear that the effectiveness of English language teaching and learning and the students' outcome in Vietnam General Education (from Grade 6 to 12) did not match.

The data claims a conflict between the practice of teaching and learning English academic writing, and the practice of English teaching and learning writing skills in Vietnam second language education at school level. The problem seems to lie with the learning outcome of UFL first-year English-major students and their GPA in English subjects in high schools. While up to 90% of students received 'distinction' and 'high distinction' grades at high school, they still underestimated their general English language proficiency. This may be surprising when we examine the Vietnam second language education policy. In the Vietnam general education system, students have to study English from Grade 6 (secondary school) to grade 12 (high school) and during this period, they take at least 945 hours of class study during the seven academic years (Ministry of Education and Training, 2007).

Furthermore, nearly 75% of students studied writing in high school, which demonstrated that writing was not a new skill to them. The 'Academic writing: the paragraph' course, was the second writing course taken when students study at UFL. The first writing course mainly focused on grammar and sentence formation. Based on this practice, it can be concluded that, in this context, there might be ineffectiveness in

English language teaching and learning in the Vietnam general education system, as well as the UFL context, which results in students' experiencing difficulties in English academic writing. The poor learning outcome at high school and teaching at UFL can be considered as the main causal contributors linked to the students' writing difficulties.

The students encountered various difficulties. Lack of vocabulary, as well as grammar and looking for ideas were three examples of difficulties, which account for over 96%. In productive skills, for example writing and speaking, lack of linguistic components, such as words and grammatical patterns were direct causes resulting in second language learners' obstacles (Smith, 2011). Learners often mentioned these factors when explaining learning barriers that they experienced. However, in the Vietnam English teaching and learning context, these linguistic barriers seem 'unreasonable'. The Vietnam second language education context had a reputation for focusing on the tests of grammar and vocabulary for many years, and since the wave of second language teaching and learning started in 1986, grammar-translation has been the most widely used teaching method in schools from primary schools to tertiary institutions (Quang, 1993).

In brief, the data demonstrated that there was no close relationship between high school teaching, and learning vocabulary and grammar, as well as the improvement of UFL first-year English major students' writing skills in the context. Moreover, in comparison to students' typical difficulties in writing in other learning contexts, UFL first-year students' difficulties seemed different. Discussing the difficulties in academic writing, both Kobayashi and Rinnert (2008) and Elfatah and Ahmed (2016) claimed that various factors impact students' second language writing, such as first language writing ability, second language proficiency, and writing experiences in both languages. Eckstein and Ferris (2017) believe that writers from different first language backgrounds often write differently, depending on how they learn writing styles in their first culture. Many linguistic researchers suggest that second language learners' first language writing capacity is the main element that determines their second language writing performance (Petric & Czarl, 2003; Bamanger & Alhassan, 2015). Obviously, there is a transfer in writing-skill between first language and second language. Therefore, the learners' first language difficulties could mirror as obstacles in their second language studies. From this perspective, we assumed that the difficulties the students experienced, may partly be from the weakness in their Vietnamese first language teaching and learning. Moreover, when comparing the difficulties experienced by students, with other academic writing difficulties of students in other contexts, we concluded that UFL first-year students were in the low level of learning academic writing skills, both in the terms of linguistic factors (as mentioned earlier), and in understanding the principles, as well as elements necessary for successful academic writing learning.

Studying the problems students encountered in ESL academic writing classes at West East Institute, Al Badi (2015) stated that students encounter several major problems: paraphrasing, referencing, and citation; language coherence, and cohesion; expressing own voice; significant topic and relevant reference. These problems, rather than being linguistic factors, concentrate on culturally determined composition skills of constructing the whole paragraph or essay. While 75% of our students declared that they encountered problems in organising ideas and had insufficient vocabulary for good writing, 80% stated that the main reasons causing these difficulties were a lack of reading and writing practice, and a lack of courses on academic writing skills in their mother tongue.

The UFL first-year students used different methods to improve their writing. Reading books (31%), and learning vocabulary and grammar (24%) were the main methods used. As mentioned above, lack of vocabulary, grammar and ideas were three kinds of difficulties in students' academic writing in this context. The methods that students used seemed (for them) appropriate for their academic writing improvement. However, in comparison with specific methods, that some other students in Yuen and Mussa's (2015:139) research used, *"reading more academic articles, and having more writing practices"*; the methods implemented in UFL context were too general and inadequate. We believe that improvement of any specific language skill requires the direct practice of this skill. For example, progress in writing mainly requires the writing practice; TELL can be used together with the textbook for a much more in-depth learning experience (Sangeetha, 2016). Similarly, with other skills, such as listening, the students could only enhance this receptive skill through practicing this skill regularly. Learning vocabulary and grammar should be only supplementary elements.

Finally, based on the discussion of the causes and difficulties above, we suggested some contextually innovative solutions for those problems in academic writing that UFL first-year students encounter. The first solution was that the UFL Department of Foreign Languages should implement introductory courses in writing focusing on the improvement of linguistic components, such as vocabulary and grammar, which are highly practical and should support the following course in academic writing. These should also be courses (both in English and Vietnamese) in the principles of academic writing, providing students with an overview on this important skill. Secondly, students' self-study writing should be given more attention – the students needed more post-class writing practice therefore, teachers in charge of these courses should ask students to finish more assignments, observe their progress and offer support when needed. The final practical solution was for the school to create a specific learning resource for multi-level writing skills. This resource should include materials such as books, relevant articles and guidelines, designed to assist writing courses at UFL.

The practice of using digital technologies and digital devices at UFL
Our findings revealed that digital technologies had been popular with students at UFL with over 90% of students using digital devices in their daily lives, and a similar number using computers or other electronic devices for studying at home. This practice was positive, as it was a prerequisite for integrating information technology into classrooms that the (Vietnamese) Ministry of Education and Training (2008) had already launched in 2008. According to an earlier unofficial survey at UFL, over 75% of students originated from urban areas, such as Ho Chi Minh City or central cities in the Mekong Delta provinces. In these areas, more than 50% of citizens had access to the internet, and 90% of the population used digital devices in their daily lives. This practice indirectly brought advantages for education in general, and second language teaching and learning in particular.

However, the findings about students' use of digital technology at UFL, do not support language learning in general. Although the Vietnam population experienced a growth of digital devices from China since 2000, the real digital boom in Vietnam (especially in central cities), officially started in 2008 when a wave of smartphones and individual devices invaded the Vietnamese market. Despite Vietnam being one of the developing South East Asian countries that experienced this digital boom, the individual use of digital devices, especially smartphones and computers, has not yet been fully integrated into the education environment.

More than 61% of our students mainly used digital technologies for finding learning materials, and nearly 21% used digital technologies for completing their assignments. The main use of digital technologies by the students, related to the use of an internet search engine, such as Google, a globally used search engine. The responses did not mention the combination of various e-learning tools and learning resources to support their study. This combination was the target for application of information technology in education (Ministry of Education and Training, 2008).

The solution for improving the use of computers and digital devices at UFL lies mainly in innovative lecturer practice, and instruction and learning orientation that include e-learning trends. All UFL lecturers, not only those teaching academic writing courses, should pay more attention to teach students how utilise the benefits of computers and other digital devices. These guidelines need to be included in the UFL teaching syllabi. In addition, the school should provide extra computer-based short courses for all students. The peremptory implementation is necessary in this situation to improve the quality of language teaching and learning in general.

The support for digital technology use in English academic writing for experimental group students (90%) was much higher than for the control group students (48%). The experimental group students studied academic writing in a computer laboratory with internet connection, while their control group counterparts studied writing in a traditional classroom with a white board; with no digital technology use in the formal teaching sessions during the 10-week semester. However, postclass, the use of digital technologies was not observed in either group. As noted in Section 3, 'the students' familiarity with digital technologies' and the data reflecting the percentage of students' 'use at home' (92%), we could not confirm that there was no use of digital technologies at home amongst students in the control group.

After 10 academic weeks, results indicated that students who had studied in class with the assistance of digital technology, appreciated the benefits of this technological integration on their academic writing.

Investigating the reasons behind this comment, we identified some differences. The control group students in the control group paid more attention to the use of dictionary software (21%), and only 17% stated that they use the internet to search for writing related ideas. However, 36% of experimental group students confirmed the use of e-dictionaries; 38 % considered using a search engine as the main factor that promoted the use of digital technologies. The significant contrast in these percentages between the two groups concluded that the integration of digital technologies benefited the students' during their academic writing course at UFL.

According to the data, the students' attitudes to the internet benefited their learning. While around 60% of the control group students believed in the benefits of the internet on their writing, over 74% of experimental group students confirmed this trend. Although our focus was not on the technical aspects of the digital technologies or the use of the installed software during the course, the researchers also aimed to gain an overview of the trend of software usage amongst the students, as well as their preference. The analysed data indicated that around 65% of students, who experienced the digital technology integration in formal learning sessions, recognised that installed software was useful to their study. The combination of these results indirectly indicated that the formal, blended classroom instruction positively influenced students' awareness about the benefits of software usage.

The final discussion in this section reports on the practical effectiveness of computer use on students' writing outcome, through their final mark. The students' average GPA in the control group was 6.00 while, in the experimental group, students averaged 7.04. In addition, the percentage of students' mark in the experimental group was in levels of nine (8%), eight (24%), and seven (39%) and was higher than those of the students in the control group. In summary, the use of digital technologies in classrooms at UFL had a positive impact on students' learning outcome, especially in improving their GPA marks.

The impact of TELL on students' motivation in academic writing at UFL

The final data driven discussion involved the impact of TELL on the motivation of first-year students in English academic writing at UFL;

through the questionnaires, ample data was collected. The first impact of TELL on students' motivation shows through the percentage of students who actively studied after class. Such findings align with Aikyo et al. (2018:15), who stated that the *"use of technology has shifted the role of the teacher/educator from instructor to facilitator, and the role of the students from passive learners to active learners"*. Locke and Lathem's (1994) goal-setting theory claims that human action is caused by internal and/or external purpose(s) and, based on this theory, we inferred that students' writing after class could be influenced by teachers' demands or their own goal setting.

The percentage of students writing post-class in the experimental group (62%) was much higher than the percentage from the control group (35%). Examining the reasons behind this data, we found that finishing an assignment was the main force in both groups. This data alone cannot help to confirm the impact of digital technologies on motivation. However, through qualitative data collected in the interview session with the teacher, question 3: 'Do you often use computers in your classes?', the response was as follows: *"I use computers frequently for my teaching. … that there is a computer with available software is very convenient for teaching because I do not need to bring my laptop. I just store my stuff on the cloud and open when I come. There will be time for me to ask students to practice writing as well as have opportunities to give more exercise for their home study…"* (sic). From this qualitative data, we concluded that although TELL did not directly affect students' learning motivation, their appearance in the classroom could support teachers' instruction, which indirectly could improve teaching quality. In other words, TELL in the classroom could help the teacher to improve students' extrinsic motivation, which refers to doing something because it leads to a separable outcome (Deci & Ryan, 1985).

Another significant finding was students' preference in writing using digital technologies. Interest in writing is extremely important to the writers in any situation. This interest was considered to be a type of intrinsic motivation, which refers to doing something because it is fundamentally interesting or enjoyable (Deci & Ryan, 1985). With intrinsic motivation, the learners maximise their potential to complete the task. This kind of motivation originates from internal factors, one of them being the feeling of desire or self-desire. According to our analysis of the collected data, 74% of experimental group students confirmed their interest in academic writing while, compared with 48% in the control group. In addition to this data, the reasons behind the statement of both groups were completely different. The students indicated three factors: easy correction (30%), dictionary (26%), and assistance in searching ideas (22%) whereas, students in the control group offered a simple explanation, which was mainly on the use of the dictionary (53%). From, the combination of this analysis, as well as the theory of motivation mentioned above, we briefly conclude that TELL did impact on students' intrinsic motivation in academic writing.

The last discussion concluded with students' interest in academic writing. The impact of TELL on the students' learning interest in the experimental group (77%) was much higher than of students in the control group (54%). While students in the control group thought that the use of the dictionary (38%) and benefits of tools for searching ideas (32%) were the main causes of their learning interest, the students in the experimental group added 'spelling correction' (17%) as a reason. 'Spelling correction' is a convenient and usable feature in the writing process. It generally promoted writing quality and created a comfortable learning feeling, indirectly improving writers' interest in their work. In brief, to some extent, digital technologies with useful software inside could have motivated second language learners.

Section 4: Moving forward

Any research has its own limitations; our first limitation relates to the methodology. As planned, both qualitative and quantitative methods were used for research data collection via the questionnaires and interview sessions. However, during data analysis, we realised that we had a greater reliance on quantitative data (the questionnaires) rather than qualitative interview data. Although synthesis and analysis of quantitative data may be more convenient and concrete than that of qualitative data (Cohen et al., 2011), this imbalance might have negatively affected our findings. Secondly, another limitation was the number of students-two student groups with 30 students per group. Such small numbers do not mirror normal UFL group sizes. In this small-scale case study, this issue was not investigated intensively, more attention was paid to analysing students' difficulties and suggesting practical solutions. Bearing in mind our findings and limitations, a follow-up study in this area could adopt a mixed methodology, with a qualitative and quantitative method balance to assure validity.

Conclusion

Through our findings, this chapter has shown the significant impact of utilising TELL for enhancing students' motivation in developing their academic writing skills in the Vietnamese higher education context. Referring back to the three insights (outlined in the Introduction), we conclude this chapter by summarising our key findings confirming that *"technology is an ever-increasing part of the English language classroom"* (Sangeetha, 2016:1).

Firstly, we found that students' difficulties in academic writing at UFL mainly originated from the limitations of second language teaching and learning inherent in the Vietnamese general education system (from middle to high school), as well as the UFL-specific context. In addition, the first-year students' understanding in relation to the principles of academic writing was also limited. However, such lack of understanding can be mitigated by way of organising courses for improving students' linguistic skills, digital literacy and skills, and paying more attention to students' independent learning skills outside classes.

Secondly, we found that, although computers or digital devices were popular amongst the students, their educational use of these devices for was often ineffective. We see a clear need for new courses that designed to effectively develop students' digital literacy and skills training. Such courses would help develop students' academic writing skills more effectively.

Thirdly, we also found the benefits of utilising TELL for developing English academic writing skills, by comparing the two student groups' final marks, and analysing students' questionnaire responses. Some benefits were also found when the internet was used effectively in digitally equipped classrooms. In addition, we found that the role of the educators in a digital classroom was important, because it can determine the success of information technology applications in second language teaching and learning. Our findings demonstrate that TELL provides more flexibility in learning, in that students can learn at home independently outside the classroom, whilst also ensuring a much more in-depth learning experience when used alongside the course book.

With a specific university context situated in a non-English speaking, developing country – Vietnam, where the use of ICT is limited, we have portrayed the positive impact of TELL on the students' English academic writing skills, enhancing intrinsic and extrinsic motivation to learn and promoting positive attitudes towards learning in students.

About the Authors

Henriette van Rensburg, PhD, is an Associate Professor of Digital Literacies and Inclusion, in the School of Education, Toowoomba Campus, at the University of Southern Queensland, Australia. She can be contacted at this e-mail: vanrensb@usq.edu.au

Triet Thanh La is a lecturer of English language at Ho Chi Minh City University of Foreign Languages – Information Technology. He can be contacted at this e-mail: lth.triet@huflit.edu.vn

Bibliography

Aikyo, M., DePew, D. D., Holt, K., Rigden, K. & van Rensburg, H. (2018). An introduction to technology-based innovations in Higher Education. In Enomoto, K., Warner, R. & Nygaard, C. (Eds.), *Innovative Teaching and Learning Practices in Higher Education*, pp. 13–18. Oxfordshire, UK: Libri Publishing Ltd.

Al Abdel Halim, A. (2009). Designing a computer-assisted language learning program (CALL) and measuring its effect on Jordanian secondary school students' reading comprehension in English. *Unpublished Ph.D dissertation*. Irbid, Jordan: Yarmouk University.

Al Badi, I. A. (2015). *Academic Writing Difficulties of ESL Learners*. WEI International Academic Conference, Barcelona, Spain.

Al-Jarf, R. (2006). Integrating technology in EFL college instruction in Saudi Arabia. *Education and Psychology Journal*, 26, pp. 215–242.

Ayres, R. (2002). Learner attitudes towards the use of CALL. *Computer Assisted Language Learning*, 15(3), pp. 241–249.

Bamanger, E. M. & Alhassan, R. A. (2015). Exploring podcasting in English as a foreign language learners' writing performance. *Journal of Education and Practice, 6*(11), pp. 63–74.

Barron, K. E. & Harackiewicz, J. M. (2001). Achievement goals and optimal motivation: Testing multiple goal models. *Journal of Personality and Social Psychology, 80*(5), pp. 706–722.

Beatty, K. (2003). *Teaching and Researching Computer Assisted Language Learning*. New York: Longman.

Busse, V. & Walter, C. (2013). Foreign language learning motivation in higher education: A longitudinal study of motivational changes and their causes. *The Modern Language Journal, 97*(2), pp. 435–456.

Cameron, K. C. (1999). *CALL and\he Learning Community*. Exeter: Elm Bank Publications.

Castellani, J. D. & Jeffs, T. (2001). Reading and writing: Teaching strategies, technology tools, and the internet. *Teaching Exceptional Children, 33*(5), pp. 60–67.

Chapelle, C. A. (2001). *Computer Application in Second Language Acquistion*. Cambridge: Cambridge University Press.

Cohen, L., Manion, L. & Morrison, K. (2011). *Research Methods in Education*. 7th edition. Routledge, London.

Deci, E. L. & Ryan, R. M. (1985). *Intrinsic motivation and self-determination in human behavior*. Plenum: New York.

Delmonte, R. (2000). SLIM prosodic automatic tools for self-learning instruction. *Speech Communication, 30*, pp. 145–166.

Dobozy, E. & Nygaard, C. (2021). A learning-centred, five-tier model of innovation in higher education. In Enomoto, K., Warner, R. & Nygaard, C. (Eds.), *Teaching and Learning Innovations in Higher Education*, pp. 19–46. Oxfordshire, UK: Libri Publishing Ltd.

Dornyei, Z. (2011). *Teaching and researching motivation*. Harlow: Longman.

Ebata, M. (2008). Motivation factors in language learning. *The Internet TESL Journal, 14*(4).

Eckstein, G. & Ferris, D. (2017). Comparing L1 and L2 texts and writers in first-year composition. *Tesol Quarterly, 52*(1).

Elfatah, M. A. & Ahmed, A. S. (2016). Using Facebook to develop grammar discussion and writing skills in English as a foreign language for university students. *Sino-US English Teaching, 13*(12), pp. 932–952.

Erev, I. & Barron, G. (2005). On adaptation, maximisation, and reinforcement learning among cognitive strategies. *Psychological Review, 112*(4), pp. 912–931.

Fedderholdt, K. (2001). An email exchange project between non-native speakers of English. *ELT Journal, 55*(3), pp. 273–280.

Fellner, T. & Apple, M. (2006). Developing writing fluency and lexical complexity with blogs. *JALT CALL Journal*, 2(1), pp. 15–26.

Gardner, R. C. (1985). *Social psychology and second language learning: The role of attitudes and motivation*. London: Edward Arnold Publishers.

Hartoyo, M. (2010). *Individual differences in computer assisted language learning (CALL)*. Semarang, Indonesia: Pelita Insani Semarang.

Hoang-Giang, D. (1999). Internet in Vietnam – From a laborious birth into an uncertain future. *Informatik Forum*, 13(1), pp. 16–20.

Hoopingarner, D. (2009). Best practices in technology and language teaching. *Language and Linguistics Compass*, 3(1), pp. 222–233.

Hubbard, P. & Siskin, B. C. (2004). Another look at tutorial CALL. *ReCALL*, 16(2), pp. 448–461.

Jones, L. (2002). Using technology in language teaching and listening comprehension: Revisiting what teachers should know and do. *International Association of Language Learning Technologies Journal*, 34(2), pp. 25–53.

Jones, L. (2008). Listening comprehension technology: Building the bridge from analog to digital. *CALICO Journal*, 25(3), pp. 400–419.

Joshi, D. K. (2010). *Learning strategies of English language teachers for professional development*. Tribhuvan University, Kathmandu.

Kataoka, K. (2000). *Computers for English language learning in Japanese schools*. Hokkaido, Japan.

Kenworthy, R. (2004). Developing writing skills in a foreign language via the internet. *The Internet TESL Journal*, 10(10).

Kobayashi, H. & Rinnert, C. (2008). Task response and text construction across L1 and L2 writing. *Journal of Second Language Writing*, 17(1), pp. 7–29.

La Guardia, J. G. (2009). Developing who I am: A self-determination theory approach to the establishment of healthy identities. *Educational Psychologist*, 44(2), 90–104.

Lasagabaster, D. & Sierra, J. M. (2003). Students evaluation of CALL software programmes. *Educational Media International*, 40(3–4), pp. 293–304.

Levy, M. (2009). Technologies in use for second language learning. *The Modern Language Journal*, 93(1), pp. 769–782.

Li, L. & Tsai, C. (2017). Accessing online learning material: Quantitative behavior patterns and their effects on motivation and learning performance. *Computers & Education*, 114, pp. 286–297.

Lichtenstein, N. (1996). The effect of word processing on writing achievement. *ERIC Document Reproduction Service No. 394146*.

Locke, E. A. & Latham, G. P. (1994). Goal Setting Theory. In J. H. O'Neil, *Motivation: Theory and Research*, pp. 13–29. Hillsdale, NJ: Lawrence Erlbaum Associates, Inc.

Melendy, G. A. (2008). Motivating writers: The power of choice. *Asian EFL Journal*, 10(3), pp. 187–198.

Ministry of Education and Training. (2007). *English Curriculum*. Ha Noi: Educational Publishers.

Ministry of Education and Training. (2008). *ICT Applications in TVET Institutions in Vietnam*. Hanoi: Educational Publishers.

Mosquera, F. (2001). CALL: Exploiting internet resources and multimedia for TEFL in developing countries. *Computer Assisted Language Learning*, 14(5), pp. 461–468.

Nguyen, V. H. & van Rensburg, H. (2016) Investigating the effectiveness of Computer Assisted Language Learning (CALL) on Vietnamese EFL young learners' listening skills. In *Global Language Policies and Local Educational Practices and Cultures*, 11th ed. Deep University Press, Blue Mounds, Wisconsin, pp. 156–173.

Nihan, B. & Hüseyin, O. (2018). The role of goal setting in metacognitive awareness as a self-regulatory behavior in foreign language learning. *International Online Journal of Education and Teaching (IOJET)*, 5(3), pp. 662–671.

Nomass, B. (2003). The impact of using technology in teaching English as a second language. *English Language and Literature Studies*, pp. 111–116.

O'Bryan, A. & Hegelheimer, V. (2007). Integrating CALL into the classroom: The role of podcasting in an ESL listening strategies course. *ReCALL*, 19(2), pp. 162–180.

Peeraer, J. & Van Petegem, P. (2010, May 17). Factors influencing integration of higher education in Vietnam. In *Global Learn*, pp. 916–924. Association for the Advancement of Computing in Education (AACE).

Petric, B. & Czarl, B. (2003). Validating a writing strategy questionnaire. *System*, 31(2), pp. 187–215.

Preacher, K. J. & Hayes, A. F. (2008). Asymptotic and resampling strategies for assessing and comparing indirect effects in multiple mediator models. *Behavior Research Methods*, 40, pp. 879–891.

Quang, N. N. (1993). *English teaching and learning in the system of continuing education in Vietnam*. International TESOL Conference, Ho Chi Minh City, Vietnam.

Sangeetha, S. (2016). Rhetorical Use of Technology Enhanced Language Learning (TELL) Practices: A Pragmatic View in English Classrooms. *The Global Journal of English Studies*, 2(1), pp. 1–13.

Serdiukov, P. (2001). Online resources for ESL/EFL teachers and students: An approach to organisation and structure. In *Society for Technology and Teacher Education, International Conference*, pp. 2932–2937. Association for the Advancement of Computing in Education (AACE).

Smith, J. (2011). *Learning foreign language.* Retrieved October 20, 2020, from http://www.teacherweb.com/VA/NottowayMiddleSchool/ForeignLanguage/apt4.asp

Tafazoli, D., Parra, M. E. G. & Huertas-Abril, C. A. (2018). Cross-Cultural Perspectives on Technology-Enhanced Language Learning (TELL). In L.A.Tomei (Ed.), *Advances in Educational Technologies and Instructional Design*, pp. 1–15. IGI Global, USA.

Teng, L. S. & Zhang, L. J. (2018). Effects of motivational regulation strategies on writing performance: A mediation model of self-regulated learning of writing in English as a second/foreign language. *Metacognition and Learning*, 13, pp. 213–240.

Teo, T. (2006). Attitudes toward computers: A study of post-secondary students in Singapore. *Interactive Learning Environments*, 14(1), pp. 17–24.

Truax, M. L. (2017). The impact of teacher language and growth mindset feedback on writing motivation. *Journal of Literacy and Instruction*, 58(2), pp. 135–157.

Tsai, S-C. (2020). Chinese students' perceptions of using Google Translate as a translingual call tool in EFL writing. *Computer Assisted Language Learning*. 32(5), pp. 1–23.

Tsou, W., Wang, W. & Li, H. (2002). How computers facilitate English foreign language learners acquire English. *Computers & Education*, 39(4), pp. 415–428.

Vurdien, R. (2013). Enhancing writing skills through blogging in an advanced English as a foreign language class in Spain. *Computer Assisted Language Learning*, 26(2), pp. 126–143.

Ybarra, R. & Green T. (2003). Using technology to help ESL/EFL students develop language skills. *The Internet TESL Journal*, 9(3), pp. 1–5

Yuen, C. K. & Mussa, I. H. (2015). Academic writing difficulties of Iraqi postgraduate students in Malaysia. *International Journal of Education and Research*, pp. 135–142.

Zha, S. (2006). The effects of a technology-supported training system on second language use strategies for international teaching assistants. *Unpublished doctoral dissertation*. Columbia, USA: University of Missouri.

Chapter 8

Using Arts-based Instructional Strategies in E-learning to Increase Students' Social-emotional Learning Outcomes

Beth Perry and Margaret Edwards

Introduction

With our chapter, we contribute to this book, *Teaching and Learning Innovations in Higher Education*, by describing several arts-based instructional strategies (photovoice, parallel poetry, poetweet, word sculptures, and my music moments) that we created and evaluated in an e-learning environment, as a product innovation. Our chapter shows that these types of instructional strategies (those founded on the arts that contain elements of creativity and human emotion) increased digital caring and helped learners achieve social-emotional learning outcomes, as they studied online. Referring to the learning-centred five-tier model of innovation in higher education (Dobozy & Nygaard, 2021, Chapter 2 in this book), our product innovation draws on a constructivist perception of learning. Perceiving learning as constructivist, we primarily see our product innovation as a means to assist students in achieving social-emotional learning outcomes, and to help e-learners experience a sense of community and social connection in their e-learning classes. As we will see, implementing and using a constructivist innovation has implications for both students and teachers.

In the chapter, our innovative teaching and learning is situated in the context of the online learning environment. Education is undergoing an explosive and seemingly unstoppable transformation that embraces online teaching and learning, sometimes referred to as e-learning. Rapid advances in technology are influencing how we teach and how we learn. Online education has become an integral part of education globally. Many students, from all levels and disciplines, now engage in e-learning for at least a portion of their programs of studies. There are many catalysts of this acceptance, including advances in technology, increased digital fluency and literacy, and the requirement to learn in isolation due to health concerns related to large in-person gatherings of students.

For many teachers and students, e-learning is new. Most have progressed through the education system engaged in face-to-face teaching and learning in traditional classrooms. Now many are embracing online instruction and learning. For educators, this is an innovation that requires an adjustment in many aspects of teaching, including preparing the curriculum of studies, developing means to assess achievement of learning outcomes, and finding new ways to provide for interaction in group activities. Educators need to focus on creating new ways to maintain the essential social and human presence when education moves to the e-learning milieu.

Early approaches to e-learning often focused on one-way communication with limited interaction among students in a class or between students and educators. Students and teachers often found online learning isolating and uninspiring (Choudhury & Pattnaik, 2020). Yet, arts-based instructional strategies are innovative because they propel course participants to engage in energetic discussion about course topics, humanise and invigorate the online learning environment, and help to create a culture of community (Janzen et al., 2019). Such arts-based instructional strategies also increase digital caring and help students meet social-emotional learning outcomes in the e-learning environment. Our focus is particularly on social and emotional presences of the Community of Inquiry (CoI) model (Anderson et al., 2001; Cleveland-Innes & Campbell, 2012) and the carative factors in Watson's Model of Human Caring (2008). These models are used to frame the analysis and discussion around our innovation, which was implemented in graduate courses at Athabasca University, an online and distance education university located in Canada. In this chapter, we describe several arts-based instructional strategies (photovoice, parallel poetry, poetweet, word sculptures, and my music moments) that we found increased digital caring and helped students meet social-emotional learning outcomes in the e-learning environment.

Reading this chapter, you will gain the following three insights:
1. using arts-based instructional strategies in online teaching can create a learning experience founded on key concepts in Watson's

(2008) theory of human caring including the authentic presence of teachers and learners, multiple ways of knowing, reflective approach, and creativity leading to wholeness;

2. arts-based instructional strategies can be translated to teaching and learning in a variety of disciplines in both face-to-face and e-learning environments; and

3. arts-based instructional strategies may be an approach that helps learners achieve a domain of learning (social-emotional) that goes beyond the traditional domains of learning (cognitive, psychomotor, and affective) and that helps students achieve these presences in the CoI model.

Overview of main sections

The chapter has four main sections. In Section 1, we discuss the background related to why we developed arts-based instructional strategies to use in e-learning environments. In Section 2, the arts-based instructional strategies we developed and used in online graduate education are described. Then, in Section 3a, we describe students' reflections on using the innovation, and in Section 3b, we describe teachers' reflections on using the innovation. Finally, in Section 4, plans for future research related to arts-based strategies (many yet to be developed) are discussed to determine if certain strategies apply to specific learning outcomes.

Section I: The Background

In this section, we explain how we first realised that using arts-based instructional strategies in our online graduate courses potentially had many benefits for learners. Utilising technology as either a supplement to traditional face-to-face education or as the primary mode of teaching, only came into existence as technology availability and use became more ubiquitous (Tomei, 2003). As Tomei (2003) notes, early forays into e-learning focused on the use of word processing, spreadsheets, and databases. Interactions within e-learning classes were largely one-directional, text-based, and asynchronous. We had been adapting a participatory action research methodology called photovoice (PV) (Wang & Burris, 1997) to make it an instructional strategy. As a research approach, PV focused on engaging research participants in telling their stories using photographic images. The idea that images convey meaning seemed equally applicable to learning as students need ways (other than written text) to share their beliefs and knowledge with classmates and instructors. PV, as a teaching strategy, was at first quite rudimentary, as the instructors posted a digital image in an online graduate course on change management and asked learners to comment on what they saw in the image that helped explain change theory. The response was overwhelmingly positive. The image seemed to capture students' interest, and learners quickly posted links between theory and what they saw in the photo. Class discussion resulted as learners compared their analyses of change theory and the image. The depth of analysis, and amount of interaction, was remarkably positive. PV as a teaching strategy was refined and became an approach used in many courses for several purposes.

We began to question why PV had such a positive effect in the online classroom and hypothesised that it was because it was founded in the arts. The arts that can include literary, visual, musical, or dramatic elements are infused with emotion and humanity. The arts emphasise aesthetics and links to creativity. Our research focus was on understanding how giving learners the opportunity to be creative and interact with one another on a human level changed the online learning environment (which has been criticised for being socially isolating and lonely).

With the anecdotal success of PV as an instructional strategy, we embarked on a series of research studies to try to answer why arts-based instructional strategies like PV had a positive impact on learning and to create and evaluate other arts-based instructional strategies. Other strategies that were developed (and tested) included parallel poetry, poet-weet, digital storytelling, and music moments. Our research with online graduate and undergraduate learners demonstrated that arts-based instructional strategies helped provide a real and authentic medium for instructors and students to engage with one another, creating e-learning environments that students and teachers experienced as inviting due to enhanced interaction between course participants (Perry et al., 2012). Further, the use of arts-based strategies stimulated creative thinking and captured student attention, enhancing the achievement of learning outcomes (Perry et al., 2012). Finally, these approaches helped learners to develop social connectedness and a sense of community in their classes, in part because participants were comfortable communicating with one another and they got to know each other on a deeper level.

Section 2: The Practice

2a: An introduction to the innovative practice

Arts-based instructional strategies usually include literary, visual, musical, or drama elements. They are distinguished from traditional pedagogies in part by their emphasis on aesthetics and their link to creativity. Effective online teaching and learning require innovative instructional strategies that help learners achieve social-emotional learning outcomes. Using arts-based instructional strategies in online teaching can create a learning experience founded on key concepts in Watson's (2008) theory of human caring. Watson's concepts include the authentic presence of teachers and learners, multiple ways of knowing, a reflective approach, and creativity leading to wholeness (2008). Also, arts-based approaches help create a learning experience that promotes social, cognitive, teaching, and social-emotional presences (Cleveland-Innes & Campbell, 2012; Anderson *et al.*, 2001).

2b: A brief overview of the curriculum

We define curriculum as the knowledge and skills students are expected to learn when engaging in the arts-based strategies. In brief, these learning activities cultivate multiple ways of knowing, encourage reflection, encourage creativity, and help students achieve social-emotional learning outcomes (Perry *et al.*, 2012). Online, they create a learning experience where students feel there they are not learning in isolation, even though they are not in the same room as other students and their instructor (Janzen *et al.*, 2019). Finally, these arts-based approaches help students achieve sustained meaningful communication while learning remotely (Janzen *et al.*, 2019). This dialogue is foundational to achieving learning outcomes.

In part, the knowledge and skills students gain when they participate in arts-based strategies are achieved as a result of the intersection of the presences in the CoI model (Rourke *et al.*, 2001; Cleveland-Innes & Campbell, 2012) introduced earlier in the Introduction. The elements of the CoI model include the following four presences that overlap to create the educational experience (Figure 1):

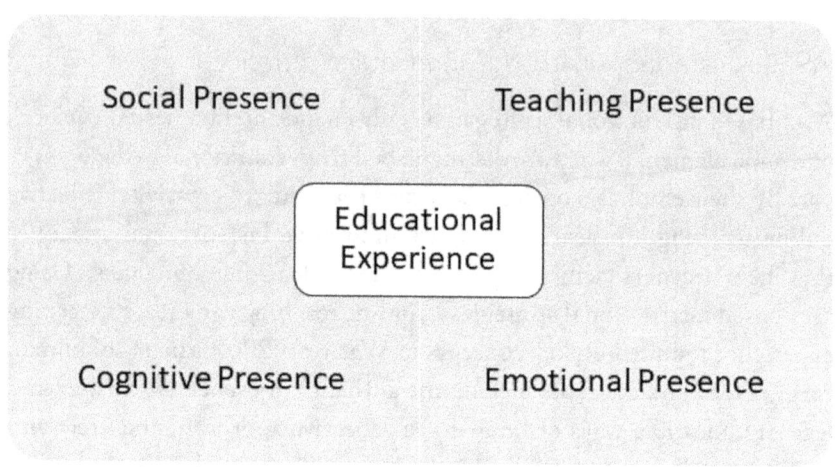

Figure 1: Community of Inquiry Model (adapted from Cleveland-Innes & Campbell, 2012; Anderson et al., 2001).

Moving to online teaching requires more than simply uploading teaching materials and resources to an online learning platform, for students to access via computers. Teaching in this new reality requires educators to be mindful of the four presences depicted in the CoI model (Cleveland-Innes & Campbell, 2012; Anderson et al., 2001; Carloni, 2021, Chapter 9 in this book also refers to the first iteration of the CoI model):

1. teaching presence, *"the design, facilitation, and direction of cognitive and social processes for the purpose of realizing personally meaningful and educationally worthwhile learning outcomes"* (Rourke et al., 2001:51);

2. cognitive presence, *"the extent to which the participants in any particular configuration of a community of inquiry are able to construct meaning through sustained communication"* (Rourke et al., 2001:51);

3. social presence, *"the ability of learners to project their personal characteristics into the community of inquiry, thereby presenting themselves as 'real people'"* (Rourke et al., 2001:51);

4. emotional presence, *"the outward expression of emotion, affect, and feeling by individuals and among individuals in a community of inquiry, as they relate to and interact with the learning technology, course content, students, and the instructor"* (Cleveland-Innes & Campbell, 2012:283).

When students experience teaching, social, cognitive, and emotional presences in the e-learning milieu, they find themselves immersed in a learning climate where they are supported to take risks, discover their creative side, and achieve their potential. The climate is supportive, encouraging, and engaging, which provides a foundation for learners to move out of their comfort zone, propelling them to achieve higher-order learning outcomes. These learning outcomes are largely cognitive and social-emotional and include evaluation, creation, analyses, application, and reflection on one's values, biases, stereotypes, and emotions.

2c: Organisation of the innovative practice

Next, we describe each of the arts-based instructional strategies we have developed and used in online graduate education. In PV, a photographic image (chosen by the instructor) is displayed with an accompanying reflective question. Students are invited to respond to the question with the image in mind. An example of a PV that we have used is an image of a butterfly going through the last transition of metamorphosis. An accompanying reflective question could be *"How is your transition from fourth-year nursing student to new graduate like this image"*? Students share their interpretations of the image in a written posting within a conference forum, where they can compare their interpretations to those of their classmates.

With parallel poetry, the teacher writes (or chooses a poem from published poetry) and shares a poem with the class related to a complex course theme or concept. Students are invited to write a parallel poem of their own which has a topic, cadence, and form that parallels the instructor's poem. Students claim they find inspiration (and a type of template) for their poems in the instructor's version and find the opportunity to express their feelings and experiences in poetry can be a helpful, creative outlet. The two poems together often create a more complete explanation of a concept or experience than the one poem alone would provide. Further, crafting a poem requires students to grasp the concepts, attitudes, and nuances reflected in the instructors' poems. Parallel poetry demonstrates achievement of higher-order learning outcomes such as analysis, evaluation, and reflection. For example, the following poems (Table 1) illustrate parallel poetry from a nursing course on nurse-patient communication and the development of the therapeutic relationship:

Instructor Poem – The Abyss	Student Poem – The Ravine
There are times	There are times
Patients find themselves	When patients are caught in the ravine
On the edge of the abyss.	Cold, hungry, destitute, and in despair.
On the verge	We as nurses, reach out our hands to them.
Of losing hope	
And fearing abandonment	
They reach toward us...their nurses.	They reach upward with feeble hands
	And take our hands:
In moments of	Warm, comforting, and strong
Pain, anguish, or fear	And we help pull them out.
We reach back	Always with the promise
Only as we know how.	That we will never abandon.
Our words, our actions,	
Our very presence—	
Communicates our promise	
That we will never abandon.	

Table 1: parallel poetry from a nursing course.

Poetweet is also based on the art form of poetry that combines the idea of a poem and the format of a social media tweet. Poetweet is a form of micropoetry first used by Sebald and Tripp (2004). A poetweet poem is limited to 140 characters, but there are no requirements for specific rhyme or rhythm schemes. No emojis or short forms of words are allowed (i.e. no lol, *etc.*). The forced conciseness of this form of expression is important for causing students to reflect deeply on concepts they are attempting to express in their poetweets because every character must be a precise choice. For the activity, students are invited to create and share with the class a poetweet about a concept currently being discussed in class. The poetweet collection is often a great starting point for class discussion of the topic addressed in the short poems. An example of a poetweet on the concept of abuse of the elderly transpired: *"The abuser is coming, Demanding and terrorizing, you can't run for your life."*

A variation on the micropoetry form called poetweet is the twaiku (Pryor, 2009). A twaiku (another form of micropoetry) is a haiku posted on Twitter and thus is limited to 140 characters. The character limit means that most twaikus do not meet the traditional haiku form precisely. However, as an arts-based instructional activity, a twaiku also requires learners to be knowledgeable about a course concept to pull out the essence of the idea that they will include in the micropoem.

Word sculptures use the artform of sculpting to encourage students to convey course learnings, solidify learning about a series of ideas, and to share complex concepts by crafting artefacts using words. In e-learning classes, students can use various software programs (i.e., Paint, Word, or Word Cloud) to create virtual word sculptures on course themes or topics that they can then share with their instructors and class members. One approach used in the word sculpture activity is to have learners generate a list of words that come to mind related to a course concept or theory as a starting point for their sculpture. Next, they arrange their words in a manner that conveys more than would be conveyed by simply reading the list of words. For example, if the concept they are working with is disease prevention, and they want to convey the essential value of immunisation, they may put their words in the form of a hypodermic needle. The image reinforces the topic and the message in the words. Once created, word sculptures can be shared with the entire class in a virtual art gallery, and the group can "walk" through the gallery and view the art. Viewing the word sculptures can spontaneously help learners create connections with one another (helping to build class community) or the sculptures often generate discussion of concepts depicted. This discussion can be left to happen naturally, or it can be facilitated by the instructor through a set of questions students answer related to what they are seeing (or experiencing) in the word sculptures (Figure 2).

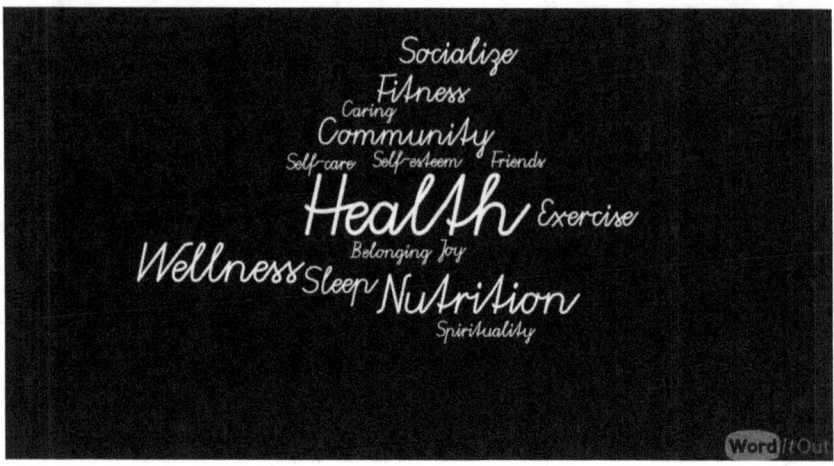

Figure 2: An example of word sculpture on the topic of the importance of personal health and wellness.

Finally, music is a powerful form of human expression and the arts-based strategy of music moments capitalises on the emotion of this art form. In the strategy we developed, called my music moments, learners are asked to find (and share) a music selection that appeals to them, and that helps to explain a course concept, idea, or theme. Both the lyrics and the melody of the music are considered as students make their choice. They share their selection with the class along with a narrative (written or oral) related to why they made the specific choice and explaining how the music relates to the course material. Complex and emotional topics such as palliative care, mental illness, ageing, and violence are often suitable for my music moment activities. Students report learning from the search for the music selection, from creating the narrative that explains their choice, and from the discussion that results in the class when music moments are shared. Online students can easily locate open access music selections on websites such as Jamendo. These sites feature a searchable database of selections that make it simple for students to locate and download music that is available free to use for educational purposes.

The five arts-based strategies explained in this section are examples of the many approaches we have used in our attempts to use art as an instructional approach in e-learning. We have researched the effects of these types of teaching approaches and shared the findings (and the strategies) in various publications and conference presentations. Many have commented that they thought they could use this innovation in their teaching. Many instructors (face-to-face, blended, and online) commented on how easy it was to use one (or several) of the strategies in their teaching, with only slight modifications to make the strategy fit their discipline or topic. Others noted that because these strategies are very low-tech, and require little infrastructure to enact, they are cost-effective approaches. Furthermore, instructors who tried our strategies found that they were equally useful in undergraduate and postgraduate education. One person who attended a conference where we shared our strategies commented: *"I think I could use PV in the course I am teaching tomorrow."*

2d: Preparation of the innovative practice

Preparing the arts-based instructional strategies begins with defining the specific learning outcome to be achieved. For example, if the goal is to have students achieve the social-emotional outcome of self-awareness (the ability to see themselves clearly and objectively through reflection and introspection) then learning activities need to be created to facilitate achievement of this outcome. Arts-based approaches are well-suited to this goal. For example, the educator might use PV (for example images depicting various human scenarios, such as a dying person or two people arguing) and ask students to reflect on how the scenario makes them feel. Alternatively, parallel poetry can be used, and students invited to reflect on a time when they may have had feelings similar to those experienced by a character in the poem. Taking this activity further, after creating their parallel poem, students could draw a picture to describe how they responded in a similar situation to one faced by a character in the poem. The focus of these arts-based interventions is to help learners develop enhanced self-awareness. Educators can use existing arts-based strategies (or create new ones) to help students achieve specific learning outcomes.

Chapter 8

Section 3: The Outcome

As noted, we have formally studied the effects of arts-based instructional strategies on teachers and learners at both the postgraduate and undergraduate level. Most of our research has focused on online teaching and learning. However, currently, we are comparing the effects of arts-based teaching strategies in online, hybrid, and face-to-face scenarios.

Specific to the effects of the innovation on online postgraduate students, our research, course evaluations, and feedback from students and instructors have shown that there are positive outcomes related to humanising the learning environment, creating a sense of community in the online class, and enhancing student engagement with the course content leading to increased student achievement. Of importance is that arts-based instructional strategies can help learners achieve social-emotional learning outcomes that go beyond the traditional domains of learning (cognitive, psychomotor, and affective) (Bloom, 1956).

Firstly, arts-based strategies humanise the learning environment. Teaching innovations that humanise the learning environment are particularly essential in e-learning. It is common for online learners to experience feelings of isolation and disconnection from the teacher and other learners, which negatively influences their learning experience, course effectiveness, and student retention rates. Human connections can support learners toward success as they can create feelings of closeness and connectedness. The positive outcome of feeling connected to others is enhanced feelings of belonging and engagement, which is motivational for learners. Learning outcomes that focus on higher-order affective domain competencies such as responding to phenomena, valuing, and internalising values, are often best facilitated through human interaction and interpersonal communication. As one student noted: *"I felt like there were other people with me during this learning experience because we all shared our feelings and personal experiences. Writing poems and sharing my music were great ways for me to safely share my feelings."*

Graduate online learners in classes which featured the use of the arts-based instructional strategies reported that incorporating human images in PV, and poems infused with human emotion, helped them feel less isolated and alone in their online classrooms. Just "seeing" and "feeling" elements of humanity in their learning activities gave them a sense of others being part of their learning. When they were invited to interact with other students in their courses, through activities such as sharing of their micro-poems in the gallery of poems, again students expressed that they felt a sense of camaraderie, reduced social isolation, and increased social presence.

Secondly, arts-based approaches can create a sense of community. Our research also showed that arts-based approaches helped to foster a sense of togetherness in the online course. When teachers and students interact, collaborate, communicate, and share a social presence in the online learning milieu, a culture of community is established. From a social constructivist point of view, learning is shaped by context, and people learn from each other (Vygotsky, 1962). Learners are more likely to engage with their education and persist with their studies when they feel connected to, and involved with, other members of the learning community. When students learn in community, they can work together to make sense of information being presented and are exposed to diversity in ways of knowing and interpreting knowledge.

Further research has shown that when learners experience high perceptions of social presence in their learning environments (particularly in online settings), they have increased learning satisfaction (Alsadoon, 2018) and they also feel more satisfied with their teachers (Richardson & Swan, 2003). Therefore, social presence, facilitated by these arts-based instructional strategies, is important for learner engagement, persistence, satisfaction, and for increasing capacity to learn from others, so that they see the world through diverse realities. One graduate student wrote in the course evaluation:

- *"Using teaching strategies such as photovoice really helped me realize how we all see different things in the same photo. It reminded me that we need to not make assumptions about how others view a situation."*

Furthermore, the sense of community is likely to prove the most fundamental element for the creation of learners' relationships with other learners and with the teacher. Models of teaching and learning, that feature interaction and engagement with others, help to create a social presence. Social presence can be experienced when learners and educators project themselves socially and affectively into the learning milieu. Any activities that help learners and educators get to know each other, to sense a connection to the group, and to feel they are not alone, can contribute to social presence and community development. When educators create opportunities for participants to share some of their most profound and personal thoughts (such often happens in parallel and micro-poetry or word sculptures), it can foster the community feeling. The sharing of human experiences through the arts-based approaches helps learners recognise their commonalities and helps them know one another on a personal level that promotes even more collaboration and communication in a cycle of positive relationship formation and mutual support. A student posted this comment in her final course activity:

- "I used to dread group work in my online courses but this time was different because I got to know you all other students [sic] on a different level as we shared so much of ourselves in the course activities."

Thirdly, using arts-based teaching approaches can enhance student engagement, and engaged students learn. Milburn-Shaw and Walker (2017) note that engagement influences the quality of the learning milieu and the educators' and learners' well-being. When students and educators are engaged, they become increasingly motivated. Also, the learning environment becomes a positive energised space where learning is valued, input is valued, and diversity of thought is encouraged. Engaged learners have improved focus on academic goals and improved academic performance (Milburn-Shaw & Walker, 2017). The other arts-based strategies, such as music moments and word sculptures, students experienced as enjoyable activities. When learners have "fun" learning, they are more likely to be energised to tackle delving deeply into complex and demanding discussions. The fun provided by the arts-based activities generated an atmosphere of momentum that propelled students to embrace the hard work of learning. Many students commented specifically in the course evaluations on how much "fun" the course was, and that because it was fun, they were eager to participate. The comments we received included: "I couldn't wait to sign on to my course each evening"; "who knew learning course could be this much fun!"

The arts-based learning strategies enhanced student engagement with the course materials, with other learners in the course, and with themselves in that they reported being more intensely self-reflective in relation to course topics. Strategies such as PV, students reported, were particularly engaging. Several noted that they logged into their courses often to see if there were new images and questions (PV activities) for them to participate in. They found the PV activity was a "hook" that caught their attention and helped them to focus on the course theme associated with the PV question. When the instructors used digital images for the PV activity that had personal relevance for them (i.e., a photo of a nature scene that indicated to learners that the teacher appreciated the outdoors or a photo of a soccer player which students believed told them their teacher was a sports fan) students found this gave them a glimpse into the personality of their teacher, which students reported as helping to engage them in their learning.

The poetry-based teaching strategies help students make an emotional connection to their learning, stimulating creative and critical analysis of course content. Art moves learners to look at the broader view of concepts and ideas, increasing the number of lenses they use to help them understand complex concepts. The arts-based strategies encouraged learners to see knowledge as whole entities rather than as discrete elements, making learning holistic, rather than a checklist or assembly line of linear thoughts. As one learner stated: *"I really got to know myself this term and to see the inherent connections between things I didn't really think about before."*

Finally, arts-based instructional strategies can facilitate social-emotional learning. One interesting observation is that all of the arts-based instructional strategies help learners achieve social-emotional learning outcomes that go beyond the traditional domains of learning (cognitive, psychomotor, and affective) commonly described in Bloom's taxonomy (1956). Astleitner (2018) and Cleveland-Innes and Campbell (2012) describe a category of learning outcome called social-emotional. Social-emotional outcomes relate to the emotional attachment students experience while acquiring knowledge and skill, and this can range from distant to closeness (Astleitner, 2018). More specifically social-emotional learning outcomes are focused on helping learners foster identity, feel emotions, discover similarities and differences between them and others, reduce prejudice, mature their self-awareness, and develop secure attachments facilitating resilience (Astleitner, 2018). To meet these outcomes, Astleitner suggests learning activities that help learners feel enjoyment, cause emotion, help develop a sense of belongingness, and encourage creativity all within a non-threatening environment. A high-achieving student wrote: *"this course really pushed me outside of my comfort zone, which was such a good thing."*

The arts-based innovations seem to meet all the requirements for achievement of social-emotional learning outcomes, in that learners report they are fun and novel, that activities which incorporate poetry and music are especially emotionally moving, the sharing of their arts-based creations with the class increases their sense of community belonging, and that these activities challenge them to be creative. Finally, since all activities are non-graded, and the instructor and classmates celebrate all contributions, the learning environment is non-threatening. Therefore, the use of arts-based instructional strategies has been valuable and has contributed to an enhanced student experience in many ways:

- humanising the learning environment, creating a sense of community in the online class, and enhancing student engagement with the course content, leading to increased student achievement;
- enhancing engagement with the course materials, with other learners, and with themselves through enhanced self-reflection;
- stimulating creative and critical analysis of course content;
- facilitating achievement of social-emotional learning outcomes; and
- making learning fun and novel enhancing student engagement.

3a: Student perspective

As explored in the previous section, students experienced a more humanised learning environment, a sense of community in their classroom. They increased engagement with course materials, their class members, and with themselves. In this section, evidence of these outcomes is presented in the form of narratives from students. Additionally, a discussion of the theoretical explanation for these positive outcomes is presented.

In relation to experiencing the learning environment as less socially isolating and more infused with human presence, learners explained their experience this way. One online graduate learner said when speaking of PV: *"Participating in PV gave me an outlet to get to know people and their perceptions."* Another student reported that PV was a way to: *"get to know* someone without the …scholarly talk." These quotes demonstrate that PV was particularly useful in helping learners experience that others were sharing their learning journey, reducing the sense of isolation.

Student quotes also helped us conclude that arts-based approaches help create the culture of community. For example, one learner said they collaborated and were: *"there for one another"*, in part because the activities encouraged them to share their personal views and values on complex topics, through the safe medium of a micro-poem. The student said: *"My point of view was acknowledged by other participants making me feel like part of the group."* This sense of belonging is essential to learning, and strategies that asked learners to disclose their emotions and experiences (such as word sculptures and music moments) helped students see that they shared many communities with others and that they were *"all in this together."*

Many students highlighted PV as a means by which they got to know one another and their instructor in a way that made them feel *"comfortable"* in the course. One learner talked about the *"connections"* made with other learners when they found they shared the same music preferences in the music activity. A student commented that the arts-based strategies encourage them to: *"communicate in a meaningful way that made the instructors feel more authentic and real."* Similarly, another commented that the activities helped students see each other as: *"real people"*. Because the students, participating in our research studies, were studying online one commented that: *"it was just like we were sitting in a face to face classroom setting."* All these reports help to show us that students found the arts-based strategies helped them connect, communicate, and see that they were part of a community which all facilitated learning.

Finally, student reports of enhanced engagement resulting from the creative, challenging, and novel nature of the arts-based strategies were common. A student who always participated enthusiastically in PV said that for her: *"PV was like a mystery…I couldn't wait each week to open the activity and see what picture was hidden behind the virtual paperclip."* Another, in noting that the uniqueness of the activities caught her attention, commented:

- *"I was a little nervous trying these activities at the beginning, but when I found out there were no right or wrong answers, and everyone was so supportive of my attempts at poetry or whatever I was encouraged to try."*

One last student simply said: *"doing PV was fun and really made the learning enjoyable, and besides that, I had many aha moments!"*

One theory that helps to explain the positive outcomes students experience when invited to participate in arts-based instructional strategies is Watson's Theory of Human Caring (2008). The theory developed for nursing care has relevance for teaching excellence. It is based on the values of honouring another's becoming, autonomy, and freedom of choice and caring as a transpersonal process (Watson, 2008). Bevis and Watson (1989), when applying this to education, note that teaching moments are potentially caring interactions and that the experience is reciprocal for teachers and students. In part the caring interactions (which we have called humanising interactions) result from what Watson (2008:10) called *"carative factors"* which include:

- *"cultivation of sensitivity to one's self and to others; development of a helping-trusting, human caring relationships; promotion and acceptance of the expression of positive and negative feelings; systematic use of a creative problem-solving, caring process; promotion of transpersonal teaching-learning; and provision for a supportive, protective, and/or corrective...environment."*

We argue that Watson's carative factors are promoted through the use of innovative arts-based instruction. For example, the activities challenge learners to become self-reflective and to consider carefully their values and emotions related to particular course topics or themes. It is impossible to express the essence of a viewpoint in a micro-poem without giving much thought to what one truly believes about the poem theme. The sharing of poems evokes a realisation others have deep feelings and profound experiences related to a course theme, and thus sensitivity to others is an outcome. Further, it takes courage to share a personal view or preference through something like a music choice. When students share their personal views and others in the class reciprocate by also sharing it is a recipe for the development of trust in the learning community. Since students realise that these learning activities do not have right or wrong answers, they feel safe in expressing their creativity and in applauding others for their contributions, again leading to community trust. Students are encouraged to be authentic and to share both negative and positive views that are possible when trust is established. The many opportunities students have to share their creations (such as poems, music, and sculptures) with the class sets up the environment for transpersonal learning. As evidenced by the student quotes, the inclusion of these learning activities in courses is an essential element for establishing a supportive learning environment where participants can challenge, question, and grow in their scholarship.

3b: Teacher perspective – our reflections

While most of our research related to arts-based strategies is focused on the student perspective, we have considered the effects on instructors. In sum, when students have a positive learning experience, then instructors are also more likely to enjoy their role. We conceived of this as a cycle with learners being engaged, asking questions, participating, having "*fun*", working to their full potential, and thus motivating teachers to do the same. As educators become increasingly present, enthusiastic, and engaged, learners are motivated to continue. The outcomes are positive for both educators and learners. Educators feel a sense of job satisfaction as they know learners are learning and that they have a positive experience.

With all innovations, there is some hesitation by some educators initially. There are questions such as: "*Is this so creative that no one will participate?*"; "*Is this so much fun that students won't take the 'real' learning seriously?*"; or "*Will others think these activities are too juvenile for graduate-level education?*" With the involvement of more educators in using these strategies, and with creditably from nationally-funded research, we have found that our innovation has gained acceptance and credibility over time.

Section 4: Moving Forward

In the future, we would like to conduct more research on specific arts-based strategies (many yet to be developed) to determine if certain strategies apply to specific learning outcomes. The potential is great to use this innovation in various disciplines ranging from humanities and social sciences to science and technology. Adapting and translating these arts-based instructional approaches to other subject areas is a goal moving forward.

Currently, we are conducting a large study looking at the effectiveness of arts-based approaches in different types of learning environments (hybrid, face-to-face, and online) with a focus on undergraduate learners. This study should provide further knowledge about how this innovation can be used with new populations of learners in the future.

Conclusion

As discussed, arts-based instructional strategies such as photovoice, parallel poetry, poetweet and twaiku, word sculptures, and music moments can be used in e-learning to help students have a more positive learning experience. Some benefits of integrating arts-based instructional strategies into online courses include humanising the learning environment, creating a sense of community in the online class, and enhancing student engagement with the course content leading to increased student achievement. Furthermore, arts-based instructional strategies help learners achieve social-emotional learning outcomes that go beyond the traditional cognitive, effective, and psychomotor, domains of learning. Watson's theory of human caring (2008) helps to explain why arts-based approaches have these positive consequences for teaching and learning, in the sense that they enhance the authentic presence of teachers and learners, allow for multiple ways of knowing, spark reflection, and create wholistic learning through the use of creativity. The low-tech, inexpensive nature of this innovation means that it is accessible to most educators. Likewise, arts-based instructional strategies, a product innovation that draws on a constructivist perspective of learning, can be easily adapted for the use of multiple disciplines. Implementing and using arts-based instructional strategies in e-learning has positive consequences for both students and teachers,

About the Authors

Beth Perry is a Professor in the Faculty of Health Disciplines at Athabasca University in Alberta, Canada. She can be contacted at this e-mail: bethp@athabascau.ca

Margaret Edwards is a Professor of the Faculty of Health Disciplines at Athabasca University in Alberta, Canada. She can be contacted at this e-mail: marge@athabascau.ca

Bibliography

Alsadoon, G. (2018). New strategies to develop effective learning environments that support learners: Real case studies. *World of Journal of Research and Review*, 5(2), pp. 25–28.

Anderson, T., Rourke, L., Garrison, D. R. & Archer, W. (2001). Assessing teaching presence in a computer conference environment. *Journal of Asynchronous Learning Networks*, 5(2), pp. 1–17.

Astleitner, H. (2018). Multidimensional engagement in learning: An integrated instructional design approach. *Journal of Instructional Research*, 7, pp. 6–32.

Bevis, O. & Watson, J. (1989). *Toward a caring curriculum*. National League of Nursing.

Bloom, B. S. (1956). *Taxonomy of educational objectives: The classification of educational goals*. David McKay.

Carloni, G. (2021). Using a community of inquiry framework to foster students' active learning. In Enomoto, K., Warner, R. & Nygaard, C. (Eds.), *Teaching and Learning Innovations in Higher Education*, pp. 195–208. Oxfordshire, UK: Publishing Ltd.,

Choudhury, S. & Pattnaik, S. (2020). Emerging themes in e-learning: A review from the stakeholders' perspective. *Computers & Education*, 144.

Cleveland-Innes, M. & Campbell, P. (2012). Emotional presence, learning, and the online learning environment. *The International Review of Research in Open and Distributed Learning*, 13(4), pp. 269–292.

Dobozy E. & Nygaard, C. (2021), A learning-centred five-tier model of innovation in highr education. In Enomoto, K., Warner, R. & Nygaard, C. (Eds.), *Teaching and Learning Innovations in Higher Education*, pp. 19–46. Oxfordshire, UK: Libri Publishing Ltd.

Janzen, K., Perry, B. & Edwards, M. (2019). *Creative arts-based instructional strategies*. Wilmington, DE, USA: Vernon Press.

Milburn-Shaw, H. & Walker, D. (2017). The politics of student engagement. *Politics*, 37(1), pp. 52–66.

Perry, B., Janzen, K. & Edwards, M. (2012). Enhancing online student engagement. *eLearning Papers*, 30, pp. 1–5.

Pryor, L. (2009, June 27). Twoets, twaiku and twoems: how the discipline of Twitter is helping to revive poetry. *Sydney Morning Herald, The (Australia)*, pp. 11.

Richardson, J. & Swan, K. (2003). An examination of social presence in online courses in relation to students' perceived learning and satisfaction. *Journal of Asynchronous Learning Network, 7*(1).

Rourke, L., Anderson, T., Garrison, D. R. & Archer, W. (2001). Assessing social presence in asynchronous, text-based computer conferencing. *Journal of Distance Education, 14*(3), pp. 51–70.

Sebald, W. G. & Tripp, J.P. (2004). *Unrecounted: 33 texts and 33 etchings.* London: Hamish Hamilton.

Tomei, L. A. (2003). *Challenges of teaching with technology across the curriculum: Issues and solutions.* Hershey, PA, USA: IGI Global.

Vygotsky, L. S. (1962). *Thought and language.* Cambridge, MA: MIT Press.

Wang, C. & Burris, M. A. (1997). Photovoice: Concept, methodology, and use for participatory needs assessment. *Health Education and Behavior, 24*(3), pp. 369–387.

Watson, J. (2008). *Nursing: The philosophy and science of caring* (rev. ed.). Boulder: University Press of Colorado.

Chapter 9
Using a Community of Inquiry Framework to Foster Students' Active Learning

Giovanna Carloni

Introduction

With my chapter, I contribute to this book, *Teaching and Learning Innovations in Higher Education*, by showing how a Community of Inquiry (CoI) framework (Garrison *et al.*, 2000; Garrison & Arbaugh, 2007) was effectively implemented to foster students' active learning. The departure from established practices took the form of a product innovation, consisting of the implementation of digitally-enhanced activities targeted at fostering active learning during emergency remote education. It was made in response to the Covid-19 lockdown and implemented in a foreign language pedagogy course at graduate level offered at an Italian university in the 2020 spring semester. Referring to the learning-centred five-tier model of innovation in higher education (Dobozy & Nygaard, 2021, Chapter 2 in this book), my product innovation draws on a constructivist perception of learning. Perceiving learning as a construction process, I primarily see my product innovation as a means to foster engagement, the co-construction of knowledge and to facilitate active learning in emergency remote education. Implementing and using a constructivist product innovation has implications for both students and teachers.

In online learning environments, students need to adapt to new practices and strategies suitable for promoting co-construction of knowledge within a socio-constructivist framework (Selwyn, 2016; Hampel, 2020). Adjusting to these new practices may be a challenge especially for learners engaged in emergency remote education, implemented as a response to a crisis, such as the health crisis caused by Covid-19 (Bozkurt *et al.*, 2020; Bozkurt & Sharma, 2020). Therefore, a distinction must be made between emergency remote education and distance education, as Bozkurt *et al.* (2020:2) note:

> • "The ...difference between emergency remote education and distance education is that the latter is an option while the former is an obligation. ...Distance education ...is a planned activity, and its implementation is grounded in theoretical and practical knowledge which is specific to the field and its nature. On the other hand, emergency remote education is about surviving in a time of crisis with all resources available, including offline and/or online. ...In this regard, it can be argued that, during the Covid-19 pandemic, with similarities and differences, ...it was emergency remote education that was applied."

Emergency remote education (Hodges *et al.*, 2020), which has become part of digital practices in higher education during the Covid-19 lockdown as Ust (2021, Chapter 5 in this book) also points out, is likely to have a profound impact on post-Covid educational practices at tertiary level (Macgilchrist, 2020; Selwyn, 2020). In this light, the present study aims to analyse students' perceptions of the effectiveness, in terms of fostering active learning within the CoI framework (Garrison *et al.*, 2000; Garrison & Arbaugh, 2007), of a foreign language pedagogy course implemented as emergency remote teaching. Perry and Edwards (2021, Chapter 8 in this book) have adopted the same CoI framework and learning model in their study.

The course was transitioned online soon after its start due to the global Covid-19 emergency lockdown. The findings of the study may be especially useful in designing effective blended and/or fully online courses in the aftermath of the Covid-19 pandemic.

The present chapter aims to provide insights into three specific areas:

1. how to devise online teaching during a time of crisis, suitable to promote active learning;
2. how to sequence activities effectively in synchronous online classes so as to foster students' active learning; and
3. how far students perceived the digital learning experience implemented during a time of crisis as empowering.

Overview of main sections

The chapter is divided into four main sections. In Section 1, I explain the background to my product innovation. In Section 2, I describe the product innovation in more detail. In Section 3, I document the success of facilitating active learning through the use of the CoI framework. In sub-Section 3.4.1., I describe students' reflections on using the innovation, and in the following Section 3.4.2, I describe my reflections on using the innovation. Section 4 is devoted to a brief consideration of how to move forward from here.

Section I: The background – the challenging digital learning experience

Due to the Covid-19 disruption, universities have engaged with emergency remote teaching (Hodges *et al.*, 2020) to continue providing students with education worldwide. The investigation of emergency remote instruction is pivotal to understanding how students have reacted to this mass emergency education, and to learn how to design and implement similar blended and/or fully online courses in the future.

As a response to the Covid-19 threat, the foreign language pedagogy course focusing on CLIL (Content and Language Integrated Learning) (Coyle *et al.*, 2010) transitioned online soon after the first few face-to-face classes. Students thus experienced a format of blended learning, which entails the combination of face-to-face and online modes (Graham, 2006; Garrison & Vaughan, 2008; Allen & Seaman, 2010; Vaughan *et al.*, 2013). While the course was in progress, emergency remote teaching was added to the face-to-face mode almost overnight to continue providing students with education during the pandemic.

The CoI model holds that effective online learning is the result of the interaction of social, cognitive and teaching presence, operationalised from a socio-constructivist perspective conceiving learning as socially constructed (Garrison *et al.*, 2000; Garrison & Arbaugh, 2007; Vaughan *et al.*, 2013). Social presence refers to *"the ability of participants [...] to project their personal characteristics into the community, thereby presenting themselves to the other people as 'real people'"* (Garrison *et al.*, 2000:89). In contrast, cognitive presence refers to *"the extent to which learners are able to construct and confirm meaning through sustained reflection and discourse in a critical community of inquiry"* (Garrison *et al.*, 2001:11). Teaching presence *"is associated with the design, facilitation, and direction of a community of inquiry. This unifying force brings together the social and cognitive processes directed to personally meaningful and educationally worthwhile outcomes*" (Vaughan et al., 2013:12). Furthermore, it is noteworthy that social expression, a previous component of social presence (Garrison et al., 2000), has recently developed into emotional presence, i.e. "*the outward expression of emotion, affect, and feeling by individuals and among individuals in a community of inquiry, as they relate to and interact with the learning technology, course content, students, and the instructor*" (Cleveland-Innes & Campbell, 2012:2).

Social presence, targeted at enhancing relationship-building among all the interactants in online learning environments, is pivotal to making students, engaged in synchronous and asynchronous learning, feel members of a cohesive group (Garrison et al., 2000; Garrison & Arbaugh, 2007; Guasch et al., 2010; Baran et al., 2011; Garrison, 2011; Bates, 2016). Activities fostering social presence online can thus help learners to feel and see each other as real people (Coker, 2018; Corfman & Beck, 2019). Social presence as a form of caring is especially important in times of crisis (Bozkurt et al., 2020). In this light, online collaborative learning, where students co-construct knowledge within a socio-constructivist framework (Vygotsky, 1978; Lantolf, 2000; Meyer & McNeal, 2011; Selwyn, 2016; Cope & Kalantzis, 2017; Weller, 2020), may be suited to enhancing a pedagogy of care (Gómez-Rey et al., 2018; Bozkurt et al., 2020) while promoting student-content and student-student interaction (Garrison et al., 2000; Garrison & Arbaugh, 2007; Vaughan et al., 2013).

Authentic assessment, an aspect of the teaching presence (Garrison et al., 2000; Vaughan et al., 2013; Conrad & Openo, 2018), is especially suitable for online collaborative learning. In this respect, authentic assessment can be implemented through real-world professional tasks operationalised as student-centred collaborative learning (Goff et al., 2015; Trammell & LaForge, 2017; Conrad & Openo, 2018; Martin et al., 2019). Likewise, digitally-driven skills development collaborative learning may represent an effective online assessment strategy fostering deep learning (Conrad & Openo, 2018). The instructor's formative assessment is crucial for collaborative learning to be successful (Vaughan et al., 2013; Conrad & Openo, 2018), especially for asynchronous learners.

Section 2: The practice – a technology-enhanced course during a lockdown

The foreign language pedagogy class, targeted at to-be teachers, transitioned online due to the Covid-19 pandemic in early March, 2020. Almost from one day to the next, the course switched from a face-to-face to an online format. As a result, students had to adjust to new online learning environments and approaches while coping with a worldwide health and psychological crisis. When the course moved online due to the pandemic, the instructor decided to modify some of its components to foster engagement and active learning. Fostering active learning through digitally-enhanced activities during emergency remote teaching is quite a disruptive practice since emergency remote education is likely to call for more instructor-controlled learning.

Working with the CoI framework, the activities implemented were thus targeted at promoting students' active learning. In keeping with the CoI framework, the instructor consistently scaffolded social presence online (Garrison *et al.*, 2000; Garrison & Arbaugh, 2007; Vaughan *et al.*, 2013). In this respect, for example, at the beginning of each weekly live class, the instructor implemented digitally-enhanced ice-breaker activities; furthermore, the instructor provided extensive formative assessment during synchronous and asynchronous learning.

As online pedagogy suggests, during synchronous online classes, held in Blackboard Collaborate web conferencing, activities were organised in small chunks (Bates, 2016). At the beginning of live classes, digitally-enhanced interactive activities were implemented, targeted at activating students' prior knowledge; short, instructor-delivered lectures followed. After being introduced to new subject-specific concepts through short lectures, students applied the newly presented concepts by engaging in digital interactive activities devised with open educational resources. Student-centred learning was thus consistently implemented through digitally-enhanced activities from an open pedagogy perspective.

Moving the course online entailed the instructor's switching the focus from content to skills development in keeping with online pedagogical approaches (Trammell & LaForge, 2017; Martin *et al.*, 2019). As the core component of emergency online teaching, the instructor implemented a collaborative learning experience, targeted at enhancing students' CLIL materials design skills development. Collaborative learning and skills development were integrated in keeping with the CoI framework, which *"speaks to the ideals of a collaborative constructivist educational environment and how we create and sustain purposeful learning activities"* (Vaughan et al., 2013:29). The CoI framework expects learners to take more responsibility for their learning process (Vaughan et al., 2013), which is a key component of collaborative learning. In the pivoted course, digital tools were used as mediating artefacts (Hampel, 2020) targeted at scaffolding student-centred interaction-based learning processes in general, and students' collaborative creation of digitally-enabled artefacts in particular.

After a series of activities designed to help the students learn (individually) how to use free digital tools to create various types of CLIL digitally-enhanced activities, the students carried out the final course assignment collaboratively. Students thus worked online in groups of six or seven to create CLIL digitally-enhanced interactive teaching units in English. This authentic assessment also worked as the course summative assessment. It is noteworthy that a higher percentage of the course summative assessment was assigned to the online collaborative task, in order to make students more aware of the value of collaborative work. They wrote a CLIL lesson plan first and created a CLIL digitally-enhanced unit afterwards, using a wide array of free educational technologies. In addition, personalisation was also enhanced by allowing learners to represent multimodal knowledge with the digital tools they preferred (Windham, 2007; Conrad & Openo, 2018). While working collaboratively, students received consistent synchronous, asynchronous, written, audio, and video feedback from the instructor (Vaughan et al., 2013:33) who also provided groups with customised group feedback upon completion of the CLIL units. Formative assessment was provided in keeping with *"a constructivist approach that views assessment and evaluation, and the tools that frame them, not only as opportunities for interaction among learners and instructors, or between learners, but also for increased growth and learning"* (Conrad & Openo, 2018:104).

In this context, it is essential to mention that to foster inclusion and equity – values which emerged unequivocally as central to emergency remote learning – the instructor used open educational resources to devise technology-enhanced activities. Likewise, students used free educational technologies to create CLIL digitally-enhanced teaching units collaboratively. Indeed, to date, there is little by way of literature available on students' perceptions of the effectiveness of online collaborative learning, targeted at skills development and implemented through digitally-driven practices as emergency remote teaching during the Covid-19 lockdown. This makes the topic cutting-edge and ripe for investigation in the aftermath of the pandemic, since the emergency remote education implemented during the lockdown is likely to have a significant impact on post-Covid educational practices worldwide (Macgilchrist, 2020; Selwyn, 2020).

The effectiveness of emergency remote teaching implemented during the Covid-19 disruption requires investigation to plan better education in the post-pandemic context. The present study aims to investigate this pivotal pedagogical aspect. Thus, it aims to examine students' perceptions of the effectiveness of emergency remote teaching, especially in relation to the development of CLIL professional skills through digitally-enhanced collaborative learning.

Section 3: The outcome

3a: Research questions

The study addressed the following research question: *"To what extent did students perceive the effectiveness of the emergency remote teaching in general, and to professional skills development in particular, within a CoI framework?"*

3b: The participants

The cohort for the present study consisted of twenty Italian students attending a foreign language pedagogy course at the graduate level at an Italian university.

3c: The method

Descriptive research was carried out through a mixed-methods approach. In particular, a semi-structured online questionnaire was administered to students at the end of the course, thereby providing the data for the study. The two types of questions featured in the questionnaire, i.e.

closed-ended and open-ended questions, complemented each other. Most open-ended questions were follow up questions to closed-ended questions, which enabled students to explain, from a personal perspective, the choices made in the closed-ended questions. A comparison of quantitative and qualitative data was thus used to gather insights based on informants' experience.

3d: Results and analysis

Student perspective

The data analysed in this section come from the questionnaire filled in by the students at the end of the course. The data investigated, which consist of students' perceptions, are not the result of a controlled experiment. The number of students involved in the study is too small to get conclusive results; some interesting phenomena may, however, be identified and further investigated in future studies.

Data show that most students felt that the delivery method of the online classes supported their learning to a very high degree (65% strongly agreed, 25% agreed, and only 10% – two students – were neutral). While engaged in emergency online learning, the majority of students felt comfortable (60% strongly agreed, 25% agreed, and 15% were neutral). In particular, students felt relaxed (80%), motivated (75%), part of a learning community (65%), and confident (50%). Only two students felt confused and/or lonely and/or anxious. In a follow-up question, data confirmed that most students felt themselves members of a learning group (55% strongly agreed, 20% agreed, and 5% – one student – was neutral). Identifying themselves as members of a cohesive group is probably the reason why almost all students felt comfortable asking questions (65% strongly agreed, 30% agreed, and 5% were neutral). The positive feelings that students experienced, while engaged in online learning, were likely to be enhanced by the instructor's social presence, which emerged as pivotal in general and especially meaningful during collaborative learning, and by the feeling of being part of a cohesive group where they felt safe. In this respect, students claimed that the instructor made them feel valued, appreciated, confident, satisfied, at ease, cared for, supported, and motivated.

Students held that the instructor made them feel like real people whose feelings, opinions and ideas mattered. The timely feedback provided was probably also instrumental in fostering the instructor's social presence. All students (85% strongly agreed and 15% agreed) stressed the effectiveness of the written, audio, and video feedback the instructor gave them, while they were creating their CLIL lessons collaboratively. Furthermore, when asked to identify the main benefits of emergency online learning, students selected: the opportunity to get more feedback from the instructor (60%), the opportunity to carry out more interactive activities (55%), feeling less intimidated when asking questions (55%), the feeling of belonging to a learning community (45%), more interaction with the instructor (40%), more active learning (35%), the chance to ask more questions (30%), the possibility of engaging more fully in the co-construction of knowledge (20%), and the feeling of having a closer bond with the instructor (20%). The instructor's social presence, facilitation, formative assessment, and support skills seem thus to have positively affected students' online learning experience in relation to students' engagement with content, peers, and instructor.

In terms of skills development, most students (75%) indicated, as being especially useful, the collaborative task requiring them to create a CLIL digitally-enhanced teaching unit in English. As part of collaborative learning, multiple ways of knowledge representation were encouraged, thereby fostering differentiation and personalisation (Meyer et al., 2014; Nelson, 2014). In a follow-up question, most students described the experience as skills-empowering, interactive, innovative, and motivating. Students' positive perceptions of the effectiveness of online collaborative learning were connected, in particular, to its skills development learning objective, whose accomplishment students described as highly scaffolded by the instructor's consistent formative assessment. In another follow-up question, students – who had singled out, as very effective, the strategies used and the activities implemented to get them actively involved in the learning process (75% strongly agreed and 25% agreed) – further identified collaborative learning, targeted at the development of professional skills, as an added value of the online learning experience. Being engaged in collaborative digitally-driven skills development learning made students feel more motivated and involved in active learning while promoting a sense of being members of a cohesive group. Students would have probably appreciated being engaged even more in collaborative learning, since they highlighted little interaction with their peers (35%) as a negative aspect of online classes. They described, in particular, devising a lesson plan and creating the relative CLIL digitally-enhanced activities collaboratively as the strategy which best helped them develop the pedagogical skills the course targeted. In this respect, most students either strongly agreed (65%) or agreed (30%) – only one student was neutral – that they had developed the skills necessary to create effective CLIL teaching materials collaboratively.

The results show that students perceived as effective, both emergency remote teaching in general, and online collaborative digitally-driven skills development in particular. They seem to have adapted rather well to emergency online learning also, thanks to the focus on collaborative skills development. Such collaboration was instrumental in making them feel even more part of a learning community in keeping with the CoI framework. Students' positive perceptions of collaborative digitally-driven skills development may also depend on the metacognitive component of this pedagogical practice, which helped learners realise, through the co-creation of CLIL digitally-enhanced artefacts, the extent of their academic achievements, i.e. how far they had accomplished the course learning outcomes. In this light, it is noteworthy that students also pinpointed the need to foster more peer-to-peer interaction in online classes; the peer-to-peer interaction dimension thus needs to be further enhanced, while re-designing similar courses in a blended, or fully online format, for the next student cohorts.

Teacher perspective
The experience made the instructor realise that although active learning was fostered during emergency remote teaching, more peer-to-peer interaction and group work could have been implemented to further enhance students' engagement and social presence during synchronous classes. As a result, while designing future blended and/or fully online foreign language pedagogy courses for to-be teachers, synchronous and asynchronous collaborative activities, supported by the use of breakout rooms, will be implemented more extensively throughout the course. Towards this purpose, as part of her teaching presence, the instructor will design highly structured collaborative tasks, suitable for scaffolding students' active learning effectively. More student-centred learning will thus be implemented to enhance social and cognitive presence, active

learning, co-construction of knowledge, and critical thinking within a socio-constructivist framework.

Section 4: Moving forward

The affordances and challenges of the emergency remote teaching investigated will be shared with the university faculty through webinars, so as to provide colleagues with pedagogical suggestions useful in planning effective, flexible student-centred learning in post-pandemic education. The orchestration of the various digitally-enhanced activities, successfully inaugurated in the foreign language pedagogy course during emergency remote teaching, can be applied across disciplines to design blended and/or fully online courses targeted at fostering students' active learning.

Conclusion

The findings indicate that students perceived emergency remote teaching to be successful in fostering active learning and skills development, while also making them feel members of a learning community. Thus, even though emergency remote teaching was implemented almost overnight, as a response to the Covid-19 disruption, students' perceptions suggest that a successful digital learning experience emerged as a result of an appreciable degree of interaction between cognitive, social, and teaching presence, as advocated by the CoI framework (Garrison *et al.*, 2000; Garrison & Arbaugh, 2007; Vaughan *et al.*, 2013).

The product innovation devised, supported by the findings of the study, can be especially useful for higher education institutions which need to re-design blended and/or entirely online and/or digitally-enhanced foreign language pedagogy courses in a post-pandemic context.

About the Author

Giovanni Carloni is a lecturer in Foreign Language Education and Corpus Linguistics at the University of Urbino, Italy. She can be contacted at this e-mail: giovanna.carloni@uniurb.it

Bibliography

Allen, I. E. & Seaman, J. (2010). *Class Differences: Online Education in the United States*. Sloan Consortium.

Baran, E., Correia, A.P., Thompson, A. (2011). Transforming online teaching practice: Critical analysis of the literature on the roles and competencies of online teachers. *Distance Education, 32(3),* pp. 421–439.

Bates, T. (2016). *The 10 Fundamentals of Teaching Online for Faculty and Instructors*. Thunder Bay, Ontario, Canada: Contact North.

Blackboard Collaborate, https://www.blackboard.com/teaching-learning/collaboration-web-conferencing/blackboard-collaborate

Bozkurt, A., Jung, I., Xiao, J., Vladimirschi, V., Schuwer, R., Egorov, G., Lambert, S. R., Al-Freih, M., Pete, J., Olcott, D., Rodes, V., Aranciaga, I., Bali, M., Alvarez, A. V., Roberts, J., Pazurek, A., Raffaghelli, J. E., Panagiotou, N., de Coëtlogon, P., Shahadu, S., Brown, M., Asino, T. I., Tumwesige, J., Ramírez Reyes, T., Barrios Ipenza, E., Ossiannilsson, E., Bond, M., Belhamel, K., Irvine, V., Sharma, R. C., Adam, T., Janssen, B., Sklyarova, T., Olcott, N., Ambrosino, A., Lazou, C., Mocquet, B., Mano, M. & Paskevicius, M. (2020). A global outlook to the interruption of education due to Covid-19 Pandemic: Navigating in a time of uncertainty and crisis. *Asian Journal of Distance Education, 15(1),* pp. 1–126.

Bozkurt, A. & Sharma, R. C. (2020). Emergency remote teaching in a time of global crisis due to CoronaVirus pandemic. *Asian Journal of Distance Education, 15(1),* pp. i–vi.

Cleveland-Innes, M. & Campbell, P. (2012). Emotional presence, learning, and the online learning environment. *The International Review of Research in Open and Distributed Learning, 13(4),* pp. 269–292.

Coker, H. (2018). Purpose, Pedagogy and Philosophy: 'Being' an Online Lecturer. *The International Review of Research in Open and Distributed Learning, 19(5),* pp. 128–144.

Conrad, D. & Openo, J. (2018). *Assessment Strategies for Online Learning Engagement and Authenticity*. Edmonton, AB, Canada: Athabasca University Press.

Cope, B. & Kalantzis, M. (2017). Conceptualizing e-learning. In B. Cope and M. Kalantzis (Eds.), *E-Learning Ecologies: Principles for New Learning and Assessment*, pp. 1–45. New York and Abingdon: Routledge.

Corfman, T. & Beck, D. (2019). Case study of creativity in asynchronous online discussions. *International Journal of Educational Technology in Higher Education, 16(1),* 22.

Coyle, D., Hood, P. & Marsh, D. (2010). *CLIL Content and Language Integrated Learning*. Cambridge: Cambridge University Press.

Dobozy, E. & Nygaard, C. (2021). A learning-centred five-tier model of innovation in higher education. In Enomoto, K., Warner, R. & Nygaard, C. (Eds.), *Teaching and Learning Innovations in Higher Education*, pp. 19–46. Oxfordshire, UK: Libri Publishing Ltd.

Garrison, D. R. (2011). *E-learning in the 21st Century: A Framework for Research and Practice*. London: Routledge/Falmer.

Garrison, D. R., Anderson, T. & Archer, W. (2000). Critical inquiry in a text-based environment: Computer conferencing in higher education. *The Internet and Higher Education*, 2(2–3), pp. 87–105.

Garrison, D. R., Anderson, T. & Archer, W. (2001). Critical thinking, cognitive presence, and computer conferencing in distance education. *American Journal of Distance Education*, 15(1), pp. 7–23.

Garrison, D. R. & Arbaugh, J. B. (2007). Researching the community of inquiry framework: Review, issues, and future directions. *The Internet and Higher Education*, 10(3), pp. 157–172.

Garrison, D. R. & Vaughan, N. (2008). *Blended Learning in Higher Education*. San Francisco, CA: Jossey-Bass.

Goff, L., Potter, M. K., Pierre, E., Carey, T., Gullage, A., Kustra, E., Lee, R., Lopes, V., Marshall, L., Martin, L., Raffoul, J., Siddiqui, A. & Van Gastel, G. (2015). *Learning Outcomes Assessment: A Practitioner's Handbook*. Toronto, ON: Higher Education Quality Council of Ontario.

Gómez-Rey, P., Barbera, E. & Fernández-Navarro, F. (2018). Students' perceptions about online teaching effectiveness: A bottom-up approach for identifying online instructors' roles. *Australasian Journal of Educational Technology*, 34(1), pp.116–130.

Graham, C. R. (2006). Blended learning systems: Definition, current trends, and future directions. In C. J. Bonk and C. R. Graham (Eds.), *The Handbook of Blended Learning: Global Perspectives, Local Designs*, pp. 3–21. San Francisco, CA: Pfeiffer.

Guasch, T., Alvarez, I. & Espasa, A. (2010). University teacher competencies in a virtual teaching/learning environment: Analysis of a teacher training experience. *Teaching and Teacher Education*, 26(2), pp. 199–206.

Hampel, R. (2020). *Disruptive Technologies and the Language Classroom: A Complex Systems Theory Approach*. New York: Palgrave Macmillan.

Hodges, C., Moore, S., Lockee, B., Trust, T. & Bond, A. (2020). The Difference between Emergency Remote Teaching and Online Learning. *Educause Review*, March 27.

Lantolf, J. (2000). Introducing Sociocultural Theory. In J. Lantolf (Ed.), *Sociocultural Theory and Second Language Learning*, pp. 1–26. Oxford: Oxford University Press.

Macgilchrist, F. (2020). Three stories about Edtech after the Corona pandemic. *Techlash*, June, pp. 12–16.

Martin, F., Ritzhaupt, A., Kumar, S. & Budhrani, K. (2019). Award-winning faculty online teaching practices: Course design, assessment and evaluation, and facilitation. *The Internet and Higher Education*, 42, pp. 34–43.

Meyer, K. A. & McNeal, L. (2011). How online faculty improve student learning productivity. *Online Learning*, 15(3), pp. 37–53.

Meyer, A., Rose, D. H. & Gordon, D. (2014). *Universal Design for Learning. Theory and Practice*. Wakefield, MA: CAST Professional Publishing.

Nelson, L. L. (2014). *Design and Deliver: Planning and Teaching Using Universal Design for Learning*. Baltimore: Paul H. Brookes Publishing.

Perry, B. & Edwards, M. (2021). Using arts-based instructional strategies in e-learning to increase students' social-emotional learning outcomes. In Enomoto, K., Warner, R. & Nygaard, C. (Eds.), *Teaching and Learning Innovations in Higher Education*, pp. 173–194. Oxfordshire, UK: Libri Publishing Ltd.

Selwyn, N. (2016). *Education and Technology. Key Issues and Debates*. London: Bloomsbury.

Selwyn, N. (2020). Digital education in the aftermath of Covid-19: critical concerns and hopes. *Techlash*, June 8–10.

Trammell, B. A. & LaForge, C. (2017). Common challenges for instructors in large online courses: Strategies to mitigate student and instructor frustration. *Journal of Educators Online*, 14(1), pp. 1–10.

Ust, S. (2021). Emergency remote teaching in interior architecture: a necessary shift. In Enomoto, K., Warner, R. & Nygaard, C. (Eds.), *Teaching and Learning Innovations in Higher Education*, pp. 109–127. Oxfordshire, UK: Libri Publishing Ltd.

Vaughan, N. D., Cleveland-Innes, M. & Garrison, R. (2013). *Teaching in Blended Learning Environments: Creating and Sustaining Communities of Inquiry*. Edmonton, AB: Athabasca University Press.

Vygotsky, L. S. (1978). *Mind in Society: The Development of Higher Psychological Processes*. Cambridge, MA: Harvard University Press.

Weller, M. (2020). *25 Years of EdTech*. Edmonton, AB: Athabasca University Press.

Windham, C. (2007). Why today's students value authentic learning. *Educause Learning Initiative*, ELI Paper 9.

Chapter 10

An Innovative Assessment Method to Evaluate Independent Learning and Academic Writing Skills

Richard Warner and Kayoko Enomoto

Introduction

With our chapter, we contribute to this book, *Teaching and Learning Innovations in Higher Education,* as we showcase an innovative assessment method developed to evaluate the independent learning skills and academic writing skills of English as an additional language (EAL) students. The innovative assessment process is a part of the Pre-enrolment English Program (PEP) curriculum in the English Language Centre at the University of Adelaide, Australia. The PEP is an enabling program tailored for international EAL students and serves as a direct pathway into the University. The PEP curriculum is structured to develop and assess four major categories of skills:

(1) Reading and Writing Skills;

(2) Speaking Skills;

(3) Listening Skills; and

(4) Independent Learning Skills.

To pass the PEP, students typically need to achieve a minimum of a Pass grade that is aligned with the International English Language Testing System (IELTS) 6.5 in the traditional language skill areas: reading, writing, listening and speaking. In addition, both the (above) Reading and Writing Skills and the Independent Learning Skills (ILS) are hurdle requirements for passing the PEP. The ILS aspect takes students beyond the traditional examination of language skills and into demonstrated understandings of academic culture and its values, including ways of thinking and expression thereof – learning how the university 'ticks'. ILS are complex and difficult to measure, which is why we have developed a new and innovative method for assessing students' ILS in tandem with developing their academic writing skills. To do so, we have designed a comprehensive and equitable assessment process, utilising the expertise of both faculty-based academics and English for Academic Purposes (EAP) instructors, which includes four assessment panels: Moderation, Consultancy, Screening and Appeals. This contrasts with more traditional assessment methods such as IELTS, TOEFL (Test of English as a Foreign Language) and PTE (Pearson Test of English) for EAL students wishing to enter Australian universities; IELTS, TOEFL and PTE focus solely on the examination of language ability in the four skill areas of reading, writing, speaking and listening.

Referring to the learning-centred five-tier model of innovation in higher education (Dobozy & Nygaard, 2021, Chapter 2 in this book), our process innovation draws on a constructivist perception of learning. As constructivists, we view learning as a social activity, which has both a subjective (individual) dimension and an intersubjective (sociocultural) dimension to it. Students construct knowledge in a relationship between self and environment. Thus, we focus on aspects including student self-conception (see also Rowley, 2021, Chapter 17 in this book), self-efficacy, self-regulation, student autonomy and responsibility in the PEP. This is why the assessment of ILS is important for us and is highly relevant in the PEP.

Thus, our innovative assessment method is different from more traditional assessments (such as IELTS, TOEFL and PTE) of EAL students. Such traditional English language assessments are built upon a cognitivist perception of learning and, therefore, test students' cognitive abilities to master the English language. For us, this is an incomplete way to screen prospective students before they begin their studies at university, because life as a university student is a constructivist learning process, balancing individual and sociocultural aspects.

Reading our chapter, you will gain the following three insights:

1. the importance of embedding the development and assessment of Independent Learning Skills in a university pathway program;

2. how to design an equitable, rigorous assessment method to evaluate both Independent Learning Skills and Academic Writing Skills; and

3. how to incorporate assessment panels in a comprehensive, staged process, involving both faculty-based academics and EAP instructors.

Overview of main sections

In Section 1, we outline more about the background of the PEP. Then, in Section 2, we discuss the theoretical underpinning of the PEP curriculum that double-tasks ILS with academic writing skills development. This is followed by Section 3, where we explain our innovative assessment method in relation to the four assessment panels in detail. We discuss the outcomes of our innovative assessment method in Section 4, before exploring ways to move forward in Section 5.

Section 1: The background

International students, who are predominantly EAL students, are a large and rapidly increasing business commodity and therefore, are of significant importance to the Australian economy today. In 2019, there were 442,219 international students in higher education nationwide, compared with 1994, when the numbers totalled only 35,290 (Commonwealth of Australia, 2020). That is, the number of international students has multiplied 12 times over the past 25 years. For many Australian universities, international EAL students are particularly important, because not only do they provide a richer cultural diversity and internationalisation of the university community, their fees also bring in substantial funding for the running of the University.

Traditionally, if international EAL students wished to study at Australian universities, there were two major routes from which to choose. Firstly, such students could do their final years of high school in the Australian secondary school system, following a similar study and examination pathway to tertiary education as their Australian counterparts, but with an EAL assessed component. This route still exists, but the proportion of international students entering via this pathway dropped by 30% in the period between 1994 and 2019 (Commonwealth of Australia, 2020). Secondly, and much more commonly, students take -and often retake – pre-university language examinations such as IELTS,

TOEFL or PTE. Studies, like that of Thorpe et al. (2017) have addressed the issue of pre-university English language examinations as a predictor of future performance at university and found only "... *an established, if weak, inverse relationship between levels of English language proficiency and academic performance in higher education*" (Thorpe et al., 2017:5).

There appear to be other factors impacting upon whether or not EAL international students succeed in their higher education endeavours. One important factor is the recognition that English language ability is only part of the bigger picture. For many EAL students, Australian educational, cultural experiences and expectations may be substantially different from their own experiences and expectations in their home country's academic culture. These differences can provide challenges in terms of their behaviour and emotional wellbeing and can therefore affect their studies. Such difficulties are shown in the wide-ranging literature covering the difficulties EAL international students can encounter when studying in Australia. These studies include the broader issue adjustments to academic requirements and study demands style (Wearring *et al.*, 2015); the culturally marked issue of academic feedback (Warner & Miller, 2015); problems in communication (Park *et al.*, 2017) and lack of local friendship circles (Gomes, 2020). These studies clearly indicate that EAL student English entry level is but one element in a range of elements influencing academic success.

English language examinations, such as IELTS, TOEFL and PTE, by their very nature, cannot interrogate the cultural, behavioural and emotional challenges in the context of a particular university. This is because these examinations are generic and point-in-time, rather than being pertinent to the specifics of a localised higher education setting. The existing evidence for EAL student experience, inclusive of the lack of significant correlation between English language examination score and future academic success, were drivers (alongside market advantage) that led to our development of PEP for international EAL students, which provides them with a direct-entry pathway into both undergraduate and postgraduate studies. As a result, the PEP curriculum includes significant coverage of EAL student academic acculturation, namely the ILS assessment components, alongside the academic English language assessment components. The curriculum was co-written by senior faculty-based academics with an EAL background with consultative input from senior

EAP instructors in the English Language Centre. In Section 2 below, we outline the theoretical underpinning of the PEP curriculum that helps bridge the gap manifested in the aforementioned traditional English language testing.

Section 2: Double-tasking ILS with academic writing skills development

The PEP was inaugurated in 1999, and is currently in its 21st iteration, and offers four different principle durations (25, 20, 15 or 10 weeks). Each student's PEP duration is determined by their existing IELTS score (or equivalent) and successful completion of the PEP, in most instances, is equivalent to an IELTS 6.5 score – the minimum score required for University entry. From the outset, the PEP was structured to parallel the language skills-based approach of IELTS, but notably at the same time, develop more than just language skills. Thus, heavily drawing upon a constructivist perception of learning, the PEP curriculum was designed to enable students to develop a much wider range of academic writing skills and cultural understandings, under the skill set labelled Independent Learning Skills (ILS) (Warner & Enomoto, 2015). Our innovative assessment method embedded within the PEP curriculum strongly recognises that promoting the ILS aligns with and compliments developing the academic writing skills of the PEP students.

The ILS aspect of the curriculum builds upon the traditional English for Academic Purposes (EAP) language skills development (reading, writing, speaking and listening) into the particular context of studying at the University. The following can-do statements describe expected student outcomes concerning the ILS aspect:

- Can negotiate their independent and class learning schedules with classmates, team members and class teacher;
- Can negotiate individual learning needs with classmates, team members and class teacher;
- Can apply problem-solving processes to successfully address and solve learning problems;
- Can reflect on learning; demonstrate initiative and autonomy in learning in order to demonstrate overall progress;

- Can seek and respond appropriately to feedback and provide effective peer feedback and assessment;
- Can develop self-editing skills;
- Can research a topic area independently;
- Can work collaboratively on group projects;
- Can develop an awareness of strategies used in intercultural communication;
- Can recognise which independent learning skills need further development and take action to assist with this (adapted from the University of Adelaide, 2020:31).

During their time on the PEP, students have access to university facilities, including library services and the University's learning management system. Thus, they can use these University's learning facilities to support the development of their ILS during the PEP. Moreover, to help simulate University learning experiences, the students not only receive input in their classrooms from their EAP instructor(s), they also have direct input from faculty-based academics through the 'PEP Lecture Series'. In this series of lectures, senior faculty-based academics focus on issues concerning successful academic study at the university, so students receive confirming faculty-based academic voices, complementing the voice of their EAP instructor(s). This lecture series was implemented to illustrate to students, the close correlation between the PEP and desired behaviours and outcomes required for both the PEP itself, and beyond into their intended degree programs. Together, these innovative elements of the dual input (from EAP instructors and faculty-based academics) to the PEP curriculum and beyond, can benefit PEP students with a multi-dimensional experience, incorporating not just EAP focused learning, but rather targeting their immediate development alongside their future needs when studying in their future degree courses at the University.

Such an embedded simulation in the PEP curriculum can help the students recognise the relevance of developing their ILS in the PEP and beyond. Over the years, we experienced how the development of ILS has proven to be of particular importance to help EAL students: *"...face [the] cultural, behavioural and emotional challenges which they must deal with effectively if they are to study successfully at an Australian university"* (University of

Adelaide, 2020:10). Therefore, we decided to strengthen the aspect of ILS and further develop the PEP curriculum by way of designing an innovative assessment method, which we describe in Section 3.

The PEP curriculum recognises the significant impact of the ILS aspect upon the development of EAL students' academic writing skills. The curriculum incorporates the four traditional language skills (reading, writing, speaking and listening) and the ILS aspect, in a communicative and genre-based approach. The significance of being able to recognise how genres/texts function in the area of writing seems not often to be understood by either (EAL) international or local students (University of Adelaide, 2020). Indeed, the nexus between ILS and academic writing skills lies in students' reflective ability to conduct genre/text analysis independently. That is, students, through their reflective practices, become able to understand that genres or text types vary in relation to purposes and intended audiences. Such an ability to analyse genres/texts independently is fundamental for students who will later be expected to present their written work in line with their discipline requirements. Therefore, in the PEP curriculum, our innovative assessment method double-tasks ILS with the development of academic writing skills.

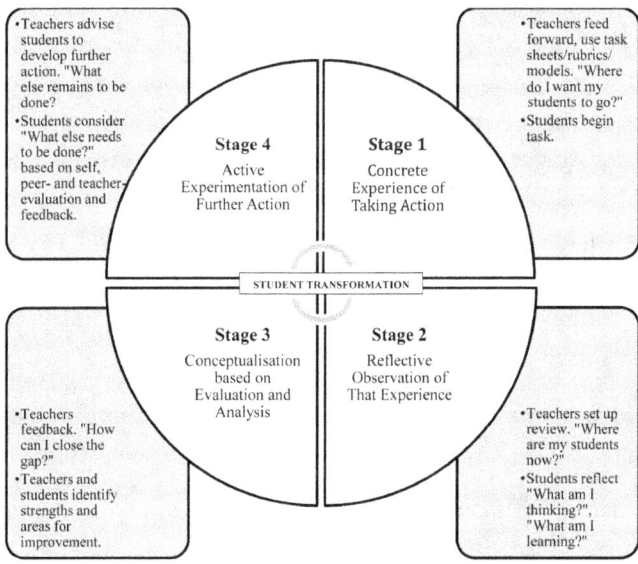

Figure 1: The Teaching-learning Cycle, adapted from Caon-Parsons & Dimmell (2016:46); Kolb & Kolb (2005).

The PEP curriculum is underpinned by the Teaching-learning Cycle model (Figure 1) that encourages students to gain strategies for independent learning in tandem with developing academic writing skills. This cyclic model provides a structured, regularly repeated method for teachers and students to engage actively in the critical reflection to evaluate and analyse progress. With the students having to be reflective and active participants in this cyclic model, they are empowered to gradually take control of their learning in the process of developing their ILS. The Teaching-learning Cycle follows the principles of experiential learning (Kolb & Kolb, 2005; Kolb, 1984) leading to students' transformation (Mezirow, 1991, 2000; Deveci, 2014) in their overall ability to navigate – with confidence – the academic, linguistic and cultural challenges at an Australian university. Mezirow (1991) emphasises the crucial role played by critical reflection in enabling student transformation, resulting from what he defines as 'disorienting dilemma' that helps students *"become aware of the realities that give shape to their lives"* (Deveci, 2014:3). In the context of PEP, this disorienting dilemma can facilitate students to transform their previously held perspectives through their critical reflection and awareness within a different academic, linguistic and cultural environment.

Figure 1 illustrates how student transformative outcomes are facilitated through concrete experience (Stage 1), reflective observation of that experience (Stage 2), conceptualisation of that reflection (Stage 3) followed by active experimentation of further action (Stage 4). The cyclic model is designed to mitigate PEP students' dilemmas in a different academic, linguistic, and cultural environment in Australia. The Teaching-learning Cycle is a crucial mainstay of the eight objectives of the PEP curriculum, which are to assist students in developing:

1. Oral communication: a willingness to speak out and participate actively in spoken discourse;

2. Significant autonomy in learning and initiative in self-directed study;

3. Familiarity with, and skills in, Australian tertiary academic styles of thinking, learning and presentation of ideas;

4. An understanding of genre analysis and skills in presenting ideas in a number of written genres in English;

5. Skills in editing their own work for grammatical correctness, and continuous development of command of more complex grammar;

6. Ability to participate actively, productively and equally as a member of a group;

7. Intercultural communication skills to participate confidently in global contexts;

8. Familiarity with, and confidence in, accessing and using student facilities and services (University of Adelaide, 2020:11).

To help the students to achieve these objectives, they are required to undertake a variety of assessed tasks (University of Adelaide, 2020:7):

1. Academic Group Reports;

2. An Academic Poster and Issue Analysis document;

3. Final Exam Essay *(Part of the four-stage panel assessment process)*;

4. Independent Research Paper *(Part of the four-stage panel assessment process)*;

5. Research e-portfolio *(Part of the four-stage panel assessment process)*;

6. Reflective Blogs *(Part of the four-stage panel assessment process)*;

7. Integrated Reading and Writing Tasks; and

8. Oral Presentations.

In addition, of the eight assessed tasks above, three key assessments, Independent Research Paper, Research e-portfolio (including reflective journals) and Reflective Blogs relate to the ILS assessment category (Figure 2).

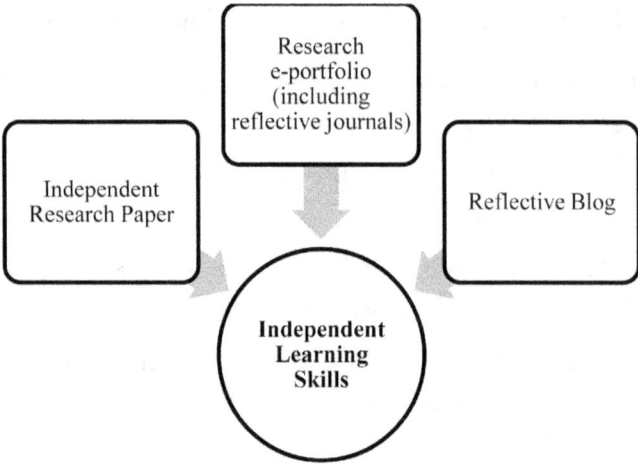

Figure 2: Assessment components of the independent learning skills category.

In the processes of completing these ILS components, the EAP instructors provide students with regular Course Progress Consultations to help encourage student initiative and autonomy (including time management) (University of Adelaide, 2020). Through these regular teacher-student consultations, the EAP instructors gain insights into the development of individual students' ILS. These insights, accompanied by relevant ILS-related comments, are recorded in each student's folder. Therefore, the process of completing the three ILS assessment components involves not just students' writing and submitting their written work, but importantly developing their reflective ILS through the Teaching-learning cycle model. This is how we facilitate our students to achieve all the aforementioned can-do statements encompassing the ILS aspect.

Section 3 explains how we utilise these students' folders containing such insights and relevant ILS-related comments during the final two panels of our four-stage panel assessment process (Figure 3). It should be noted that the focus of Panels 1 and 2 is on the Final Exam Essay, to be followed by Panels 3 and 4 that extend the focus onto those ILS-based assessment tasks seen in Figure 2. We begin Section 3, however, by detailing the University structure responsible for conducting the four-stage panel assessment process.

Section 3: The innovative assessment method in more detail

3a: PEP Advisory Committee (PAC)

To bring about the demonstrated understandings, paramount in the framing of the PEP is recognition of the value of collaboration between EAP instructors and faculty-based academics who teach into various degree programs to which the PEP students are aiming to gain entry. Academic program oversight of the PEP is enacted through the PEP Advisory Committee (called PAC). The PAC functions as an official assessment committee of the University, and follows normal University protocols. The PAC is composed of senior EAP facilitators in the PEP, the PEP Program Manager, the PEP Education Advisor, several current faculty-based academics (with an EAP background and experience) who teach into undergraduate and postgraduate programs. The inclusion and collaboration of both EAP instructors and faculty-based academics are deliberate and important aspects of our innovative approach. The PAC is co-chaired by a senior faculty-based academic and the PEP Education Advisor. The PAC is responsible for curriculum maintenance and development, including such responsibilities as:

- Modifying or changing tasks for students;
- Overviewing determination of examination questions;
- Running professional development for PEP instructors (actioned by PEP Program manager) on PEP course-related issues, such as feedback;
- Running professional development on sessions university academic-related issues (by the academic co-chair of the PAC);
- Giving a Lecture Series during the PEP – relevant to academic skills and independent learning- to all PEP students on the main University campus (by academic staff members of the PAC);
- Evaluating and advising on curriculum redesign and development and preparing review documents to recommend appropriate PEP development;

- Conducting professional development for inexperienced screening panel academics;
- Working with the Director of Studies, PEP Coordinators and instructors on streamlining administrative processes, assessment protocols and materials development;
- Participating in student appeals and complaints procedures.

Thus, through the PAC, student learning is facilitated and supported by formalised dual input from staff collaboration between the EAP instructors and current faculty-based academics. Their collaborative input informs the PEP curriculum content, its delivery and assessment process, helping to scaffold students' development pertinent to their immediate needs within the PEP. Crucially, such input from current faculty-based academics can help provide understandings and strategies which students can further utilise when they commence their degree program at the University.

3b: The innovative, collaborative assessment process

One unique feature of staff collaboration lies in their overseeing and taking part in the grading process of the Final Exam Essay, and importantly, any instance where a student has not passed the ILS assessment category. In this collaboration, EAP senior facilitators and faculty-based academics agree to the exact wording of the Final Exam Essay question. This ensures that the question structure is clear, relevant and academic in style. The topic covered in the Final Exam Essay is one that the students will have covered in some depth already during their PEP studies. Furthermore, both EAP instructors and faculty-based academics collaboratively implement stages of the assessment process in the four panels: 1) Moderation, 2) Consultancy, 3) Screening and 4) Appeals (Figure 3). In this process, both internal (EAP instructors) and external (faculty-based academics) markers grade and moderate assessment work to ensure equity and fairness for the students.

An Innovative Assessment Method to Evaluate Independent Learning

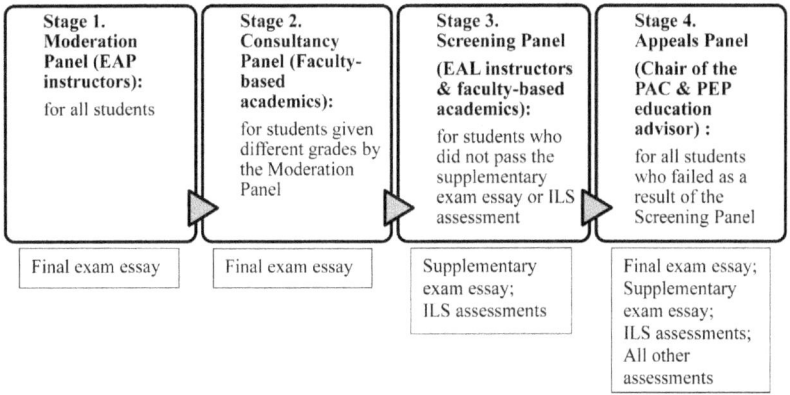

Figure 3: The four-stage panel assessment process.

Collaboration between faculty-based academic and EAP instructors is not especially 'new' as such. However, as Figure 3 illustrates, the innovation in this lies in how we carefully planned and designed our assessment process with the four-stage panels, using grading processes and screening discussions involving both parties. During collaborative screening discussions (Stage 3 – Screening panel), internal and external panel members refer to individual students' folders that contain all of their graded assessments, plus relevant comments and insights that the EAP instructor/s previously made during regular teacher-student Course Progress Consultations. Indeed, as Figure 3 shows, both the Screening and Appeals panels serve as a vehicle for scrutinising a student's ILS – a hurdle requirement for passing the PEP. As such, the four-stage process was carefully structured to maximise academic rigour and equity in our assessment method. It is this unique collaborative assessment process that is innovative, rather than the collaboration itself.

3c: Organisation of the innovative assessment practice

As described in the sub-section above, our innovative assessment practice involves internal grading and moderation from the EAP instructors, coupled with external grading and moderation (of the same tasks) from the faculty-based academics. The innovative assessment process is comprised of 1) Moderation, 2) Consultancy, 3) Screening and 4) Appeals panels (Figure 3). This structural format of the innovative assessment process is a direct extension of our Teaching-learning Cycle model that underpins the PEP curriculum. The curriculum has at its core, the development of the requisite intercultural competency, communication and language skills, and ILS that are necessary for students' active participation in the academic culture of the University.

Stage 1 – Moderation panel (EAP instructors)

Preparatory to the Moderation panel itself, an internal process takes place to help ensure inter-rater reliability between different markers. Once all students submit their Final Exam Essays, the senior EAP facilitators select three essays across different grade bands. They record and electronically save the grades and justification comments for the EAP instructors (and later for faculty-based academics in Stage 2 – Consultancy panel) to access online through a secure intranet. Following this preparation, three EAP instructors from different PEP classes are assigned to one Moderation panel. Each instructor is given copies of the same three (sample) essays together with the senior EAP facilitators' grade justification comments at the start of the panel to ascertain inter-rater reliability. Then, each Moderation panel receives around 16 Final Exam Essays belonging to students who are not taught by any of the instructors in that panel. Each of them in the panel blind-marks their assigned Final Exam Essays, in response to each of the marking criteria using the marking rubric and complete their (1st marker's) grade for each Final Exam Essay.

All three instructors in the Moderation panel, now act as a (blind) second internal marker to one of their colleagues in the panel, following the same protocols to give the 2nd marker's grade. This means that this important written assessment component is blind-marked by two different EAP instructors, who do not teach the students whose essays they receive. Examination moderation like this is not an unusual concept. However, an important and equitable part of the PEP assessment process occurs at this juncture.

Stage 2 – Consultancy panel (faculty-based academics)

The Moderation panel process is followed by a Consultancy panel, composed of two faculty-based academics – the external markers – who, if there is a difference between the 1st and 2nd markers' grades, can be called upon to assess the particular Final Exam Essay in question and make a final decision as to the grade awarded. Therefore, a Consultancy panel is held for students who have been given 'different' grades (regardless of passing or failing the Final Exam Essay), that is, whenever there are cases of any disagreement between the two internal markers as a result of the Moderation panel. Despite the rigorous process of ascertaining inter-rater reliability prior to the Moderation panel, such cases of disagreement do happen. The Consultancy panel process enables an objective (faculty-based) academic determination of the final grade.

If the Moderation panel and Consultancy panel processes for the Final Exam Essay have occurred, and a student does not gain a pass (in the Reading and Writing Skills category), they are allowed to take a Supplementary Exam Essay. This Supplementary Exam Essay question also relates to a topic that the students have already covered during the PEP, so that the content is not new to them. The Supplementary Exam Essay question again entails the essay title being agreed upon, following the same internal and external input process as for the Final Exam Essay question.

Stage 3 – Screening panel (EAP instructors & faculty-based academics)

Once the Supplementary Exam has taken place, the essays are collected, as they were for the Final Exam Essay. However, following this collection of the essays, the grading process for the Supplementary Exam Essay varies from that of the Final Exam Essay. In this stage, each essay us concurrently graded by the student's EAP instructors (internal markers), and two faculty-based academics (external markers). When the internal and external markers have finished grading their copy of each essay, they meet as a Screening panel (with an administrative support person) to compare their grades for each essay. Thus, the two faculty-based academics (who do not know the students) and the student's own EAP instructors form the Screening panel to determine the final grade of individual students. If the markers concur on a grade, then the student is awarded that grade. However, grade differences may exist amongst the panel members. In such cases, a discursive process is put into place, giving the external markers (faculty-based academics) a chance to examine the student's previously graded assessments throughout the PEP to give them a 'bigger picture' perspective. Simultaneously, the internal markers (EAP instructors) can converse with the external markers to discuss issues which are not immediately apparent 'on paper' and which could affect the student's overall performance. In this respect, the screening panel also functions as a forum for scrutinising a student's overall ILS grade, as the student cannot pass the PEP without passing the ILS category. The students are not just graded by their EAP instructors, but also equitably by the faculty-based academics to help ensure both rigour and equity during the final phase of the PEP assessment process.

This discursive Screening panel is a direct manifestation of the innovative assessment process of (external) faculty-based academics' collaboration with (internal) EAP instructors; these objective faculty-based academics can offset some of the 'instructor subjectivity', which can sometimes occur. This process combines systemic understandings of faculty-based academics' expectations of students in university degree programs, together with a detailed picture of the EAL student's current position in terms of academic writing skills and demonstrated ILS. The access to individual students' folders enables assessors to consider previous grades and relevant comments and insights provided by EAP instructor/s from their regular Course Progress Consultations with each student. The final decision, regarding the student's grade for the Supplementary Exam Essay, can thus be informed by detailed discussion. This process extends beyond the marking rubric and permits consideration of other factors that might influence the student's future academic success in their intended degree program.

If students have already passed all the assessment components under the Reading and Writing Skills category, they do not need a Supplementary Exam Essay. However, because the ILS is also a hurdle requirement for passing the PEP, if students do not pass the ILS category, their ILS-related issues must be scrutinised by this panel. The panel typically discusses the student's performance in at least two out of the three assessment components under the ILS category: Independent Research Paper, Research e-portfolio (including reflective journals) and Reflective Blogs (see Figure 2). During this screening process, the panel members refer to the expected can-do statements encompassing the ILS aspect (outlined in Section 2), whilst examining the three already graded ILS components. All of these components require students to have exercised their own reflective ILS to analyse genres/texts in their academic writing, which is encouraged through the Teaching-learning Cycle.

The faculty-based academics on the Screening panel have the power to overturn existing grades in the ILS assessment components, should the information they examine, receive and discuss, warrant this. Such a power to overturn previous grades enables equity in the screening process. It is again informed by discussions and negotiating a final agreement between the EAP instructors and faculty-based academics. The students then receive their grades for the PEP overall and, if not satisfied with any grade(s) they have the right to appeal.

Stage 4 – Appeals panel (Chair of the PAC & PEP education advisor)

In the final stage of our innovative assessment process, student performance is reviewed by an Appeals panel comprising the PEP Education Advisor and the senior faculty-based academic who together co-chair the PAC. Therefore, this final stage of the assessment process also has both internal and external academic input and collaborative oversight. The process involves assessment of the appeal letters from the students, together with any documentary support for the students' claims. The panel has full access to the individual student folders – containing copies of all the graded assessments and other documentation including marking rubrics and any 'student at risk documents' issued during the PEP. If the panel, after perusing the student's written appeal and all the appropriate other documentation, decides that there might be a case for appeal, the student is then invited to have their appeal heard orally. The student can also bring a support person (usually one of their peers) to be with them at the oral appeal. The Appeals panel can overturn any assessed grade that the student might previously have received on the PEP, should they feel it be warranted. This Appeals panel process allows the student voice to be heard outside of the subjectivities of the classroom relationship between EAP instructor and student, with their voice being heard by disinterested parties, neither of whom are involved in that student's teaching.

Moreover, the faculty-based academic can provide detailed understandings of what might 'lie beyond' for the student on their degree programs, more than the understandings of their EAP instructors alone. The final outcome for the PEP student who appeals is determined by means of this long, yet equitable process, which includes knowledge from the different stakeholders, teaching and faculty-based academics, rather than just from the EAP instructors only.

Section 4: The outcome

4a: Student outcomes

In the PEP, students experience a direct-entry pathway program that is carefully designed and delivered to bring about a transformative learning experience (Mezirow, 1991, 2000; Deveci, 2014) following the Teaching-learning Cycle. The PEP curriculum double-tasks the ILS with academic writing skills development to achieve the ILS-related can-do statements (outlined in Section 2) that are highly pertinent to their future success in their future degree programs at the University. Successful completion of the PEP means that students can move into their intended degree programs, with both the four traditional EAP skills (reading, writing, speaking and listening), and with insights to, and experience of, how to continue developing ILS within the broader parameters and demands of the University.

Through the transformative learning experience in the PEP, the PEP graduates are likely to continue onto their degree programs with a heightened degree of confidence in their ability to succeed. One major factor helping these graduates to move forward with greater self-efficacy is the fact that the PEP curriculum, including the aforementioned final assessment process, was collaboratively designed and enacted by their EAL instructors and faculty-based academics. Nowhere is this collaborative innovation better exemplified, than in the assessment process for the final assessment components in the PEP, where these EAP instructors work alongside the faculty-based academics, in helping to ensure an equitable, rigorous assessment process for every student. This unique, innovative collaboration in this pathway program can enhance student self-efficacy to continue their transformation (Mezirow, 1991, 2000; Deveci, 2014) – initiated in the PEP through the Teaching-learning Cycle – within their degree programs.

One indicator for the success of the PEP is represented by a study of the Grade Point Average (GPA) of PEP graduates in their subsequent (undergraduate and postgraduate) degree courses. Compared with 47% by those EAL students who directly entered via the IELTS pathway, 68% of PEP graduates showed a GPA of 4 (Pass) or above (out of 7), (University of Adelaide, 2012). Furthermore, over the past two decades, the University has seen a growing number of students entering the undergraduate and postgraduate programs via the PEP pathway, starting from around 50 in 2001 to around 800 in 2016. At the end of 2017, the higher IELTS requirement (changed from 6.0 to 6.5 minimum) for the direct entry pathway was introduced. As a result, the enrolment number was somewhat reduced. However, even with the impacts of Covid-19 in 2020, we are still seeing a significant number of offshore students remotely completing the PEP pathway.

4b: Staff outcomes

The PEP has a clear focus upon stated and achievable student outcomes, as outlined in Section 2. However, there are significant positive outcomes for staff as well, both for the EAP instructors and the faculty-based academics involved. The instructors get the chance to work with the faculty-based academics for mutual empowerment in a variety of different ways. In terms of co-curricular design, both the faculty-based academics and the senior EAP instructors bring their understandings and expertise 'to the table', and the design and foci of the PEP curriculum reflect this dual input. Adjustments are only made to the curriculum through the auspices of the PAC, with both faculty-based academic and EAP instructor input. This dual input role is also highly visible in the final assessment process, where faculty-based academics and EAP instructors can work together to ensure rigour and equity for the students. Moreover, the professional development sessions held by the faculty-based academics for the EAP instructors can help facilitate mutual systemic academic understandings and unpack the localised academic culture and its values. All of these interactions between faculty-based academics and EAP instructors, regarding the PEP, can serve to 'de-mystify' each other's perspectives and roles and lay the foundations for greater mutual co-operation, collaboration and teamwork, which are desirable outcomes in themselves.

Section 5: Moving forward

In its 21-year history, the PEP has seen many changes to the curriculum, all of which are indicative of the ongoing strength of the relationship between the faculty-based academic staff and the senior EAP instructors on the program. Such changes are appropriate as any curriculum which 'stands still' runs the risk of becoming less relevant or even outdated, particularly in the increasingly online world in which we now operate. What is crucial for the PEP, is that this innovative duality of staff collaboration remains in place, as the benefits that this combination brings – which have been outlined in some detail above – remain in place, but that there also be a regular re-evaluation of the program in terms of its oversight, the curriculum (and its delivery) and assessment. For example, looking at possible ways whereby the four-stage panel assessment process could be made even more equitable and rigorous for the students' benefit.

With the advent of Covid-19 and its worldwide impacts on student lives, we have had to adopt a remote teaching delivery of the PEP swiftly. This has included not only synchronous and asynchronous remote teaching and learning, but also the showcased collaborative assessment moderation process conducted in a virtual space. One challenge relates to how the PEP remote learning delivery can equally facilitate students to navigate disorienting dilemmas (Mezirow, 1991, 2000) in our virtual teaching and learning space. This does not appear to be an impossible challenge, as even as far back as 2008, Xing and Spencer reported that it was possible in an asynchronous online course for EAL international students to acquire academic skills, through exercising reflection. The digital technologies of today, such as ZOOM, can enable high-quality virtual and synchronous face-to-face interactions.

A further challenge, however, could lie in the collaborative assessment moderation process being conducted in a virtual space. The logistics of the collaborative innovation in PEP requires new skill sets development on the part of both faculty-based academics and EAP instructors. Yet, it could also prove time-saving in terms of travelling to moderation meetings.

Conclusion

The PEP has a possibly unique organisational structure by way of university pathway programs for EAL students in Australia. The dual input by both faculty-based academics and EAP instructors into curriculum design, development and delivery, is innovative in itself. Moreover, assessment – particularly within the latter stages of PEP curriculum – has significant input from disinterested faculty-based academics through the Moderation, Consultancy, Screening and Appeals panel processes. This systematic four-stage process works towards greater student equity than would likely be the case if the panels were solely comprised of EAP instructors. Furthermore, the input and continuing overview from faculty-based academics (with appropriate levels of expertise) are not typical of other pre-university EAP Programs, as such input helps 'tailor' the PEP towards the specific realities faced by and expectations of, graduating PEP students at the University.

The students on the PEP, receive a pathway program tailored to the particular university they are hoping to enter, rather than studying a more generic pathway program offered by private providers, not necessarily attached to a particular university. Maximising learning outcomes for their EAL students is a goal for all Australian universities, but this maximisation is not a 'quick-fix' in respect to academic pathway programs. PEP offers a robust and innovative model designed to facilitate learning as transformation (Mezirow, 2000) which can help EAL international students bridge the gap between English language skills and successful adaptation to the University academic culture with all its demands. Our challenge now is to effectively adapt this innovative assessment method in the remote delivery mode – precipitated by Covid-19 – to maximise learning outcomes for our PEP students.

Chapter 10

About the Authors

Richard Warner is an Adjunct Lecturer in the School of Education in the Faculty of Arts at the University of Adelaide, Australia. He can be contacted at this e-mail: richard.warner@adelaide.edu.au

Kayoko Enomoto is a Senior Lecturer, Head of Asian Studies and Director, Student Experience in the Faculty of Arts at the University of Adelaide, Australia. She can be contacted at this e-mail: kayoko.enomoto@adelaide.edu.au

Bibliography

Caon-Parsons, S. & Dimmell, P. (2016). *Pre Enrolment English Program (PEP) Review – Stage 2 December 2016*. English Language Centre, University of Adelaide.

Commonwealth of Australia (2020). International Student Enrolments in Australia 1994–2019, *Australian Government Department of Education, Skills and Employment*. Accessed September 9, 2020 from https://internationaleducation.gov.au/research/International-Student-Data/Documents/INTERNATIONAL%20STUDENT%20DATA/2019/2019%20Time%20Series%20Graph.pdf

Deveci, T. (2014). The Transformative Learning Experiences of Learners of English as a Foreign Language at a University Preparatory Programme. *Transformative Dialogues: Teaching & Learning Journal*, 7(3), pp. 1–19.

Dobozy, E. & Nygaard, C. (2021). A learning-centred five-tier model of innovation in higher education. In Enomoto, K., Warner, R. & Nygaard, C. (Eds.), *Teaching and Learning Innovations in Higher Education*, pp. 19–46. Oxfordshire, UK: Libri Publishing Ltd.

Gomes, C. (2020). Living in a Parallel Society: International Students and their Friendship Circles, *Journal of International Students*, 10(1), pp. xiii-xv.

Guanipa, C. (1998). *Culture shock*. Retrieved October 13, 2005, from San Diego State University Website: http://edweb.sdsu.edu/people/CGuanipa/cultshok.htm

Kolb, A. Y. & Kolb, D. A. (2005). Learning styles and learning spaces: enhancing experiential learning in higher education. *Academy of Management Learning and Education*, 4(2), pp. 193–212.

Kolb, D. A. (1984). *Experiential Learning: Experience as the Source of Learning and Development*. Eaglewood Cliffs, N.J.: Prentice Hall.

Mezirow, J. (1991). *Transformative Dimensions of Adult Learning*. San Francisco: Jossey Bass.

Mezirow, J. (2000). *Learning as Transformation: Critical Perspectives on a Theory in Progress*. San Francisco: Jossey Bass.

Park, Klieve, E. H., Tsurutani, C. & Harte, W. (2017). International students' accented English—Communication difficulties and developed strategies. *Cogent Education*, 4(1), pp. 1–15.

Rowley, J. (2021). Discovering professional musician identity through reflective narrative writing: a case study of pedagogic proficiency. In Enomoto, K., Warner, R. & Nygaard, C. (Eds.), *Teaching and Learning Innovations in Higher Education*, pp. 357–373. Oxfordshire, UK: Libri Publishing Ltd.

Thorpe, A. Snell, M., Davey-Evans, M. S. & Talman, R. (2017). Improving the academic performance of non-native English-speaking students: the contribution of pre-sessional English language programmes. *Higher Education Quarterly*, 71(1), pp. 5–32.

University of Adelaide (2012). *Review of English Language Admission Requirements & University Language Services and Student Support Report*.

University of Adelaide (2020). *Pre-enrolment English Program Teacher Handbook Semester 1, 2020*. English Language Centre, University of Adelaide.

Warner, R. & Enomoto, K. (2015). The Pre-enrolment English Program: a pathway program for learning to research. In Nygaard, C., Bartholomew, P. & Guerin, C. (Eds.), *Learning to Research – Researching to Learn*, pp. 19–38. Oxfordshire, UK: Libri Publishing Ltd.

Warner, R. & Miller, J. (2015). Cultural dimensions of feedback at an Australian university: a study of international students with English as an additional language. *Higher Education Research & Development*, 34(2), pp. 420–435.

Wearring, A., Le, H., Wilson, R. & Arambewela, A. (2015). The international student experience: an exploratory study with students from Vietnam. *The International Education Journal: Comparative Perspectives*, 14(1), pp. 71–89.

Xing, M. & Spencer, K. (2008). Reducing cultural barriers via Internet courses. *Innovations in Education and Teaching International*, 45(2), pp. 169–181.

Chapter 11
Affirm – Apply – Advance: Transitioning Undergraduate Students through their Theory-into-practice Journey

Michelle Bissett and Melanie Roberts

Introduction

Our chapter contributes to this book, *Teaching and Learning Innovations in Higher Education*, as we present a process innovation which scaffolds the knowledge and skill development of students in a four-year undergraduate health program at Griffith University in Queensland, Australia. We designed four annual 'transition workshops' at program-level to support students' theory-into-practice translation. We define innovation as a new and sustainable curriculum approach which addresses a recognised professional challenge, that enhances the student experience, and has been evaluated through research.

Integration of theory-into-practice is widely acknowledged as challenging in many health care disciplines, including occupational therapy (Ajani & Moez, 2011; Beane *et al.*, 2017; Dobson & Beshai, 2013; Hatlevik, 2012; Jackson *et al.*, 2013; Rodger & Turpin, 2011). Typical university program design, where students are required to complete a set number of courses to satisfy degree requirements, can compartmentalise learning and subsequently, challenge students' ability to integrate known knowledge in new or applied contexts. In recognition of this challenge, four annual 'transition workshops', underpinned by an 'Affirm–Apply–Advance' framework were developed and implemented to ensure students were supported to *affirm* theoretical knowledge, *apply* it to practice examples and *advance* their knowledge and skills for the coming academic year.

The workshops are underpinned by four theoretical pillars articulated in our program's philosophy: (i) evidence-based practice, (ii) client-centred practice, (iii) theory-driven practice, and (iv) occupation-centred practice. The workshops are implemented at key points across the four years of the program, in order to ensure students share a collective understanding of theoretical concepts and their application to occupational therapy practice, and a successful transition between the years of the program. This annual program-level approach differs from traditional models of health care education, which contain a collection of courses and expect that students are capable of integrating learning and applying it to real-world practice. This program-level approach takes responsibility off individual educators to address the theory-into-practice challenge and, instead, enables them to align their teaching with the transition workshops and shared program definitions and language for our pillars. A co-teaching model is used, whereby two occupational therapy educators, from within the program, deliver the workshop in combination, so that students are exposed to professionals who deliver content in different ways.

Referring to the learning-centred five-tier model of innovation in higher education (Dobozy & Nygaard, 2021, Chapter 2 in this book), our process innovation is underpinned by a constructivist approach of learning. Through a constructivist perspective, we see our process as a strategy to support students' knowledge of, and confidence in, applying occupational therapy theoretical concepts to contemporary practice.

Reading this chapter, you will gain the following three insights:

1. a program-level approach can support students' theory-into-practice integration;

2. an *"Affirm–Apply–Advance"* framework may be applicable for implementation in other undergraduate programs;

3. co-teaching has perceived benefits for students and educators when addressing key curriculum content.

Overview of main sections

This chapter has four main sections. In Section 1, we describe the challenge student occupational therapists experience when attempting to translate theory into their clinical practice. We provide an overview of the four theoretical pillars underpinning our undergraduate program and an initial description of our innovative program-level strategy to address theory-into-practice integration. Section 2 explores the development and implementation of our annual 'transition workshops' which address theory-into-practice translation. We describe our 'Affirm–Apply–Advance' framework, which underpins the workshops, and provide curriculum examples of each aspect of the framework. We expand on the roles of educators and students within the learning experience and the pragmatic steps administered before, during and after workshop delivery. In Section 3a, we describe students' experiences of our innovation, and in Section 3b, we describe our educator perspectives of developing and implementing the innovation. Further, we detail our mixed-methods evaluation of this innovation and provide insights into our key learnings, which we consider may be of assistance to other educators in their creation of program-level curriculum initiatives. Lastly, in Section 4, we describe our future aspirations in the area of theory-into-practice translation. We also share our plans for dissemination of our work to enable other educators to consider the implementation of a program-level curriculum approach, to address profession-specific curriculum challenges.

Section 1: The background

Albert Einstein asserted: *"In theory, theory and practice are the same. In practice, they are not".* This rhetoric resonates in health care education. While required knowledge can be taught in orderly segments of content, actual practice is more complex and requires students to integrate a range of diverse and even competing knowledge and skills. In occupational therapy, the implications of this for graduates is that they may not provide appropriate evidence-based services (Curtin & Jaramazovic, 2001) or that the services they offer, while evidence-based, may be incongruent with the profession's organising concept of occupation (Gustafsson *et al.*, 2014). Thus, the challenge for educators is to bridge the gap between university and the world beyond it (Stein *et al.*, 2004) by providing students with a sound understanding of professional theory coupled with the skills to apply this theory in real-life contexts.

Our Bachelor of Occupational Therapy program is underpinned by four theoretical pillars which position graduates to practice in contemporary and future areas of professional practice. The pillars, and our definition of them, are presented in Figure 1. When the program commenced in 2014, educators crafted pro-active strategies to make links from theory to practice explicit for students. The first two years of the program contain significant theoretical information as students are introduced to the philosophies, theories, models and frameworks underpinning occupational therapy.

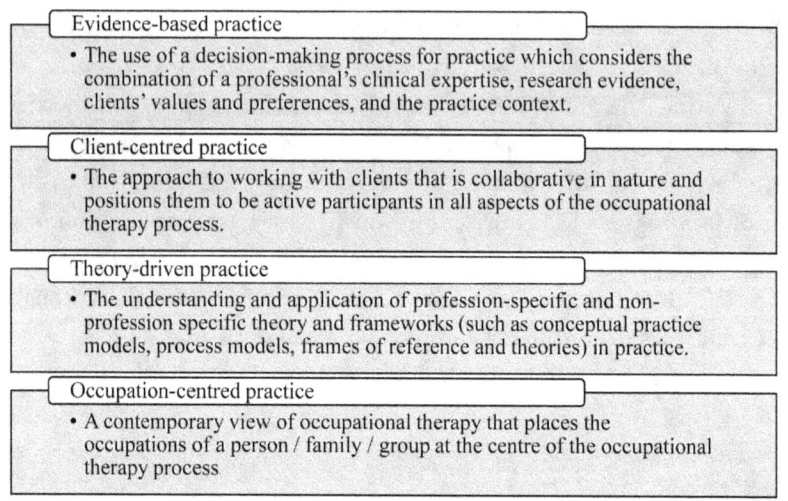

Figure 1: *Theoretical pillars underpinning the undergraduate program.*

As the program progressed, it became apparent that students compartmentalised their knowledge between the years of the program and the teaching periods. This is consistent with published literature which reveals that students view knowledge acquisition as being composed of remembering isolated facts (Chew, 2014). This approach is not student-centred and positions the students as passive recipients of education. Further, this is problematic as it fails to support students to *"...develop a connected understanding or how to reason with and apply concepts"* (Chew, 2014:216). We perceived that the university's introduction of a trimester model further impacted, as our program content is only delivered in Trimesters 1 and 2. Consequently, some students experienced a four-month break between academic years, where they had no contact with the university or occupational therapy program. Across the program, students expressed difficulty recalling the considerable content they had previously learnt. When recalling prior learned knowledge, their descriptions reflected knowledge from primary textbooks and only the practical links that had been demonstrated in class. This made teaching difficult as student performance was not congruent with educator expectations. Consequently, educators were using their own unique approaches to address the integration of theory and practice, not necessarily in collaboration with other staff and only within the context of their trimester-long course. This strategy had limited effectiveness and failed to address or support students' ongoing development of theory-into-practice integration. This is because it failed to incorporate an understanding of students' prior learning and the extent of how much more advanced, and undelivered, content remained in the curriculum.

A possible strategy, in the form of a full-day 'transition workshop', was conceptualised by the authors of this chapter. It is important to note here, that the terms 'transition' and 'transition pedagogy' in higher education are synonymous with supporting the experience of new university students transitioning into their first year of university (Kift, 2015). Key features of this model, include an intentional focus on the curriculum to enhance the student experience. In our innovation, transition aligns with traditional definitions, but covers transition across Years 1, 2, 3 and 4 of our program.

As course convenors for Years 2 and 3 courses, we compared the expectations of students to ensure that the transition between years was developmental, and that Year 3 content 'met' students at the level of their finished Year 2 content. We conceptualised a teaching session at the commencement of Year 3 that would effectively 'transition' students from their previous year of learning to the next. We trialled the first transition workshop with Year 3 students in January 2018. For each of the four theoretical pillars (as shown in Figure 1), educators identified key learning outcomes based on troublesome knowledge for students – concepts that were "...*difficult to grasp... or conceptually challenging, requiring the unlearning of earlier perspectives*" (Rodger *et al.*, 2015:546). We drew upon previously published literature about troublesome knowledge in our discipline (e.g. Rodger & Turpin, 2011) and troublesome knowledge we identified from the previous year's curriculum. Learning objectives were established for each theoretical pillar using language presented in Bloom's revised taxonomy of learning (Anderson *et al.*, 2001).

In the workshop, students completed rotations through each theoretical pillar, after which they engaged in group reflections on their learning. These sessions were based on pedagogical approaches to learning (including active learning) and methods for learning discipline-specific knowledge (Shulman, 2013). Student knowledge and confidence were compared pre and post-workshop; the results demonstrated that knowledge was significantly higher for all four pillars, and confidence had significantly improved post-workshop for three of the four pillars. We were confident that existing knowledge from Year 2 had been transitioned and we had calibrated cohort knowledge on theoretical pillars in line with program expectations for Year 3. We hypothesised that taking a program-level (rather than course level) perspective, using targeted annual workshops, would enable us to transition and support theory-into-practice translation effectively across the curriculum. In doing so, we could:

(i) create and standardise opportunities for students which anchored the theoretical pillars across our curriculum and demonstrated their relevance and application to contemporary occupational therapy practice;

(ii) establish year level expectations for pillar mastery; and

(iii) explicitly demonstrate the value we, as educators, placed on the value of theory-into-practice translation in the program.

Based on this workshop's success, we received a university teaching and learning grant to develop and implement the transition workshop model across all four years of our program.

Section 2: The practice

In this section, we explore the development and implementation of our transition workshops within our program. This is achieved through a detailed explanation of the context of our program, the needs of our students, an example of workshop structure and content, and management of the initiative as a routine part of our curriculum.

Our program is delivered across two campuses of the university. We accept approximately 50 new students on each campus each year. These relatively small numbers enable us to work closely with our students, and become familiar with individual or specific student strengths and challenges within each cohort. The goal of our program is to graduate occupational therapists who can work in contemporary and future health and social care delivery models. All teaching is underpinned by shared beliefs that students bring knowledge to the classroom and the constructivist view of student learning (Ertmer & Newby, 2013).

The transition workshops aim to address a long-standing challenge within our profession– the integration of theory into practice. Traditionally, individual course convenors have attempted to integrate this theory-practice gap in individual courses within the curriculum. Our innovation focuses on using a program-level 'scaffolding' strategy (Enomoto, 2011), where students are able to revisit key concepts which increase in complexity over their degree. By taking this approach, we provide focused annual developmental opportunities for theory-into-practice exploration. This approach aligns with the notion of the spiral curriculum (Harden, 1999; Woodward, 2019), a constructivist approach which includes four features: (i) key topics are revisited, (ii) each revisiting adds increasing levels of difficulty, (iii) new learning is related to previous learning, and (iv) student competency increases over time. These learning opportunities create a central point from which course-level teaching and activities can be aligned or expanded across the subsequent year. To our knowledge, we are the first program in our profession to take an annual program-level approach to this challenge.

2a: An introduction to the innovative practice

The primary aim of the transition workshops is to increase students' understanding of, and confidence in, occupational therapy theory and its application to professional practice. The transition workshops are implemented each year in the program. For Year 2, 3 and 4 students, this is typically the first teaching class of the year. The Year 1 transition workshop occurs at the commencement of the second trimester. At this point, students have very preliminary knowledge of relevant theory, and this workshop provides an opportunity to label trimester one learning, and re-emphasise its importance within our curriculum. Students attend one workshop per year. They are contacted prior to class and provided with key information relevant to the workshop. A minimum of two educators, typically who would be working with students in the trimester, co-teach each workshop. The Year 1, 2 and 4 workshops are a half-day in length. The Year 3 workshop, provided at the midway point of the program, is a full-day workshop. This is longer, in order to support student's knowledge and confidence in the pillars, before their first full-time practice education experience. Student and educator workbooks are used to ensure consistency in the delivery across our two university campuses.

All permanently employed educators within our team (n=9) were invited to participate in the development and implementation of the original workshops. Two working groups created the content (either Years 1 and 2 or Years 3 and 4), under the leadership of the chapter authors. Educators were allocated to the working groups based on where, in the curriculum, they completed the majority of their teaching. In this way, they could ensure learning activities for Year 1 were consistent with content provided in Trimester 1. They could also share an understanding of Year 1 content to enable the Year 2 transition workshop to be aligned with knowledge levels from the end of Year 1. The two lead educators ensured congruence between the work developed by the working groups. In the development of each workshop, educators considered:

- What knowledge and skills should students have at this point of the curriculum for each of the four pillars?

- Are there areas of troublesome knowledge that could be addressed in workshops to support students' understanding of the four pillars?

- What are the appropriate learning outcomes for the transition workshop for each of the four pillars?

Educators identified that congruence between their own understanding of the pillars was essential in the delivery of the workshops. As a team, we agreed to align concepts and language with a key discipline textbook – which we had already adopted for wide use across the program. This text provides the foundations of the occupational therapy specific theory that we draw upon and, by aligning with it, we could ensure students were receiving consistent definitions of concepts. We encouraged educators to bring these concepts to life for students by sharing, in the workshops, their own unique examples from their careers.

The 'Affirm–Apply–Advance' framework (Figure 2) underpins all transition workshops. This equates to students having an opportunity to 'affirm' their existing knowledge, 'apply' this knowledge to practice scenarios and consider how they will 'advance' their knowledge and skills in the coming year (described in more detail later). Other consistency features are that workshops address all four theoretical pillars, have the entire campus cohort present in the same workshop and include a minimum of two educators and adopt an active, authentic and collaborative teaching and learning approach.

Some intentional differences exist across the four transition workshops. We recognise that student exposure to, and knowledge of, the pillars varies across the years of the degree. Consequently, although all theoretical pillars are addressed, the expectations of students vary between the pillars in the same year. The intentional separation or integration of the pillars in the workshop design is another aspect of difference. For example, in the Year 3 workshop, the four pillars are kept discrete. This is because integration requires thorough knowledge and educators need to ensure that students are accurate in their knowledge at the program midpoint. The Year 4 workshop, in comparison, addresses the pillars in separate activities and compels students to make consideration of the other pillars. As integration of theoretical pillars is essential for practice, we need to ensure our Year 4 students are competent to do this in the classroom.

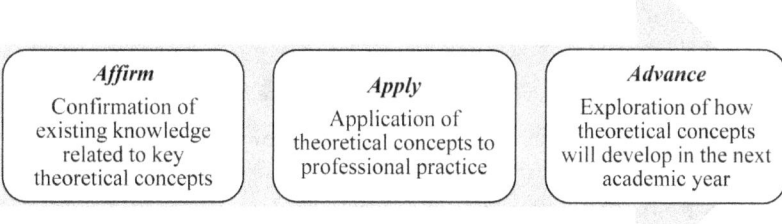

Figure 2: The 'Affirm-Apply-Advance' framework underpinning all transition workshops.

2b: A brief overview of the curriculum

The transition workshop format and content is best described through the illustration of the common aspects of all workshops. These are now described, and illustrations from the workshops are provided. An overview of the Year 3 workshop is provided in Table 1, providing details of how the 'Affirm–Apply–Advance' framework is implemented for two of the theoretical pillars – occupation-centred practice and evidence-based practice.

Introduction to the workshop: Educators introduce the session and outline their role as facilitators throughout the class. Educators provide an overview of the purpose of the workshop, a five-minute re-cap of program courses from the previous year (or trimester for Year 1 students) and an insight into the upcoming courses for the year with reference to key knowledge and skill development. The re-cap is kept intentionally brief; it is done so to ensure that students understand that the workshop's purpose is not to re-teach the entire content from the previous year.

Sample Transition Workshop Content – Year 3

Welcome to session (30 *minutes*)

- Introduce the session and explain the workshop purpose.
- Recap Year 2 curriculum, including occupational therapy and non-discipline specific courses and summary of learning outcomes already achieved from the program (PowerPoint) (Academic 1).
- Overview Year 3 curriculum (including discussion of upcoming courses, practice education experiences, expectations of students in relation to knowledge and skills, introduction to key staff) (Academic 2).

Occupation-centred practice (75 *minutes*) – *Led by Academic 1*

- **Affirm** (15 minutes) – In small groups, students review the impact of personal and environmental factors that influence occupational performance and engagement.
- **Apply** (35 minutes) – Firstly, in small groups, students are provided with a clinical scenario related to a person with a physical or mental health condition and an occupation (e.g. catching public transport). They are required to provide examples of three adaptations that can be applied to the occupation which considers the relevant person (e.g. low vision) and environmental factors (e.g. physical environment of the local area). Secondly, students are required to prepare a summary of their proposed occupational adaptations and key learnings and prepare any questions they have relating to occupational adaptation.

- **Advance** (15 minutes) – Students lead a full group discussion in which all small groups summarise their learning. Staff use generic prompts to extend student feedback by asking:
    o What was the key learning from this session?
    o Did any content connect with what you have learned in other courses? If so, what?
    o Was anything confusing?
    o What is the biggest question you still have?
    o How will you use what you have learned about this pillar this year?

Both staff members highlight examples of their own use of occupational adaptation in practice, and discuss how this knowledge of personal and environmental factors and the skill of occupational adaptation will feature in the forthcoming year of curriculum (i.e. in class content, assessments, practice education).

Short break (10 minutes)

Theory-driven practice (75 *minutes*) – *Led by Academic 2*

Affirm (15 minutes)

Apply (35 minutes)

Advance (15 minutes)

Lunch (60 minutes)

Evidence-based practice (EBP) (75 *minutes*) – *Led by Academic 1*

- **Affirm** (15 minutes) – In small groups, students review one of the four elements of EBP and develop an explanatory statement to share with their peers.
- **Apply** (35 minutes) – In small groups, students consider the identification and application of evidence to a clinical scenario. Firstly, they explore how they will address the element of EBP (as explored in the Affirm stage) in relation to the scenario. Secondly, they develop a 'fact sheet' about the element to enable their peers to implement EBP in their upcoming practice education successfully. *(This resource is collated and shared to the cohort post-workshop)*.
- **Advance** (15 minutes) – Students lead a full group discussion in which all small groups share their element summaries and overview of how it applied to the clinical scenario. Staff use generic prompts to extend student feedback asking:
    o What is challenging about using evidence in practice?
    o Who can help you find and synthesis evidence for practice?
    o What is the biggest question you still have?
    o How will you use what you have learned about this pillar this year?

Staff highlight clinical examples of how they have accessed, synthesised and used evidence in their own practice. The staff discuss common challenges for implementing EBP and provide resources to support students in the coming year. Students examine aspects of the curriculum where they will need to implement EBP in the coming year and what strategies they will initiate to support their skill development to ensure successful completion of assessments and practice education.

Short break (10 minutes)

Client-centred practice *(75 minutes) – Led by Academic 2*

- **Affirm** (15 minutes)
- **Apply** (35 minutes)
- **Advance** (15 minutes)

Conclusion *(30 minutes)*

- Staff thank students for their engagement in the workshop and provide verbal feedback on student knowledge and skill level based on observations from the day. This includes identifying areas of students' strengths and areas for potential development (Academic 1)
- Staff respond to any last-minute questions about theoretical pillars and how they will be addressed and expanded in the upcoming year.
- Students complete reflection on their learning from the day. They are encouraged to identify personal knowledge and skill development and prepare an action plan to further their skills in the coming year. (Academic 2)
- Data collection for concurrent research evaluation of innovation.

Table 1: Sample transition workshop.

Students' experience of workshop content: A combination of individual and small group activities, underpinned by active learning approaches, are utilised. Each group is encouraged to convert their student workbook into a electronic shared document to enable them to take notes and record their work and learning from the session. As illustrated above, the students work through an 'Affirm', 'Apply' and 'Advance' framework as they address each pillar. Table 2 provides examples of these activities across the year groups related solely to the client-centred practice (CCP) pillar. Through this illustration, it is possible to demonstrate the scaffolding of pillar complexity across the years of the program.

	Affirm	**Apply**	**Advance**
Year 1	Students are presented with a definition of client-centred practice (CCP) congruent with class content and discussions from Trimester 1.	Students observe a client interview and are required to identify instances where the therapist implements CCP principles.	Students make individual notes regarding how to ensure that they will be client-centred in their upcoming interview with a client.
Year 2	Students discuss CCP and why this is important in health care.	Using a case study, students consider how they can be client-centred in a hospital environment and possible barriers which may challenge their ability to be client-centred. Students complete a simulated client assessment incorporating CCP principles.	In small groups, students provide peer feedback on client assessments to enhance students' knowledge and skills during interviews. Students keep a record of the feedback so they can improve their performance in upcoming simulation activities.
Year 3	Students discuss: (i) the key components of client-centred practice, (ii) why client-centred practice is important in occupational therapy and (iii) how they know if their practice is client-centred.	Students apply CCP principles to a group (rather than individual clients). Students reflect on their effectiveness to be client-centred with this new type of occupational therapy client.	Students reflect on the similarities/ differences that exist between being client-centred with individuals versus groups. Students are directed to read academic literature relating to CCP in group/community practice contexts in preparation for their Trimester 2 classes and practice education.
Year 4	In small groups, students are asked to share examples of how they have been client-centred in their interactions with clients in the previous year.	Students consider a client scenario in which the client is planning to make an unsafe medical decision. Students discuss how they might be client-centred with consideration to other relevant frameworks such as ethics and dignity of risk.	Students reflect on how they embed CCP in the context of legislation and work environments and how they will navigate and communicate their professional decision making with clients on upcoming practical placements.

Table 2: Example of a transition workshop focus related to client-centred practice.

Large group discussions occur at various points to enable students to reflect on their learning for each pillar. Educators facilitate these large group discussions using observations from the group discussions, pre-determined prompt questions and illustrations from their own careers. Students are encouraged to ask questions and/or seek clarification of their interpretation of theoretical concepts. Educators finalise the discussion by highlighting how students' knowledge and skills of the pillar will be advanced in the forthcoming year of the curriculum.

Educators role in the transition workshop: Educators act as facilitators throughout the workshops and lead the large group discussions. This approach ensures that all relevant content is explored to the depth expected for the year level. Facilitators move between the groups and support students with concept clarification and practice examples, to develop their knowledge and skills, and to ensure students receive a diversity of feedback and examples. Staff within the occupational therapy program are readily able to enact a facilitation role as this approach is commonly used across our curriculum.

Feedback from the workshop: Students are encouraged to provide feedback using an online survey. This feedback is used in the refinement of the workshops. Educators liaise with each other throughout the session to generate feedback for students at the workshop's completion. Educators also advise students of strengths in their knowledge and skills and areas needing further development. When areas of development are identified, students are directed to learning resources that may support them. Students appreciate this feedback as it enables them to benchmark themselves against the expectations of the program.

2c: Organisation of the innovative practice

Students are contacted one week before class, via e-mail, to welcome them to the new year (or trimester for Year 1 students) and orient them to the upcoming workshop. Students are directed to an organisational site within the Blackboard Learning Management System (LMS) which provides the student workbook (inclusive of an outline of the workshop), pre-reading list (as appropriate) and small group allocations for the session. Students are expected to be active participants in the workshops.

They are well versed on this expectation through the structure of other aspects of our program.

Educators orientate themselves to the workshop's aims and content through a facilitator workbook. This is located on a shared drive and the LMS site. This workbook includes the content from the student workbook and provides a range of notes to assist the facilitation of the workshop. For example, key references are included, and educators are given an indication about aspects of content that may be particularly challenging for students. Prompt questions are provided to support educators and ensure consistency across the two campuses. Educators meet in advance to discuss delivery of the workshop, including who will be responsible for covering specific content and leading group discussions. Educators are encouraged to contribute their knowledge and clinical examples throughout the workshop to aid students to integrate theory-into-practice. After the workshops, educators meet to debrief and provide feedback on the class activities, including timing and whether task difficulty was appropriate for the student cohort. This information is used as part of a quality improvement process.

Educators' commitment to this curriculum innovation has been fundamental to the success of this initiative. Because they are involved in the development, review and refinement of the workshops, educators have experienced a personal connectedness to the initiative and value its inclusion as a new addition to our program. Furthermore, educators report benefits from co-teaching with a colleague, which, in turn, has a positive impact on their commitment to the innovation.

2d: Preparation of the innovative practice

We engaged a mentor to support the development, implementation and evaluation of our innovation. This person was a senior health academic with expertise in teaching and learning. During mentoring sessions, we updated them with our progress and sought critical feedback on our ideas, particularly in relation to how our work was, or could be further, aligned to broader university teaching and learning strategies. Amongst a range of feedback responses, our mentor encouraged us to create a program that could have an application to other programs within the university. As an example, this assisted us in developing a workshop framework using language not unique to our discipline.

The transition workshops were created with consideration to pragmatics, resourcing and sustainability within the program. While the initial implementation was supported by an institutional grant, we were conscious that, for the content to become a standard part of our curriculum, the delivered workshops needed to have low cost and resource demands. Consequently, we use basic tools that are available for use in our workplace, including the LMS, online survey collection tools and literature freely available through the university's library collection. Additionally, we use on-campus large flat-floor teaching spaces to enable group activities and large group discussion. Case studies used in workshops are developed in-house to avoid costs associated with licenced products. Our workbooks are copyrighted to the university, and we have embedded creative commons licencing, so that our work can be distributed to other disciplines within our university or occupational therapy programs across the country. As a consequence of this thrift and pragmatic design, we perceive that other programs could easily replicate our annual workshop underpinned with the 'Affirm–Apply–Advance' framework.

Section 3: The outcome

The transition workshops have been evaluated as part of a research project using both quantitative and qualitative approaches. Students, educators and a project advisory group (including practising occupational therapists, existing students and graduates) provided feedback on the curriculum initiative. The project advisory group members gave critical feedback on (i) authenticity of the class activities to teach practice concepts; (ii) whether the knowledge and skills potentially attained by students were relevant to contemporary practice; and (iii) the applicability of content to a range of occupational therapy practice contexts (such as hospitals, community care, individuals, groups, physical health, mental health etc). Minor changes to case studies were made to reflect the nuances of practice in the local area. Collectively, the feedback has been very positive.

3a: Student perspective

Students (n=229; 91%) voluntarily completed surveys at the beginning and end of each workshop to measure their knowledge and confidence in the four theoretical pillars and the usefulness of the transition workshops. We allocated time for survey completion within the workshops in an attempt to obtain a high response rate. Knowledge and confidence were reported on a bespoke survey, and the pre and post data were analysed using Wilcoxon signed-rank tests. Results show a statistically significant increase ($p < 0.05$) in students' knowledge and confidence after the workshops, with small or medium effect sizes, except for knowledge of evidence-based practice which declined after the workshop. The survey also included one subdomain (usefulness) from the Intrinsic Motivation Inventory, which required students to indicate agreement with a range of statements about workshop usefulness on a Likert scale *(1 = not all true, 7 = very true)*. These results revealed that students perceived high levels of benefit from the workshops with a mean score of 6.53 (SD = 0.73).

In the post-workshop survey, students were asked to complete the sentence: *"This workshop has ..."*. To date, 97% of the responses have been positive. Example comments include:

- *"...been great for revision and also for a window into the coming year."* (Year 2 student);
- *"showed me where there are gaps in my understanding of the theory;... has also shown me I need to learn how to explain the content with my own voice, and not textbook."* (Year 3 student).

The remaining students indicated that workshops were not beneficial or of mixed benefit (benefit in some areas but not in others). Primarily, these students wished that there was further application and demonstration of occupational therapy practice:

- *"I would have enjoyed a little more application of each practice. I understood each theory and example of it, but I am seeking a more workplace utilisation."* (Year 1 student).

The post-workshop survey provided students with the opportunity to volunteer to participate in a focus group about the transition workshops. Separate focus groups were held for each student cohort, and 18 students participated. Focus groups were conducted by staff who had not delivered the respective workshop. We funded a research assistant to complete data analysis to minimise the risk of bias. Data were analysed using thematic analysis, and three key benefits were identified. In summary, students believed that the workshops:

(1) facilitated revision and primed them for further learning.*"It gives you an insight into trimester 2 and what you're going to investigate and learn. ... It gives you a summary of trimester 1 but also introduces what you're going to do in trimester 2."* (Year 1 student);

(2) enabled them to understand how theory can be applied to occupational therapy practice: *"Helped me to understand how we apply some of the theory we have previously learnt, into a clinical/practical setting."* (Year 3 student);

(3) supported them to feel confident and prepare for workplace learning:*"It just really set us up well to get into practice education."* (Year 4 student).

Students enjoyed the experience of co-teaching by the team of educators. They appreciated when they observed consistency between the educators.

- *"Yeah they bounced off each other quite a bit... and I thought it was good because they kind of built on what the other one was saying."* (Year 4 student).

Students also appreciated discovering that educators may offer differing applications of theory:

- *"Because when it's just one staff member you feel like you have to agree with them because there's no-one there challenging them, but if there's someone there challenging it you're like, yeah it's okay that I can think another way, it will still be okay."* (Year 3 student).

The repeated, deliberate and explicit teaching of the four pillars is particularly helpful for students in preparation for their practice education experiences. They voice feeling more comfortable and confident articulating their professional practice (and corresponding decision making) to supervisors, other health professionals, clients and families. We attribute this to the spiral curriculum design (Harden, 1999), which enables students to continuously add depth and complexity to their understanding of our four program pillars. Further, the use of engaging pedagogical practices, including personal reflection, relational learning, 'real world' case-based discussion and co-teaching contributed to creating a beneficial learning experience. These active, authentic and collaborative approaches have been valuable to students as they have enabled students to move safely out of their 'comfort zones'. Therefore, they develop knowledge and skills required for professional practice and are more articulate when discussing how occupational therapy practice is supported by theoretical constructs. Anecdotally, in 2020, we have witnessed students arrive at workshops ready for content to be delivered using the Affirm-Apply-Advance framework and with theory-to-practice questions that they need resolved. We have also observed them refer to, and draw upon, transition workshop content throughout the year, which we hope demonstrates they are less compartmentalised in their learning. Evaluation of the student experience is ongoing, and we intend to explore students' perceptions of the entire program of four workshops when the first cohort completes the suite in 2022.

3b: Teacher perspective

Educators revealed benefits from engaging in the transition workshops and they valued the co-teaching model:

- *"I think it's got multiple layers of advantage; for us, for them, for the curriculum."* (Educator);
- *"Actually for me that was really nice to see the way that X teaches... I've taken some things away from that that I can do in other years."* (Educator).

As leaders of this innovation, we have learnt four key lessons. Firstly, we (and the broader team) have confirmed the importance of conceptualising, planning and implementing theoretical content at a program level. In doing so, we can effectively apply taxonomies of learning to ensure that workshop content is pedagogically sound and developmental across the program. This shift is also of benefit to our students as it provides expectations for theoretical knowledge relative to the stage of their degree. As all program educators have been involved in the transition workshops (either in development or delivery) it has centralised our own language and interpretation of the program theoretical pillars. This is important, as it ensures that students are receiving consistent information about key practice concepts. Furthermore, the realisation that students hold different levels of pillar knowledge and skill competence at different stages of their degree has shifted educators' expectations in other teaching, learning, and assessment tasks. For example, educators are now adjusting assessment stimuli and marking criteria to reflect that students have greater knowledge and skills in client-centred practice than evidence-based practice in Year 3 of the program.

Secondly, engaging a mentor for this curriculum change was critical to our success. This enabled us to obtain a perspective beyond that of our own discipline, which was important to ensure we avoided 'group think'. She assisted us in ensuring that our project aligned with university strategic goals around teaching and learning. Our mentor was a 'critical friend' who gave us educated, objective and supportive advice.

Thirdly, we experienced an energising focus group with our teaching colleagues. They spoke positively about the outcomes they experienced–particularly in relation to their affirmative experiences of co-teaching and learning from each other. We learnt that curriculum change requires a team approach with commitment from colleagues. Our innovation could capitalise on the collegiality that already existed within our program staff, who are united in their mission to provide high-quality education to our students.

We acknowledge that this curriculum change would have been impossible without the support from our Head of Program and occupational therapy colleagues. Lastly, this innovation illuminated the significant contribution students can make to the refinement of the curriculum. This was illustrated through survey feedback, focus group discussions and by having students on our advisory committee. Consequently, we see the potential for pro-actively (beyond routine student evaluations) including students in all aspects of planning, designing and evaluating future teaching and learning initiatives.

Section 4: Moving forward

As a program, we aspire to be international leaders in theory-into-practice translation in occupational therapy education. The innovation, now a routine part of our program, strengthens our commitment to this goal. Our student's professional identity is strengthened through our commitment to supporting their understanding of theory and its application to practice throughout their program journey. We have observed students willingly attending these classes as they now perceive a 'value-add' to their curriculum.

We recognise the value in continuing to engage our program staff in the ongoing review and refinement of this innovation. This is essential to ensure that workshop content remains contemporary but also to ensure that program staff feel invested in, and committed to, the workshops. We do this, primarily, by seeking staff feedback and by sharing this (and student) feedback with the team in meetings. We are aware that the involvement of all program staff in workshop delivery has enabled educators to direct students back to transition workshop content whilst working on other activities in the following year. We are also sharing this approach with potential new students at university Open Days as an innovation that exists within our particular occupational therapy program. We remain committed to a co-teaching model which requires considerable evidence to be justified as a routine part of our curricula within the budget-conscious university sector.

We plan to disseminate our work through university forums as we perceive our model may have applicability to other health (and potentially non-health) programs where students are required to base practice on theoretical concepts. In future iterations of the program, we envisage incorporating simulated clients in the latter transition workshops. This would enhance the authenticity of the experience for students and enable us to include the valuable contribution of consumers in the delivery and evaluative components of our work consistent with national accreditation guidelines (Occupational Therapy Council of Australia, 2018). Our work is being prepared for dissemination through publication and conference presentations. Lastly, we remain committed to the dissemination of our work to other university programs which may experience similar theory-into-practice challenges and could implement an annual transition workshop underpinned by our 'Affirm–Apply–Advance' framework.

Conclusion

This chapter described the implementation of a program-level initiative to address a well-established theory-into-practice challenge that exists within our profession. It outlined the development and implementation of annual 'transition workshops' which, underpinned by constructivist theory, used an 'Affirm–Apply–Advance' framework to support students' learning across the four years of their curriculum. Evaluation of our work identified that the workshops facilitated revision for students, increased their understanding of how to apply theory in practice and supported their confidence in preparation for workplace learning. The co-teaching delivery model adopted in the workshops supported students learning whilst also providing professional development for educators. We perceive that a program-level approach to the integration of theory-into-practice may be of relevance and significance to other health and non-health disciplines as it addresses the compartmentalisation that can occur when students study discrete courses. We encourage teaching programs to consider the introduction and use of an annual learning experience that utilises an 'Affirm–Apply–Advance' framework to student learning.

About the Authors

Michelle Bissett is a Senior Lecturer in the Discipline of Occupational Therapy in the School of Allied Health Sciences at Griffith University, Australia. She can be contacted at this e-mail: m.bissett@griffith.edu.au

Melanie Roberts is a Senior Lecturer in the Discipline of Occupational Therapy in the School of Allied Health Sciences at Griffith University, Australia. She can be contacted at this e-mail: melanie.roberts@griffith.edu.au

Bibliography

Ajani, K. & Moez, S. (2011). Gap between knowledge and practice in nursing. *Procedia-Social and Behavioral Sciences*, 15, pp. 3927–3931.

Anderson, L. W., Krathwohl, D. R. & Bloom, B. S. (2001). *A Taxonomy for Learning, Teaching, and Assessing: A Revision of Bloom's Taxonomy of Educational Objectives* (Complete ed.). New York: Longman.

Beane, A., Padeniya, A., De Silva, A., Stephens, T., De Alwis, S., Mahipala, P., Sigera, P., Munasinghe, S., Weeratunga, P. & Ranasinghe, D. (2017). Closing the theory to practice gap for newly qualified doctors: Evaluation of a peer-delivered practical skills training course for newly qualified doctors in preparation for clinical practice. *Postgraduate Medical Journal*, 93(1104), pp. 592–596.

Chew, S. (2014). Helping students to get the most out of studying. In Benassi, V. A., Overson, C. E. & Hakala, C. M. (Eds.), *Applying Science of Learning in Education: Infusing Psychological Science into the Curriculum*, pp. 215–223. Society for the Teaching of Psychology.

Curtin, M. & Jaramazovic, E. (2001). Occupational therapists' views and perceptions of evidence-based practice. *British Journal of Occupational Therapy*, 64(5), pp. 214–222.

Dobozy, E. & Nygaard, C. (2021). A learning-centred five-tier model of innovation in higher education. In Enomoto, K., Warner, R. & Nygaard, C. (Eds.), *Teaching and Learning Innovations in Higher Education*, pp. 19–46. Oxfordshire, UK: Libri Publishing Ltd.

Dobson, K. & Beshai, S. (2013). The theory-practice gap in cognitive behavioral therapy: Reflections and a modest proposal to bridge the gap. *Behavior therapy*, 44(4), pp. 559–567.

Enomoto, K. (2011). Fostering high-quality learning through a scaffolded curriculum. In Nygaard, C., Courtney, N. & Holtham, C. (Eds.), *Beyond transmission – Innovations in University Teaching*, pp. 167–184. Oxfordshire, UK: Libri Publishing Ltd.

Ertmer, P. A. & Newby, T. J. (2013). Behaviorism, cognitivism, constructivism: Comparing critical features from an instructional design perspective. *Performance improvement quarterly*, 26(2), pp. 43–71.

Gustafsson, L., Molineux, M. & Bennett, S. (2014). Contemporary occupational therapy practice: The challenges of being evidence based and philosophically congruent. *Australian Occupational Therapy Journal*, 61(2), pp. 121–123.

Harden, R. M. (1999). What is a spiral curriculum? *Medical Teacher*, 21(2), pp. 141–143.

Hatlevik, I. K. R. (2012). The theory-practice relationship: reflective skills and theoretical knowledge as key factors in bridging the gap between theory and practice in initial nursing education. *Journal of Advanced Nursing*, 68(4), pp. 868–877.

Jackson, A., Bluteau, P. & Furlong, J. (2013). Interprofessional working in practice: Avoiding a theory-practice gap. *International Journal of Practice-based Learning in Health and Social Care*, 1, pp. 90–92.

Kift, S. (2015). A decade of transition pedagogy: A quantum leap in conceptualising the first year experience. *HERDSA Review of Higher Education*, 2(1), pp. 51–86.

Occupational Therapy Council of Australia. (2018). *Accreditation standards for Australian entry-level occupational therapy education programs*. Retrieved from: https://www.otcouncil.com.au/wp-content/uploads/OTC-Accred-Stds-Dec2018-effective-Jan2020.pdf

Rodger, S. & Turpin, M. (2011). Using threshold concepts to transform entry level curricula. In Krause, K. Buckridge, M., Grimmer, C. & Purbrick-Illek, S. (Eds.), *Research and Development in Higher Education: Reshaping Higher Education*, pp. 263–274. Refereed proceedings of 34th annual HERDSA international conference, Gold Coast, Australia.

Rodger, S., Turpin, M. & O'Brien, M. (2015). Experiences of academic staff in using threshold concepts within a reformed curriculum. *Studies in Higher Education*, 40(4), pp. 545–560.

Shulman, L. S. (2013). Those who understand: Knowledge growth in teaching. *Journal of Education*, 193(3), pp. 1–11.

Stein, S., Isaacs, G. & Andrews, T. (2004). Incorporating authentic learning experiences within a university course. *Studies in Higher Education*, 29(2), pp. 239–258.

Woodward, R. (2019). The spiral curriculum in higher education: Analysis in pedagogic context and a business studies application. *E-Journal of Business Education & Scholarship of Teaching*, 13(3), pp. 14–26.

Chapter 12

An Innovative Model for University-industry Collaboration in Course Design and Delivery

Sami Heikkinen

Introduction

With my chapter, I contribute to this book, *Teaching and Learning Innovations in Higher Education*, as I present an innovative model for university-industry collaboration. The model has been used to govern course design and delivery of an online course at The LAB University of Applied Science in Lahti, Finland. The course is an elective course, *Introduction to insurance business*, offered for bachelor students. I show how using this model for university-industry collaboration results in more up-to-date knowledge within the course. The industry partner collaborating makes its expertise visible and is able to improve its corporate image in the eyes of the students, leading to an increasing number of potential recruits at the time when these students are graduating.

Referring to the learning-centred five-tier model of innovation in higher education (Dobozy & Nygaard, 2021, Chapter 2 in this book), my process innovation draws on a constructivist perception of learning. Perceiving learning as a constructivist, I primarily see the process innovation as a way to facilitate student engagement in generative learning (Wittrock, 1974). Generative learning means that the students integrate new learning ideas into their existing realm of educational experiences. By creating a mental web of experiences, students understand how the principles that they learn, connect to their world, and how such learning can be beneficial for themselves. Implementing and using a constructivist process innovation has implications for both students and teachers.

Reading this chapter, you will gain the following three insights:
1. how to establish collaboration with industry partners to create industry-driven course content;
2. how to set shared goals for university-industry course content production;
3. how to build an online course in collaboration with industry.

Overview of main sections

The chapter has four sections. In Section 1, I present the background of the model. Then, in Section 2, the practice itself is explained in detail. Following on from this explanation, in Section 3, the outcomes of the innovative practice are evaluated by way of utilising students' reflections (Section 3a) and the teachers' reflections (Section 3b) on using the innovation. Finally, in Section 4, I focus on how to develop the established innovative practice even further.

Section 1: The Background

'What to teach in a university course?' is a difficult question to answer. The course content should be topical and academically canonised. Yet, finding an appropriate balance between these two factors can be difficult. The knowledge transfer between university and industry is often understood as a one-way process from university to industry (Bekkers & Freitas, 2008 and Ankrah & Omar, 2015). However, the counterpart from industry to university remains a somewhat unknown subject. Much contemporary research focuses on issues related to the from-university-to-industry-process (e.g. Bekkers & Freitas, 2008 and Ankrah & Omar, 2015). From the perspective of curriculum development, the knowledge transfer situation is problematic. Typically, new industrial practices have to be approved as shared understanding within the industry before they reach the university curriculum. Achieving this position, requires the emergence of shared understanding, which in turn requires the emergence of established best practices. From this continuum, it can be concluded that things taught at university, on knowledge-based courses, can become outdated before they end up being the subject of teaching. Considering that students, who participate in such studies, may still spend some years studying before their graduation, the skills of the graduate can be outdated at the time of graduation.

An alternative to this long and slow process of getting state of the art knowledge from industry to university is work-integrated learning (Cooper et al., 2010). A recent example of work-integrated learning is the hugely popular *Elements of AI* (artificial intelligence) course, designed in 2018, in a collaboration between the industry partner Reaktor and the University of Helsinki. AI is a buzzword, and there appears to be substantial interest in gaining knowledge about what exactly AI encompasses. Together, the industry partner and the university were able to offer this online course available globally. Whereas practitioners such as Vihervaara (2015), have identified that industry-specific courses can offer a beneficial added value to the course content, yet research, such as that of Wit-de Vries et al. (2019) on knowledge transfer, has focused on research related perspectives. This has meant, that the practical dimensions of facilitating knowledge transfer remain somewhat undetermined.

An opportunity for exploring new practices to facilitate knowledge transfer, began to arise at the beginning of 2020 as the LAB University of Applied Sciences was founded. LAB came into being as its predecessors, Lahti University of Applied Sciences and Saimaa University of Applied Sciences, merged. Along with the establishment of a new university, the role of the university is in a state of change. According to the new strategy, LAB now has its focus on innovation, industry and commerce (LAB University of Applied Sciences, 2020). Based on the Universities of Applied Sciences Act (2014) in Finland, universities such as LAB have to regenerate the industrial structure of the region. Realising this strategy requires new forms of collaboration with industry. A merger such as ours gives a fresh start and enables new initiatives for new kinds of collaboration with the industry.

Luckily, everything did not have to start from very beginning as a relevant initiative was already in existence. During 2019 LAB (then known as LAMK) started a project for defining new forms of collaboration; one of these forms was the design and delivery of a course in collaboration with an industry partner. This has resulted in a newly developed course. The production process of developing this course is described in this chapter.

Chapter 12

Section 2: The Practice

Designing and delivering a course in a university-industry collaboration has many benefits for both parties. The collaboration itself, provides the university with up-to-date information concerning the current workplace requirements in the industry. At the same time, such collaboration gives up-to-date content for the course, providing students with timely expertise, that is requisite in their future transition to the workplace. Many companies are currently facing difficulties in recruiting skilled labour (Ministry of Economic Affairs and Employment, 2019), and this model of collaboration may help industry solve this problem as the university students are potential future employees.

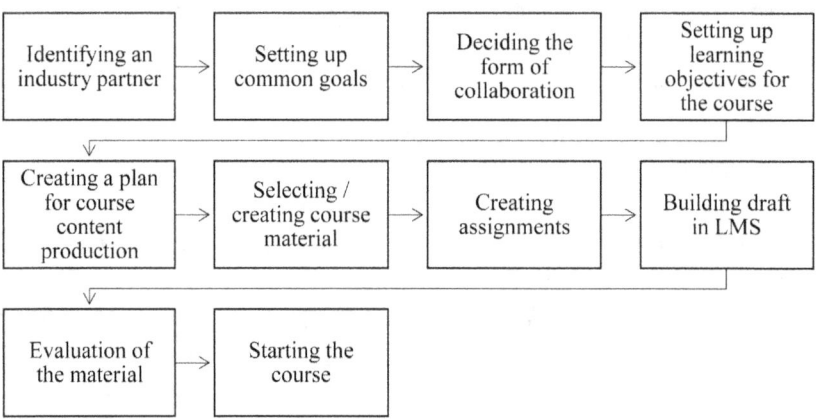

Figure 1: The model for university-industry collaboration in course design and delivery.

Figure 1 shows the model for university-industry collaboration. The starting point for the design of the course is identifying an industry partner (referred company) which has common needs with the university. The directionality of this process is normally initiated by the company(ies) who contact the university and present their current challenges. The contact person at the university then tries to ascertain what would be the best way to resolve the challenges. Sometimes, the initiatives can be discerned, based on any previous collaboration. Therefore, it is vital to have good relations between university and industry. Furthermore, if the university and the participating company do not have achievable benefits for both through the collaboration, any such collaboration cannot lead to a desired outcome. When the university chooses a partner for collaboration, the company must have an interest in collaborating. The company does not just create material for goodwill, rather they will also want to receive tangible benefits. Therefore, it is advised that we do not offer partnerships to any company, but to a potential partner that can benefit from the collaboration. The design of the joint course aims to enhance both the image of the company itself and thus the image of the company as an employer of choice. This objective has been pursued in the past, for example, through guest lectures, but this model will further deepen collaboration.

Once a suitable company partner is found, the next thing to solve is to combine the interests of university and company. As part of its curriculum, and for ethical reasons, the university cannot promote the processes of a single company solely. Therefore, we must implement the contents of the course on a more general level, so that the perspective is in a broader description of the field of business and its operations. In our case, it meant that the course could not be focused solely on the operations of our partner company. Instead, we had to include information about the industry, and other competitors as well. In the early stages of the collaboration, it is important to find the right balance between the presentation of the partner company and the information presenting a general view of the business field.

The next step is to consider the form of collaboration. The implementation of the joint course, moves beyond the more traditional idea of guest lectures. Instead, the partner company participates within each theme of the course. In addition, the form of course execution must be decided, be it contact teaching, online learning or perhaps blended learning. In our case, we decided to design an online course, because it would enable us to scale up the from the regional to the national level if needed. This aspect was considered because the partner company operates at a national level. This gives maximum benefit, from the company's perspective, for participating in the course.

Once the form of collaboration has been found, the next question is to consider what the learning objectives of the course are. At this stage, alongside the needs of the company, the objectives defined by the university curriculum must be considered. The acquired skills must meet the definitions of the European Qualifications Framework (EQF). This sets the standard for the material produced by the company.

After defining the learning objectives, the next step is to plan how the course will be produced. In our case, we decided that the company produce the electronic learning material. Along with the texts, some video materials are used. The video materials are the same materials that the company already use as a part of their internal human resource development. The material is available for enrolled students, from the starting date of the course until the end of the semester. At this phase of the process, it was noticed that there was an employee in the company, currently studying in the university. This was considered as a connective asset worth utilising. The student could bring the student perspective, at the same time as her knowing the company from inside. We decided to give her a major role in the evaluation process to determine what kind of materials and assignments should be used within the course.

The learning objectives were the basis for this selection. The university teacher prepared a draft of the assignments to be used to assess the achievement of learning objectives. It is important to allocate sufficient time to reconcile materials and assignments. This is vital because this is the part of the process that is most likely to fail, as the different partners produce the different sections (learning material and assignments). This challenge was tackled through project meetings. In these meetings, the company presented the materials produced, and university representatives explained how the material is used, as a basis for an assignment and for an evaluation of the learning outcomes. As a part of our project, the workgroup meeting was scheduled monthly. We decided to use Microsoft Teams as a platform for material sharing and communication in between meetings.

Along with the monthly meetings, the scheduling aspect of the overall process must be considered. The schedule of the university's academic year determines the deadline by which the course must be available to students. Counting backwards from the deadline allows one to define how the available timespan can be divided into different parts of the process. In our case, the production of materials and assignments for the course was started in January and completed in August. In this way, the course is available in September, at the beginning of the autumn semester. By delivering the course in the autumn semester, it enables the company to recruit students from the course as part-time employees for the spring semester. During the spring semester, they get used to the work and its requirements. By this means, such part-time employees are fully qualified to start full time work next summer after the course has ended. This is the season when the company has a great demand for its workforce due to summer holidays.

Our decision to execute the course online required the selection of a Learning Management System (LMS). We chose Moodle as the LMS, because it was already in use at the university. In addition, using the existing LMS reduces administrative workload, such as creating student IDs. Furthermore, Moodle is deemed as an appropriate option for upcoming use, as it enables the enrolment of non-university students onto the course. This makes it possible to offer the course also to company staff members and students of other higher education institutions.

Online courses require extensive production of the material. In our case, the company already had in-house training material that could also be used in this course. However, the company still had to produce more material for the course themes, as there was no existing material available. Besides this, students have to search for a part of the material needed for the course, as a part of the assignments. On some themes, company material available online can also be used as a part of the material for the course. For example, the marketing material of the company is used in assignments where students need to familiarise themselves with the products of the company and its competitors.

This method has similarities with the student as producer model (Neary & Winn 2009) and with the concept of student as co-producer (McCulloch 2009). As presented by Dobozy and Nygaard (2021, Chapter 2 in this book), this kind of role of students is one of the distinctive features of constructivism. At the same time, the role of the teacher changes. Instead of imparting the knowledge, the teacher becomes the knowledge curator. As an example of the producer role of the student, in the competitors' product comparison assignment, the student conducts a product comparison based on mystery shopping. Here, the student appears as a fake client and acquires an offer for the service of a competing company. When the student has done the same operation in the company's service, they can compare these options with each other and assess the competitive factors of different actors. As the student is taking active actions to gather the information needed, it helps to get closer to the learning objectives and create more durable learning outcomes. This method has been proven to be suitable, for example, in making comparisons between the options accessible for students.

When materials and assignments begin to form, the technical script of the course must also be prepared. The online form also sets the requirements for the diversity of the content. This means that the material must utilise a variety of media to make the course interesting. The integrated HTML5 package (H5P) system in Moodle gives a wide range of opportunities for partial integration of assignments into materials. Already in the early stages of this process, there must be a draft. The final version takes shape as the selection of materials and assignments produced begins to emerge. After that, the way in which the course is to be built must be considered.

When the course reaches the stage whereby it is available to students, there must be a clear plan about how the course proceeds. The logical sequence of progress is considered in the pedagogical script performed at the initial stage. It must also take into account the tasks of the teacher during the course. In our case, it was decided to implement a part of the course assignments automatically, taking advantage of the possibilities offered by Moodle and H5P. The teacher's contribution during the course is to evaluate and give feedback for essay assignments and for these assignments, it is important to have a rubric guiding the evaluation of essays. This will be especially important if the implementation of the course is scaled up to meet national needs. This means that the course may have more than one teacher, and all of them must be able to evaluate essays based on the same criteria. In addition to assessing essays, the teacher's task is to answer questions that arise from the students. Careful analysis of the questions is important because they can identify potential development areas that need to be considered in the future, together with the university and the company.

Organisation of the innovation

The course is delivered online. When the implementation of the course begins, a schedule is given to enrolled students for completing the course assignments. The course consists of three main themes, each of which includes materials and assignments. The subject of the first theme is the industry of the company. The second theme deals with typical products of the industry. The third theme focuses on the competencies required by the employees of the industry. Each theme has a deadline by which the assignments of this theme must be completed. Roughly, one month is allocated for each theme. Within this month, the student will be able to make their scheduling quite freely. The online course does not include predetermined time-specific meetings, allowing students to plan their schedule with some freedom.

The course structure follows the cycle (Figure 2): material -> assignment -> feedback -> material. Students proceed individually according to this model from theme to theme. Some assignments are assessed automatically via the LMS, whereas the teacher assesses some of them (e.g. essay assignments).

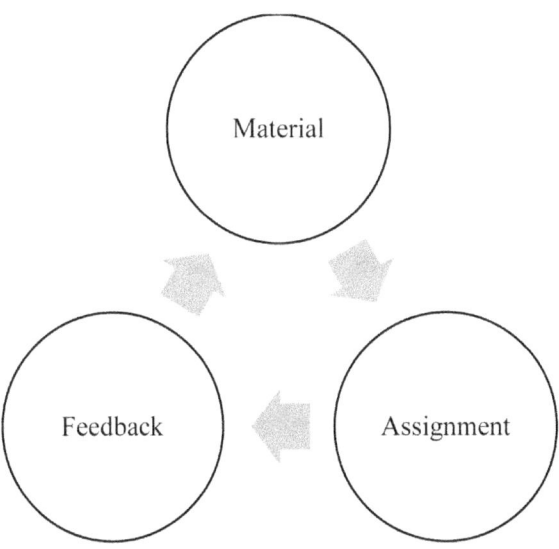

Figure 2: The cyclic structure of the course content.

This course is part of the complementary studies in the curriculum. Since this is not a compulsory course, both the planning and implementation of the course has been very flexible. If the need for the course is recognised, the topical theme offering relevant competencies, the planning and including such a course into complementary studies should be very flexible.

This course is not included in any of the modules or specialisation options currently available in LAB University of applied sciences. On the other hand, one might think that this is more about hybrid know-how, combining the contents of different themes. Thus, it offers a good opportunity to supplement their skills for students of different disciplines (e.g. marketing and financial management).

Preparation of the innovation

If a teacher feels like they would like to implement a course of contemporary content together with a company, they will need to pay attention to the following issues. First, they should find a corporate partner who feels that producing a joint course is useful for themselves. This is best achieved when the course allows a company to build a new channel for recruitment, although there might be other objectives the companies may have. Once a company has been found, it is of mutual benefit to define together the objectives by which both parties' benefit. When setting goals, it is important that content complements the curriculum. As the objectives have been defined, the next step is to draw up a pedagogical script. At this juncture, it is an appropriate moment to decide roles and responsibilities for both the university and the company. An LMS system also needs to be selected. If LMS use is mainly controlled by the university, then the university's LMS can be used. If the company has used its own material, within the confines its own LMS, then this raises the possibility of using the company's LMS, or selecting a completely external system for this purpose. The format of the materials and assignments to be produced is determined by the pedagogical script and the LMS used. Once these choices are made, the material can be produced.

During production, it is important to arrange meetings between different parties to ensure that there is appropriate directional movement and the quality criteria associated with content production are met. It is important to schedule meetings right at the beginning of the project, because finding suitable dates can prove challenging later. When materials and assignments are completed, they must be transferred to the LMS and tested. This will help ensure that everything works as planned. After this, the course is ready for enrolment. This does not mean that everything is ready, as the content must constantly be kept up-to-date, and this responsibility has to be considered beforehand. This ensures that course content remains as contemporary as possible for the short-term future.

Section 3: The outcome

3a: Student perspective

Students wish to have contemporary knowledge in the content of their courses. A large-scale study shows that 71 % of students studying in Finnish universities were satisfied with the content of the university courses (Potila *et al.*, 2017). Even though that percentage satisfaction is high, at the same time it means that there remains a gap for contemporary course content. That gap is what the new innovation presented in this chapter aims to address. Even though the course presented in this chapter has a focus on the knowledge and skillsets of the insurance industry, part of these capabilities can be understood in a wider context as a part of the 21st-century graduate skill set (Stevens, 2012).

We address the needs of students in this course by involving a student in the planning of the course. This has been possible because the company involved has already recruited students who continue to pursue their degree at the university. As mentioned previously, one of these students has been involved in the planning of the course. This is in order to incorporate student insight and input into our consideration of types of materials and assignments. Indeed, designing assignments together has made it possible to find the types of assignments that are engaging for students. This approach ensures that the planning team work together to proactively meet the needs of our students:

- "This has been an interesting process [in which] to participate. I strongly feel that I have had a chance to tell what I would like to have. What is even better, I have seen with my own eyes, that my wishes are now a part of the assignments." (Student who participated in the course production process).

The final version of the course material consists of three themes focusing on the specific industry. In the first theme, students learn the basic principles about the industry, the different kinds of companies in the business and the competitive situation in the field. In the assignments they have to, for example, find different kinds of information from the statistics and internet sites to compare different companies. In the second theme, students gain familiarity with the products of the industry. In this theme, students do mystery shopping to find out how the different companies are building their competitive edge. The third theme focuses on the skills required of the employees working within the industry. In this theme, the assignments are focused on simulations presenting the typical situations employees are facing and how to adapt to different kinds of situations. Within every part of the course, the materials and assignments mirror to the actual work-life practices as much as possible.

During the first iteration of the course, the feedback from students was analysed to verify, as far as possible, that all possible errors, ambiguities and other possible problems have been removed from the course. Some errors remained due to students being unable to access some materials, as well as some problems with assessment details in automated assignment settings. At the same time, we also gathered information on the functionality of the course and found that overall, the students positively perceived our up-to-date and concrete content of the course. For example:

- *"This has been an interesting course to participate [in]. I have never seen such up-to-date content. It almost feels that I am already taking part in the company's activities."* (Student enrolled on the course);
- *"I would surely like to have more courses like this. I especially liked the assignments – they were so fresh and educative."* (Student enrolled on the course).

3b: Teacher perspective

The implementation of this course has been fruitful for the teacher. When participating in this kind of process, the teacher receives confirmatory support and insights from industry partners for doing their work. This ensures that the course content aligns with contemporary industry needs and practices. What is more important, a teacher's professional competence develops as they can see the challenges of everyday life in the companies involved. Yet, it requires a new skill set from the teacher, as effective communication and project management skills are required to ensure the project is going in the right direction at the right pace.

When this kind of process is put into practice for the first time, sufficient effort must be made to establish a common understanding between participants. Such common understandings are in relation to expected learning outcomes, learning materials and assignments, evaluation criteria and time management; using time for this purpose helps to create better results. Working together with the company is not an easy or simple way to design a course, nevertheless it is a methodology which offers so much more than the traditional model used to plan the teaching. That is why it is worth persevering with the methodology, even if it is both cerebrally challenging and labour intensive for its creator.

Moving forward

Whilst the themes and materials of the course are currently up to date, it is important to remember that being up to date is in itself, transient. Therefore, we must prepare an updated plan for the course at the end of the course production process, at least annually. It would be wise to consider this as a requirement, when planning the course content for the subsequent iterations. For example, it would be helpful to refer to the latest statistics in the industry, rather than to include figures directly from the materials, should they differ. Thus, this update work should be carried out collaboratively between the university and the company. Such a collaboration can not only help reduce additional upgrade needs in the long term, but also help ascertain whether more extensive updates should be made to the course, ensuring that the material remains contemporary in the future.

Conclusion

Creating course material in innovative collaboration with industry partners offers significant benefits to three stakeholder groups. First, the university receives up-to-date knowledge relevant to the needs of the industry. Second, students can be sure that the content they study is up-to-date in relation to the skills required to work in the industry. Third, companies brighten up their corporate image and will attract more motivated recruits to apply for work.

This chapter presented a model of partnership that can be used to develop or refine a university curriculum. Specifically, the model explored how to establish collaboration with industry partners to create industry-driven course content. The model showcased in this chapter helps to set common goals for university-industry course content production.

Furthermore, this innovation follows a step-by-step process for building such an online course in collaboration with an industry partner. The example provided in this chapter was positively received by students who perceived that content and assessments aligned with contemporary business practice. One key element for delivering this experience was using a student as a co-producer in the production process. This practice ensures the course content is contemporary and student-oriented. As Skillicorn (2016) defines, innovation is a practice successfully translating an idea into a process, creating value for one or multiple stakeholder groups. Within this practice, all stakeholders: university, company and students have gained added value. This practice can be implemented as a truly innovative win-win collaboration for all parties.

About the Author

Sami Heikkinen is a senior lecturer in LAB University of Applied Sciences, Lahti, Finland. He can be contacted at this e-mail: sami.heikkinen@lab.fi.

Bibliography

Ankrah, S. & Omar, A. T. (2015). Universities–industry collaboration: A systematic review. Scandinavian Journal of Management, 31(3), pp. 387–408.

Bekkers, R. & Freitas, I. M. B. (2008). Analysing knowledge transfer channels between universities and industry: To what degree do sectors also matter? *Research Policy*, 37(10), pp. 1837–1853.

Cooper, L., Orrell, J. & Bowden, M. (2010). *Work-integrated learning: A guide to effective practice*. London: Routledge.

de Wit-de Vries, E., Dolfsma, W. A., van der Windt, H. J. & Gerkema, M. P. (2019). Knowledge transfer in university-industry research partnerships: a review. *The Journal of Technology Transfer*, 44(4), pp. 1236–1255.

Dobozy, E. & Nygaard, C. (2021). A learning-centred, five-tier model of innovation in higher education. In Enomoto, K., Warner, R. & Nygaard, C. (Eds.), *Teaching and Learning Innovations in Higher Education*, pp. 19–46. Oxfordshire, UK: Libri Publishing Ltd.

European Union. (2020). Description of the eight EQF levels. Retrieved from: https://europa.eu/europass/en/description-eight-eqf-levels

LAB University of Applied Sciences. (2020). *The Best of Both Worlds LAB Strategy 2030*. Retrieved from: https://lab.fi/en/info/about-us/strategy.

McCulloch, A. (2009). The student as co-producer: Learning from public administration about the student–university relationship. *Studies in Higher Education*, 34(2), pp. 171–183.

Ministry of Economic Affairs and Employment. (2019,). *Occupational Barometer: Labour shortage in many occupations*. Retrieved from: https://tem.fi/en/-/ammattibarometri-tyovoimapula-vaivaa-yha-useampaa-ammattia

Neary, M. & Winn, J. (2009). *The student as producer: reinventing the student experience in higher education*. In Bell, L., Stevenson, H. & Neary, M. (Eds), *The Future of Higher Education: Policy, Pedagogy and the Student Experience*, pp. 192–210. London: Continuum.

Potila, A. K., Moisio, J., Ahti-Miettinen, O., Pyy-Martikainen, M. & Virtanen, V. (2017). Opiskelijatutkimus 2017.

Skillicorn, N. (2016). Infographic: 15 Experts on What Innovation Actually Means. *Inc.com*. Retrieved from: https://www.inc.com/nick-skillicorn/9-defining-characteristics-of-successful-innovation.html

Stevens, R. (2012). Identifying 21st-century capabilities. *International Journal of Learning and Change*, 6(3–4), pp. 123–137.

Universities of Applied Sciences Act 2014. 932 (Finland).

Vihervaara. T. (2015). *Yritysyhteistyö opetuksessa – käytännön käsikirja yliopistoille ja yrityksille*. Helsinki: Aalto-yliopisto.

Wittrock, M. C. (1974). Learning as a generative process. *Educational Psychologist*, 11(2), pp. 87–95.

Chapter 13

Project-Based Learning in a Japanese University: A Disruptive Innovation in Business Education

Sarah Louisa Birchley, Keiko Omura and Kayoko Yamauchi

Introduction

With our chapter, we contribute to this book, *Teaching and Learning Innovations in Higher Education*, by illustrating how we have implemented Project-Based Learning (PBL) as a disruptive product innovation in curriculum design and delivery. PBL is defined as: *"a teaching method in which learners gain knowledge and skills by working for an extended period of time to investigate and respond to a complex question, problem, or challenge"* (BIE, 2003:307). PBL may not be considered as overly innovative in other educational contexts, but in the context of language education, in Japanese higher education, it is still a novel method. Taking a bottom-up approach to bring about this innovation has helped students at the Faculty of Business Administration at Toyo Gakuen University, Tokyo, Japan, to develop those language skills, business content knowledge, and 21st-century skills necessary for employability in the new knowledge economy.

Referring to the learning-centred five-tier model of innovation in higher education (Dobozy & Nygaard, 2021, Chapter 2 in this book), our product innovation draws on a constructivist perception of learning. Perceiving learning as constructivist, we primarily see our product innovation as a means to support students in developing their English language skills, their business content knowledge and more importantly, their employability. Implementing and using a constructivist product innovation has implications for both students and teachers. We define innovative teaching and learning as an open and brave mindset that encourages both teachers and learners to respond to change creatively. To use new knowledge and understanding to experiment starts with the question: *"what is best for our learner?"* and then relies on collaboration, reflection and creativity to redefine the power/possibilities of learning. We argue that:

- innovative teaching occurs as a by-product of educators' continuous learning within a supportive community; and
- innovative learning occurs in between people when they feel safe with each other, casting constructive questions about the existing curricula, delivery, and value.

Reading this chapter, you will gain the following three insights:

1. an innovative way to approach language teaching that integrates content and language through a PBL pedagogy;
2. the challenges educators face in implementing new innovations in this context; and
3. what we can learn from the literature on business and management that can be applied to educational contexts.

Overview of main sections

In Section 1, we provide the background and context to our innovation. Section 2 details the practice of PBL, providing an overview of our curriculum and how we organised the innovation. Section 3 describes the outcomes of, and reflections upon, the innovation as they relate to the students and educators, while Section 4 details how we are moving forward. We will now describe what we define as our faculty-driven, disruptive innovation to the well-established language teaching program at our university in Tokyo, Japan.

Section 1: The background

As educators in the management faculty; with one author having an academic background in educational management, we felt it useful to take an interdisciplinary approach and explore the management literature, as well as education, to ground our innovation. In the management literature, innovation is seen as a process, more specifically, a problem-solving process (Dosi, 1982) and a diversified learning process whereby learning may arise from different issues: learning-by-using, learning-by-doing or learning-by-sharing (Cohen & Levinthal, 1990; Dogson, 1991). Taking a multidisciplinary definition – also included in Enomoto et al. (2021, Chapter 1 in this book) – innovation is the: *"multi-stage process whereby organisations transform ideas into new/improved products, service or processes, in order to advance, compete and differentiate themselves successfully in their marketplace"* (Baregheh et al., 2009:1334). In our context, our organisation (the university) is, to some extent, transforming our ideas into new/improved products (curriculum) to advance our learners and essentially broader society.

Idea Initiation

Initially, we felt there was a need for innovation as the Japanese government revised standards for education in 1991, and Japanese universities were given greater discretion in constructing their curriculum. In terms of English teaching, at most universities, this reform resulted in cookie-cutter type compartmentalization. In our context, since the unified curriculum was designed for students, regardless of their majors, it has been difficult to introduce even a small change to its content, so the need to change arose out of frustration with the system. We argued that our learners were obviously disengaged in their current freshmen English classes, proficiency levels were not increasing, and the overall Freshman English program of the university felt stunted and out of date. This meant we remained unable to equip students with the skills and mindset necessary for employability in the 21st century knowledge and skills economy (see Dobozy & Nygaard, 2021, Chapter 2 in this book, for a more in-depth explanation of 21st-century skills and the benefits of including them in curricula).

In our context, being disruptive, in terms of the management literature, is seen as positive. We are disrupting the current curriculum and working, bottom-up, to innovate and make change. In the context of management, *"disrupters first appeal to low-end or unserved customers and then migrate to the mainstream market"* (Christensen et al., 2015:6). In our context, we are attempting to appeal to our customers, both students and their future employers, by providing them with content knowledge, English language and employability skills. We are starting with one program, in the hope that it will expand and become more mainstream within the faculty and possibly the university. Similar to disruption in management, our disruption is not just a product but also a process, as it does not happen at one fixed point, rather it is an evolution over time.

Previous research on PBL in language education in Japan shows a positive effect. Williams (2009) reported that when taught, in an elective course with a PBL approach, university students with limited proficiency in English learned a great deal of English and academic skills, such as how to use the library and multimedia technology effectively. Kiyokawa (2018) reported on a small-scale qualitative research on PBL for learners at a university in Japan. The results showed that after completing a project, learners who had had no experience with or very limited knowledge of PBL reflected a positive attitude (such as build teamwork and learn deeply) towards this approach. This study concluded that learners benefit from PBL implemented into their instruction, as a tool to raise awareness of 21st century skills. Hennessy and Malcom (2017) reported on their PBL English language courses for non-English majors at a national university in Japan. Themes developed from their data analysis suggested both positive and negative attitudes towards PBL, such as unease, frustration, satisfaction, and cooperation. Their study is similar to ours in the way in which they engaged their fellow faculty to develop the course content collaboratively. However, a major difference is that their PBL course was 100% voluntary, unlike ours which is a core course, with credits necessary for graduation.

To conclude this section in our university context, PBL can: 1) help students become more familiar with basic business knowledge, 2) help improve their English proficiency, and 3) raise their awareness of the 21st-century skills necessary for employability. It has the potential to better educate the future generation of Japanese employees. The way we implement PBL is as a bottom-up, faculty-led, disruptive innovation to the current curriculum.

Section 2: The practice

2a: An introduction to the innovative practice

Our innovation was to incorporate a PBL pedagogy in the required, general English classroom for business students. This was so that our learners are not only engaged in English but also developing knowledge of business concepts that mirror what they are studying in their specialist courses in Japanese, and acquiring additional 21st-century skills necessary for their future career. We argue that this approach results in an increase in English proficiency and skills development, whilst also cultivating a collaborative and supportive classroom environment, where both learners and educators are active and keen to participate in class. The class is mandatory; we believe that this learning community helps alleviate the business students' reluctance towards learning English.

In our context, innovation was brought about by three educators, with varying educational and cultural experience. As knowledge guides actions and informs decisions, recognising the context of collaboration between different types of educators with varying experience is an important aspect of this study. Innovation is driven by people; educators share roles of being experts, process or relationship promoters as well as champions for the innovation. Institutional memory and identity as an educator are two key aspects when considering delivery of innovation in educational contexts.

In terms of institutional memory, two professors have worked at the institution over 15 years and thus they have an extensive institutional memory. They understand how the program 'was' and how it developed over the last 15 years which is an important foundation that can be brought to bear on present decisions (Walsh & Ungson, 1991). They benefit from more tacit knowledge; the personal, context specific knowledge of the organisation that is at times difficult to formulate and communicate. They share a sense of 'know how' of how the institution functions and their way of interacting with the institution is embedded within the minds of the people in the organisation.

Our identity as educators is shaped through our formal education and our cultural background. We are two educators born in Japan, but having experienced higher education overseas and one born in the UK with fifteen years' experience working in Japanese higher education. All of us involved in delivering our innovation have shared explicit knowledge of language teaching that is packaged, easily codified, communicable, and transferable. We have diverse cultural and academic backgrounds that converge; this inclusion of diversity and collaboration, we argue, contributes to the success of our innovation.

2b: A brief overview of the existing curriculum

PBL within the curriculum

Currently, at the university, there are three types of classes, English classes, *Kyoyo-kyouiku* classes (general liberal arts education) and *Senmon-kyouiku* classes (specialist subjects related to a major). Only 11 English classes out of 350 (3%) state in their syllabus that they have any kind of 'project' component. Additionally, just 9 courses out of 600 specialist courses in the university (1.5%) have a 'project' component. These figures include both core and optional courses. Thus, we argue that to bring in a full project-based, mandatory course for first years into the university is, of itself, an innovation.

The English curriculum

The university has a compulsory English curriculum for freshman and second-year students that has been run by the English Education Develop Center (EEDC) since 2006. The EEDC is a cross-faculty centre providing a unified curriculum. On the first day of class, the students are given a placement test and divided into 4/5 levels based on proficiency and split into their major (Business Administration, Human Sciences and Global Communications). All Business Administration students are split into eight classes of around 30 students. All freshmen, regardless of their major are required to take four 90-minute classes per week, for 15 weeks a semester, over two semesters. Overall, there has been no major overhaul or innovation in the curriculum since its inception in 2006.

The new PBL curriculum

The new PBL curriculum for the business faculty students consists of four projects taught in and through English, that the students must complete in groups, over two semesters. Each project is conducted in five stages: conception; definition and planning; launch and execution; performance and control, and project close, based on guidelines on project management from the Project Management Institute and their Project Management Body of Knowledge, more commonly known as PMBOK®. However, considering contextual factors, such as the number of classes per week, class time, semester length, and most importantly, learner characteristics, it was adapted for our context (Table 1). Each project starts with an orientation phase which explicitly teaches what is expected in the course and the skills needed for success in the course. Each project begins with a project question, drawn from tasks that are centred around the needs of the faculty, external stakeholders, and the learners; the key business concepts mirror themes that are introduced in the specialist classes. The themes reflect the transition between high school and university, which also aim to help the learners with no previous PBL experience feel comfortable in learning through PBL (Kiyokawa, 2018). This is achieved by incorporating projects that support student learning about the university and its surrounding areas, while encouraging them to think about jobs in the future.

Project Question & PMI Framework	*How can you promote the Faculty of Business Administration and the skills you will get for your future via a short PR video?*
Week 1 Initiation	As a whole class, students study about the 4Ps of Marketing, SWOT analysis, University PR, purpose of education and education management.
Week 2 Planning	Students work together in project teams to plan how they will answer the project question.
Week 3 & 4 Execution, Monitoring & Controlling	Students work on the project in their teacher facilitated project teams and engage in weekly reflection tasks.
Week 5 Closing	Students give a final presentation to share the outcome of the project. Reflection tasks, self-peer-evaluation.

Table 1: Sample Project.

When creating the above curriculum, we considered: 1) following the five stages (guidelines) in the syllabus coherently, 2) identifying the transferable skills needed for the learner to succeed in the course as well as their future, 3) setting appropriate project questions to meet the needs of all the parties involved, and 4) selecting appropriate themes/topics/projects for our particular student body.

2c: Organisation of the innovative practice

In this subsection, we will explain what goes on inside and outside the classroom for both the educators and learners. Firstly, educators take on multiple roles inside and outside the classroom, with the key roles including *researcher, communicator, persuader, curriculum planner, coach, facilitator, mediator, assessor, and cheerleader*. Outside the classroom, in order to successfully implement the innovation, the teacher needs to first be a *researcher;* to find out what the needs of the learners, the faculty, institution and society as a whole are and to understand the pedagogical changes necessary to implement PBL. Through focus groups with various stakeholders, the teacher can ascertain the needs to be met and gain an insight into the wider context within which the innovation will take place.

Secondly, the educators must take the roles of *communicator and persuader*, working with senior faculty and management to be given the freedom to implement the innovation. It is the responsibility of the educators to be able to clearly and concisely present their idea and show that they possess sufficient knowledge to successfully implement the innovation. Once the freedom to pilot and innovate has been granted, the teacher needs to *plan* the curriculum, prepare all necessary materials to run the innovation and keep in close contact with the team, to reflect and share experiences and encourage the progression of the innovation. Inside the classroom, the teacher no longer takes a traditional teaching role, but one of a *coach/facilitator*. They must learn how to *mediate* between students who may face disagreements in teamwork, present lesson and project objectives in a way that the learners can comprehend, be objective in their ability to *assess* students, and support and *cheerlead* for students as they navigate the innovation.

Regarding the learners, outside the classroom, they need to become *independent, autonomous learners*, with advanced time management skills, communication skills and a willingness to step out of their comfort zone.

They need to *cooperate* and *communicate* with their classmates on homework assignments and work as a team. They need to use technology to communicate with their peers and take leadership roles when appropriate. All these skills need to be taught, practiced and developed, as often students do not begin university with this skill set. This new value is communicated to the students through having them engage with the career center on campus, communicate with other faculty members and their *sempai* (senior students) and alumni, thus extending the concept of social constructivism outside the classroom. Being largely used to traditional Confucius style classrooms, functioning as passive receivers of knowledge, seldom engaging in critical discussions with other classmates or their teachers, nor initiating their learning actively, students need to become open to a more Socratic experience. For them, the Socratic classroom may feel like utter chaos, with a lack of teacher-led order or control.

2d: Preparation for the innovative practice

This section explores how we prepared for the innovation and the materials necessary to implement the innovation from the educator's perspective. Through our process, nine important considerations emerged from our reflections when developing and implementing our innovation (1. recognition, 2. needs & engagement, 3. idea development, 4. environment, 5. technology, 6. materials, 7. implementation, 8. reflection, 9. communication). The first two elements of recognition and needs and engagement should be placed first, though there is not necessarily an order to the latter half of the preparation, owing to many of the elements being inter-reliant.

Recognition

Innovation potentials are the triggers for innovation. In the business field, there are many sources of innovation potential, for example, client needs, market environment, trends and future projections, new technologies, individual strengths and digitisation. In our educational context, the teachers initially recognised the need for innovation by considering the market environment and future trends. To ascertain the innovation potential of our students and to further develop the basis for the recognition, we needed to conduct a needs analysis, to assess where we were and plan where we wanted to go.

Needs & Engagement

We used a variety of strategies to ascertain the needs of our learners, the program itself, and additional stakeholders. We conducted three focus groups; one with the English teachers in our faculty, one with our business faculty colleagues, and one with the university administrative support staff of various sections of the university. Each focus group was transcribed and analysed to find common themes among how the stakeholders viewed the English program, the skills of the business students and the needs of society. In addition, we conducted a needs analysis survey of the learners themselves and a general survey for English teachers who had taught business faculty students in the past. For anyone seeking to implement an innovation, we argue it is vital to ascertain how the internal stakeholders view a potential innovation as it is one means of gaining support for implementation and finding projects that fit the needs of the learners.

Idea Development

Based on the needs analysis, the next step was to develop the curriculum. In our discussions, we worked through various ideas of what kind of curriculum would be most appropriate and decided on PBL. We drew up a list of potential projects and then looked at what kind of structure would be most suitable, settling on a loose version of the Project Management Institute framework for PBL lessons, however we adapted it to our context.

Environment

We soon realised that the classroom environment would play an integral part of the success of the innovation (for further details on how different types of classroom layout relate to communication see Forasacco, Chapter 4 in this book). A traditional classroom, with desks arranged facing the front, would not be conducive to the kind of collaboration and conversations necessary for project work. Thus, we needed to negotiate with the academic affairs and facilities administrators to be timetabled in an appropriate classroom. A co-working space is when people assemble in a neutral space to work independently on different projects, or in groups on the same projects. We envisioned a classroom or space on campus that replicated this new co-working style, with circular tables, access to internet, space to move around between groups; generally a non-traditionally academic layout that is more conducive to collaboration and close interactions. We found many groups chose to work outside the classroom in other spaces on campus that better suited their needs.

Technology

Generally, consideration should be given to the extent to which students are trained to use technology. It is worth conducting a small survey on the students to discover their degree of comfort with specific devices and tools and if they have access to them. A simple online task could also be given to check their proficiency. For our students, in addition to the physical environment of the classroom, we needed to ensure that the multimedia tools would be available to them. It was vital that the room was fully connected to Wi-Fi, that students had access to mobile phones, and had easy access to laptops, desktop computers and video equipment. The university library has a laptop and iPad rental system which was useful. However, we encountered problems with the speed of the Wi-Fi and the teacher consoles were not updated with the latest software to support the websites we used.

Materials

As there was no textbook, we needed to create handouts, PowerPoints and additional materials to make the course successful. We took a somewhat ad-hoc approach to creating materials on a weekly basis, based on how the learners responded to each lesson, the next step in the project process and time taken for each section. The three instructors shared ideas and materials for each class, by explaining how each used the materials via email and sharing the actual materials in Google Drive. In this way, each teacher was able to share, collaborate and adapt their materials for their specific group of students while also maintaining the aims and integrity of the overall course.

In addition, a project class of this nature also requires learners to have access to resources from which to create products and services. Specifically, students need access to stationery such as large pieces of paper, pens, markers and glue, and various creative tools. Therefore, we made boxes of project kits that we could bring to class and that were available outside of class hours for the students to access freely. Aside from traditional teaching materials, we also wanted students to engage with and identify other available resources at hand, that could link to their projects. As we have an English Lounge on campus, which is designed to support autonomous learning and language practice, we envisioned students using and interacting with resources and additional materials in that space, as they worked on their projects.

Implementation

We successfully ran the initial pilot classes over 30 weeks of the school year at three different levels during 2019–2020. A second pilot was conducted at the start of 2020, however, the implementation stage was radically different, as all classes had to be held online due to the Covid-19 pandemic. In this case, two pilot classes were run via Microsoft Teams. Students were put in virtual groups to work on digital projects. During this time of emergency remote teaching (ERT) we were able to cover the same content as the previous year but had to make exceptions for issues with technology. It was estimated via a survey that 1/3 of the learners did not have access to a laptop or tablet and were engaging in classes via their cell phone. Thus, in terms of implementation, we quickly ascertained the challenges in running the same kind of course but 100% online. Initial feedback and class evaluation surveys suggest that the students were relatively comfortable with the experience online and coped better than we had expected. We did not have to deviate from the content at all and were able to find workable solutions in lieu of working face to face.

Reflection

As a means of self-reflection, we used several different tools; journaling, post-lesson email feedback, informal chats and meet ups, and formal focus groups. As soon after each lesson as possible, teachers shared their lesson plans and reflections with each other (an analysis of the emails sent throughout the academic year can be found in Section 3b).

Communication

We also needed to be mindful of how to report the findings and progress of the innovation to other stakeholders. We did this by feedback to the English Center via regular meetings, casual anecdotal conversations with colleagues, bringing the innovation on table at crucial meetings with senior management, and a presentation to the faculty and other stakeholders.

Section 3: The outcome

In order to triangulate the data, we collected feedback from several different sources using various approaches to gauge the learner perspective on the innovation and their outcomes. To examine the learner perspective, we adapted Zuniga's (2019) epistemological stance based on the concept of constructivism to ascertain how individuals construct knowledge based on their experience of the project. We used data collection approaches that aligned with the theory of autonomous learning; based on the concepts of learner responsibility and independence, and how they reshape the view that the learner is responsible for learning, teachers do not abdicate their responsibilities of teaching in the language learning process and, on the contrary, teachers become the primary agents on fostering the development of learner autonomy within the classroom context. The questions we asked students were grounded in the ideas of self-reflection and self-assessment, calling on them to assess their fundamental beliefs and assumptions about learning themselves. We were also driven by the theory of self-regulation, which refers to self-generated thoughts, feelings, and behaviours oriented towards attaining goals (Zimmerman, 2000).

In addition, for the teacher perspective, we have taken a co/autoethnographic approach (Taylor & Coia, 2009) as our methodology for exploring teacher innovation and reflection, as it helps to show how we, the participants were engaged and: *"the intersection between theory and practice, research and pedagogy"* (LaBoskey, 2004:827). Our research was: *"generated from the lived experiences, past and present, of [us as] teacher[s]"* (Coia & Taylor, 2009:11). Throughout the course of the year we wrote to each other, sharing lesson plans, reflections and narratives of experience, met face to face for reflection meetings, and a more formal post-course focus group. As Coia and Taylor (2009:12) ascertained in their co/autobiographical research the: *"process is messy. Sometimes the writing flows and other times it is laboured. Our conversations often help us to get through the tensions."* As we are experiencing change and innovation in our pedagogy and action and agency as educators, we expected there to be tension to deal with.

Part of our teaching innovation in this context was to stress the importance of reflection in our teaching and learning journey through PBL. In the same vein as Dewey (1933), we use reflection as a means by which we can act with foresight and devise a plan based on our learning from past classroom experiences. Moon (1999) puts forth a list of behaviours which characterise reflective practice. These include, the mental processing of reflection; a critical element; self-development or professional development; emotional involvement; or, enhanced by the sharing of reflection with others. This collective reflection as seen through the emails and focus group, is the way we gain collective knowledge of the innovation in our classroom and the change process.

3a: Student Perspective

We conducted surveys in all classes (one per project, per class), peer evaluations, open-answer reflective writing tasks and a focus group at the end of the course to ascertain the student perspectives of PBL. Figure 2 shows the conceptualisation of the learner perspectives and Table 2 the evidence of the learners' metacognitive awareness. Referring to the literature, we could ascertain that learners were engaged in not just learning English and business content, but also social and emotional learning (SEL): self-awareness, self-management, social awareness, relationship skills, and responsible decision-making.

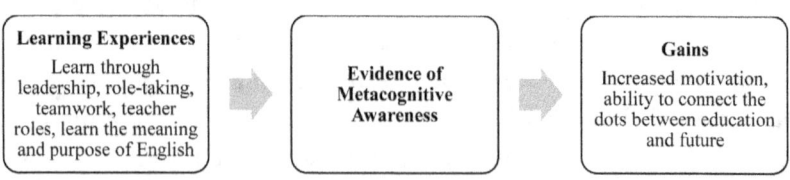

Figure 2: Conceptualisation of Learner Experiences & Gains.

Previous research has shown that SEL is one learning strategy that developed from the need to improve the social interactions among learners when working together, aimed at enhancing learners' ability to apply what they know, as well as their attitudes and skills, to *"understand and manage emotions...establish and maintain positive relationships, and make responsible decisions"* (Weissberg & Cascarino, 2013:10).

Through the analysis, it was immediately apparent that the learners could clearly articulate their learning experiences, stating examples of how they learned through leadership, through teamwork, taking different roles, and through observing the role of their teacher (that they recognised differed from other student—teacher interactions). They could also express the meaning and purpose of English, providing strong evidence of metacognitive awareness. We saw that learners were "thinking about thinking." They were aware of their acquired knowledge and were often able to verbalise and reflect on their own learning (see Box 1). Through this, we could see gains in increased motivation and an ability to connect the dots between their education and their future career.

Learner self-identified issues	Learner self-identified solutions to overcome issues in future projects	Learner self-identified gains
English language proficiency.	Better collaboration.	Improved communication skills.
Communication.	More communication.	Better collaboration skills.
Technical (PC skills, etc.).	Self-help.	Improved teamwork skills.
Collaboration.	Delegation of tasks.	English proficiency.
Absences (in the lower level classes).		Autonomy.
		Planning skills.
		ICT skills.

Table 2: Evidence of Learners' Metacognitive Awareness.

Our findings were similar to those of several other researchers. Zuniga (2019) examined American high school students' perceptions on collaborative work in a project-based learning class. She noted that in PBL:

"emotional issues are one of the foundational obstacles to collaboration in teamwork versus loosely working together in a group" (Zuniga: 2019:11). However, she found that these obstacles can be overcome when students increase their positive perceptions of working with others and better understand their emotional intelligence related skills. It implies that if students can learn to manage their emotions, there could be more improved collaborative experiences, as they can learn through social interactions(Vygotsky, 1978, cited in Zuniga, 2019).

Similar to our study, Styla and Michalopoulou (2016) studied the effectiveness of the teacher's role in the development of the social skills of high school students using the PBL method within their new curriculum of literature. They found that social skills of low level learners can be increased when taught through PBL. Such skills include inclusion of shy and isolated learners into cooperative activities and introverted ones gaining confidence. We also found initial evidence of this, however a deeper analysis in future studies is warranted. Styla and Michalopoulou (2016) also noted the importance of harmonisation of the teachers with the requirements of PBL as they help facilitate such social learning. Interestingly, we found that it is through the teacher collaboration "process" that helped shape this "product" of a PBL curriculum. Similarly, Visschers-Pleijers and colleagues (2006) found that in a PBL setting collaborative knowledge construction amongst learners occurred more frequently than any one learner's elaboration of knowledge. Additionally, Nokes-Malach *et al.* (2015) theorise various social and cognitive mechanisms exist to support and to cause failure in settings where there is collaboration among learners. Social mechanisms that influence failure in collaborative learning include: (a) social loafing, or the belief held by some learners that other group members will pick up their slack and therefore they do not feel responsible for contribution to the co-production of knowledge; and (b) fear of evaluation by group members, stemming from a sense of discouragement from contributing to the conversation due to fear of being negatively evaluated by their group members (Nokes-Malach et al., 2015).

- *I was reminded of the importance of communication. Since the project was in an English subject, I thought that language skills and slide making skills would be important. But more than that, I felt that we need to work together as a team to complete the project and help each other.*
- *What I learned in this class was the ability to communicate and produce something in groups. I improved my communication skills by up working strangers and talking to them. The more times we did this, the more conversations we had, and the more we got to know each other after only three times of group work, the better chance we had of getting to know each other. I wasn't sure if I would be able to make friends after entering the university, but I'm glad that I made friends in this class. I wasn't very good at meeting new people, but I was able to open up to them in a normal way, and I think that communication skills are important. I realised that we can work smoothly in group work by getting to know each other first and then creating the work.*

Box. 1: Learner Reflections.

Our findings are also in line with the underlying philosophies of another component of our university's English program, as mentioned previously, our English Lounge. This is a dedicated "third space" on campus for students to interact in English and develop social and cultural capital. It was based on the concept from Vygotsky (1978) that individuals learn through social interaction. We found that learners were able to tie some aspects of the projects in our course to the English Lounge and also used the space to work.

Our biggest take away from this initial analysis is that our learners are displaying a developing metacognitive awareness, that is in line with other research on the topic and to a lesser extent, gains in language proficiency and business knowledge.

3b: Teacher perspective – Our reflections

In order to ascertain the teacher perspective, we utilised two kinds of data: 1) an analysis of weekly email reports and 2) an auto-ethnographic reflection analysis. This section of the chapter presents the perspective of this team of teachers--what the teachers in this team 'did' during the pilot program, how they did it and how they felt about it.

Chapter 13

Discourses of collaboration

Discourses are embodied in sets of texts which come in a wide variety of forms (Grant *et al.*, 1998; Taylor & Van Every, 1993) and researchers must examine sets of texts that describe the organisational realities (Phillips & Hardy, 2002). In this research, we explore two conversations: one conversation through weekly email exchanges and one conversation through an auto-ethnographic focus group interview. A conversation, in this instance, is defined as a set of texts produced as part of an interaction between two or more people and are linked together both temporally and rhetorically (Ford & Ford, 1995).

Through these conversations, we can see the role of language in the organisation and how it deals with change (in this case, pedagogical and curriculum change). Ford and Ford (1995) argue that the forms of conversation associated with initiating organisational innovation and change are those that establish a need for change. Using an analysis of the weekly emails, we establish the process of change and through the auto-ethnographic interview we present a reflection on the change.

1) Weekly email analysis

The analysis focused on what Perer *et al.* (2005) describes as archived, organisational messages. From April 1st, 2019 to January 10th, 2020, 129 emails were extracted for analysis. Taking a socio-centric perspective, we looked at our collection of email messages as the raw data to help identify the many facets of the collaboration and how we processed change and extracted patterns of its structure.

2) Auto-ethnographic focus group

We also engaged in an auto-ethnographic focus group held for one-hour, at the end of the academic year. The focus group was transcribed and analysed. As a result of the coding and analysis of the emails and focus group, there were three main overarching and closely integrated themes that emerged: a) teacher identity, b) teacher agency, and c) program delivery. Teacher identity refers to the occasions where the teachers questioned their identity; attempting to ascertain what made them capable teachers who were able to deliver innovation. Teacher agency refers to the capacity of teachers to act purposefully and constructively to direct their professional growth and contribute to the growth of their colleagues and highlights discussions throughout the year when teachers showed their capability for growth. Finally, delivery refers to exchanges where the teachers discussed how to implement the innovation (Table 3).

A) Teacher Identity	Experience	The experience of the teacher (as a teacher) and experience of the teacher (as a learner). The teachers explored how they reflected on and felt about each aspect and to what extent their prior experience had an impact on them now as educators.
	Skills	The teachers debated their own skills and the skills of their learners, including how to measure them and how to classify them.
	Self-confidence	The teachers questioned and exhibited increasing levels of self-confidence throughout the journey.
	Value and purpose of education	The teachers discussed at length the value and purpose of what they were doing; continually questioning its value for the learners' future.
	Teacher Role	Actions that the teachers took in the classroom called them to question their roles, such as how they monitor and facilitate group work, how they take leadership of the class, mediate disagreements between learners and how they give praise.

B) Teacher Agency	Interaction with external stakeholders	Teachers stepped up to continually communicate with colleagues in the faculty and English center. They shared progress and examples of best practice.
	Emotions & Feelings (teachers)	Teachers used the focus group and email communication to express their emotions (Confusion, Fear, Questioning identity as educator. Lack of confidence/self-doubt, Surprise, Excitement, Frustration, Guilt, Enjoyment, Stress, Exhaustion, business, amazement).
	Collaboration	Teachers shared resources, collaborated on ideas, helped each other out with material and idea development.
	Visioning	Teachers shared the same visions; a desire for better facilities, images of what a future program and curriculum would look like.
C) Program Delivery	Image Reality	Teachers discussed their expectations and the source of their expectations, as they relate to their experience.
	Evaluation	Teachers shared thoughts on course objectives: -measurement of / -level of tangibility / Peer-evaluation; -issues surrounding how to evaluate learners and the program.
	Preparedness	Teachers questioned their level of preparedness, how to manage time for preparation and in the classroom and how to develop materials.
	Learner Experience	Teachers reflected on the learners' level of maturity, issues with transition from high school and how that would impact the delivery, their ability to reflect, their learning styles, their personality and their attendance.
	English	Teachers discussed at length the use of English in the classroom, how to police English use (if at all), discussed explicit versus implicit teaching.
	Overall Curriculum	Teachers questioned how to fit the innovation with other courses both English and subject courses (drawing cross-curricular comparisons). And how to help learners make connections with the real world.

Table 3: Key themes of teacher discourse during the innovation.

By reflecting on our exchanges, it became obvious that we made certain choices and took actions to make change. Many of the choices we made were mediated by our identity and experience as educators. What we purposefully do (agency) and how we see ourselves and our roles as teachers (identity) dynamically interact during the delivery of the innovation. It was particularly insightful to read through the transcript of the focus group and analyse the email exchanges to see the process of how we felt and what our primary concerns were moving forward.

What is of most importance in these findings, is that innovation in this context was not an individual journey, it required collaboration, nurturing, and essentially a deep trust among those involved in order to successfully navigate the stages.

Section 4: Moving forward

To move forward we need to reflect on our findings and have applied them to the literature on innovation in management. We argue that the overriding factor to the success or failure of a disruptive innovation in this context is collaboration. More specifically, the role of trust in innovation management, coupled with the importance of social capital and presence of learning communities that are open to innovation within organisations.

Within an educational institution, collaboration is often used for the purpose of making important educational decisions. Research suggests that in professional learning communities, change is more likely to be effective when those responsible for implementation and delivery are included in the shared decision-making process (Louis et al., 1996; Preskill & Torres, 1999).

As such, institutions often call for educators to work in self-managing teams to develop goals, curricula, instructional strategies, and staff development programs; known as a form of distributed leadership. In this case, we came together to form a self-managing team tasked with overhauling the current English language business curriculum. This approach is suitable for an organisation that wants to take a flat hierarchical structure, filled with skilled and motivated professionals, who group as necessary to become self-managing, flexible teams. In such teams, there are often individual leaders and individuals who have strong interpersonal connections. The conversations that occur within these teams, becomes the *"medium for interaction; analysis of discourse becomes, then, analysis of what people do"* (Potter, 1996:146). As was evident in the teacher reflections and their engagement in the innovation, there were strong interpersonal connections between us. We are planning on expanding these self-managing teams through collaboration and continuous professional development (similar to that presented by Scott-Webber *et al.*, 2021, Chapter 3 in this book); we also see value in engagement and collaboration.

In practical terms, in order to spread our findings within our institution we have already begun to hold professional development and faculty development sessions and have sought to gain support from senior management by applying for funding to raise awareness and disseminating this practice in various forms. As for the next step, we hope educators at other universities in Japan, who are interested in PBL, can learn about our journey through academic publications and presentations, as well as through official PR activities conducted by our university. Furthermore, we are interested in reaching out to schools both inside and outside Japan that are using PBL, to set up joint projects, and ideally would like to engage with industry, both domestic and international, on collaborative materials development (akin to Heikkinen, 2021, Chapter 12 in this book).

Based on our study we can share what we think are the seven prerequisites for innovation in similar contexts, those being: 1) capacity and knowledge among faculty and staff, 2) a clear organisational structure that facilitates change and innovation, 3) strong leadership and opportunities for communication within the institution, 4) creativity and dedication of individual teachers, 5) opportunities for organisational learning, 6) shared value: ensuring others buy-in to the innovation and 7) evidence of sustainability; ability to ascertain the extent to which the change is sustainable. To conclude, Figure 3 summarises our experience of the innovation.

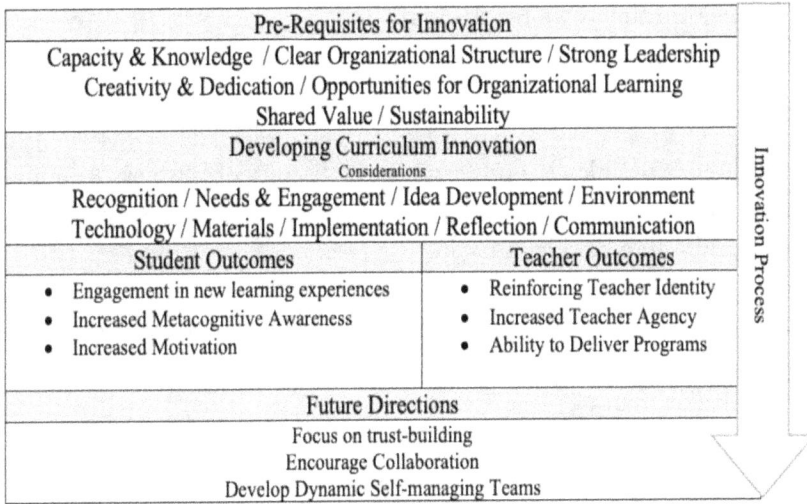

Figure 3: Summary of our Innovation Process.

Conclusion

In this case of innovation in teaching and learning, we used the concept of disruptive innovation to develop a concept (in this instance a new PBL curriculum) that created new value in our institution, by disrupting the existing curriculum (Bower & Christensen, 1995). We have offered an innovative way to approach language teaching that integrates content and language through a PBL pedagogy. We have also learned that challenges related to teacher identity, teacher agency, and program delivery can be resolved when there is a collaborative and supportive learning community. Finally, we recognised the importance of taking an interdisciplinary approach, by engaging with literature in the fields of business and management, and how that can be applied to educational contexts for a better understanding of the innovation process.

We aim for this innovation to be incremental, in that it will gradually build improvements into the already existing English language teaching curriculum. This chapter has laid out the process of our bottom-up innovation and after reflection and analysis, has provided an insight into the lessons that can be learned from the experience and how they relate to the literature on innovation in business and management. We hope this chapter has inspired other educators to collaborate and be agents of change within their own institutions.

About the Authors

Sarah Louisa Birchley is a professor in the Faculty of Business Administration, Toyo Gakuen University, Tokyo, Japan. She can be contacted at this e-mail: sarah.birchley@tyg.jp

Keiko Omura is a professor in the Faculty of Business Administration, Toyo Gakuen University, Tokyo, Japan. She can be contacted at this e-mail: keiko.omura@tyg.jp

Kayoko Yamauchi is an assistant professor in the Faculty of Business Administration, Toyo Gakuen University, Tokyo, Japan. She can be contacted at this e-mail: kayoko.yamauchi@tyg.jp

Bibliography

Alfieri, L., Nokes-Malach, T. J. & Schunn, C. D. (2013). Learning through case comparisons: A meta-analytic review. *Educational Psychologist, 48*(2), pp. 87–113.

Baregheh, A., Rowley, J. & Sambrook, S. (2009). Towards a multidisciplinary definition of innovation. *Management decision, 47*(8), pp. 1323–1339.

Bower, J. & Christensen, C. (1995). Disruptive technologies- catching the wave. *Harvard Business Review, 73*(1), pp. 43–51.

Brown, H. (2017). Why and why now? Understanding the rapid rise of English-medium instruction in higher education in Japan. *Journal of International Studies and Regional Development, 8*, pp. 1–16.

Buck Institute for Education (2020). Retrieved from: https://www.pblworks.org/

Christensen, C. M., Horn, M. B. & Johnson, C. W. (2011). *Disrupting class: How disruptive innovation will change the way the world learns*. Vol. 1. New York: McGraw-Hill.

Cohen, W. M. & Levinthal, D. A. (1990). Absorptive capacity: A new perspective on learning and innovation. *Administrative Science Quarterly*, pp. 128–152.

Coia, L. & Taylor, M. (2009). Co/autoethnography: Exploring our teaching selves collaboratively. In Fitzgerald, L., Heston, M. & Tidwell, D. (Eds.) (1990), *Research Methods for the Self-study of Practice*, pp. 3–16. Dordrecht: Springer Verlag.

Cook, V. (1999). Going beyond the native speaker in language teaching. *TESOL Quarterly, 33*(2), pp. 185–209.

Dewey, J. (1896). The reflex arc concept in psychology. *Psychological Review, 3*(4), pp. 357–370.

Dewey, J. (1933). *How we think.* New York: Heath & Co.

Dobozy, E., and Nygaard, C. (2021). A learning-centred, five-tier model of innovation in higher education. In Enomoto, K., Warner, R. & Nygaard, C. (Eds.), *Teaching and Learning Innovations in Higher Education*, pp. 19–46. Oxfordshire, UK: Libri Publishing Ltd.

Dogson, M., (1991). *The management of technological learning: Lessons from a biotechnology company.* Berlin: Walter & Gruyter.

Dosi G. (1982). Technological paradigms and technological trajectories. *Research Policy, 11*, pp. 147–162.

Enomoto, K., Warner, R. & Nygaard, C. (2021). What drives teaching and learning innovations in higher education? In Enomoto, K., Warner, R. & Nygaard, C. (Eds.), *Teaching and Learning Innovations in Higher Education*, pp. 1–18. Oxfordshire, UK: Libri Publishing Ltd.

Ford, J.D. and Ford, L.W. (1995). The role of conversations in producing intentional change in organizations, *Academy of Management Review, 20*(3), pp. 541–570.

Grant, D., Keenoy, T. & Oswick, C. (1998). Introduction: Organizational discourse: Of diversity, dichotomy and multidisciplinarity. In Grant, D. Keenoy, T. & Oswick, C. (Eds.) (1998), *Discourse and Organisation*, pp. 1–14. London: Sage.

Gray, B. 1985. Conditions facilitating interorganizational collaboration, *Human Relations, 38*(10), pp. 911–936.

Heikkinen, S. (2021). An innovative model for university-industry collaboration in course design and delivery. In Enomoto, K., Warner, R. & Nygaard, C. (Eds.), *Teaching and Learning Innovations in Higher Education*, pp. 257–271. Oxfordshire, UK: Libri Publishing Ltd.

Hennessy, C. & Malcom, W. (2017). Learner voices through journal in a Japanese University STEM project-based Learning class for EFL learners. Presented at 8th International Conference on Language, Literature, Culture and Education, Bali, Indonesia, 19th & 20th September, 2017. *IJLLCE journal, 8*, pp. 39–48.

Imafuku, R. (2011). Japanese first-year PBL learners' learning processes: A classroom discourse analysis. In Bridges, S., McGrath, Whitehill, T. (Eds.), *Problem-Based Learning in Clinical Education: The Next Generation*, pp. 153–170. Dordrecht: Springer.

Kiyokawa, S. (2018). The power of project-based learning in a Japanese EFL Classroom. *JSLA*, 10(7), pp. 7–84.

LaBoskey, V. K. (2008). The fragile strengths of self-study: Making bold claims and clear connections. In Aubusson P., Schuck S. (Eds.) (2008), *Teacher Learning and Development. Self Study of Teaching and Teacher Education Practices, vol 3*, pp. 251–262. Dordrecht: Springer.

Loughran, J. M., Hamilton, L. LaBoskey, V. K. & Russell, T. (Eds.) (2004), *International handbook of self-study of teaching and teacher education practices*, Part 1, pp. 69–102). Dordrecht: Kluwer Academic Publishers.

Louis, K. S., Marks, H. M. & Kruse, S. (1996). Teachers' professional community in restructuring schools. *American Educational Research Journal*, 33(4), 757–798.

Moon, J. A. (1999). *Reflection in learning and professional development, theory and practice*. London: Kogan Page.

Nokes-Malach, T. J., Richey, J. E. & Gadgil, S. (2015). When is it better to learn together? Insights from research on collaborative learning. *Educational Psychology Review*, 27(4), pp. 645–656.

Perer, A. & Smith, M. A. (2006). Contrasting portraits of email practices: visual approaches to reflection and analysis. In *Proceedings of the working conference on Advanced visual interfaces*. Venezia, Italy, May 23–26, 2006, pp. 389–395.

Phillips, N. & Hardy, C. (2002). *Discourse analysis: Investigating processes of social construction* (Vol. 50). London: Sage.

Potter, J. (1996) *Representing reality: Discourse, rhetoric and social construction*. London: Sage.

Preskill, H. & Torres, R. T. (1999). *Evaluative inquiry for Learning in organizations,*. London: Sage.

Scott-Webber, L., P. Loeffelman, Denison, M. & Runyan, D. (2021). Is higher education ready for the transformed learner coming from 9–12? A case study. In Enomoto, K., Warner, R. & Nygaard, C. (Eds.), *Teaching and Learning Innovations in Higher Education*, pp. 47–82. Oxfordshire, UK: Libri Publishing Ltd.

Styla, D. & Michalopoulou, A. (2016). Project based learning in literature: The teacher's new role and the development of learners' social skills in upper secondary education. *Journal of Education and Learning*, 5(3), pp. 307–314.

Taylor, J. R. & Van Every, E. J. (2014). *When organization fails: Why authority matters*. New York: Routledge.

Taylor, M. & Coia, L. (2009). Co/autoethnography: Investigating teachers in relation. In Lassonde, C. A., Galman, S. & Kosnik, C. (Eds.) (2009), *Self-study research methodologies for teacher educators*, pp. 169–186. Rotterdam: Sense Publishers.

Visschers-Pleijers, A. J., Dolmans, D. H., Wolfhagen, I. H. & van der Vleuten, C. P. (2005). Development and validation of a questionnaire to identify learning-oriented group interactions in PBL. *Medical Teacher*, 27(4), pp. 375–381.

Vygotsky, L. S. (1978). *Mind in society: The development of higher psychological processes*. MA.: Harvard University Press.

Walsh, J. P. & Ungson, G. R. (1991). Organisational memory. *Academy of Management Review*, 16, pp. 57–91.

Weissberg, R. P. & Cascarino, J. (2013). Academic learning + social-emotional learning= national priority. *Phi Delta Kappan*, 95(2), pp. 8–13.

Williams, S. M. (2009). Learning together: project-based learning in the university classroom. College of Integrated Human and Social Welfare Studies, 43, pp. 127–142.

Yokoyama, K. & Birchley, S.L. (2020). *Transnational entrepreneurship: Japanese self-initiated expatriate entrepreneurs in South East Asia*. Dordrecht: Springer Verlag.

Zimmerman, B. J. (2006). Development and adaptation of expertise: The role of self-regulatory processes and beliefs. *The Cambridge Handbook of Expertise and Expert Performance*, 186, pp. 705–722.

Zuniga, A. (2019). *Harnessing emotions: The impact of developing ability emotional intelligence skills on perceptions of collaborative teamwork in a project-based learning class*. [Unpublished doctoral dissertation]. Arizona State University.

Chapter 14

Facilitating Active Student Learning Using Innovative Approaches in Pre-Service Teacher Education

Lana YL Khong

Introduction

With my chapter, I contribute to this book, *Teaching and Learning Innovations in Higher Education*, as I show how an innovative and authentic lesson design is used to facilitate active learning opportunities for novice student teachers. 'Active learning' is defined as a theory and method of teaching that engages students in the process of thinking meaningfully and deliberately about, and then co-creating, their learning experiences (Davidson, 2018). Furthermore, in their seminal work, Bonwell and Eison (1991) extend the definition of active learning as an approach that focuses more on developing students' skills than on transmitting information and requires student participation in activities necessitating higher-order thinking, as well as an exploration of their attitudes and values. Besides, 'collaborative learning' is the term used by Smith and MacGregor (1992) to describe joint intellectual effort by students, or students and teachers together, thus forming the environment in which meaning can be actively created (Dobozy & Nygaard, 2021, Chapter 2 in this book). Selected examples of innovative lesson designs are described, including scenario-planning, experiential games, and role-plays that effectively engage undergraduate and postgraduate student teachers with the course content.

Being guided to think 'out of the box' helps Millennial (also known as Generation Y, born 1980 to 1994) and younger Generation Z (born 1995 to 2012) student teachers understand, interpret, apply and thus, be more likely to 'imprint' factual and theoretical curriculum material in ways that become more real and concrete for them. In addition, this pedagogical approach requires hands-on practice in planning and participating in lessons that are more activity-oriented and student-centred. This serves student teachers well for when they start working with their Generation Z and Gen Alpha (born 2013 to 2025) students in school during their Practicum, and post-graduation as qualified teachers.

The underlying framework for this core module in teacher preparation is one of social constructivism and active collaborative learning design, where student-designed and student-centred seminars completely replace more conventional instructor-directed lessons. This, in turn, requires the tutor to play a facilitator role, providing vital support and guidance throughout the process of seminar preparation. This account reflects my personal 'take' on the innovation. Although I am the coordinator of the teaching team, individual tutors have their own approaches, some being more didactic than others. As academics, most prefer to have the autonomy to decide how to approach the course. As such, the model described here is more about collaborative learning among students and with one tutor and a group of students, than about colleagues working together to teach a course.

My innovation is a process innovation in teaching a core Education module for trainee teachers. The innovation is a learning approach requiring students to work collaboratively to design interactive seminars for their peers. It needs to be borne in mind, that such interactivity is not of itself particularly innovative in some teaching and learning traditions. However, in the Singaporean tradition of teacher-centredness, memorisation and rote learning, it is this active-learning context which is innovative of itself. The innovation was implemented in Diploma- and Degree-level teacher training programs offered at the National Institute of Education in Singapore. Referring to the learning-centred five-tier model of innovation in higher education (Dobozy & Nygaard, 2021, Chapter 2 in this book), my process innovation draws on a social constructivist perception of learning. Perceiving learning as a constructivist, I primarily see my process innovation as a means to empower small groups of learners to work independently. They do so by responding to one another's perspectives and ideas while collaboratively designing a learning 'package' for their peers. In this learning-doing-sharing process, they engage with the curriculum in more authentic ways. Thus, implementing and using a constructivist process innovation has implications for both learning and teaching.

Reading this chapter, you may gain the following three insights:

1. Engaging students in active learning mode requires a tutor to have a mindset that encourages open-ended exploration and less structured outcomes. Tutors will ideally, therefore, embody an inquiring and curious stance as a co-learner rather than as a subject matter expert. As the innovative approach calls for some risk-taking on the part of students, the tutor needs to skilfully create a safe learning environment where students feel there are no 'wrong' answers or 'stupid' questions.

2. The student-teacher learning experience is more meaningful when they have multiple opportunities to reconnect with memories of earlier school experiences. Examining their own prior 'lived' knowledge, they can develop empathy for future students, many of whom may have similar experiences.

3. As Millennials are comfortable moving in digital spaces, the active learning approach leverages on this ability when they are given autonomy to create learning experiences involving games and role-plays within the prescribed curriculum. The freedom to design creative learning spaces engenders engagement, curiosity and excitement in learning, as well as a sense of empowerment which can drive deeper learning.

Overview of main sections

In Section 1 of the chapter, I discuss the context in which this innovative approach was developed. In Section 2, I outline several examples of how the innovation process works in practice, based on actual student group applications of the process. Section 3 shares student feedback on how the development of this learning approach has affected their learning experiences and outcomes, and finally, Section 4 imagines how it may evolve going forward, taking into consideration the enhanced calibre of students we are currently receiving into our teacher education programs.

Chapter 14

Section 1: The background

My teaching institution receives two to four cohorts annually of pre-service (pre-credentialed) students from diverse disciplinary backgrounds. The faculty run Educational and Academic Studies modules as well as supervise the Practicum to hone students' pedagogical, IT and content skills. If student performance is consistently satisfactory in all these aspects, the university then credentials them as fit-to-be teachers, serving primary and secondary schools, pre-university and junior colleges. Student cohorts (organised by program) range in size from 80 to 250 at any one time and the programs run from one to two years depending on the certifications and specialisations students are enrolled for.

The course I discuss, in this chapter, is a compulsory core module that all pre-service student teachers take in addition to their academic subject content, pedagogy and service-learning modules. It encourages students to explore the implications of being a teacher in diverse 'social contexts' of schooling in Singapore. These include types, levels, and expectations of schools, as well as gender, age, ability and family environments of students. Before the revamping of the module to its current form, the content was taught in mass lectures once a week, with smaller weekly tutorial classes to allow for teacher-led discussion around specific topics raised in the lectures. Students were also required to sit for final written examinations at the end of the module. Course coordinators felt this was inadequate in the face of evolving social, demographic and logistical concerns, and the decision was made to do away with the didactic, 'one-size-fits-all' mass delivery approach. With increasingly complex school contexts, student teachers needed to grow in their capacity for a deeper understanding of unprecedented issues arising in the 'real' world of school for which there are no 'one right' answers. Instead of written exams, the course would also be assessed differently, namely based on student seminars designed to involve active learning strategies instead of 'mini-lectures'. These are much more effective at providing a conceptual understanding of subject content than traditional approaches (Doyle, 2019).

In my experience, of both coordinating and facilitating the module in this active learning mode, most student teachers generally enjoy taking responsibility for shared peer experiences in re-constructing knowledge, finding it meaningful, thought-provoking and ultimately, more impactful. As Doyle (2019) points out, active learning gives students a chance to develop higher-order critical thinking and analysis skills. One of the primary goals for the module is to actively engage student teachers with the curriculum material, and, in so doing, gaining a deeper understanding of the overall social context of education from a classroom teacher's perspective. It was anticipated that our pre-service students would learn more when they actively participate in the process of creating authentic understandings, using small group discussion, demonstration of problem-discovery, and problem-solving through role-playing and experiential games (Deslauriers *et al.*, 2019). This is in distinct contrast to more conventional styles of teaching, even at the university level, where students are expected to listen passively, taking notes while attempting to absorb information solely curated and presented by the tutor. In our active approach, students are encouraged to design opportunities for themselves to explore their questions and engage with the material in more independent and open-ended ways, resulting in the generation of higher-order thinking.

Section 2: The practice

2a: An introduction to the innovative practice

Essentially, the changes we have made in our teaching and learning for this course relate to giving students more ownership of their learning. The focus is on inquiry and discovery based on real-world situations, and dilemmas students can relate to. In other words, as mentioned by Dobozy and Nygaard (Chapter 2 in this book), students are supported to learn, not so much what the explicit curriculum or even the experts teach, but by making sense of authentic personal 'lived' experience, a diversity of shared experience as well as through mutual exchanges among students. Under the banner of inquiry-based learning, students are engaging in learning *"that enables critical thinking, flexible problem solving, and the transfer of skills and use of knowledge in new situations… rather than being presented with essential information, must discover or construct essential information for themselves"* (Darling-Hammond, 2008:1–2). In the process, they also learn that there is rarely one right (or textbook) answer to complex situations faced in the classroom or school setting.

Small groups of three to six students (depending on the cohort size), in a tutorial class, are given a choice of five broad topics on which to firstly read text content organised by topic and uploaded onto a learning management platform. This is followed by further individual and group research, using suggested and recommended references. They are encouraged to search for other online and news sources to delve further into the topic. As a group, they design a seminar outline which they then present to their tutor in a consultation session lasting from an hour to an hour and a half, depending on their preparedness. During this consultation, the tutor plays an important role as a guide in facilitating their understanding both of content as well as pedagogy.

Two examples of topics relevant to the local school system that we include in student-led seminars are Citizenship and Character Education (CCE), and Working with School Stakeholders, both being particularly challenging aspects of a teacher's daily responsibilities. Students are also given suggested but flexible guidelines to design their interactive 90-minute seminars for their peers. The individual seminar groups are free to shape their seminars to cover pertinent sub-areas of concern within the broad topic for more in-depth discussion. Creative use of authentic scenarios for role-playing, or presenting moral dilemmas arising within a realistic classroom or school setting for experiential problem-solving, for example, have provided fertile ground for active group discovery, discussion and the formation of useful new knowledge. Divergent student perspectives have also surfaced based on the unique personalities, school histories and family backgrounds of seminar participants, resulting in richer learning environments based on mutual sharing of experiences, dialogue across differences, and peer collaboration.

In their groups, students design the 90-minute seminar, based on the course topics, to explore key issues within each broad topic. Guidelines given at the start of the course advise students to design the seminar to focus particularly on the attitudes, approaches, roles and responsibilities of teachers. Every seminar should also aim for active interaction and innovation through focused discussions, relevant role-playing, and gamified activities to engage the class in deeper learning. One-way lectures are strongly discouraged, not least since the peer and tutor seminar assessment form grades the seminar team on items such as creativity, originality, interest, and relevance. Students are also encouraged to make links to their prior experiences (if any) in school both as students as well as in their untrained status as contract or relief teachers. Often, seminar teams attend the consultation session with tutors with ideas for scenarios that they have created from scratch, which can be superficial and lack authenticity. For example, they may craft student profiles for the role plays which are too generalised and stereotypical. However, whenever they are asked to pause and think of actual students they have encountered or were themselves as students, there is often an expressed sense of recognition and relief to be able to base their scenarios on real-life situations with updated situations and some creative license. They are then able to fluently recall the difficult issues they themselves, or their own students, faced and what they or their own teachers did (or did not do) to manage and mitigate the situations. This process of recall then results in effective changes to make the scenarios much more realistic and provocative.

In the process, it is important to increase the groups' awareness that real life can often be stranger and more convincing than fiction. A key positive outcome is that their classmates also better resonate with these role plays, since the majority is likely also to have encountered similar issues and situations themselves. This clearly makes for much more engaged post-activity discussions. When the role plays and games are truer to life, players can be more immersed in the perspectives of their allocated roles. Anecdotally, it has been observed that students with a Liberal Arts or Humanities background tend to be readier to 'go with the flow' of the role-plays.

In contrast, students from the Science or Mathematics disciplines more commonly find it initially safer to pre-script their lines. This pre-scripting however, almost inevitably leads to peer feedback in the assessment forms that the role-plays seemed 'forced' and 'artificial'. It is useful therefore to sometimes ask students when they outline, say, a planned role-play during the consultation, to rehearse their parts, by the tutor assuming one of the main roles (for example, a highly-stressed parent). This gives students who may be less confident, and find it challenging to think on their feet or *ad-lib* when unexpected turns in the scenario happen, an early opportunity to try it out. Games too, such as those that track a student's 'school journey' over several years, for example, need quite a lot of thought and preparation so that it meets the purpose for which it is intended. Many are based on popular game formats such as Monopoly or Snakes and Ladders and make use of the groups' customised game boards, tokens and die to simulate the school system or utilise classroom floor space for physical movement on the 'boards' drawn out there. It has been quite insightful, facilitating groups that were able to create more complex and sophisticated scenarios and games that successfully allowed for more nuanced scenarios and moves. Still, naturally, these required a lot more brainstorming and preparation of material on the students' part.

2b: A brief overview of the curriculum

This core module for pre-service teachers partly embodies a 'flipped classroom' model (Brame, 2013) where, apart from the first introductory briefing session by the tutor, students are encouraged to read text lecture materials, do research in the library and online, have group discussions during which they have opportunities to reflect on their own experiences which can be linked to course topics. Classroom time is then better freed up to focus on the in-depth interactions and activities that can support engaged peer-to-peer learning around sub-topics, as well as allowing space for 'out of the box' thinking and collaborative work.

The curriculum of the module covers five essential topics pertaining to the social context of education that students are being prepared for during their teacher training with practicums and of course, when they graduate as qualified educators. The course curriculum starts by exploring, philosophically and practically, what it means for a school to be considered 'good', which includes an investigation of several education policies currently governing the structures and processes of local schools. This foundation knowledge is followed by delving deeper into the forms, functions and challenges of compulsory character and citizenship education. The third topic examines, more closely, the differences in learning opportunities available to varying segments of the student population and the effects differential access to resources may have on influencing student outcomes. The focus is particularly on raising awareness of the roles and actions of teachers, and the challenges they face in attempting to close some of these resource and accessibility gaps. The next topic of working with stakeholders in school challenges students to move beyond their comfort zones to consider how to engage with and influence their Gen Z students, parents of these students, and beyond school walls to the wider community. Finally, the seminars conclude with a reflective interrogation of the multiple aspects and attributes of being a 21st C teacher as well as how students would personally take on the challenges therein. The final essay also refocuses students on this personal aspect.

I have been both course coordinator and course tutor in this module that entire cohorts of students in graduate and postgraduate programs are required to take. The tutor is responsible for facilitating students during the small group consultations through an initial problem-finding, problem-discovery and problem-framing process before they conduct their seminars. The small groups participate in a reasonably intensive consultation session, which gives the students the necessary individual and collective opportunity to think more deeply, ask and respond to critical questions and comments from the tutor as well as their peers. They are given time and space to brainstorm and refine creative ways to design and conduct reflective seminars that consider possible authentic paths on which beginning teachers can approach real-life teaching and learning challenges. Ideally, in the process of tailored 'experiential' learning during the seminars, the student teachers are presented with several challenging issues that require them to interrogate their mental models further, as well as their teaching and learning approaches.

2c: Organisation of the innovation

Before the start of the course, the Course Notes for Students document is uploaded to an online platform (in our case, Blackboard) where students can read clear guidelines on the course format, structure and assessment requirements as well as foundational overviews of each topic. The course is fairly unique in the institution in taking this active student-led seminar approach, and both the graduate and non-graduate students are unlikely to have a similar experience of the approach in any other course they take. Hence, the first whole-class session focuses on going through the details to familiarise students with what is expected of them. The class is then split into five seminar groups, and students choose (or are allocated) the topic on which they will work together over the next two to four weeks to prepare their seminar. Good samples of actual seminar plans produced by their predecessors are shown to the class to give them concrete ideas of what they could create. Consultation slots of a minimum of an hour are booked with the tutor for in-depth discussion of the group's seminar plan. These administrative details are completed within the first hour of the two-hour class. The second half is allocated to providing an overview of the course content and, at the same time, to possibly also experience a range of interactive pedagogies led by the tutor.

The tutor-group consultation session is the first of four assessment components whereby students are evaluated both individually and collectively on criteria such as preparedness and contribution. Originally, the consultation was non-assessable, but we found that some students would take advantage of that to be non-participative or arrive unprepared at the session. The situation improved substantially when we allocated 20 percent of the course marks to this pre-seminar session. Tutors lead the session by facilitating the conversation first to understand the group's intentions and objectives for the seminar, asks clarifying questions about content and processes, suggests relevant information and ideas, and ideally, stretches the group to consider ideas and areas they may not have thought of. As a tutor, I consistently encourage students to continue thinking together and take full ownership of the final design. After this often-intense session of active value-added tutor and student brainstorming, students often agree that they would want to modify their plan before the seminar. Based on the pre-seminar consultation assessment rubrics, the tutor then allocates scores to individual students as well as the group after the group has left. Pre-set individual rubrics made known to students before the session are attitude, knowledge/understanding, contribution, while group rubrics are coherence and documentation.

The seminar is wholly conducted by the seminar group from start to end, unless the tutor chooses to 'jump in' to add comments or clarify instructions; the tutor's role throughout the session is to actively observe and offer additional value in her/his final concluding remarks. Tutors also spend some post-seminar time with the group giving targeted feedback on how the seminar went, asking the members for their perspectives of whether their objectives were met, what worked or did not work after the rest of the class have left. The following suggested format mostly guides groups:

Seminar introduction: 5 to 10 minutes. This may be approached in various ways, e.g. a skit, a video clip, a jigsaw or word search puzzle. These tuning-in activities help stimulate active class interest and attention and can generate useful initial information (such as good definitions of key concepts) for seminar discussion.

Seminar activities led by the presentation group: 70 to 80 minutes. The whole class should arrive punctually and come prepared, having read through the lectures and additional resources themselves, and be fully ready to engage in the seminar actively. In the end, the presentation group will summarise and conclude the seminar, including offering their views on the main focus questions (if they did not do so earlier).

Seminar assessment is peer- and tutor-based using a standardised evaluation form rating the group on ten rubrics – five on content and five on presentation – including creativity, critical analysis, interest, teamwork, time management and coherence. Qualitative comments on learning points that class members gained as well as suggestions for improvement provide a reflective component for the participants. The debrief tutors have with the seminar group also provides an opportunity for self and group reflection on the seminar.

2d: Preparation of the innovation

As mentioned earlier, different tutors approach the facilitation role differently. Having acted as both a coordinator and tutor over several iterations of the course, I have chosen to share my own practices here. Personally, working with this constructivist learning approach has encouraged me to shift my own perception of the most useful tutor role to assume, and I have increasingly adopted a 'guide on the side' rather than the traditional 'sage on a stage' role (King, 1993). To realise the innovation, the following steps were taken to strengthen the value of the consultations to students. Teacher experience and expert knowledge can be effectively curated and shared through relevant stories and authentic examples to fill in the gaps of limited student knowledge and first-hand experience, as well as to modify misperceptions or easy assumptions; additional materials, for example, ministerial policy speeches reflecting official mandates or perspectives, research findings, video clips and newspaper commentaries on topically relevant issues, can be introduced as supplemental reference resources if necessary; high-quality student work such as game boards depicting individual student journeys along different levels and pathways of schooling can be shown to the groups. These often spark off creative imaginations as to what is possible. Students can also be encouraged to think out of the box (literally) and use outdoor spaces for generating active learning. As a result, students have designed adventurous 'treasure hunts' around the campus and created challenging 'obstacle courses' in an adjacent classroom for their peers to safely navigate around when blindfolded. Others have made use of video documentaries and movie clips, and written tailored scripts for role-plays involving, say, parents, students and teachers embroiled in realistically-framed conflict situations (for the topic on School Stakeholders). Using video editing technology, students have also been able to 'invite' experienced school leaders, senior teachers, parents and students into our classroom through pre-recorded and 'live' interviews. Overall, this open-ended learning approach engages students in creating and sourcing their own teaching materials, all useful skills for future classroom teaching.

Section 3: The outcome

3a: Student perspective

Student responses shared here are elicited from the qualitative portion of mandatory end-of-course Student Feedback on Teaching evaluation forms which are completed anonymously. These would thus represent honest student comments based on their first-hand perceptions and experience of the innovation. Not surprisingly, there is a range of different student responses to this learning approach. Over time, my observation is that students generally offer two types of response, the first being from those who are used to learning in a passive, teacher-directed mode, intent on acquiring 'safe or right answers'. They are often uncomfortable with having to design their own learning without clear directives or specific instructions. They dislike the 'open-endedness' of the format, often require a lot of hand-holding, and constantly ask for reassurance that they are 'on the right track'. In the seminars, they are also clearly uncomfortable with the interactive facilitation role they need to play in enacting their plan, as opposed to the more familiar, arguably easier 'one-way teaching' role. Some will inevitably express their frustrations with and resistance to the innovation in negative teacher evaluations at the end of the course, as shown below.

The active learning approach of this innovation certainly requires that students step out of their comfort zone and this category of students may find it extremely challenging to do so especially since the course duration is only between six to eight weeks. In general terms, and there are many individual exceptions to this, student teachers who are training to be Mother Tongue (second-language) teachers fall into this first category especially those who are less fluent in the English language, for example, international students from other countries. Most, if not all, local students selected to teach in a non-English medium are comfortably bilingual after their years of schooling. Interestingly, again with many exceptions, another group of students I would include in this first category are those training to be Science or Mathematics teachers, probably because they have been deeply ingrained in 'fact- and formula-based' modes of content learning. They often focus on finding 'the right answer' to apply in different scenarios and can find it challenging to understand that there are often no 'predetermined' answers to tackling real-life issues that teachers today face in schools. The younger Diploma and undergraduate Degree level students also generally lack the confidence of the Post-graduate Diploma students, many of whom may already have several months of 'contract teaching' experience under their belts, as well as earned overseas Masters level degrees, being older in years. An increasing number are also mature 'mid-career' switchers who have been working for several years in other industries such as accountancy, marketing, or finance.

On the other hand, students from the Arts and Language paths often (though not always) revel in this approach and express themselves very fluently and vividly in dramatic role-playing scenarios as well as in debates and presenting arguments. They also tend to be better critical thinkers and question the status quo, being steeped in Humanities subjects such as Literature and Social Studies and thus, have developed greater comfort when faced with more ambiguous situations.

However, most, if not all, students are initially taken aback when they recognise the nature of the course format as being so much more student-centred than they are used to. A very small minority might have had occasional experience with something similar in the higher education space they inhabit, but that would be reasonably infrequent. Many do quickly find their feet and can actively rise to the new expectations, ask questions to clarify, think out of the box, and design engaging and enjoyable outcomes co-learning with and facilitating their peers. These divergent outcomes usually are reflected in student feedback at the end of the course, and certainly affect the teacher evaluations received, both positive and negative. Extensive examples of each of these types are drawn upon below in the selection of student comments shared in formal feedback evaluations, and which are based particularly on the consultation sessions where the tutor's teaching and facilitative role is most evident. It is also less than helpful to our team that the official evaluation forms are still not geared to accommodate this innovative approach to teaching and learning, being based on the traditional teacher-directed information-delivery mode. This inevitably may put pressure on some tutors to assume a stronger 'teaching' role so as to receive more positive evaluation scores.

Student comments are not uniformly positive as the following indicates. A first-year Degree student pointed out that: *"There shouldn't be such a high percentage of marks given during seminar consults as this creates a structured and rigid environment. Trust that everyone, as student teachers, will participate actively in the group. If need be, there could be a peer evaluation form...when someone doesn't speak during consultation it doesn't mean that he or she did not provide any inputs."*

Several prefer *"more concrete content teaching"* as *"there could have been more learning in the classroom, but it didn't happen."* *"It feels like we are just watching ourselves fumble over and over..."* Similarly, a young Diploma student commented, *"Learning was based on autonomy [sic] learning where we are expected to learn independently."* These comments reflect the fact that some young people prefer the tried and tested path to learning and are uncomfortable with being stretched beyond the familiar. Deslauriers *et al.* (2019) have highlighted the intriguing finding that students often prefer the passive learning mode because that makes them *feel* like they are learning more, when in fact, because of the increased cognitive effort required in active classrooms making them feel like they learn less, students actually end up learning *more*.

On the other hand, students in these very same cohorts who had more positive experiences and better learning outcomes with this innovation commented that:

- *"(You) stimulate us to think through your questions, always there to guide us and make us think."*

- *"(You are) open-minded and open the floor for many interesting discussions. Many new perspectives were discussed during (your) lessons, using higher-order thinking skills which expands our knowledge."*

- *"The questions asked during the consultation were really good, and I appreciated the input given to help improve the (seminar) presentation."*

A postgraduate Diploma student gave detailed feedback:

- *"… after consultation with (you) my group felt we had a much clearer idea on where the presentation was heading, …(you) provided us with constructive feedback, provoking us to think further on how we could improve our activities to better tailor to the topic."*

Another student gave her frank feedback:

- *"After the session with you, I was totally drained out, probably due to your high expectations of us and the need to modify our lesson plan. But it was this provoking session with you that set us thinking, which led to a successful seminar later. To me, this effort paid off with your valuable inputs."*

In a similar vein,

- *"I found your observations to be very sharp and your criticism constructive…while it was daunting for our lesson plan to be scrutinised so carefully, the entire process was very helpful in guiding us along to make the seminar more focused for the class…it allows the group to really take the initiative and move the discussion in the way they want to, as opposed to it turning into a teacher-led discussion."*

A final piece of feedback that was offered by a senior colleague who had sat in on my consultation sessions affirms the direction that tutor guidance needs to go to support this practice:

- *"Your questions shape their thinking and force them to think critically and at a higher level than they might have been…I saw them eager to share their ideas with you and very willing to receive your critiques and suggestions."*

Based on the range of narratives offered here, it seems critical that a strong positive foundation in the tutor-student relationship needs to be laid quickly and well in order to support the innovative yet unfamiliar format. This would pre-empt some students feeling vulnerable because they need to continuously put in the effort to meet the assessment requirements, as opposed to the more straightforward and simpler requirement of sitting for a final written exam at the end of the course. Some need explicit instructions at the start and consistent, friendly tutor guidance throughout. This category of students is usually anxious as to whether they are "on the right track" and need continuous assurance that there can be several 'right tracks'. Others who are more confident and self-directed need guidance for working within the course guidelines, with additional content input where necessary, so that they have the freedom to be innovative and think out of the box without going off on less relevant tangents.

3b: Teacher perspective – my reflections

Observing and listening to my students run their seminars, I have frequently found myself gaining new perspectives on old issues, getting better insights into the perspectives of my Millennial students and their closer-to-the-ground experiences of schooling and the impacts of schooling on the current generation of students. This innovative practice is certainly not perfect and has room for improvement, given the varying feedback I have received from different cohorts of students. For me, it is still a balancing act between 'control' and 'letting go', between intellectual rigour and the 'joy' of discovery and inquiry learning to optimise classroom learning. This is a continuing process with every fresh and unique cohort I teach. Setting expectations at the start and reiterating these in the consultations seems to be essential for preparing students for what is to come. These are re-visited after each seminar to elicit their reflective feedback on whether and how they managed to meet their learning objectives. Comments on 'strengths' and 'areas of improvement' penned by their classmates, as part of the peer assessment component provide useful feedback on what was learned by individual members of the class, and whether the group's teaching intentions were effectively fulfilled.

Given this diverse range of student types, I am aware that as a tutor, I will have to 'switch different hats' when interacting with them. It is challenging, in the normally short time given, to get to know students well enough to understand their preferred learning styles and tailor appropriate responses to their learning needs, whether in the early preparation phase or in the feedback and evaluative phase. Not effectively closing this gap may result in student anxiety and a struggle to learn optimally. To better support students, tutors will require strong observation and communication skills to dynamically respond and scaffold student learning at different levels of learning needs. They need to be comfortable with 'messy' thinking around a broad question as only general guidelines are provided. Instead of providing 'right' answers, tutors can best serve the deepening of student thinking skills by carefully framing thoughtful, open-ended questions, while seizing opportunities to highlight contemporary events as authentic examples. This can support students as they grapple with constructing meaningful connections between prior understandings and experiences, and the facts and frameworks they are encouraged to learn.

Section 4: Moving forward

Over a few years, it can be observed that the students taking this course are discernibly different in their learning approaches and abilities. More recent cohorts are much more confident and willing, even forcibly so, to share their critical views, compared with earlier cohorts who are less sure of themselves and their own opinions. The local education system of the 20th century has tended to produce graduates who have generally been trained to do as they are told and were more compliant, both in their perspectives and behaviours. Many now enter our institution with international exposure having studied in different systems around the world, and some come to us already having earned higher degrees in their teaching subjects or, as mentioned earlier, with a few years of working experience under their belts. They are also generally academically of higher calibre since the entry requirements for the teaching profession have also become more discriminating. They are, therefore, more open to the innovative approach taken in the course, and display more enthusiasm when asked to take on more ownership for their learning.

As a direct result, tutors facilitating this course need to modify their teaching competencies including the ability to assume a different instructional role, that of allowing for more student agency. Those on the staff team who are more 'old-school' may find it less satisfying to work with our current generation of student teachers who are likely to challenge their long-established notions of 'right' and 'wrong', especially in discussions of moral and ethical issues. On the other hand, the team also needs to temper a more liberal and open attitude to alternative student views, with the realisation that they are being prepared to teach in a system that still retains many regulatory elements, and that may sit uncomfortably with young, idealistic, passionate, and outspoken student teachers.

This chapter has outlined the format of the course, which I feel offers a more productive approach for engaging student teachers in safe learning environments, where there is rarely only 'one right answer' to the complex dilemmas they will face in the world of school. Teaching as a profession, is not just intellectual or cognitive work but very much so, if not more, to do with 'emotional labour', as many educational researchers have discussed. In a looser learning format, students are given creative space to choose what to examine more in-depth, based on relevance or personal concerns they may have at this early stage of their career. Furthermore, our perception is that they are definitely not 'blank slates', just waiting to imbibe the wisdom of academic faculty, but come with a wealth of real-life prior knowledge and experience that are rich veins a skilful educator can tap on to contribute to collective class learning. Unfortunately, time is always a limited resource and students not only have multiple other courses and responsibilities that require their focused attention at the same time, but also the allocation of face-to-face time for this module is restricted to just six weekly sessions of two hours each, plus an additional hour or two per group at the consultations. A key challenge then is how to best optimise learning within the time constraints. I would need to scaffold the process by providing additional guidance and resources, for example, lesson templates, extra readings, video clips and/or other online links, as well as preparing myself psychologically to energetically influence and inspire better thinking in my face-to-face time with students, as well as to frame my words carefully and positively in the direction of better learning. A more current limitation to this innovation would arguably be that it works best when face-to-face immediate physical student interaction is allowed, and probably less well if physical proximity and movement are restricted in the light of 'social distancing' rules.

Conclusion

The active learning approach discussed in this chapter indeed serves to engage students in useful learning much more than if course, or topic, contents were merely downloaded to them as one-way content-heavy lectures. Moreover, such active learning in itself is innovative as it flies in the face of the more traditional teaching methods still endemic in the Singaporean classroom. In addition to the student teachers actively socially constructing their own deeper learning of the course content, they also get to directly experience the challenges of actively facilitating learning in the classroom setting. Indeed, constructivist learning theory highlights the fact that individuals learn through building their knowledge, connecting new ideas and experiences to their existing knowledge base and lived experiences to form new or enhanced understanding (Bransford *et al.*, 1999). Furthermore, as Dobozy and Nygaard (2021, Chapter 2 in this book) state, knowledge is perceived, not as a commodity external to the learner but rather, is the outcome of the process of individual and collective construction.

This module thus provides a path for students to take greater ownership of their professional growth, and also demonstrates explicit models for what they can do in future. By requiring them to work together to solve issues and challenges in small group discussions, exploring the nuances of interesting case studies, meaningful role-playing, and games, they experience the situations 'first-hand' to some extent and are able to empathise with school stakeholders' challenges as well. The group work for seminar design and facilitation also engenders a shared sense of responsibility, with every member bound by a sense of obligation to work collaboratively to create an interesting seminar for the class. A side benefit of this is an enhanced sense of friendly competition for groups who have experienced an earlier seminar where standards have already been set at a high level as it motivates them to try to outdo their peers, which raises the learning level for all.

The group debriefings and reflective activities that follow innovative simulations, role-plays and games, provide important opportunities for students to uncover, analyse and verbalise their personal assumptions, feelings, beliefs, thought processes, and projected actions as future professional educators. Debriefing for the seminar teams, held immediately after the seminar, is also an informal aspect of formative assessment, whereby the tutor helps to shape students' attitudes, skills and knowledge, by providing constructive feedback based on actual shared classroom situations. The student teachers also consistently hear from their peers' points of view, so this exercise in perspective-taking is also valuable for developing a wider and deeper appreciation for the diversity of experiences in the real world of school (and life). These learning conversations could certainly contribute to their continued socialisation into competent teacher professional identities. Training our future teachers to be reflective practitioners is vital because it helps develop the fundamental competencies of self-awareness and self-management. They can then more confidently role-model these skills for, and strongly influence, their students to develop these 21st-century competencies to fortify them for a volatile present *and* future.

About the Author

Lana YL Khong is a Lecturer at the National Institute of Education, Nanyang Technological University, Singapore. She can be contacted at this e-mail: lana.khong@nie.edu.sg

Bibliography

Bonwell, C. C. & Eison, J. A. (1991). Active learning: creating excitement in the classroom. *ASH#-ERIC Higher Education Report No. 1*, Washington, DC: The George Washington University, School of Education and Human Development.

Brame, C. (2013). *Flipping the classroom*. Vanderbilt University Center for Teaching.

Bransford, J. D., Brown, A. L. & Cocking, R. R. (Eds.) (1999). *How people learn: Brain, mind, experience, and school*. Washington, DC: National Academy Press.

Darling-Hammond, L. (2008). Introduction: Teaching and learning for understanding. *Powerful Learning: What We Know About Teaching for Understanding*. San Francisco, CA: Jossey-Bass, pp. 1–9.

Davidson, C. N. (2018). *10 Key Points about Active Learning*. Retrieved from: https://www.insidehighered.com/views/2018/01/25/how-think-about-active-learning-and-its-benefits-opinion

Deslauriers, L. S. M., Miller, K., Callaghan, K. & Kestin, G. (2019). Measuring actual learning versus feeling of learning in response to being actively engaged in the classroom. *Proceedings of the National Academy of Science*, USA. September 24, *116*(39), pp. 19251–19257.

Dobozy, E. & Nygaard, C. (2021). A learning-centred five-tier model of innovation in higher education. In Enomoto, K., Warner, R. & Nygaard, C. (Eds.), *Teaching and Learning Innovations in Higher Education*, pp. 19–46. Oxfordshire, UK: Libri Publishing Ltd.

Doyle, L. (2019). *The benefits of active learning in higher education*. Retrieved from: https://www.northeastern.edu/graduate/blog/active-learning-higher-education/

King, A. (1993). From sage on the stage to guide on the side. *College Teaching*. *41*(1), pp. 30–35.

Smith, B. L. & MacGregor, J. T. (1992). What is collaborative learning? In Goodsell, A. S. (Ed.), *Collaborative Learning: A Sourcebook for Higher Education*, pp. 9–22. University Park, PA: National Center on Postsecondary Teaching, Learning, and Assessment.

Chapter 15

Innovative Assessment in Higher Education: A Public Dissemination Assessment Model for Language Students

Rhiannon Evans

Introduction

With my chapter, I contribute to this book, *Teaching and Learning in Higher Education*, by presenting a public dissemination assessment model for language students, whereby they communicate their research and knowledge in a format easily accessed and understood by the general public. I also demonstrate that this type of authentic assessment is adaptable and can develop communication skills in almost any discipline. The innovative assessment method was implemented in a Beginners Latin class within the Bachelor of Arts at La Trobe University, Australia. Although the example delineated here is taken from teaching Ancient Roman culture and language, the model could be much more widely applied to any aspect of specialised knowledge that is susceptible to being shared with a non-specialist audience.

The chapter shows that authentic assessment can broaden students' transferable skills, particularly in communication, while at the same time strengthening their discipline-specific skills. Referring to the learning-centred five-tier model of innovation in higher education by Dobozy and Nygaard (2021, Chapter 2 in this book) – my process innovation draws on a constructivist perception of learning. Perceiving learning as constructivist, I primarily see my process innovation as a means to broaden the skills acquired while learning a language, and to ensure that assessments test more than the learning of grammatical forms and their usage. Implementing and using a constructivist process innovation has implications for both students and teachers.

The innovation can also meaningfully engage students who have never learned a (second) language in high school, including those from low socio-economic backgrounds or who are first in the family to university. This issue of engaging such non-traditional learners drew me to finding this innovative approach. Engagement can be particularly difficult in a short time frame, such as a 12-week semester, and it may not be easy for students to form an instant connection with the material taught – in this case, the students are divorced from the material by 2000 years of history and by the fact that the language is no longer widely spoken. In the chapter, I define innovative language teaching and learning as modes of instruction and assessment, which move away from instructivist methods, such as lectures and quizzes. Innovative teaching and assessment serve to encourage students to extend their learning beyond disciplinary confines. Innovative teaching and learning should embrace new and exciting means of instruction and assessment, allow students to explore new technologies, and involve outcomes which are transferable to other aspects of study and to life beyond university.

This chapter's case study shows how language students are assessed on their ability to transmit both linguistic and cultural information via an easily-consumed, popular medium, such as a podcast or a tourist brochure; it will also demonstrate that this is easily adaptable in a broad range of disciplines. I have called this method of assessment the 'public dissemination' assessment model. This chapter shows how setting an assessment task which encourages students to explain an area of their study to a general public audience has several benefits for the student. Not only does the student have to master (often complex) concepts and narratives, but they must then reconfigure information in terms which would be understandable to a non-specialist. This process encourages the student to see themselves as the expert, thus building self-esteem, while allowing them to build skills outside of the traditionally narrow confines of disciplinary knowledge and methodologies, namely it requires the ability to communicate high-level concepts to a non-specialist audience without over-simplification. Authentic assessment has been shown to increase the power of learning (Brown, 2015); and this 'real world' model of assessment enables employability skills while deepening discipline-specific knowledge.

Reading this chapter, you will gain the following three insights:
1. the ability to communicate with the public is a valuable skill which should be fostered;
2. this transferable skill may be applicable to many discipline areas in Humanities, STEM and beyond; and
3. an explanation of how to construct an authentic and engaging assessment.

Overview of main sections

The chapter has four sections. In Section 1, I explain the pedagogical issues involved in teaching and setting assessment that applies only to a narrow disciplinary setting. In particular, I address language learning and assessment and explain that a close focus on only grammar and translation results in lower levels of engagement and poorer outcomes for some students. In Section 2, I explain the principles and logic of the public engagement assessment model, and how assignments can be engineered to ensure that students can demonstrate their strengths, by showing an understanding of the wider context as well as difficult concepts, and by effectively communicating their knowledge to non-specialists. Section 3 describes the outcomes after I administered this assessment over four semesters, and how this assessment method resulted in a wide range of imaginative and engaging submissions, which sometimes showcased the abilities of weaker language students. This is followed by Section 4 that explains how I have already made some changes to the administration of the task, and how it could be easily modified to provide an engaging assessment technique in the teaching of any number of scholarly disciplines.

Section I: The background

The idea for this innovation was expanded from an assessment set in La Trobe University's Human Physiology Department by Drs Louise Lexis and Brianna Julien (Lexis & Julien, 2019). One of their students had made an animated children's book to explain the path of a cell in the human body (Resai-Kashkooli & Leslie, 2019). I was looking for a way to increase engagement and invigorate assessment in Humanities subjects involving history, culture and language-learning. My discipline is Classics and Ancient History, which includes many subjects taught through English, but also incorporates two 'dead' languages, Latin and Ancient Greek. Assessment in these subjects traditionally revolves around research essays, close readings, and quizzes which test either uptake of historical information or grammatical forms.

Our language subjects, in particular, had a fairly staid assessment regime, based on rote-learning and the reapplication of learned forms. Although knowledge of grammatical concepts and forms is a significant and unavoidable part of language learning, I hoped to encourage students to incorporate more cultural information in their learning. Previously this had been confined to lectures and a tiny component of quizzes. In part, this concentration on learning the structures and forms of language comes about because semesters are short (in our case 12 weeks) and most universities require that students should acquire sufficient language ability to understand and make use of the language after one or two semesters. Indeed, students themselves might rightly feel short-changed if they cannot use their knowledge in unfamiliar language situations after a year of study. Such an impetus might (and often does) drive us, as teachers, to 'get through' the grammar or the textbook. Although this does work well for students with a talent for the strictures of highly inflected languages like Latin and Ancient Greek, it is less suited to those who find memorising difficult, or who become demoralised when translation becomes difficult. Most students will eventually build confidence and language capacity, but we are almost certainly failing to retain some students who could succeed with some alternative models of assessment.

Indeed, there has long been a scholarly discussion of language learning, indicating that concentration solely on grammar and syntax leads to less satisfying outcomes (Richards & Rogers, 2001; Carvajal, 2013). If students learn about language in the contexts in which it is used, they not only discover additional historical and cultural breadth but also develop a deeper fluency and understanding of the language itself (Allen, 2002; Chafee, 1992). Amongst those involved in Ancient Greek and Latin pedagogy, the issue has been how to do this easily while teaching a dead language, where it is less easy to relate language-learning to travel, current affairs or contemporary cultural phenomena (Gruber-Miller, 2007). For example, in teaching Spanish, the teacher might ask students to watch a Mexican film or research the political situation in Venezuela, then talk or write about it. The other hurdle for ancient languages is that oral competency has rarely been tested or thought important, although some teachers, particularly at the primary and secondary school level, are now adopting spoken Latin (and occasionally Ancient Greek too) as a mode of learning (Bailey, 2017).

Experience has demonstrated to me that asking students to speak Latin takes time and dedication; as such, even when embraced, it is often a casualty of reduced face-to-face time in tertiary settings, leaving the teacher to fall back on the 'nuts and bolts' grammar and syntax model. Instead, I opted to focus on changes to the curriculum and particularly to assessment, which could easily be incorporated into the constraints of class time without detracting from the scaffolding needed for language understanding. Rather than asking students to translate an invented and simplified passage of Latin, this mode of assessment – the 'public dissemination' assessment model – pushes students to connect ancient Latin writing to its original context. Further, it encourages them to think about how they might transmit their learning to a broader audience, mirroring the increasing drive for academics to share their knowledge. Universities call this 'public scholarship' or 'public engagement' – something which often involves experts being asked to engage with the public through radio interviews, television documentaries, blogs, podcasts, and so on. Corker and Holland (2016:1) define public engagement as *"the way in which the higher education sector connects with a wider audience – people who do not already have a formal relationship with higher education"*. The phrase much more commonly refers to academics (teachers and/or researchers) engaging with a non-academic audience. In doing so, academics must consider the appropriate tone, standard and level of detail to adopt, to ensure that their audience will understand and be engaged with subject matter which may be complex and esoteric.

The goal of public engagement is to foster interest in academic material, which might otherwise be seen as confined to an ivory tower and of little relevance to the public at large. As well as encouraging lifelong learning outside of formal education, there is a pragmatic reason to engage with public scholarship, since universities are increasingly being asked to justify their funding by governments. Thus, there is more involved than an expert 'talking down' to non-experts, instead, there is a potential dialogue involved. The National Co-ordinating Centre for Public Engagement (NCCPE) defines public engagement as *"the myriad of ways in which the activity and benefits of higher education and research can be shared with the public. Engagement is, by definition, a two-way process, involving interaction and listening, with the goal of generating mutual benefit"* (NCCPE, 2016:np). The innovative assessment – described in this chapter – allows students to perform a similar operation of cultural translation for and in conversation with those without prior knowledge. In this way, the assessment performs a paradigm shift by asking students to act not only as researchers but also as experts and communicators.

Section 2: The practice

2a: An introduction to the innovative practice

The public dissemination assessment model transforms traditional, niche assessment, which tests only disciplinary knowledge, by adding an additional layer of communication skills. It creates an assignment which requires students to demonstrate their understanding of a particular topic in a fashion which can be consumed by the general public. It requires them to research and master an area of the curriculum, and then to transpose that knowledge into a short video, podcast, brochure, comic book or blog. The model is transferable to almost any area of study: all disciplines have specific or specialised areas, which might well interest the public if they – the public – could access the basic knowledge needed to understand it. The goal is not that members of the public become instant experts, but that they can appreciate a specific area of a wider discipline. The real goal is to ask students to master material which would be esoteric to a non-specialist (in this case, someone with little or no knowledge of Latin and Ancient Roman culture), and to be able to communicate it successfully. To do this successfully, students learn to modify their style and tone according to the needs of their reader, thus learning to adopt different registers and employ them in an appropriate medium.

The teacher sets up the task, giving a set topic or choice of topics, and some advice to students on where to find sources to research the topic. Students could be given free rein to choose any subject area within the discipline, but this should probably be restricted to advanced students, as those with less experience may pick a topic which is difficult to research or for which resources are not easily available. As a general rule, though, choice in an assessment of this type helps to develop student skills in self-directed learning (Johnson 2006): they may lightly research a number of different areas before finding the best one for their chosen medium, or the topic which interests them most. Depending on the year level and ability of the students, the teacher may also have introduced the topic(s) briefly in class. Students may be asked to take on the task individually, in pairs or in small groups. The students then choose a medium for their engagement with the public; they conduct their research on the topic, and then work on *adapting* that knowledge to a form which could be consumed by a member of the public. The adaptation is the real goal of this assessment form, as it asks students to think about the most effective way to communicate their knowledge in the medium they have chosen. Moreover, they must consider whether it is best conveyed with the use of images, visualisations, audio clips or other means; they consider who the video or brochure is aimed at, and the appropriate language to use for that audience. Students must make a variety of decisions about how to present their assignment while balancing this presentation with the need to convey their specialist knowledge. As they need to make a number of decisions about how to communicate, it may be advisable to give some examples of previous year's student work or a sample submission devised by the teacher, in order to guide the students.

2b: A brief overview of the curriculum

This model has been used over a two-year period by a Humanities class in Beginners Latin. This is a one-semester class of twelve weeks, in which students gain a basic knowledge of Latin vocabulary, syntax and grammar. By the end of the course, they are able to translate simplified Latin into English and to understand core grammatical terms and forms. In the not too distant past, this language was taught through the translation of fairly dry sentences and passages, tending to concentrate on military exploits. More recently, there has been a welcome broadening of topics in textbooks, to reflect the diverse nature of the Roman empire and to include women, slaves and non-Romans in their narratives. Nevertheless, most

Latin assessment remains wedded to a narrow window of grammar quizzes and translation, to the exclusion of the cultural background in which this language was used. However, a language is inevitably embedded in one or more cultural contexts (Kramsch, 1993), as is evidenced by vocabulary which is not easily translated into another language and whose resonance might differ depending on the cultural baggage of the translator (Kramsch, 2003). For example, in Latin, the word *pietas* is often translated as 'piety', but is really closer to 'duty' or 'obligation', and could indicate duty to one's family, the state or to the gods. It is difficult to translate it consistently throughout a text: there is no one English word which fits. A student who has investigated Roman religion, as well as the political and social structures of ancient Mediterranean societies, will be better placed to understand the nuances of this word and the best way to translate it in context.

The innovative assessment described in this chapter aims to reflect these changes in language teaching and in the curriculum, by extending this broader outlook to the mode of assessment. It assesses our students' ability to discuss the cultural background of the language they are learning.

2c: Organisation of the innovative practice

The teacher explains to students that the assessment will be a little different from those they have encountered so far in this and other classes. The teacher asks students to choose a topic from a list. In my case, I allow students to look at provincial uprisings in Britannia by the Iceni queen Boudicca, or the Caledonian chieftain Calgacus, or look at Roman ethnographies of northern 'barbarians'. I give them links to online sources along with references to useful passages in Latin and English. As these students are at beginners' level, I do not expect them to read the passage entirely in Latin, as they do not yet have the tools to read an extended passage of 'real' Latin. However, I tell them that they should look at the Latin in parallel with the English translation, as part of the exercise is to demonstrate an understanding of key vocabulary and forms. I also provide a short secondary bibliography so that they can research Roman attitudes to ethnic difference.

Students are asked to transform their chosen narrative into a form which would appeal to the public. This is best done at least a few weeks into a semester – a sufficient amount of time to feel comfortable with independent research. As my students are at beginners' level, they complete this assignment in week 9 of a 12-week semester. They are shown an example of a submission which addresses a different topic (in this case a Latin text about Africa). They read the primary and secondary sources on their chosen topic; they then write a version of that narrative and convert it into a form suitable for public consumption, which may involve filling in some historical or social background. For example, if they choose Boudicca's uprising in modern East Anglia, they may include some contextual information on when the Romans invaded Britain and how they co-opted local leaders as client kings, in order to explain Boudicca's status. They then need to convert the narrative into a medium, style and tone which is appropriate to the intended audience: for example, if they are creating a history worksheet for children, they will retell it in fairly simple language and might include comic book-style images of Romans and Britons, as well as other 'fun' items, like Latin word searches. If they plan to produce a podcast for adult listeners, they can include a more sophisticated analysis of the historical period and adopt a different register. On the other hand, if they choose to create a museum or tourist brochure, they should adopt language which promotes local history or the area in which the uprising occurred, and might include images of Roman and British artefacts found in East Anglia or of the local landscape. Students should be told that, in order to plan their submission, they may need to look at similar materials aimed at their target audience, so that they can judge the best way to frame their work.

As they create this 'product', students must find a way to engage with a historical text written in Latin, and convey to their audience how and why the language of the text is important. To gear students towards doing this, there is a compulsory language component, as students are required to discuss and analyse five Latin phrases from the original narrative, choosing those which are particularly dramatic or significant in the original text. For example, the Britons are described by the historian, Tacitus, as 'a womanish and fanatical crowd' (*muliebre et fanaticum agmen* Tacitus *Annals* 14.15), terminology which demonstrates the Roman contempt for northern barbarians, as well as their gendered outlook. A student creating a podcast or blog could use this opportunity to explain the vocabulary, and briefly discuss Romanocentric and patriarchal attitudes found in this and other texts.

2d: Preparation of the innovative practice

This innovation does take a little organisation, and it is recommended that the instructor talks students through the task a couple of weeks (at least) before the assessment is due. As the task is probably quite different from anything students have completed in a Humanities subject, the teacher needs to explain it in detail and to allow time for questions. With lower-level students, in particular, the teacher might need to create a sample assessment piece so that students have a clear idea of what is required. Some preparation might depend on the materials or sources being studied and the need to explain to students how they can obtain these materials. Students need access to source materials and additional research materials through their university library or a free online source. In my case, all the ancient sources in the Latin original are out of copyright and available on websites such as the Latin Library or Perseus. However, English translations generally appear on the internet only when the copyright period has ended; it is, therefore, important that I explain to students that these translations might be dated and a little harder to read. Fortunately, our library now has a license to the online Loeb Classical Library, a collection of Ancient Greek and Latin texts with parallel English translation.

The teacher does not require many materials themselves. However, in order to give the students as much scope as possible, it is advantageous if the students have institutional access to programs like Prezi, Microsoft PowerPoint or MS Sway (which allows them to build a multimedia presentation). Adobe Photoshop and graphic design programs could be used to design professional looking books, pamphlets and worksheets, but high-end programs are not necessary, and this should be made clear to students. Blogs can be created on free website platforms like WordPress and Wix. In addition, students can create a video or audio presentation with a laptop or mobile phone app. In order to ensure a level playing field, students should have the opportunity to voice any concerns about technology, bearing in mind that most higher education institutions have the facility to lend devices to students where necessary.

Section 3: The outcome

3a: Student perspective

Students in the Beginners' Latin class generally did well in this assignment. Some of them put an enormous amount of effort into the task, even though it was worth just 10% of the overall mark, and they produced very professional-looking media. One even made a full board game, based on Monopoly! A deaf student produced an Australian Sign Language (Auslan) video retelling of their narrative, complete with subtitles, which the rest of the class enjoyed watching.

I was pleasantly surprised to see that some students, who struggled in quiz situations, were able to shine in this assignment, and showed a commendable ability to engage with the language when asked to explain it to a non-specialist audience. Some students did treat it very procedurally and provided a very bare looking pamphlet in a Word document, but many of them had fun with it. In addition, students showed good engagement with the requirement to adopt an appropriate medium and tone for their intended audience. For example, one student submitted a folded, paper 'mini-zine' for a young audience. As it unfolded, a different part of the Boudicca story was unveiled, along with a word game or cartoon image of a Briton or a Roman soldier. This student found an appropriate way to convey the complexities of Latin and Romano-British history (in fact, quite a brutal history) to a primary school audience. Another student produced an audio recording which mimicked the tone and register of a public history podcast or radio documentary, of the type aimed at a non-specialist audience of history enthusiasts.

Students said that they enjoyed the assessment, via informal feedback and formal teaching surveys, e.g. one student comment on anonymised survey said: *"this was the most imaginative assessment I've done in a language class"*; and *"I felt like I learned more than just how the Romans spoke and what they did"*. Some felt that it was too onerous a task for 10% of their total grade, and one did express the view that there was potential *"to be marked on presentation, not just knowledge of Latin"*. When I asked the students, who submitted the most interesting work, whether I could show their work in a Scholarship of Learning and Teaching presentation, they were pleased and happy to give permission.

3b: Teacher perspective – my reflections

The teaching staff learned that non-traditional assessment can engage and extend students who are not 'natural' language learners. We also learned that a small amount of thought and effort in assessment design can have a significant outcome. Language assessment—particularly in the area of Classical languages—tends to focus on a narrow area (grammar and vocabulary acquisition) and, as a result, assessment modes tend to be ingrained in the test and/or translation format.

One key takeaway is that asking students to imagine that they are communicating with the wider world, rather than only within the artificial circle of students and teachers, engages and challenges them. The assessment task expands the skillset acquired by a language student and gives them clear, transferable skills, such as the ability to create a simple podcast or a brochure, and the confidence that they can adopt the appropriate tone and language for a specific genre and audience. At the same time, it asks students to engage with the language and the society which produced the original text.

I have run this assessment successfully over two years now, with excellent results. In future, I would consider expanding the percentage attached to this assessment and suggest that students carry out more extensive research into both the historical background and language use in their chosen narrative. I have already begun to replace some of the remaining quiz format assessment with similar tasks which draw on contextual as well as linguistic knowledge.

Section 4: Moving forward

As this innovative assessment has proved successful and popular with Beginners Latin students, I shall continue to use it with this class. However, taking the feedback from students into account, I shall consider whether this assignment should attract more marks, or whether it should be made clearer to students that their submission does not need to be professionally polished: a thoughtful submission with appropriate use of language and images which hits the right tone for the intended audience is sufficient.

This practice could be fruitfully used in many other disciplines, and I hope to extend it to some of the non-language, history and literature-based classes at my university, as well as inspiring teachers in other disciplines to consider similar strategies, just as my desire to develop this assessment model drew on the ideas of my own colleagues. It should be possible for STEM disciplines, as well as those in Business, Commerce and the Social Sciences to find topics which students could research and communicate to a general audience.

Such a practice would help our students to develop a wider range of communication skills than those normally found in classes focussing on acquiring and analysing complex and niche material. It would also build a skill frequently sought by employers: the ability to transmit ideas fluently and communicate effectively with non-specialists both within and outside of their organisations.

Conclusion

The public dissemination assessment task has proved to be one of the most popular and engaging of those I have set Latin students. While there is still a place for exam-based assignment or translation exercises, it is important to introduce innovative assessment like this into the mix, not only to keep the process of learning interesting to students, but also for the purpose of equity: many hard-working and talented students do not flourish in exam situations. In addition, many universities now value and encourage public scholarship and the ability to communicate research to the general public. However, it is often difficult for academics to accomplish this, as their training often prioritises communication with peers. The public dissemination assessment model trains students to act as experts who are able to share their knowledge and experience with a wider audience. It thus assesses disciplinary knowledge *and* the ability to communicate that knowledge beyond the classroom.

About the Author

Rhiannon Evans is Associate Professor of Classics and Ancient History and Head of the Department of Languages and Linguistics at La Trobe University. She can be contacted at this e-mail: r.evans@latrobe.edu.au

Bibliography

Allen, L.Q. (2002). Teachers' pedagogical beliefs and the standards for foreign language learning. *Foreign Language Annals, 35*, 518–29.

Bailey, J. S. (2017). The persistent perks of speaking Latin. *Eidolon*, January 24, 2017.

Brown, S. (2015). Authentic assessment: using assessment to help students learn. *Electronic Journal of Educational Research, Assessment & Evaluation, 21*(2), pp. 1–8.

Carvajal, C. A. B. (2013). A 'Grammatical translation' method, a historical linguistic error of perspective: Origins, dynamics and inconsistencies. *Praxis & Saber, 4*(8), pp. 243–263.

Chafee, J. (1992). Teaching critical thinking across the curriculum. In Barnes, C. A. (Ed.), *Critical Thinking: Educational Imperative*, pp. 25–35. San Francisco: Jossey-Bass.

Corker, C. & Holland, S. (2016). Using public engagement to enhance student engagement: An example from history. *Student Engagement in Higher Education Journal, 1*(1), pp. 1–8.

Dobozy, E. and Nygaard, C. (2021). A learning-centred five-tier model of innovation in higher education. In Enomoto, K., Warner, R. & Nygaard, C. (Eds.), *Teaching and Learning Innovations in Higher Education*, pp. 19–46. Oxfordshire, UK: Libri Publishing Ltd.

Gruber-Miller, J. (2007). Communication, context, and community: Integrating the standards in the Greek and Latin classroom. In Gruber-Miller, J. (Ed.), *When Dead Tongues Speak: Teaching Beginning Greek and Latin*, pp. 1–18. Oxford: Oxford University Press.

Johnson, J. A. (2006). Beyond the learning paradigm: Customizing learning in American higher education: 10 Bellwether principles for transforming American higher education. *Community College Journal of Research and Practice, 30*(2), pp. 97–116.

Kramsch, C. (1993). *Context and Culture in Language Teaching*. Oxford: Oxford University Press.

Kramsch, C. (2003). From practice to theory and back again. In Byram, P. M. & Grundy, D. P. (Eds.), *Context and Culture in Language Teaching and Learning: Context and Culture in Language Teaching and Learning*, pp. 4–17. Bristol: Channel View Publications.

Lexis, L. & Julien, B. (2019). Private communication.

National Co-ordinating Centre for Public Engagement (NCCPE) (2016). *What is public engagement?* Retrieved from: https://www.publicengagement.ac.uk/explore-it/what-public-engagement

Perseus Collection: Greek and Roman Materials (2020). Retrieved from: http://www.perseus.tufts.edu/hopper/collection?collection=Perseus:collection:Greco-Roman

Resai-Kashkooli, R. & Leslie, C. (2019). *The Little Cell Who Lost Its Way.* Melbourne: La Trobe University e-Bureau. Retrieved from: https://library.latrobe.edu.au/ebureau/ebook.html#littlecell

Richards, J. & Rodgers, T. (2001). *Approaches and Methods in Language Teaching.* Cambridge: Cambridge University Press.

Tacitus (2008). *The Annals.* Yardley, J. C. & Barrett, A. (Eds.). Oxford: Oxford University Press.

The Digital Loeb Classical Library (2020). Retrieved from: https://www.hup.harvard.edu/features/loeb/digital.html.

The Latin Library (2020). Retrieved from: https://www.thelatinlibrary.com

Chapter 16

Teaching from the Native American Circle: An Innovative Teaching Framework

Diana Schooling

Introduction

With my chapter, I contribute to this book, *Teaching and Learning Innovations in Higher Education,* by illustrating an innovative teaching framework based on what is called the Native American Circle. I show how to use the Native American Circle as a foundation for both teaching and learning. This innovative teaching framework has proven to have a high impact on student learning. Since 2007 it has been implemented by a succession of school boards in the largest Bureau of Indian Education (BIE) school in the U.S. The success of the framework is evidenced by its spread to other schools in the BIE system, wholly tribally operated schools outside the BIE system, and also to public schools with a high ratio of Native American students across the U.S. Furthermore, resulting from the work of Consultants for Indian Progress over the past three years, the framework has been implemented in various higher education institutions in the Puget Sound area, and more committedly in some of the Native American institutions in the area. For example, the Muckleshoot Tribal College has embraced it most recently, and is building their new doctoral program on these practices (Lyng-Olson, 2020).

Referring to the learning-centred five-tier model of innovation in higher education (Dobozy & Nygaard, 2021, Chapter 2 in this book) my process innovation draws on a constructivist perception of learning. Perceiving learning as constructivist, the innovative teaching framework is seen primarily as a means to achieve diversity in actual teaching and learning practices. It is evidence-based, shown in the behavior of teacher and students alike, and shown in the quality of content achieved by the student when they feel respected and empowered to embrace their own learning. Teaching from the Native American Circle (Teaching from the Circle for short) increases both teacher and student engagement and retention. It also returns the benefit of the knowledge gained to the community, which ensures the instruction, learning, and return-of-benefit connection remains sustainable and scalable.

Implementing and using a constructivist teaching framework has implications for both students and teachers. Here students are respected, and know that they are, authentically, partners in their own education – future equal Subject Matter Experts – then they are inspired to achieve mastery of the subject content that is being taught with this framework. This helps mitigate the engagement and retention issues, which can be a factor affecting students' mental health. My own and teachers' reflections on using the innovation (outlined further in Section 3) show how it empowers introverts to share observations and practical experience, especially in the critical area of washback, i.e. student feedback and end-of-course surveys. Moreover, the innovation tempers the extrovert, focusing on core methodology informed by the pedagogy, to 'trim the fat' in classroom/coursework communication. Together, it assists reclaiming what has been called 'classroom management' from a dictatorial standpoint, while facilitating even the newest pre-service teachers in setting boundaries wherein true learning can develop (see Khong, 2021, Chapter 14 in this book).

Teaching from the Circle is both a bottom-up and strategic approach. It is bottom-up not just as foundational, but also as a method by which the instructor becomes a mentor, by emphasizing the focus of education as multilateral collaboration, through fostering mutual understanding as the foundation, not as an end-outcome. It sets the foundation for diversity by connecting excellence in education via different domains, thereby increasing the capacity for global learning, research and continued innovation. It supports the European University Association (EUA)'s standards for efficiency. Also, it can lead us to meet the common global concerns addressed in the European University Initiative, and to address the benchmarks expressed in Erasmus+ and the Lisbon Treaty (European Commission, 2019). These benchmarks are equity, inclusion, a cohesive intercultural understanding that ensures professionalism, and a sense of belonging and being heard.

Teaching from the Circle ensures that we are all 'speaking' in a way that can be understood by others, so it facilitates authentic collaboration, research sharing, and enables reliable synergies from the bottom-up. Institutional autonomy is empowered to develop cohesive strategies in a way that will be understood by all, because it generates from a foundation of real, mutual respect, not 'lip-service'. Teaching from the Circle is both explicit and implicit, preserving uniqueness in a world of global connections, creating a level playing field for innovation and the sharing of research, regardless of how large or small a university may be. Moreover, research is of very limited value if the wider community and stakeholders are neither able to grasp its importance nor to understand why it needs to be implemented.

Reading this chapter, you will gain the following three insights:

1. education cannot be effective if it comes from a mindset that believes it is a commodity;

2. teaching from the Circle ensures that nothing is missed. Students see and experience how all content is connected. Educators can see that everything is checked off and that content is mastered;

3. the 7 Sacred Directions Pedagogy is an example of Civil Rights in action – illustrating, modeling, guiding and physically doing the whole of Civil Rights. It shows the connection between vocabulary and practical action.

Overview of main sections

This chapter has four main sections. Section 1 outlines the background of how I came to develop this teaching framework. It explains the journey that has led me here, functioning to help the reader gain insight into why I believe that without Civil Rights as an actionable foundation-process in education, the result is education being built on shifting sands. I encourage the reader to please think back on their ancestry, life journey, how their educational experiences affected all that, and how we are, indeed, all related. In Section 2, I describe the Native American Circle teaching framework in more detail, explaining its practical implementation, as we verbally move around a Medicine Wheel or Circle, and how the different areas complement and are connected to each other. In Section 3, we return to the 'top of the Circle', and tie in measurable student outcomes. We see how mastery of content is achieved through trauma-informed instructional methodology that ameliorates Civil Rights abuses, which affect excellence in learning (see Kalyn et al. 2021, Chapter 18 in this book). Section 4 presents my takeaway guidelines for institutional administrators, showing how it amplifies their reputation for educational excellence. Finally, I conclude by showing how everything is truly connected, and our scholars and stakeholders work as team members for a better world, without abandoning our cultures and unique perspectives.

Section 1: The background

My work with the Native American Circle teaching framework origins from my own personal background. I am directly descended from three different Native American tribal nations, including two tribal chiefs. Those nations are Muscogee-Creek, Seminole, and Cherokee. Cherokee is the language of my mother's people and the language of my greeting to you: 'Osiyo!' (Hello) and 'Wado' (Thank you). I also have Swiss, Scottish, and Norwegian ancestry, being directly descended from Harald Fairhair, the first king of Norway. These ancestors and seeing my childrens' BIE teachers having to write their own entire curricula, or heavily modify what their school board had purchased, are the reasons why I returned to the field of education.

I originally developed a 'research Medicine Wheel' to organize and keep track of my 2015 project proposal. The project explored how Native American tribal nations can alter state and federal educational standards under the Indian Self-Determination and Educational Assistance Act of 1975, in order to ensure that their future leaders are being properly trained. This 'research wheel' did not just include which parts of my project proposal plugged into which Sacred Direction or element, but also included *me*. All things are connected, and the person writing the project proposal must naturally be a factor in it. Comments included on it were remembering to eat, sleep, and drink enough water for proper cognitive function, not to fixate on pre-conceived ideas, the mid-point is where projects, written or being executed, tend to lose momentum. As the Circle returns around to the beginning, completing my 'end' notes involved letting the data, visuals and interviews teach me how it should be presented. It can be likened to 'The Big Push' philosophy for European readers, and I can happily report that, due to the self-care that is threaded through anything Circle-based, there were no casualties in this project proposal.

It made me see that, to be effective in any element of Native American education, a law degree would be required. Therefore, enrolling at the University of Oklahoma College of Law for a Master in Legal Studies-Indigenous People's Law (including International Indigenous People's Law) taught by renowned professors and tribal court endowed chairs, Lindsey Robertson and Tiawagi Helton, was a logical next step. Professor Robertson was a rapporteur to the United Nations for its development of the Declaration of Indigenous Rights. During these courses, proving the content in light of the education demographic, as a whole, was a concern, because most Native American students are actually enrolled in public schools, not in tribal or Bureau schools, and there are few Native American post-secondary institutions. The degree courses showed that, as a Native American, as an Indigenous person, nearly everything I do is founded in one federal law or another. The end goal of my first project proposal had been to create leaders who could walk and speak from 'both sides of the fence.' Leaders who could explain, in Native American concepts, what the federal government or corporations wanted to do, and then accurately communicate back to the federal government or corporations why that would or would not work and what next-steps there would be, if any, in their own non-Native way of speaking.

I observed, through my law degree, that our ancestors' rights were abrogated and they lost the bulk of their natural resources because neither the federal government, nor corporations, were going to tell them what their rights are. This led to me to apply to Arizona State University to earn a Master's in TESOL – with a declared focus of teaching English via Civil Rights legislation and policy. It is not just sufficient to know our rights, we also need to know what the rules are on how to hold violators accountable. Teaching English as an International Language, or TEIL, was one of the very first classes. Here, I found the element I was searching for in my enrollment, in the first place. English has always been a *lingua franca* for my people. The question was, then, how to tie it all together, given the way the English language has been used to abuse and abrogate rights over large portions of the globe. The teacher for that TEIL course would also teach four other classes over the course of my degree, including the Capstone project, which is a two-day seminar presentation, and my research Medicine Wheel emerged from its cocoon with the title, 'Decolonizing Instruction: A 7 Sacred Directions Pedagogy'.

Section 2: The practice

Teaching from the Circle is an actionable pedagogy – words and actions meet and agree here. If we think of the old adage: "*Actions speak louder than words*", it resonates through into civil rights and communication via every part of life. Who we are in academia, whether students or teachers, is not separate from who we are at home. We are all human beings, looking for a way to move our communities forward through life.

Our movement forward can literally be enabled through teaching in a Circle. Some with anxiety might think this would be disadvantageous to them, but it actually facilitates listening and hearing better than being in the back of the room. Beyond just being able to hear more clearly, students are visually focused on the board behind the instructor and taking notes, rather than looking to the left or right. A circle also precludes imperious, take-all-the-attention students from being so. There is a wide literature on the value of classroom circles as a learning space tool. For example, Satt (2017) notes such circles can help develop a sense of classroom community. Likewise, Caine and Caine (2020) focus on the value of classroom circles in teacher professional development. Garnett et al. (2020) show how classroom circles can function as classroom community restorative practices. Indeed, some of the disrespect that academia has tolerated in the classroom, could well be facilitated by the seating chart. A full or semi-circle seating chart also makes better use of the lighting, which can affect such variables as mood, and attention deficit. Actions, and that includes seating charts, put our minds in the proper context before learning begins. Nevertheless, it is not always possible to have such a seating chart, especially when faced with instructing 5,000 students in a lecture hall. However, it can be set by giving verbal instructions of the process expectations at the outset, which may, depending on the context, need to be at least partially restated sometimes throughout the term. It is highly recommended that this to be done verbally, as well as stated in the syllabus, especially for students who are only just being exposed to this diversity, equity and inclusion foundation to instructional practice and classroom expectations. We make mistakes when we jump to conclusions, and that includes assuming students know this well enough or will remember this as they go deeper into the course content. Teaching from the Circle shows the connection between vocabulary and practical action. It enables content to be learned in digestible, 'bite-sized' pieces.

2a: An introduction to the innovative practice

Teaching from the Circle is non-linear instruction, grounded in critical thinking and being mindful that all things are connected. Figure 1 (below) depicts the essentials of circle-based instruction in the Native American Circle innovation framework, which derives from the concept of the Medicine Wheel, or Circle by Cote-Meek (2016) covering learning and healing. The 'Medicine Wheel for Learning and Healing' by Cote-Meek (2016) consists of a large circle with the center of it as an X, not a cross or plus sign. There are description bubbles at the center of the X, as well as at the top, right, bottom, and left. The top of the circle, sectioned off by the X is white (North). The next section, working down around to the right, is yellow (East). The bottom section is red (South). The left section is black (West).

Based largely in the Lakota Medicine Wheel, which is a Sacred Symbol of Knowledge that recognises the 4 Elements, the Circle that I have designed and developed further includes the Cherokee 7 Sacred Directions, as Figure 1 illustrates. In my Circle innovation, 4 Elements are similarly represented via a color wheel: yellow (sun, illumination, the Morning Star), red (wisdom, good health, growth), black (rain, purity of water), white (warmth, happiness, generosity, nourishment), as well as the vocabulary of empathy, gratitude, love, and compassion. The Cherokee 7 Sacred Directions are: North, East, South, West, Down, Center, and Up. These bring in the elements of forgiveness, peace, healing, and truth. With knowledge at the center, these comprise what I call the '7 Sacred Directions Pedagogy.' We begin in forgiving ourselves first, since we are often our own worst enemy, by self-examination, and correcting attitudes and actions. Inductive reasoning starts first, realising that wisdom is not exemplified in excessive verbiage, and that the process of forgiveness as described above, is empowering and foundational to everything that we do, in and out of the classroom or lecture hall. Truth and compassion are the elements that 'close the Circle'.

Chapter 16

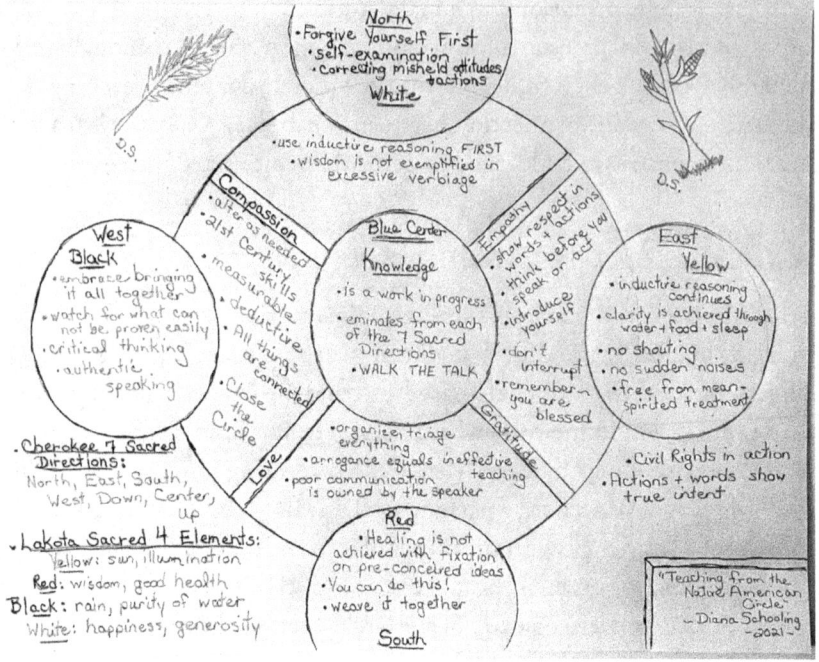

Figure 1: Essentials of circle-based instruction (drawn by Schooling, 2021).

2b: A brief overview of teaching from the Circle

In Figure 1, at the very top, it is white and corresponds to the Sacred Knowledge Elements/Colors for happiness and generosity. The side of the X that creates a border on the right-hand side of that section is labelled 'empathy.' It has a bubble at the top, labeled 'North.' Inside the bubble, at the very top, under the label 'North,' we see the following two bullet points: (1) self-examination, (2) correcting misheld attitudes and actions. Inside the white section, underneath that, next to the part of the X bar that is labelled 'empathy', we see these bullet points: (1) inductive reasoning *first*, and (2) wisdom is not exemplified in excessive verbiage.

The right-hand side, where it is yellow, corresponds to the sun, illumination, and the Morning Star. The bar of the X there is labeled 'gratitude.' It has a bubble on the side, labeled 'East,' and has these bullet points: (1) inductive reasoning continues, (2) clarity is achieved through water+food+sleep, (3) no shouting, (4) no sudden noises, and (5) free from mean-spirited treatment. Inside the yellow section, next to the part of the X bar that is labeled 'gratitude,' we see these bullet points: (1) show respect in words + actions, (2) think before you speak or act, (4) introduce yourself (5) don't interrupt, and (6) remember you are blessed.

The bottom section of the X, where it is red, corresponds to: wisdom and good health. The bar of the X, there, is labelled 'love'. The bubble at the very bottom of this section is labelled 'Red.' ' Inside this red bubble, we see these bullet points: (1) Healing is not achieved with fixation on pre-conceived ideas, (2) You can do this!, (3) begin to weave it all together. Inside the red section, next to the X bar that is labelled 'love', we see these bullet points: (1) Organize, triage everything, (2) arrogance equals ineffective teaching, and (3) poor communication is owned by the speaker.

Moving along the Circle, from the bottom to the left, that area is black. That corresponds to: rain, purity of water. The bar of the X, there, is labelled 'compassion'. The bubble at the far left is labelled 'West'. On the left-hand side is where we begin to 'close the Circle'. Inside that bubble, we find these bullet points: (1) embrace bringing it all together, (2) watch for what cannot be proven easily, (3) critical thinking, and (4) authentic speaking. Inside the black section, next to the X bar labeled 'compassion', we see these closing bullet points: (1) alter as needed, (2) 21st Century skills, (3) measurable, (4) deductive, (5) all things are connected, and (6) Close the Circle.

In the very center of the X, is a large blue bubble. It is labelled 'Blue Center'. Closing the Circle, we bring our vision, our focus, to the center bubble, where it is labelled, 'Knowledge.' There, we see these bullet points: (1) is a work in progress, (2) emanates from each of the 7 Sacred Directions, (3) WALK THE TALK. The left upper corner has a sketch of a Native American feather, and the right upper corner has a sketch of a corn stalk, or maize plant.

2c: Organization of the innovative practice – teaching from the Circle

Teaching from the Circle is suitable for all demographics, because it can effectively help ensure that nothing is missed. Students can see and experience how all content is connected. Teachers can 'see' in the Circle that everything is checked off and that content is mastered. The Circle innovation utilizes the 4-stage scaffolding (shown in Table 1), following Fisher and Frey's work (2009) examining experience in schools with a high percentage of students with English as a second language background. Furthermore, the Circle innovation framework also addresses Tier 5 (implementation fidelity) of the learning-center five-tier model discussed by Dobozy and Nygaard's (2021, Chapter 2 in this book) in terms of ensuring the Circle innovation is implemented as intended via assessments. The Circle innovation can present the evidence of performance fidelity in the forms of end-of-course assessments, student experience surveys, and the organic piece (truth and compassion) that closes the Circle of the whole innovation framework. Indeed, all the elements in the Circle (Figure 1) need to be married together by various assessments, or the validity of the 4-stage scaffolding cannot be ascertained (Brown, 1995).

Stage 1: Focused Lesson	Modeling: explains out loud that students should think through	Verbal, visual, and physical learners are engaged	Following directions, acquiring strategies
Stage 2: Guided Instruction	Students join in, start modeling	Listening + repeating	Practice, learning how to produce something similar
Stage 3: Collaborative work	Rephrasing, working together, manners, integration of knowledge	Thinking how to solve problems & accomplish tasks	Memory work, remembering what was said, understanding
Stage 4: Independent work	Combines everything learned in Stages 1–3, competence + performance	Enables students to mentally close the Circle, all steps included	Enables students to verbally/physically (words, graphs) to close the Circle, prove mastery of content

Table 1: Teaching from the Circle: a modeling of 4-stage scaffolding.

Moreover, teaching from the Circle innovation is underpinned by the view that knowledge cannot be taught from a mindset of education as a commodity. The current status of teaching as a commodity has created the situation where miseducation in competencies remains entrenched in what does not work. Miseducation in our various educational competencies is similar to trying to drive a car with one spark plug that is not fully functional. Moving down the road will still be possible, but not at the speed, agility, or effectiveness that would be possible, if they were all working together.

2d: Example of the innovative practice – teaching from the Circle

This sub-section outlines the beginning of a course that I designed on Civil Rights and Responsibilities. This example demonstrates that anyone can 'plug and play' their own nations and locations, including the specific details of Erasmus+: equity, inclusion, cohesive intercultural understanding that ensures professionalism, and a sense of belonging and being heard (European Commission, 2019). These details apply to practitioners' own situations, showing how to set up Circle-based respect and expectations at the course beginning:

- *Purpose of this Unit*: To inform and empower Indigenous students of individual and community rights and responsibilities as applicable to their Nation-Within-A-Nation status.

- *Goals*: The student will become well-informed on individual and community rights and responsibilities as a U.S. Citizen, a Puyallup Nation Citizen, and Muscogee-Creek Nation Citizen, and a Washington State Resident. By the end of the course, the student:

1) will know their rights and responsibilities in and out of the classroom, on Reservation and off;

2) will know how to recognise the subtle ways these rights may be repressed or infringed upon, as well as when and where to speak up or keep silent, including the consequences of both; and

3) will be aware of the various ways in which language, including literacy, is a part of a judicious classroom, judicious community, and a judicious nation.

Chapter 16

At the end of this course, the student will be able to show mastery of the above information, set forth in the goals (above), via a PowerPoint, live or video dramatisation. The students can choose and emphasise what is more important based on what speaks to the students the most from the material presented and discovered. However, all points must be touched upon in their final presentation. Students who choose the live or video dramatisation may work together and receive their separate grade, given that they have brought their ideas to the instructor beforehand so s/he may assist in documenting their individual contributions to satisfy state and federal school requirements. Regardless of topic, I use the introduction (below) in all instructions:

- *Introduction*: We are all connected. This course will be presented within the Circle. As we progress together, we will learn how all things have a basis and are all woven together even when the true purpose is obscured from view by nature or design.

"It is in the hearts and minds of men and women where a Nation and its rights survive—or not." (by Professor Rees Davies).

This introduction is designed for the first day of class, and should be in the syllabus for students who might forget, because this may be new to them. Then, I verbally cover the whole innovative practice process, unpacking the Teaching from the Circle, ensuring that the 'show what you know' element (below) is characterised by frank discussions. The first day is the day to set the stage, therefore, it is vital to make sure that we are all on the same page, and that we are 'speaking the same language' from the onset. That is, the vocabulary we are using is understood by all, regardless of the students' mother tongue or the language being utilized for instruction.

- *Unit Outline*: All classroom discussion will be done in the Circle. Other materials will be also presented as physically Circle as possible.

- *Classroom Welcome*: is conducted in English, German, Mvskoke, Cherokee and Twolshootseed.

- *The First Greeting*: is spoken in our host Nation's language: Twolshootseed, German, Mvskoke and Cherokee greetings will be presented for educational purposes, being the other ethnic languages of the instructor.

- *Show What you Know*: classroom discussion of student rights and responsibilities, in the classroom, on the Reservation, in the general population, including but not limited to:

  1) Electronics, personal and others – publicly, tribally, or someone else's;
  2) Disciplinary actions – appropriate and not appropriate;
  3) Physical property – same ownership as 2); and
  4) Confidentiality – what is personal, what is keeping a confidence, when something needs to be brought to staff attention for assistance.

To assist administrators & School Board members to teach from the Circle, teaching from the Circle can be presented as the short-description of best practices. Such guidelines for best practices can facilitate measurable student outcomes, leading to less substandard instruction on the part of the teacher and less bad habits/behaviors on the part of the student. The guidelines for best practices can bring about connections between vocabulary and action that encourages mastery of content, illustrating best practices strategies by identifying student learning styles. Teaching from the Circle respects and trains all student learning styles organically. This, in turn, proves measurable student outcomes and adequate yearly progress with ease. A considerable amount of blank space should be allowed at the end of the guideline package, so attendees could write or draw what stood out most to them, and also space to write what they wanted to point out to their governing bodies, once they returned to their home institutions.

Section 3: The outcome

The outcomes from this innovative pedagogy are the ease with which educators, in conjunction with their institutions, can achieve the Erasmus+, the European University Initiative, the Lisbon Treaty (European Commission, 2019), and the new Diversity Equity and Inclusion legal requirements in the USA.

3a: Student perspective

The European University Initiative and Erasmus+ have the lofty and attainable goals of education as an area of collaboration, fostering mutual understanding, showing the value of multilateral collaboration: i.e., because we are all 'speaking' in a way that can be understood by others (European Commission, 2019). This cannot be done without the students. We are training them to join us in the venture, to change the world for the better.

Teaching from the Circle builds on diversity, connecting excellence in different domains, increasing the capacity in global learning, teaching, research, and continued innovation. Students gain critical confidence in their abilities, being empowered to find their 'voice,' which is the goal of the Lisbon Treaty (European Commission, 2019). Being heard, being valued, being included, having a sense of belonging, being treated as helpful budding professionals, are all – as we have seen by the description – in every element of Teaching from the Circle.

Virtually every discipline, every class, can be proven by a final project, as suggested in the list above, rather than a written exam, and this shows mastery of content in a way no written exam ever could. Writing is already the foundational component of any project, for every discipline. In some disciplines, a glossary quiz may be necessary, and in languages, we always have our oral conversational assessments.

Students who have had this foundational basis to their learning experience have excelled in all content areas, including their class standing, ability to craft scholarship essays, and increase the number of higher education institutions to which they are accepted. When moving into the world of higher education, to an institution that does not employ this innovation framework, we have seen a return to lower grades, less understanding of the content, and multiple experiences with academic suspension, even in areas where they consistently made only the highest marks before. Under this burden, only the most tenacious students achieve their desired degree, and usually not on time.

Whether K-12 or higher education, the lack of diversity, inclusion, and respect in the learning process has a significant impact on acquiring the credentials needed for the rest of adult life. Remembering that our society only can move forward successfully, together, makes this an immediate concern. These are our future leaders, and the quality of leader from whom we have to choose in the future, is in school today.

3b: Teacher perspective – my reflections

Teaching from the Circle supports the EUA standards of efficiency, facilitating authentic collaboration, sharing of research, and enables reliable synergies (European Commission, 2019). It saves time. It saves wasted motion, wasted speaking, and wasted activities/assignments that do not plug into the EUA standards. It makes it easy to see which motions, lectures—both in content and length, or assignments have not actually been serving our instructors or students.

The issue of time is crucial in Native American culture, as the most disrespectful thing one can do is to waste someone's time. Any teacher feeling that they need to talk for two hours should consider whether that is really a necessity. In a world where employers want to see graduates who have the knowledge, but also already have experience applying it in real-world contexts, Teaching from the Circle facilitates a 10–20 schedule; 10% verbal/written instruction, and 20% projects/assignments. We succeed when our students succeed.

Section 4: Moving forward

Moving forward with Teaching from the Circle is not devoid of non-diversity related hurdles. School districts, superintendents, principals, academic deans, institutional presidents, and academic boards want value adding innovation. Some are hesitant to implement it, not because they are exclusionary in their vision, but because they are the ones who have to answer for it, in case it does not deliver the measurable outcomes needed. They are fearful of falling short, or of failing altogether, especially if they are previously unfamiliar with these concepts.

The fact that it is an innovative framework process, not a high cost technology, can be a worry for those who believe that the higher the cost of implementation, the more likely success is achieved. The cost factors involved here are the removal of the possibility of lawsuits for failure to teach, or for Civil Rights violations, which is not immediately evident. To those, the point needs to be made that mitigating risk is always a wise choice. And with all those concerns in mind, they are addressed in the following guidelines, as part of my recent Capstone presentation on why we need to implement Teaching from the Circle:

Furthermore, teaching from the Circle eradicates generational substandard language instruction and ameliorates the trauma of emotionally abusive classroom practices. To realize this, inductive reasoning is used to promote respect as the classroom standard. Teaching from the Circle facilitates discrimination and negative treatment to be eliminated through a classroom environment that prevents such negativity from developing. For example, in the (above) course on Civil Rights and Responsibilities, we can show an example of Civil Rights in action by way of illustrating, modeling, guiding, and physically covering the whole of the Civil Rights dimension. Teaching from the Circle allows us to show the connection between vocabulary and practical action. When we respect others, we can alter weave all the content together, while keeping an eye for what cannot be easily proven.

Conclusion

Some readers may still be thinking that they do not see why this innovation framework should be something to consider implementing, much less implementing now. However, the response to this is a simple one. If education is not effective; i.e., students are not functional in the content, then it cannot be said to be truly education. Treating it as a commodity, rather than the service that it is, both compounds the problem and prevents real solutions from happening (Sanchez *et al.*, 2017).

The 'Teaching from the Circle' connection of vocabulary and practical action, which creates authentic critical thinking, that then births societal and economic innovations, cannot exist without effective communication. The foundation of education is communication. There is only one reply to those who would continue the twenty-plus year-old argument, that we have to wait until X, Y, and Z are accomplished: It is only too late if we do not start now.

About the Author

Diana Schooling has just completed her term as the Educational Specialist on the Board of Directors at Consultants for Indian Progress. She can be contacted at this e-mail: ProfDSchooling@icloud.com.

Bibliography

Brown, J. D. (1995). *The Elements of Language Curriculum: A Systematic Approach to Language Development*, Boston, MA: Heinle & Heinle Publishers.

Caine, R. & Caine, G. (2002). *Learning to Learn: How to Develop Process Learning Circles. First Steps.* Government of South Australia Department of Education and Children's Services.

Dobozy, E. & Nygaard, C. (2021). A learning-centred five-tier model of innovation in higher education. In Enomoto, K., Warner, R. & Nygaard, C. (Eds.), *Teaching and Learning Innovations in Higher Education*, pp. 19–46. Oxfordshire, UK: Libri Publishing Ltd.

European Commission. (2019). *Education*. Retrieved from: https://ec.europa.eu/info/education_en

Fisher, D. & Frey, G. (2009). *Guided Instruction*. Alexandria VA: Association for Supervision and Curriculum Development.

Garnett, B. R., Kervick, C. T., Moore, M., Ballysingh T. C. & Smith, L. C. (2020). School Staff and Youth Perspectives of Tier 1 Restorative Practices Classroom Circles. *School Psychology Review*, 19, pp. 1–15.

Kaylyn, B., Brenna, B. & Jaunzems-Fernuk, J. (2021). Using Fiction and Non-fiction Literature to Teach Sensitive Health Issues in Teacher Education. In Enomoto, K., Warner, R. & Nygaard, C. (Eds.), *Teaching and Learning Innovations in Higher Education*, pp. 375–403. Oxfordshire, UK: Libri Publishing Ltd.

Khong, L. YL. (2021). Facilitating active student learning using innovative approaches in pre-service teacher education. In Enomoto, K., Warner, R. & Nygaard, C. (Eds.), *Teaching and Learning Innovations in Higher Education*, pp. 301–321. Oxfordshire, UK: Libri Publishing Ltd.

Lyng-Olson, H. (2020). *Advanced degree program launched by Muckleshoot Tribe, UW Tacoma*. Retrieved October 28, 2020 from https://www.thenewstribune.com/news/local/article244149207.html.

Marsh, T., Cote-Meek, S., Young, N., Najavitis, L. & Toulouse, P. (2016). Indigenous Healing and Seeking Safety: A Blended Implementation Project for Intergenerational Trauma and Substance Abuse Disorders. *International Indigenous Policy Journal*, 7(2), pp. 1–37.

Sanchez, M, Garcia, O. & Solorza, C. (2017). Reframing language allocation policy in dual language bilingual education. *Bilingual Research Journal*. 41(1), pp. 37–51,

Satt, J. (2017). *Developing Communities through Classroom Circles. New York: United Federation of Teachers.* Retrieved from: https:www.uft.org

Schooling, D (2021). *Essentials of Circle Based Instruction*, custom drawn diagram.

Chapter 17

Discovering Professional Musician Identity through Reflective Narrative Writing: A Case Study of Pedagogic Proficiency

Jennifer Rowley

Introduction

With my chapter, I contribute to this book, *Teaching and Learning Innovations in Higher Education*, by providing an innovative learning framework for tertiary educators to engage students in developing a professional musician identity. The innovative learning framework utilises the Arts-based Learning Model (ABLM) (Rowley & Munday, 2020) to analyse student reflexive narratives for capturing their transition from student to professional. Using the ABLM as an analysis framework is novel, as it originally emerged as a graphic summary of learning as a result of an artistic mentoring practice with middle school students in rural Victoria, Australia. The school students were engaged at the time in discovering their Australian Indigenous heritage and exploring personal self-identity. The flexibility of this innovative tool was demonstrated by its use for analysis of undergraduate music student reflexive narratives created in online portfolios. This utilisation of the ABLM took place in an internship placement elective course offered at the Sydney Conservatorium of Music. The ABLM framework was used as a lens to explore student reflexive narratives about their learning, who they were becoming and their future professional musician practice. Burgeoning utilisation of an online portfolio (henceforth, ePortfolio) for documenting an individual's learning journey has seen higher education music learners practise skills of critical thinking and reflection within both formal and informal assessment. Reflective narrative writing provides the benefit of aiding assessment, student learning, and professional development, as it often reveals known effective practices and unknown areas needing improvement.

I define innovative teaching and learning as approaches that support the aim of higher education to improve knowledge, skills, and competencies of students to prepare them for their future musician lives and careers. Transitioning from proficient student to novice musician professional is a journey that many higher education students find challenging, as it requires explicit translations of attributes and skills from one of facilitated learning to one of independent discovery. The ABLM is a framework that allows for identity development in its use as a pedagogic tool for analysing student transitions to professional and is the innovation detailed in this chapter. As a learning model, the ABLM encourages learners to improve their digital literacy utilising an art, language, music and intercultural competency mentoring approach. This approach to pedagogic proficiency relies on utilising artist mentors to deliver authentic cultural and professional knowledge around the artistic practice and for students to write reflectively on that experience. Students engage in 'storying' (writing narratives) to explore the process of transforming from student to professional in the ePortfolio, which has been established as a personal learning space.

Reflective writing is used across disciplines, but it most widely accepted as a pre-professional practice, as educators believe in the value of reflecting on one's knowledge and practices, such as in Schön's (1985) seminal reflective practitioner work. As a creative and reflective narrative writer, a student has the opportunity of being less tacit in their understanding of how to construct meaning generally in what might be a new content discipline. When engaging in what is a spontaneous, intuitive explanation of the actions of everyday life, they show themselves to be knowledgeable. However, at times, learners cannot clearly express what they know. When trying to describe a specific knowledge of something, they are often at a loss and produce written or oral descriptions that are somewhat inappropriate. The act of 'knowing' is ordinarily tacit, implicit in patterns of action and in the feel for the knowledge that we process. A major contribution of reflective writing within a digital space for students is that it allows them to examine their tacit understandings to see where and how this knowledge might be elaborated for the complex and/or uncertain rhetorical contexts they need to use as future professionals in a career that they are yet to be sure of.

Referring to the learning-centred five-tier model of innovation in higher education (Dobozy & Nygaard, 2021, Chapter 2, in this book), my process innovation draws on a *constructivist* perception of learning. Perceiving learning as *constructivist*, I primarily see my process innovation as a means to encourage the transitioning from proficient student to novice professional. Implementing and using *a constructivist process* innovation has implications for both students and teachers, which I cover in the chapter.

Reading this chapter, you will gain the following three insights:

1. how the ABLM described in this chapter articulates the positive impact of combining creative and artistic practice with the pedagogy of ePortfolio thinking and processes to improve learning engagement;

2. how the ePortfolio has become widely used as a flexible digital literacy tool for students to document learning and achievement within a safe personal learning space; and

3. how the utilisation of artistic mentors assists students to build possible 'self', personal identity whilst growing social awareness and resilience.

Overview of main sections

This chapter has three main sections. In Section 1, the design of the innovative learning framework is described within the context of supporting learners' discovery of personal 'self' and the impact of the artistic mentoring provided to assist in that seeking of self-identity. The ABLM emerged as a framework for identity development, and it was subsequently used to analyse University students' self-reflections and this chapter describes that process. In Section 2, the process of ePortfolio thinking through reflective narratives is described, as this was added to the artistic practice and learning about self, both cultural and future thinking, as part of a program of developing the employability of the tertiary music students. Section 3 describes the outcomes of the innovation in teaching and learning in higher education in evidence-based best practice, using the students' commentary as evidence of the success of the ABLM as an analysis tool. The resources utilised along with the framework are open source and as such others are encouraged to apply the framework within their specific disciplines and tertiary institutions.

Section 1: The background

There exists a challenge surrounding engagement for students and, according to current University strategy, we need to employ creative practices to ensure students reach mandated graduate outcomes (e.g. communication, influence, interdisciplinary effectiveness, critical thinking, cultural competence, an integrated professional, ethical and personal identity). Universities globally seek to ensure that they prepare the graduate for professional practice at the conclusion of their studies where the student demonstrates a greater awareness of identity and a connection to the cultural background (for example) contributes significantly to students developing a positive sense of a future possible 'self' (Bennett *et al.*, 2017) and thus extends their learning engagement, health and well-being through enabling educational equity.

Preparing students for a learning engagement strategy must be done within the context and knowledge of the program, institution and desired learning outcomes for students. In this particular context, the ABLM was used to analyse student reflexive writing about their professional practice experience, which was a program of work-integrated learning (WIL) for undergraduate final year music students. A series of workshops were held before the WIL where three specific objectives were sought:

1. to expose students to the benefit of reflective practice in developing essential competencies in writing personal narratives about their experiences;

2. to encourage students to consider the role of mentors and mentees in building collaborative knowledge and practice through an artistic pursuit;

3. to help students understand the role of the ePortfolio as a personal learning space and how digital literacy is of benefit to other literacies required for future career considerations.

Section 2: The practice

A successful model of arts-based learning was created in regional Australia as a result of lunchtime visual art classes with Middle School students who identified as First nations/Australian Indigenous people, where artistic mentors are employed to work with students in a mentoring capacity creating original artistic practice and imparting knowledge of cultural heritage, experiences and techniques. The 2019 Closing the Gap report on Indigenous Australians, states that *"attendance rates fall throughout the secondary grades, declining with increasing year level"* (Commonwealth of Australia, 2019:54). Therefore, engagement strategies to encourage students to continue their learning become very important in these vulnerable adolescent years. The report states that a greater awareness of identity and connection to background contributes significantly to Aboriginal students developing a positive sense of a future 'possible self' and thus contributes to their learning engagement, health and well-being through enabling educational equity (Rowley & Munday, 2020).

Students have many needs for continued engagement, including understanding and involvement in learning about themselves, culture and community. The ABLM was developed as a tool for identity development and is presented below. It demonstrates how we, as educators, can assess the impact of combining creative art practice with narrative reflective writing to improve self-efficacy, digital literacies and cultural knowledge. The process of utilising this innovative framework as part of teaching and learning through active artistic mentoring combined with student reflexive narrative allowed positive engagement outcomes to emerge. These are presented in Figure 1.

Suppose we start at the centre of the diagram and follow the roads out. In that case, there are specific aspects of student learning engagement and measured learning outcomes discovered through a student's artistic practice. The four main components of the model (growing social awareness, building identity and resilience, belonging and future work/education) assists the students to build 'possible' self. The corners are combinations and strengths of each aspect: passion, well-being, engagement and the value of being mentored. The students are at the centre of the diagram, inside the circle, and represented within the unbroken cycle at any point of their learning (Rowley & Munday, 2020). The four clear segments indicate that students have the potential to make different combinations at different times of their learning, engagement and success.

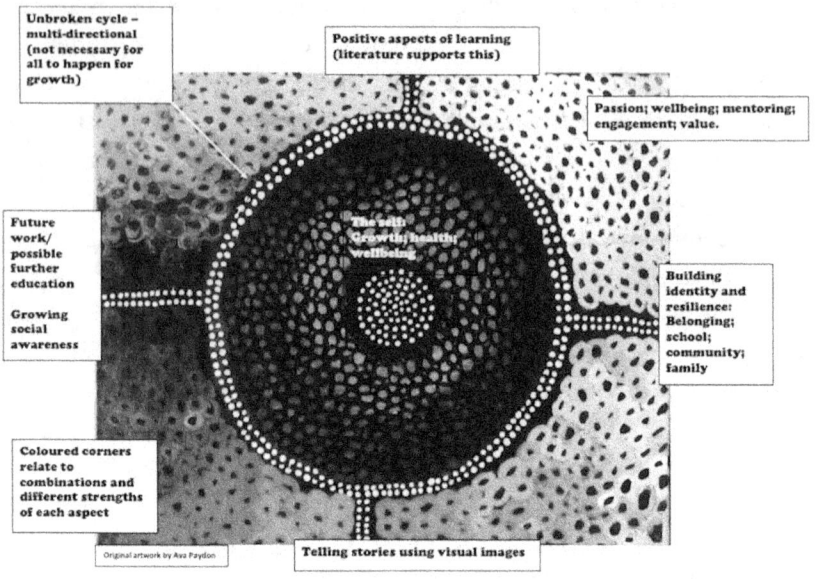

Figure 1: ABLM – An Arts-Based Learning Model (Rowley & Munday, 2020).

2a: An introduction to the innovative practice

The ABLM was created and tested on vulnerable students in regional Australia, and the results were transformative. Adapting this model as a framework for analysing University students' narratives showed how flexible the model was as a framework for the emerging novice professional. After many years of researching the use of the electronic portfolio (ePortfolio) to assist students in collecting evidence and reflecting on their learning development, an opportunity to combine a mentoring role within the digital literacy space provided a lens into the necessary steps undertaken by the student to transition to a professional artistic 'self'.

The literature detailing youth resilience-building indicates that available pathways and supports that enable and facilitate self-regulation toward sustainable livelihoods are quite thin, inconsistent, or missing in the lives of many young people (Rowley & Munday, 2020). It is important for all students beyond the western corpus to understand better the ideas that are inherent in the world (Arvanitakis & Hornsby, 2016). One of these elements is the understanding of our intangible cultural heritage and the realisation of becoming a contributor to the whole society's cultural consciousness. Here then, there is a potential impact of the curriculum to develop these competencies for social citizenship to thrive beyond their *"disciplinary reach"* (Arvanitakis & Hornsby, 2016:43).

There are broadening fields of thought and research around the topic of engaging young adults in learning about their future professional self at the tertiary level. ePortfolios are becoming more widely used as flexible storehouses for students to collect evidence of learning and documentation of achievement (Rowley, 2019). Developing digital literacies have proven to be a successful engagement strategy for those disengaged from secondary education. Beyond school, digital literacies enable people to find employment, improve their education, access services and connect socially (Munday & Rowley, 2019).

2b: A brief overview of the curriculum

We know that reflexive writing inside an ePortfolio has the potential to engage diverse learners. Previous work has shown that students producing an ePortfolio embedded in curriculum tend to move from states of extrinsic motivation to intrinsic motivation in their learning (Rowley, 2014). ePortfolios facilitate self-directed learning by allowing a user to collect evidence, reflect on learning and curate their personal learning space for outside audiences to read.

In our specific context, final year undergraduate music students undertaking an elective professional practice internship were at the precipice of transitioning from student to professional. For this reason, it was appropriate timing for proposing to students that they explore their employability thinking. The internship requires 80 hours of work placement and, as a credit subject, a formal assessment was designed to provide a grade and to exemplify tacit learning as a developing professional (Whitney *et al.*, 2021). As the researcher had worked within the ePortfolio space for some time, it was of benefit to continue using ePortfolio thinking as a learning practice. Moreover, with the addition of artistic mentoring, the student engagement in the learning framework -as part of the employability workshops- was expected to promote a smoother transition into professional self. Utilising the ABLM as a framework for analysing the student reflections provided evidence of its value as a pedagogic tool.

The versatility of the ePortfolio enables the collection and organisation of evidence and artefacts to demonstrate understanding. Besides, acquisition of skills can be flexibly showcased for different audiences giving the creator the ability to present their 'self' appropriately and specifically. Thus, the ePortfolio, in providing a scaffold to building digital literacies through reflective practice, offers significant possibilities for addressing professional and rhetorical literacy and learning engagement shortfalls (Bennett, 2016). Combining a mentoring aspect to the learning context instigates a trajectory of learning development where inquiry and discovery are encouraged through artistic practice (Yeo & Rowley, 2020). In our specific context, students were engaged in creating a performance of an Opera over 4 days of rehearsal and on the 5th day performed to a live audience.

2c: Organisation of the innovative practice

Explicit movement along a continuum toward professional is a difficult concept for young adults who are only managing to be students. Rowley et al. (2016) posed a dilemma faced by students who are preparing to transition from a life as a student to that of one in the professional world who is utilising the expertise learnt as a student. They conclude that the space between the two roles is a complex one that is often fraught with difficulty.

Part of a student managing their own learning is focused on gathering and selecting evidence of developing skills and attributes and weaving these together to tell a story about who they are to a particular audience (Rowley et al., 2016). Such a personal engagement in learning through creating a narrative is an experience that stays with the personal, professional and possible 'self' for life. Within this context, we might consider the notion of how we, as educators contribute to the growth of citizens who love to learn – for life. Sometimes we are caught in a dialogue of what exactly we are developing our students for in terms of future participation in our society and in so doing, we focus only on career aspirations. It is pertinent to consider, therefore, the question of how we educators as part of our social citizenship, can engage students with others so that learning is collaborative, as it is optimal for students to understand the community in which they live and work (Bennett et al., 2017). Therefore, the citizen scholar is one who has been involved in contemporary pedagogical approaches and has developed sufficient competence to carry on as independent learners in the future (Arvanitakis & Hornsby, 2016).

2d: Preparation of the innovative practice

A total of 25 local tertiary students participated in the project and were engaged in an undergraduate elective where they worked with an artistic mentor over a one-week (equivalent) period of internship which was set up as a WIL program. The mentors were selected for their professional artistic expertise and their willingness to inspire students into a mode of professional thinking (Yeo & Rowley, 2020). The period of internship was practical hours spent with a mentor after the workshop experiences and the building of an ePortfolio with evidence of their transition and growth as a professional.

The ABLM was used as a framework for analysing student experiences to assist in seeking the desired outcomes in their transition from student to professional. It is important to note that each student was encouraged to consider their future as a professional artist and in doing so, become aware of their own cultural background. Testing the ABLM as a framework for analysing written narratives about tertiary students' readiness for professional practice was based on the previous results of two pilot studies where the model was utilised with secondary students in regional Australia to explore how the narrative writing in the ePortfolio assisted with the development of a sense of 'possible' self (Munday & Rowley, 2019).

Section 3: The outcome

Possible selves (Markus & Nurius, 1986), are the selves that people would like to become, expect to become, and wish not to become. Researchers of possible 'self' have demonstrated the value of this approach in helping learners find the relevance of their learning and in driving motivation (Hardgrove et al., 2015). At the crux of possible selves is an empirically grounded conclusion that imagined futures only produce motivated action when there is viable self-regulation that can be directed towards desirable future states (Bennett et al., 2017). The students who participated in this internship were working within a regional context and preparing for a performance being mentored by artistic professionals, whilst also mentoring the younger regional music school students. The ABLM acted as a framework for interpreting the resulting reflexive narratives as written in the ePortfolio by the tertiary students. Being part of a mentoring program, the undergraduate students were able to receive and give mentoring to the individual benefit of the mentee. They had role models in the artistic mentors they worked with as professionals in the arts industry they provided real-world, authentic work experience (Yeo & Rowley, 2020). Through their reflective narrative writing, the students gleaned aspects of artistic development to pass onto the younger students they mentored. No data were collected from the younger mentees and hence, are not included here.

For the educators, a sense of authentic yet rigorous learning engagement was provided to the student as they navigated an evaluation of the experience within their own terms of reference and future career thinking. The ABLM provided a clear framework for analysis, as it provided the following headings to guide the interpretation of the student reflections: growing social awareness, building identity and resilience, belonging and future work/education. By tabulating phrases under these headings, I was able to determine the individual's sense of self and transition from student to professional artist.

3a: Student perspective

Findings from the student experience were analysed using the ABLM to see growth, identity, belonging and future professional self. The benefit of the artistic mentoring was unique to the professional practice for many of the students involved. Students' narratives showed an understanding of the aims and outcomes of the project, including high levels of transformative language in their reflections (Yeo & Rowley, 2020). The first two extracts are examples of belonging:

Discovering Professional Musician Identity through Reflective Narrative Writing

- "*The principal artists sat down with the Sydney Conservatorium cast and asked about our aspirations for the future. Hearing about the many directions both their professional lives as musicians and other areas of work have taken them, inspired me greatly as I have often been confused as to what will happen after I graduate.*" (Female, 4th-year student).

The ePortfolio housed student responses under the following headings: summary of learning; learning objectives and outcomes; the translation of theory to practice; self-reflection; future opportunities. The narratives demonstrated that the artistic mentoring experience was transformative for the undergraduate participants in the internship program, as it showed that authentic, real-life experiences were powerful in assisting students, both in skill building and in creating a valuable toolkit for use in their future professional self.

- "*As a performer, I have been inspired by the conduct of the Principal Artists during both the rehearsal and performance process. The attitudes of all the professionals to the entire cast of various ages and abilities were instructive in the way we are expected to help and exemplify the appropriate and most constructive attitudes of a performer.*" (Female, 4th-year student).

Student narratives as an authentic, reflexive practice showed themselves in the present and future as professional musicians. They were encouraged to creatively assess the experience by documenting and curating their growth by articulating the practice of professional performance through experiencing in. The following extract exemplifies such growth:

- "*I heard experience and stories from these professionals who further illustrated to me the importance of self-belief and staying strong within yourself as a performer.*" (Male, 4th-year student).

It is clear that this process relied heavily on experiential learning to give an insight into the challenges of future work and served as an example of reflection-in-action (Schön, 1985). The following two quotes show that the students do think of themselves in the present and reflect on what they might become in the future:

- "*This experience was very valuable as it allowed me to get a taste of professional practice, as well as observe the automatic reactions and challenges I face when I perform, and additionally, learning not to be too critical of myself when I have finished a performance."* (Male, 4th-year student).

Another student who was preparing to be a music teacher added to the sentiments by specifically stating:

- *"The lessons and concepts I have internalised from this experience are some that I plan to use within my own teaching and future performance opportunities. I hope that by sharing this experience with those who are under my instruction will, in turn, help their musical development and performance ability, as well as increase their appreciation for art forms such as opera."* (Female, 4th-year student).

Thinking about your future professional self is not often explicitly asked of tertiary students although within the WIL literature it is strongly recommended. The next extract shows how the student considered who she might be once the tertiary studies end.

- *"After reflecting on the experience and the learning opportunities, I felt that there were a few main things I could incorporate into my practice as a performer. While I am still working on my vocal technique, the internship gave me insight into how my current technical skill handled and appeared in the performance setting. I felt that it was able to handle the professional criteria that were required; however, I look forward to further improving and solidifying areas of my technique that may need work for future performances."* (Female, 4th-year student).

Following is a screenshot from one of the ePortfolio pages of a final year undergraduate Music student who clearly narrates where she believes she is in the transition from student to professional and is an example of future work/education.

Figure 2: An example of ePortfolio page.

By students reflecting on who they are as musicians, performing artists and who they are becoming, a pattern of future goals and aspirations emerges (Blom & Hitchcock, 2017). The following extract is an example of identity:

- *"Being part of a medium-sized opera had its ups and downs. I learnt first-hand that it was imperative to come prepared with my parts note-perfect and to play as in tune as possible. This not only applies to other instances in the musical world but since it was only a 12-person orchestra, it made it very obvious when I played some things slightly out of tune and sometimes missed my entries."* (Male, 3rd-year student).

The use of an ePortfolio process within this WIL program provided a reliable personal learning space where student learning and future career thinking was scaffolded through reflexive practice. The associated ePortfolio process helps students to curate these changes in career thinking by forging a future direction imperative.

3b: Teacher perspective – my reflections

This chapter illustrates the transformative potential of using the ABLM for analysing student reflections on artistic mentoring and professional skills development, particularly for building self-efficacy and professional competencies whilst having a sense of agency in the building of the professional self. Using ABLM to interpret the reflexive comments provided a snapshot of how encouraged the tertiary music students were to reveal any shift in their perceptions about who they were. Moreover, they were able to write about these shifts inside the personal learning space of the ePortfolio. The students were challenged to interrogate themselves as a future professional and to explore their identity as a musician and the growth that the WIL experience afforded during this internship program of professional practice. As an educator, I was able to see where they were and to evaluate the experience within the context of the program learning outcomes. This provided me with the opportunity to reflect myself, re-design aspects of the program where needed and to act within a pedagogical framework according to the student feedback written in their reflections. As a facilitator of learning, I needed to reflect myself on the future design of the program so that it provided the tertiary music students with learning through an authentic WIL context. Through a deeper interrogation of their reflections using the ABLM, I better understood their learning experience and how they committed to furthering their discipline-specific musician knowledge. This allowed me to discover new approaches to managing a professional relationship with the artistic mentors.

Section 4: Moving forward

The ABLM, as an innovative framework, is discussed as a tool to analyse student learning. Also, it represents, amongst other aspects, a positive cycle of learning engagement, health and well-being, growth, resilience and cultural understanding and professional consciousness (Rowley & Munday, 2020). It has transferability potential for other disciplines, as an analysis framework for exploring how students transition from student to professional. As a mentoring model for learning, it has the potential to encourage a partnership with artistic mentors and students, as there is a sense of developing a professional through the understanding of meaningful work. It was noted in the analysis of student narratives there was an emergence, amongst the students, of a 'future' and/or 'professional self'. These selves were actioned through the created artistic practice and the accompanying digital narratives contributing to the development of the social citizen, lifelong learner and for building community awareness. Reflective writing benefits students because it helps students identify their tacit knowledge as well as gaps in that knowledge. Such reflections bring rhetorical and writing process decisions to the forefront, which can focus subsequent professional learnings and encourage growth as a future working professional within a career preparation context.

Conclusion

The student reflections, according to the ABLM analysis, showed that there were reciprocal benefits for students in all categories. The tertiary students found the mentoring of younger students to be important in the development of their musical identities, advancing the transition from music student to music professional (Yeo & Rowley, 2018). The identification of 'possible selves', noted by Markus and Nurius (1986) allowed an insight into links with the past and the present through the addition of ePortfolio thinking and processes, and its potential of documenting the narrating and demonstrating the self through evidence of accomplishment and ideas. It is evidenced through the student perspectives section that this could help progress the student thinking into a realisation of possible future career and/or professional practitioner.

The ABLM as both a framework for analysis and as a learning model for artistic mentoring provided a guide and encouragement for students to reflect on who they want to be in their future careers. Additionally, the framework enabled students to determine how their current studies can assist in distinguishing the best possible pathways for achieving desired and/or necessary graduate outcomes needed to realise themselves as a professional. As an innovation in teaching and learning in higher education, the ABLM provides a framework guiding educators to tailor discipline-specific competencies to the curriculum they design to assist in the transition from student to professional. There has been criticism of our assessment practices in higher education as typical assessment practices mask complexities and contradictions in how students write reflectively and how we, as educators, grade them. This example of the ePortfolio thinking process proposes an authentic assessment practice, based on clearer theoretical underpinnings, particularly from social theories of language and digital literacy.

About the Author

Jennifer Rowley is an Associate Professor in Music Education at the Sydney Conservatorium of Music, The University of Sydney. She can be contacted at this e-mail: jennifer.rowley@sydney.edu.au

Bibliography

Arvanitakis, J. & Hornsby, D. (2016). Are universities redundant? In Arvanitakis, J. & Hornsby, D. (Eds.), *Universities, the citizen scholar and the future of higher education*, pp. 7–20. Basingstoke, Hampshire, UK: Palgrave Macmillan.

Bennett, D. (2016). Developing employability in higher education music. *Arts and Humanities in Higher Education*, 15, pp. 386–395.

Bennett, D., Reid, A. & Rowley, J. (2017). Student musicians' experiences of reflexivity during internships: Personal narratives and complex modalities. *International Journal of Music Education*, 35(3), pp. 460–475.

Blom, D. & Hitchcock, M. (2017). Perceived usefulness and relevance of ePortfolios in the Creative Arts: Investigating student views. In Rowley, J. (Ed.), *ePortfolios in Australian Universities*, pp. 155–172. New York: Springer.

Commonwealth of Australia. (2019). *Closing the Gap Prime Minister's Report 2019*. Australian Government, Department of the Prime Minister and Cabinet.

Dobozy, E. & Nygaard, C. (2021). A learning-centred five-tier model of innovation in higher education. In Enomoto, K., Warner, R. & Nygaard, C. (Eds.), *Teaching and Learning Innovations in Higher Education*, pp. 19–46. Oxfordshire, UK: Libri Publishing Ltd.

Hardgrove, A., McDowell, L. & Rootham, E. (2015). Precarious lives, precarious labour: Family support and young men's transitions to work in the UK, *Journal of Youth Studies*, 18(8), pp. 1057–1076.

Markus, H. & Nurius, P. (1986). Possible selves. *American Psychologist*, 41(9), pp. 954–969.

Munday, J. & Rowley, J. (2019). Art and identity: Secondary students discovering a 'sense of self' through creating artworks and webpages. *ab-Original: Journal of Indigenous Studies and First Peoples' and First Nations' Cultures* 3(1), pp. 23–45.

Rowley, J. (2014). Enhancing student learning through the management of technology-rich physical learning spaces for flexible teaching. In Scott-Webster, L., Branch J., Bartholomew P. & Nygaard C. (Eds.), *Learning Space Design in Higher Education*, pp. 53–68. Oxfordshire, UK: Libri Publishing Ltd.

Rowley, J. (2019). The musician as teacher: Navigating future self for career development. In Jennifer Rowley, Dawn Bennett, Patrick Schmidt (Eds.), *Leadership of Pedagogy and Curriculum in Higher Music Education*, pp. 150–169. New York: Routledge.

Rowley, J., Bennett, D. & Reid, A. (2016). Leadership as a core creativity for musician identity. *32nd World Conference on Music Education (ISME 2016)*, Glasgow, Scotland: International Society of Music Education (ISME).

Rowley, J. & Munday, J. (2020). An arts-based learning model: Synergies of artist mentorship, ePortfolio and discovering 'possible self'. *The Australian Journal of Indigenous Education*, 49(2), pp. 89–97.

Schön, D. (1985). *The design studio: an exploration of its traditions and potentials*, London: RIBA Publications for RIBA Building Industry Trust.

Whitney, I., Rowley, J. & Bennett, D. (2021). Developing student agency: ePortfolio reflections of future career among aspiring musicians. *The International Journal of ePortfolio*, 11(1), pp, 1–18.

Yeo, N. & Rowley, J. (2018). Reflections on a three-way mentoring program using ePortfolios: I Pagliacci (Leoncavallo) in the Spiegeltent. *Music in Schools and Teacher Education Commission (MISTEC)*, New York University, Prague. 8–12 July, 2018.

Yeo, N. & Rowley, J. (2020). 'Putting on a show' non-placement WIL in the performing arts: Documenting professional rehearsal and performance using ePortfolio reflections. *Journal of University Teaching and Learning Practice* 17(4).

Chapter 18

Using Fiction and Non-fiction Literature to Teach Sensitive Health Issues in Teacher Education

Brenda Kalyn, Beverley Brenna and Judy Jaunzems-Fernuk

Introduction

Our chapter contributes to this book, *Teaching and Learning Innovations in Higher Education*, by focusing on integrating literary texts with post-secondary Health education curricula for teacher candidates (TCs) in a Bachelor of Education Program. At the forefront of our innovation was a process invitation for TCs to acquire knowledge through stories and respond to literature in ways that might parallel the responses of their future students to non-traditional content area textbooks. We hoped their course-based reading, within the context of a post-internship elective, would enter the heart as well as the mind, impact their future teaching, and shape the way they might consider subject matter through their own lived experiences. Underpinning our work is the idea of relational pedagogy from a social constructivist perspective (Crownover & Jones, 2018; Vygotsky, 1978), connected to ideas about transformational learning (Mezirow, 2000). Our work is reflected through the learning-centred five-tier innovation model in higher education (Dobozy & Nygaard, 2021, Chapter 2 in this book). We draw on the constructivist perception of learning by linking content, student responses, and the building of knowledge through relational interactions with the literature, experience, and others.

Our chapter shares thematic ideas with other chapters in this section. Schooling (2021, Chapter 16 in this book) speaks of authentic learning partnerships among subjects, learners, and instructors. Khong (2021, Chapter 14 in this book) discusses meaningful, deliberate thinking concerning the complexities of school contexts, students, and teachers, stressing the importance of understanding unprecedented issues in relation to the real world of schooling where no single right answer can suffice. Rowley's work (2021, Chapter 17 in this book) transitioning music students to novice paid professionals dialogues well with our explorations in the liminal space where teacher candidates become teachers. Evans (2021, Chapter 15 in this book) explores the dissemination of research knowledge into formats accessible to the public – an aspect of our inquiry, as we seek non-traditional required readings for teacher candidates to use for dual purposes: the acquisition of course-based knowledge and application to their classrooms.

Our inquiry's 75 TCs were enrolled in one of two elementary cohorts (grades Kindergarten to Grade 8), taking ECUR 450: *Elementary Methods in Health Education* as a post-internship elective. Our team of three researchers contributed to this project in various ways. One was the primary instructor for both cohorts, another suggested appropriate fiction texts to apply as course resources, and a third contributed to lectures and discussion. TC participation was voluntary and anonymous in the course framework; through various data collection methods, we attempted to collect their responses to the literary texts chosen as required reading, exploring how these texts served different course outcomes, going beyond the impact of traditional textbook resources. These readings were selected and applied with social learning theory in mind (Bandura, 1977) to challenge TCs to engage, through fictional and case study narratives, with ideas about how others face and manage difficult and sometimes tragic situations or circumstances. Perceiving learning as a constructivist act, we see our process innovation as a means to explore the impact of reader-response (Rosenblatt, 1978) on TCs' explorations of Health content in relation to learning and teaching.

Working with TCs in various contexts within curricula areas, and facilitating their internship practice, we have noted an increase in TCs' tensions with and exposure to a variety of behavioral disruptions or traumatic events within classrooms. TCs struggle with 'how to handle' these behaviors and, further, how to understand the root of the behaviors, if that is possible. Part of our idea for implementing literary novels within TCs' Health methods courses was to expose potential root causes for some behaviors through stories of children's lives and provide insight into understanding these behaviors. We wondered whether readings, discussions, and subsequent practices might help TCs develop a deeper understanding of the social/emotional contexts of curricula and life experiences that potentially affect classrooms—sometimes in traumatic ways. Essentially, we wondered whether our teaching itself could be transformative, probing *"the belief that instructors can promote meaningful change in students' lives if they view courses as stages upon which life-changing experiences can occur"* (Slavich & Zimbardo, 2012:576).

In November 2019, a tragedy occurred in our province, when a ten-year-old girl committed suicide. The following week there were four more suicide attempts amongst children in this community. This increasing trend in self-destruction is challenging society and has a devastating impact on students, communities, and schools. Schools temporarily close when serious events occur, and counselors are made available to help everyone cope with the emotional strain experienced. Teachers are tasked with moving forward with their students and communities, and we know that teaching cannot proceed until healing occurs. Suicide awareness and prevention are examples of contexts we considered as we selected literary content to match our school systems' needs.

Our qualitative study unfolded as we began to wonder what impact children's novels and non-fiction case studies might have on teaching elementary students' understanding of sensitive curricular issues in Health, and how resources such as these might bridge other sources when working with preservice Health educators. Implementing our constructivist process innovation thus has implications for teacher candidates as well as their future students.

Reading this chapter, you will gain the following three insights:

1. practical examples of how sensitive Health issues can be taught through the study of middle-grade and young-adult novels;

2. places of evocative intersection between Health and English Language Arts, foregrounding mutually supportive practices; and

3. illuminative narratives of TCs' experiences living their future curriculum as classroom teachers by exploring innovative knowledge expansion models to support pedagogical practice.

Chapter 18

Overview of main sections

The chapter has four main sections. In Section 1, we offer the Health education context in which our work resides. In Section 2, we outline the methodology and methods of our study. We also provide background on reader-response theory and delineate the Health methods course outcomes in which our study took place. In Section 3, we discuss the outcomes that emerged from our data, including TC voices, as these participants unpacked the impact of our required reading. In the fourth, we suggest ideas for the future regarding applications of this work and further research. Following these sections, we present a summary of key conclusions from this inquiry.

Section 1: The background

Over past decades, significant changes in Canadian Health curricula demonstrate changing societal issues represented within contemporary curricula, and the impetus for topics necessary to assist student growth into healthy citizens. Past health curricula topics included an in-depth study of the digestive system, the eyeball, cleanliness, puberty, and healthy relationships (Kogan, 1970; Ratcliff, 1982). Although these topics are relevant and somewhat embedded within current health topics, current issues such as HIV/AIDS, sexually transmitted diseases, immunization, bullying, relationships, sexual orientation, self-harm, suicide, body image, mental health, wellness, disease, and acting on one's personal well-being are primary within current Canadian Health Curricula (Saskatchewan Ministry of Education, 2010).

Tenets of contemporary curricula promote the idea that children's experiences are foundational and shape who they will become and that basic needs of love, food, and shelter must be met to provide this foundation (McLeod, 2020). Teachers might ask: is the child hungry for food, love, or attention; who cares for them; how are they cared for; what are their experiences; are they loved; what do they see; what do they experience? It is imperative to build resiliency and healthy social/emotional skills in the early years of a child's life.

Recent studies point towards children's health issues concerning eating disorders, obesity, and dramatic increases in mental health and anxiety issues. It is believed that today's youth will have a shorter life expectancy than their parents, due to a rise in severe health issues and unhealthy lifestyles (Bates & Eccles, 2008). Also, Canadian statistics estimate 1.2 million children and youth are affected by mental illness (Mental Health Commission of Canada, 2019). To address these alarming concerns, we were inspired to introduce our innovation in teaching and learning to include required post-secondary reading, currently unconventional in content-area coursework, where academic textbooks and scholarly articles have been the norm. Our goal was to stretch the contemporary boundaries of teaching Health education because *"for both individuals and communities, health literacy involves possessing not only knowledge of healthy behaviors but also the ability and willingness to translate that knowledge into everyday realities"* (Socha & Cameron, 2019:5).

Textbooks provide contemporary conceptions of health that focus on personal responsibility and the act of making the right choices. In theory, this may appear reasonable; however, scholars increasingly stress that information and facts ignore the realities and social determinants of health in students' daily lives. Raphael (2016) lists these determinants as factors that have a significant consequence on our children's health: Indigenous ancestry (that carries the trauma of residential schools); disability; education; food security; gender; housing; citizenship; income; and social safety. Socha and Cameron (2019:7) further that if teachers and curricula focus specifically on traditional messages of health and well-being through definitions and information without factoring in the lives of children and health inhibitors, we assume a definition of health *"at the expense of valuing and starting from the lived experiences of our students"*. We posit that the stories embedded within high-quality literature might be more authentic and speak engagingly of real-life encounters, societal challenges, and health determinants. Learning through literary novels and research-based non-fiction may assist in a well-rounded overview of what it means to be a Health educator.

Section 2: The practice

As we considered the outcomes for our particular target course, subsequently delivered by the lead author on this chapter, we wondered what impact realistic fiction books might have on learning about contemporary health issues. In the first year of our inquiry, we introduced the novel *Fox Magic* (Brenna, 2018), which all students read. During the second year, and based on TCs' interests, five other novels were introduced, and TCs chose which one they would read. These novels are identified below:

- *Fox Magic* (Brenna, 2018), a middle-grade story of three girls who created a suicide pact and the subsequent outcomes of this decision with a focus on resiliency for the child who chooses to live;
- *Wild Orchid* (Brenna, 2005), a young-adult novel that provides insight into a young adult who lives with autism;
- *The Moon Children* (Brenna, 2007), a middle-grade novel dealing with fetal alcohol spectrum disorder and selective mutism in the context of a supportive friendship between two ten-year-old children;
- *Sapphire the Great and the Meaning of Life* (Brenna, 2019), a middle-grade novel that explores diverse characters including the nine-year-old protagonist's gay father, as well as a neighbor who is a Trans woman, alongside themes of identity and bullying;
- *Calvin* (Leavitt, 2015), a young-adult novel that follows a teen with schizophrenia as he struggles to gain control of his mind and his destiny;
- *Jason's Why* (Goobie, 2013), a junior/middle-grade novel about a child with severe behavior challenges who transitions into a group home.

Book choices were based on previous awards and writing that contained compassion, humor, sensitivity, and clear depictions of the characters, their behaviors, and their lives. In addition to fiction, we also queried the influence of a particular non-fiction collection of case studies titled *The Boy Who was Raised as a Dog* (Perry & Szalavitz, 2017). In this collection, child psychiatrist Dr. Perry discusses a series of real-life traumatic experiences, that children have endured, and the subsequent themes of hope, care, and love that remain despite these realities. The stories address questions related to brain science: what happens to the brain during trauma, and the brain's astonishing ability to heal. Our inquiry was shaped by transformational learning theory and relational pedagogy

(Crownover & Jones, 2018; Mezirow, 2000). It was particularly directed towards how our required reading might be received, further the Health education of our teacher candidates, and what the effects might be of this reading on pedagogical considerations for future teaching in elementary schools.

Introducing these readings does not imply that all students have encountered traumatic events or societal challenges in the same way as these literary characters. The intent was to explore knowledge, understanding, empathy, experience, and messages of hope and resiliency through these stories and enhance teacher candidates' exposure to real issues. Course outcomes were met through readings, discussions, questions, and various pedagogical discourses and experiences.

Thus, we attempted to nudge TCs to adopt new pedagogical strategies, considering and trying to ease areas of potential discomfort, and interrogate their responses to this innovation as future teachers. In keeping with ideas about transformational teaching, we considered that: *"education should be more about inspiration than information... equipping students with both the skills and attitudes that are necessary for overcoming challenges"* (Slavich & Zimbardo, 2012:577). We were challenging our participants as teacher candidates/students in a university Health class and as teachers of children. Ultimately, they moved between the Health course curriculum as students and their transformation into members of the teaching profession.

As teacher educators, we are conscious of the movement of our teacher candidates (TCs) as they explore coursework that focuses on both subject area knowledge and teaching pedagogy. At times, these TCs perform as learners, navigating content. At times, they present as teachers, demonstrating awareness of future practice and pedagogies. The liminal space that encompasses both stances is described in the research as a transformative state in the process of learning that includes a reformulation of the learner's meaning frame along with a shift in the learner's ontology or subjectivity (Land, Rattray & Vivian, 2014). This liminal space is particularly intriguing to us in our context in teacher education. We wondered how together with our students we might illuminate and discuss the shifts that may be occurring in the liminal space provided by a Health education class during our study. We also wondered what teaching strategies and resources might catalyze their movement within this liminal space. We considered how we might document these catalysts as part of reflective practice.

Following the delivery of both undergraduate courses that trialed these resources, we asked TCs to complete a voluntary, anonymous, post-class survey (Section 2c) to collect data on our key research questions. Our questions attempted to activate considerations of relational pedagogy (Crownover & Jones, 2018) as well as transformational learning (Mezirow, 2000). The research questions guiding this inquiry were:

- In what ways do teacher candidates envision children's and young adult literature as a support for the Health Curriculum at particular grade levels?

- In what ways do TCs' views on the utility of children's literature change throughout one post-secondary education Health course?

- How do these views compare and contrast with practices they are currently observing in schools, particularly in relation to sensitive issues they will encounter with their students and within their schools?

- Do humanistic approaches to learning about sensitive health issues affect the connections between subject, knowledge, student, and teacher, thereby assisting TCs in navigating the liminal spaces between learning and teaching?

2a: An introduction to the innovative practice

At the heart of our innovation is TCs' intersection as a student *and* as a teacher. We used a relational framework here so that teacher candidates could respond to learning through these novels and subsequently transfer their experience into school Health curricula as teachers.

Reader Response Theory at Work

We used reader-response theory (Rosenblatt, 1978, 1982) as a framework for this inquiry, allowing that reading is a transaction involving a contribution from *both* reader and text. Reader-response theory recognizes the relationship between reader and text and suggests that reading can stir up elements of memory, experience, and consciousness within the reader

(Rosenblatt, 1982). In terms of the stance of the reader, teacher candidates were encouraged to respond both aesthetically and efferently to required readings, with an emphasis on Rosenblatt's (1982:269) concept of a *"primarily efferent stance"*, from the Latin word efferent *"to carry away"*, where the reader's attention focuses on information and meanings derived from the text. As a result of engagement with literary texts, we anticipated that TCs might make underpinning connections to issues taught within the Saskatchewan Health Curricula and experience the potentiality of course readings, both fiction and non-fiction, to inspire gains in knowledge, information, and understanding about teaching sensitive issues.

2b: A brief overview of the curriculum

Our Saskatchewan Provincial Health Curricula K – Grade 12 (2010) set the stage well for interdisciplinary work. These documents intersect within the following cross-curricular competencies: developing thinking, developing identity and independence, developing literacies; and developing social responsibility.

Elementary-level Saskatchewan Health Curricula, required to be taught 80 minutes per week (Grades 1–7) and 100 minutes per week (Grade 9), include various grade-level outcomes, focusing on topics of mental and physical health across the grades. Elementary-level English Language Arts Curricula, required to be taught 560 minutes per week (Grades 1–6) and 300 minutes per week (Grades 7–8), also present some similar outcomes from grade to grade, including goals to comprehend and respond to a variety of texts that address identity, community, and social responsibility. Besides, reader-response's general goals are intended to be applied to grade-level texts along with oral fluency and comprehension.

Post-Secondary Elementary Health Methods Course (ECUR 450)

This course, the context of our study, introduces teacher candidates to the elementary Health Curriculum and classroom practices. Health is the one subject that transcends the life-experiences of students and teachers within schools. Each day and in every way, what students and teachers experience contributes to their health and well-being. We must plan for positive learning environments and a productive, caring capacity, so everyone within the school feels valued, loved, trusted, challenged, and cared for during their time in school. The challenge lies in understanding these students and their life experiences.

ECUR 450 is meant to provide teacher candidates with an understanding of practical Health methodologies and help TCs develop knowledge about health and pedagogical skills as classroom teachers. The class assignments, discussions, and content are structured to facilitate TCs' understanding of the connection between personal health, wellness, and education from both student and teacher perspectives. The mandate in ECUR 450 is to encourage TCs to think broadly about Health education. Course outcomes include understandings of the following:

- The K-12 aim of the *Saskatchewan Health Education Curricula* is to develop confident and competent students who understand, appreciate, and apply health knowledge, skills, and strategies throughout life;

- Health education contributes to fostering improved health while recognizing that there are many *issues and factors that promote health* at every stage of a young person's development;

- *Mental health* is of primary concern today;

- Inquiry questions explore deeper understanding to assist students in negotiating the bigger questions of *decision-making and taking responsibility* for their health in relation to self-community-family-peers;

- *Teacher health* is important. Throughout this course, teacher candidates can provide opportunities to attain, maintain, and promote a healthy mind, body, emotion, and spirit (Saskatchewan Ministry of Education, 2010).

Brenda Kalyn, the first author of this chapter, was the course's primary instructor, and both cohorts received the same syllabus and followed the same instructional procedures. Beverley Brenna, the second author of this chapter, was the author of several of the novels. The third author of this chapter, Ph.D. student Judy Jaunzems-Fernuk, was a major contributor to lectures and discussions with TCs. All three worked together to understand the data collected in this inquiry and appear as authors of this chapter.

2c: Organization of the innovation

TCs in both cohorts were provided with a class overview of the readings through the course syllabi in the first week of January. However, one month before the beginning of the class, TCs were sent an e-mail explaining the books required in the class and the option of searching them out online. This provided them with plenty of time and alleviated tensions of not having the material when readings began. Discussions of the novels did not occur until March, so students had adequate time to secure their reading. The novels were provided at a cost to the students, and all books were less than $20.00 Canadian. *The Boy Who was Raised as a Dog* (2017) was ordered online or purchased by the students in the campus bookstore. We have found that students often access cheaper or used versions online and prefer this method. While TCs purchased these required resources, a small grant related to this study allowed us to offer a complimentary book of choice to all TCs following the study.

TCs were placed into reading groups based on their chosen novels; no specific numbers were required for each group. Following our reader-response framework, TCs were asked to react evocatively to the novel they read in preparation for group discussions. TCs were also required to submit written responses answering the various response questions on selected novels, which served as part of our data set as well as contributed to their group discussions:

1. Summarize the story in one paragraph.

2. As you read through your novel and prepare for class discussion, please consider: your reaction to the story as a reader and a teacher.

3. Were there one or two pieces of the story that really made you think, question, wonder, or answer a question you might have had?

4. Broad question: what did you learn from reading this novel? Was there an evocative piece in the story that spoke to you as a learner and as a teacher?

5. Before this health course, did you consider the use of fiction to extend your personal understanding of content-area outcomes? Explain.

6. Would you consider using novels about sensitive issues within your teaching? Identify the tensions and/or benefits of utilizing fiction to support content-area outcomes. Please share your rationale for thinking this way.

7. What advice would you give to authors of children's literature in making their work accessible to support content-area teaching?

The groups discussed their responses. After about 20 minutes, each group summarized the novel, and their responses, to the whole class; this provided an overview for all students to learn about the five other novels besides the one they read.

Reading the multi-case study book, *The Boy Who was Raised as a Dog* (2017), followed a similar pattern. However, at this juncture, the instructor placed the TCs into reading groups of 3–5 students. There were nine chapters/case studies chosen for reading, and students were assigned to read the introduction (Chapter 1) and assigned chapter. Subsequent group discussions occurred around a list of questions; group summaries were also presented to the class, outlining the case studies read by each group. TCs learned about the trauma identified within each chapter, the child's behavioral characteristics, treatment approaches, and outcomes. The following reader-response questions were applied to this text, answered in written form as well as verbally discussed within TC groups, adding to our data set:

1. Summarize the chapter's story in one paragraph.

2. What were the child's behaviors as a result of the trauma experienced?

3. Discuss Dr. Perry's approach to therapy for the child.

4. What did you learn about trauma and the brain?

5. Were there evocative moments in the story that spoke to you as a learner and teacher?

6. How might you apply this knowledge within your classroom?

7. Did the readings of the novel and the case studies impact your learning and/or caring for students in different ways? If so, how?

Two additional questions were asked of the TCs, who provided written responses to these and an open-ended question; verbal discussions occurred within the class based on these questions.

1. What did you learn about teaching sensitive health-related issues through reading your novel?

    a. Consider the required reading of the novel for class vs a lecture/discussion on bullying, suicide, etc. Which would you prefer, and why? What is the *value* in one or the other?

2. How did the case study book *The Boy Who was Raised as a Dog* affect you personally, professionally, or both?

    a. Is this a good approach to learning about trauma, life, outcomes, impacts on children, and above all, about hope, love, and good therapy? Please explain your thoughts.

3. Any further comments?

Table 1 identifies the process of our use of the novels and case study literature. The exploration of both types of reading material relied on independent reading and discussion in reading groups before summarizing the group responses for the class.

Novel	Case Study
1. Choose novel and assign reading groups	1. Assign chapters for reading
2. Complete reader response questions prior to due date discussions	2. Designate discussion groups based on chapters
3. Group discussions	3. Complete reader response questions prior to due date discussions
4. Summarize for the class	4. Group discussions
	5. Summarize for the class

Table 1: Process Summary.

A Post-Class Survey occurred at the end of the course requesting further information. Due to the COVID 19 outbreak, we sent this survey to our students via email:

1. Have your course-based readings and experiences this semester increased your knowledge base and/or caused any transformation in your understanding of teaching health, specifically, and teaching, in general? Please explain.
2. Do you have a preference to learn from stories such as these you have read in class, from textbooks, lectures, or a combination? Please elaborate.
3. During the course, were you aware of thinking like a teacher vs. thinking like a student, or both? Please expand.
4. Please write a one or two-sentence description of your main 'take away' from your learning experiences within the class.
5. Please list three words to describe how you were emotionally engaged by the stories and/or presentations.

In addition, as shown in Table 2, we also requested the completion of a Likert Scale response by way of rating the impact of the six course-based experiences/resources on their 'knowledge growth'.

Case studies	No Impact	Some Impact	Fair Impact	Strong Impact	Most Impact
Novel	1	2	3	4	5
In-class presentations	1	2	3	4	5
Guest speakers	1	2	3	4	5
In-class sharing of personal experiences	1	2	3	4	5
Selected readings (for Action Plan)	1	2	3	4	5
Reflective responses to readings	1	2	3	4	5

Table 2: Knowledge Connections Likert Scale Response.

2d: Preparation of the innovation: Course engagement through assignments

The course begins with an overarching look at health and wellness, health curricula, and the curricula conceptual pieces. Through a wellness survey, TCs analyze their personal health and wellness in six dimensions and subsequently move into a personal eight to ten-week Action Plan (AP), which directly reflects embedded curricula content from K-Grade 9. The desired outcome is to connect TCs to curricula and pedagogical practice through personal experience. The design is meant to encourage the intersection between the TC as a student and the TC as a teacher, thereby exploring the transitional and liminal phases of change. The big question within the assignment is preparation for the profession and the following question: *Who takes care of the teacher?* The goal is to get at the 'heart' of the TC and encourage exploration of self through their experiences, challenges, and successes.

Further assignments include exploring and presenting health issues in relation to children, classrooms, and subsequent teacher practice. Teacher 'practice' forms as a result of knowledge acquisition and exploration of real-life scenarios through discussions, reflections, readings, and student presentations. The goal is to relate to the issue as teachers and understand the implication for students and how we, as teachers, care *for our students*. Through the assignment, TCs work in groups to:

- *Understand* the *basic health issue*;
- Discuss the issue in *relation to children*, their health, and learning;
- Define the *teacher's role* in understanding the issue and its relation to teaching;
- Describe how student *health is compromised* as a result of this issue; and
- Relate this issue to the *curricula outcomes* chosen.

Guest presentations: All guests were experts in their field and brought the *human story* to their presentations. The presentations were connected to the novel character experiences and to realities of the case study stories. Guest speaker topics included: Mental Health in the Classroom (Creating

Calm Classrooms); Sexual Health; Traditional Indigenous Teachings in Health; Effects of Racism on Children; LGBTQ2 Gender Issues.

The novels and case study readings formed the umbrella framework for this inquiry. Knowledge acquisition was extended through the novels and case-studies. The *stories* embedded within this literature related to real-life sensitive health issues of children and youth. The issues are reflective of what teachers may encounter within classrooms in terms of situational contexts and behaviors. Desired outcomes from these readings included the transformation of TCs from 'student reader' to an informed teacher with a greater understanding of knowledge and strategies of care for students, exploring the realities of professional contexts. The readings were the core of the course, and all guided course experiences enfold within the context of these stories, weaving back and forth within discussions, reflections, lectures, and presentations. These pedagogical strategies were deliberate and provided TCs with the opportunities to *explore the intersection between themselves as students and becoming teachers of students*. Ultimately, health, in all of its dimensions, is at the core of healthy learners and healthy teachers. We encourage other instructors to build on their contextual processes and cultures within their classroom and the particular curricula foci they wish to enhance. Most importantly, the novels and books selected should have high ratings from peer review for literary merit and not just appeal to the curricular topic of focus.

A number of theorists make suggestions about the teacher's role in selecting and presenting literature to students (Rozalski et al., 2010; Gregory & Vessey, 2004; Prater et al., 2006). They suggest the teacher's role should include:

- choosing a responsible selection of appropriate reading material that is developmentally appropriate to the curricula issue and has valuable context to the story;

- careful scrutiny of the characters;

- drawing students' attention to the illustrations and pictures as these enhance the presentation of the story;

- evaluating the author's message to the reader;

- building suitable and inspiring lessons within the curricula content;

- creating a safe learning environment within the classroom;
- collaborating with other school or health professionals for assistance;
- providing parental information about potential topics being discussed in class; and
- building a library resource of topics and suitable reading material.

We envisioned literature as a powerful tool to teach sensitive issues in the context of our province's Health curricula. Stories are a way to engage in the realities of challenging issues, sensitive topics and can be a less threatening way to encourage students to dialogue, role play, ask questions, and seek answers. Alternative options for students to demonstrate their understanding of issues may be through puppets, artistic expression, and role play in relation to the issue. Ultimately, the result of classroom practice will involve an increased understanding of the issue, personal change, increased empathy, healing, continued wonder questions, and improved overall health.

Before the readings began in class, TCs were told the nature of the readings and that any personal sensitivities or concerns they might be feeling about the intended readings should be discussed with their instructor to eliminate any potential trauma within our classroom. There was only one TC who said she was not sure she should read the novel because she was early in her pregnancy, and she did not want to experience any negative emotional responses to the story and threaten her overall health and well-being. The course instructor discussed this with her, and they agreed it should be the TC's decision. An alternative assignment would have been presented; however, the student decided to read the novel. This points to the importance of having counseling services in place, being aware of who their students are, and recognizing the potential for sensitive issues arising from past TC experiences or from within their classroom of students. Setting a caring and respectful environment within the university classroom will hopefully alleviate any discomfort or tensions for TCs. Teacher candidates need to feel safe as adults to discuss and share their opinions and to feel the tensions that arise from discussions that occur.

The data collected from the optional post-class surveys was collected by a graduate student and stored on her password-protected computer until all marks were submitted. Names were removed from the survey questions, ensuring student anonymity. This practice was applied to address ethical considerations of potential power dynamics where instructors study student responses related to a course in session. Because this inquiry lay within the framework of typical course improvement, it was approved by our REB ethics board for exemption from further formal ethics' procedures, including participant permissions.

Section 3: The outcome

The initial health and wellness survey undertaken by TCs in class seemed very effective in inviting them to interrogate their personal health and wellness. Via their personal Action Plan assignment, TCs could implement a curriculum-related plan to take care of themselves as teachers and evaluate personal outcomes at the end of their 8–10-week plans. TCs were highly moved when sharing personal and sometimes sensitive challenges through their assignments, which they have faced throughout their lives. We believe that this precipitated for them a reflective connection regarding the evocative nature of health, upcoming readings, and subsequent connections to course material. TCs related more fully to the challenges of maintaining health on a variety of levels; this assignment was directly related to the K-8 Health curricula.

Constant shaping of discussion topics and building an umbrella of health-related conversations was primary for the instructor teaching these courses. Moving throughout the term, it was important to point out how teacher health and wellness related to students' outcomes and focused on connections within our topics of discussions. In doing so, it became visible that TCs were making strong connections, moving through thoughtful, evocative experiences, moving through the liminal space as TCs/students, and envisioning transferring this knowledge to their classrooms. They formulated ideas on how to implement stories of experience into the classroom to promote discussion, foster deeper understandings, and reach curricular outcomes.

When considering providing advice to authors of children's literature, TCs suggested writing through the child's eyes, yet keeping the topic authentic without 'putting ideas into children's minds.' A focus on healing and positivity was also stressed to encourage healthy outcomes. Including illustrations and being mindful of the language that children could understand were also recommended. According to the TCs, authentic, researched characteristics validated the storied content and contributed to validity and reliability.

The case study compilation, *The Boy Who was Raised as a Dog* (Perry & Szalavitz, 2017), provided thought-provoking insights into the trauma and tragedy that children face in their lives alongside hope and resilience in overcoming adversity. TCs came to understand knowledge about the brain and its healing capacity through appropriate counseling, the strength of inter-agencies working together, and the power in love and understanding that teachers bring to students' lives. We used this book to teach TCs about experience through content; we did not suggest reading it with elementary or secondary students.

TC commentary about their experience reading this book was positive for a variety of reasons and included these combined observations and personal responses:

- *"I loved this book... I could not put it down. It is a reminder that we can never assume where a child is from or why they are how they are"*;
- *"It made me consider and re-evaluate my approach to students...I gained a better understanding of how to be a trauma-sensitive, informed teacher"*;
- *"It provided biological, neurological information within the case study story...and how teachers can make a difference"*;
- *"I was upset at the depressing life lived by some children..."*;
- *"Made me rethink my own childhood and what therapy can do... affected me personally and professionally and reminded me how fortunate I am"*; and
- *"It serves as a reminder that students may have issues going on outside of school, and as teachers, we must consider behavioral triggers."*

3a: Student perspective

Many of the TCs surveyed self-identified that, before this course, their experience and thus their consideration of using fiction materials to support

Health Curriculum outcomes was limited. Over half of the respondents indicated that they had not previously considered using fiction to support health lessons. As one respondent stated, "*I thought of health as a matter-of-fact subject.*" Another TC indicated, "*Honestly, I didn't realize that fiction can extend my personal understanding of health curricula. I would love to hear more about similar fiction novels.*" A third TC stated that "*I honestly thought that fiction texts shouldn't be used as sources of information because the stories are not true. I now understand that there can be truth within the fiction.*" TC comments indicated that their literary reading as part of this course encouraged them to broaden their views of reading and to read more.

A minority group of students, those who had previously considered the use of fiction to extend personal understanding of Health Curricula/content area outcomes, voiced ways that the current work reinforced their views. "*A lot of fiction stories deal with personal issues and experiences that students have*", said one TC. "*I also read a lot of fiction books that helped me decide to make good choices in teen/adult years.*" Another reminded us of the importance of authentic subject matter—that we can learn from fiction, "*especially if the stories are based on research.*" Another TC said, "*I prefer to learn from stories… they leave more of an impression.*" When thinking about resources for future teaching, these TCs noted the importance of grade level when assessing the appropriateness of resources. Novels were deemed supportive for particular age groups, with some discrepancies in suggested ages, as TCs varied from advocating use in high school or Grades 6 and up, or particularly for teachers, administrators, librarians, and school counselors, while others identified possibilities for students in Grades 4 and up. A number of TCs indicated that the application of a novel might depend on the particular students involved—whether they were mature enough to handle the sensitive content. Many students indicated preferences for an additional list of related titles and based on their responses new titles will be added to the reading choices this coming term.

Rationale for Novels

Many of the TCs provided a common rationale for using a novel study in elementary and/or secondary health class settings, citing that these resources were "*engaging.*" "*People like stories and giving their opinions*", said one respondent, another adding, "*It's a necessity to discuss mental health and suicidal ideation/peer pressure in teenagers… novels would be a good way to introduce sensitive topics."* Another stated *"for students who have struggled with these issues, it may feel validating to have it discussed…"* This TC continued *"fiction provides a more personal, humanistic viewpoint of a situation…with emotional connections to the character, leading to increased empathy and understanding of mental health issues."*

These responses parallel more general reasons for sharing literature with children and young adults, connecting to a list of outcomes provided by Wason Ellam (1987) that suggest literature is important for a variety of purposes: to provide vicarious experiences; to extend linguistic options for reading and writing and to develop vocabulary and ideas. In the field of literacy, Rosenblatt's (1978) theory of reader-response is a powerful reminder of the value of literature as a pivot for personal transformation and is a common framework for English teachers. In Health education, however, it seems as if we are still working to apply what we have known in English coursework for some time: that literature has great power in catalyzing efferent as well as aesthetic reader experiences. Responses from this study also highlight the potentiality of interdisciplinary teaching, where literacy skills and content area knowledge can be enhanced together. Cohen (2002) identified how effective it is to wrap content-area lessons in fiction—illustrating the uses of textbook novels, written specifically by academics for this purpose, in post-secondary education.

Tensions in our current study related to the serious content in our resources offered particular thoughts about introducing a book like *Fox Magic* (Brenna, 2018). One TC stated, *"There is a chance students would feel uncomfortable, but it is likely they will all benefit."* This respondent went on to advise the selection of specific curriculum outcomes realizable through the use of this resource. TCs combined shared thoughts: *"It's a heavy book, so I would need to feel like my class was prepared for it…I would talk with the school counselor if a student is known to be depressed and/or suicidal prior to this topic…I would reach out to parents before bringing it into the classroom."* Another TC emphasized the importance of having *"sensitive class discussions about the heavy content in a novel"*, ensuring that students would not be left to read it on their own. Ideas that the content might be *"too graphic"* or *"traumatizing"* for those who have personal connections to the serious subject matter, or even *"triggering"* were suggested as applicable to future decisions as a classroom teacher.

Another smaller group of respondents presented their anxiety in relation to teaching serious issues. *"I think I would be more comfortable in sharing a novel to teach sensitive issues than not using a resource…however, I am still a little uncomfortable."*

Another TC posed that, *"Sometimes I think it's best to not address topics such as harm and suicide but rather focus on bettering the student with healthy coping mechanisms."* Related to this were concerns from a few of the respondents about having choices in what/how to teach. *"I would feel slightly anxious,"* said one, *"if I had to teach something that I did not feel comfortable with."*

Finally, there were respondents that reminded us about the importance of particular resources for particular subjects. *"In some cases,"* said one TC, *"I would prefer a lecture (on topics such as safe sexual practices) because the message may be clearer."* Another respondent said, *"Reading the novel allows for a slow build-up to an important conversation"*, and emphasized *"the importance of pairing novels with opportunities to expand children's background knowledge and information on connected subjects."*

The novels provided strong insight into the characteristics of the youth who were living with particular differences such as autism, fetal alcohol syndrome, mutism, foster care, parental neglect, gender issues, family disruptions, and others. TCs could relate to some of these situational contexts within the classrooms they visited throughout their internship and pre-service education. The readings became more "non-fictional" due to experiences encountered with students in classrooms who reflected the storied characters. Reality, knowledge, story, and experience intersected in new ways for TCs as a result.

Teacher Candidates Transitioning through Liminal Space

As instructors, we were curious about TCs as students and exploring their curricula experiences as a teacher. Their responses were intriguing:

- *"I considered what it would be like to be a student in my classroom"*;
- *"The concepts that we learned … caused me to think like a teacher because I was invited to reflect on how I would address these issues in my own teaching practice"*;
- *"During some of the lectures I felt like a student learning many things for the first time"*;

- "Whereas I felt more like a teacher when considering ways to teach health in my own classroom"; and

- "I was able to put myself in the students' shoes as well as the teacher's shoes. I am grateful for that experience as I see things and understand things a lot differently than I would have previous to this class."

TCs made connections between subject, knowledge, students, and the teacher; this assisted them in navigating the liminal space between teaching and learning. The humanistic nature of the readings increased TCs' knowledge of sensitive issues and the realities of the children who experience trauma and differences in their lives. As Figure 1 clearly depicts, they experienced learning and knowledge as well as increased empathy for the children's experiences.

Figure 1: Wordle Drawn from TC Responses to Literary Texts.

3b: Teacher perspective – our reflections

Instructor Perspective

Course instructors noted that integrating fiction and non-fiction case studies into this Health education course was productive, but not without challenges. As with any working group, there were some levels of discomfort when discussing difficult issues. Within the classes, there were several TCs who shared their experiences with trauma and mental health issues. Dealing with personal issues, as a teacher, became another topic of conversation and reaffirmed the importance of paying attention to teacher health, in order to effectively deal with the health of students within one's classroom. TCs varied from being excited to teach about important health issues in literary novels to being somewhat apprehensive; a few TCs said they still preferred a lecture, as they felt retention of information was better for them that way. Both the primary and assistant instructors within the course have Mental Health First Aid Training and counseling expertise, which positioned them to listen attentively to TCs and guide discussion while being attentive to TC tensions and behaviors.

The instructors noted that TCs connected as teachers, and demonstrated thinking more about their future students, than identifying as students themselves. They made the link between literary novel and case study as informative, realistic, and emotional. They broadened their knowledge and expanded their ideas of practice and being openly observant of children's behavior and considering why that behavior exists. They recognized their positioning in the classroom and identified that they are not counselors or therapists; however, they believed themselves capable of understanding the implications of experience in a student's life and how that may manifest through classroom behavior. This type of awareness evolved from their experiences with the literary material from this course, and they affirmed that this was a new and valued learning experience.

The introduction of non-conventional literary works within this health methods course affirmed the value of literature to educate and inspire new teachers as noted by this TC, "*The class structure helped me connect with the content... expert guest speakers, group and class discussions were very beneficial.*" Another TC affirmed, "*I loved the way this class was set up, and I wouldn't change a thing.*"

Section 4: Moving forward

Ultimately, it is important as course instructors to provide a wide variety of methods for TCs to explore sensitive topics and issues in Health education that may affect their classrooms and school communities. Student engagement can be heightened through reading novels and case studies. Prater et al., (2006) affirm that using literary novels has many benefits for students, including encouraging expression, dealing with and discussing problematic issues, and analyzing the thoughts and behaviors of self and others. Subsequently, these outcomes may transfer to the elementary school classroom, where children are able to share and empathize with others who struggle (Gregory & Vessey, 2004). Rozalski et al. (2010) assert that books have long been used within the areas of social studies and history to learn about the historical stories of others. It would be prudent then to follow suit within the area of Health education and learn about the sensitive issues that face contemporary teachers and children.

As instructors in higher education, we believe this innovation was important and demonstrated positive, thought-provoking outcomes for TCs who are about to embark on their careers. We realized that introducing an innovation dealing with sensitive issues was 'big' and we were under no illusion that all TCs would be comfortable with these topics within their classrooms. We were aware they might agree that this innovation is a wonderful idea yet feel a sense of *"I can't do it"*. Above all, we wanted to 'plant a seed', encourage thinking about using novels in teaching sensitive Health issues, and encourage them to work within their comfort levels. To build teacher capacity and confidence within Health education, we held professional development sessions to support learning for TCs, provided information on the Mental Health Certification Course, and shared extra resources.

We intend to continue with the implementation of a learning and exploring curriculum through novels and case studies. We posit that the realities of the human experience override the factual contexts of learning. We intentionally wanted to get at the heart of teaching, learning, and experiences. As human beings, we are *feeling* beings, and we are called to make sense of life and the world through the realities of stories that are experienced every day by others, if not ourselves. Developing greater empathy and knowledge challenge us to learn about others, apply solutions to curriculum, and forward critical pedagogies in education.

Conclusion

While deepening understandings about the variety of resources that might be utilized to achieve Health Curriculum outcomes, TCs involved in this inquiry were very receptive to these resources for supporting them in their own knowledge base. *The Boy Who was Raised as a Dog* "*affected me personally and professionally,*" said one TC "*...because it made me aware of the unknown situations my students may face*". While most of the TCs surveyed had positive responses to the idea of fiction and case study materials in support of post-secondary Health courses as well as the teaching of Health in secondary and elementary contexts, a minority stated a preference for the more traditional lecture model: "*I learn better through listening, seeing slides, watching videos than I do retaining the information in books...*" recognizing that "*...others who enjoy reading more may choose to read.*" TCs, who indicated little previous experience with using fiction in content areas such as Health, seemed to voice the greatest tensions in literary applications. "*I never had a Health class that did that, and so I never thought of it,*" stated one respondent, going on to express anxiety about teaching sensitive issues in general but also stating, "*I would like to learn more about these topics and what I can do as a teacher to help students who struggle.*"

Our constructivist process innovation, in applying unique resources to this Health education setting, is really just the beginning of our explorations with non-traditional required reading for our students. It would be interesting to follow our TCs into their early teaching experiences, identifying whether fiction and case-study materials are used to support their elementary or secondary students in content-area learning. Tensions identified by in-service teachers related to sensitive Health Curriculum outcomes might assist us in circling back to our practice and re-considering key resources and their application. We are heartened by the positive responses from our TCs in terms of the benefits of the novels and case study materials we shared and continue to imagine places of evocative intersection between content-area teaching and English Language Arts.

Further research is recommended on the application of a variety of resources in elementary and secondary settings, considering the value of these resources for students at every age level, and exploring the teaching practice of Health instructors who seek to deliver the very best program possible in reaching curricular outcomes for the health and well-being of their students. Such research is important in recognizing the multiplicity of roles played and the understanding of techniques needed, by the 21st-century teacher, ourselves included. Drawing from interdisciplinary solutions to challenges faced is one approach that may facilitate the work of educators. Innovations here showcase an extension of the role of 'teacher', as well as shifting student roles and ways of learning.

About the Authors

Brenda Kalyn, PhD is an Associate Professor in Curriculum Studies, College of Education, University of Saskatchewan. She can be contacted at this e-mail: brenda.kalyn@usask.ca

Beverley Brenna, PhD is a Professor in Curriculum Studies, College of Education, University of Saskatchewan. She can be contacted at this e-mail: bev.brenna@usask.ca.

Judy Jaunzems-Fernuk, PhD is a sessional lecturer in the College of Education, University of Saskatchewan. She can be contacted at this e-mail: judy.fernuk@usask.ca

Bibliography

Bandura, A. (1977). *Social learning theory.* Englewood Cliffs, NJ: Prentice-Hall.
Bates, H. & Eccles, K. (2008). *Wellness curricula to improve the health of children and youth: A review and synthesis of related literature.* Ministry of Education Alberta Education: Edmonton, Alberta.
Brenna, B. (2005). *Wild orchid.* Calgary, AB: Red Deer Press.
Brenna, B. (2007). *The moon children.* Markham, ON: Red Deer Press.
Brenna, B. (2018). *Fox magic.* Markham, ON: Red Deer Press.
Brenna, B. (2019). *Sapphire the Great and the meaning of life.* Toronto, ON: Pajama Press.
Cohen, P. (2002). *Teachers wrap lesson in fiction.* Retrieved April 11, 2019, from https://www.nytimes.com/2002/11/16/books/teachers-wrap-lessons-in-fiction.html
Crownover, A. & Jones, J. R. (2018). A relational pedagogy: A call for teacher educators to rethink how teacher candidates are trained to combat bullying. *Journal of Thought*, 52(1–2), pp. 17–28.
Dobozy, E. & Nygaard, C. (2021). A learning-centred five-tier model of innovation in higher education. In Enomoto, K., Warner, R. & Nygaard, C. (Eds.), *Teaching and Learning Innovations in Higher Education*, pp. 19–46. Oxfordshire, UK: Libri Publishing Ltd.

Evans, R. (2021). Innovative assessment in higher education; a public dissemination assessment model for language students. In Enomoto, K., Warner, R. & Nygaard, C. (Eds.), *Teaching and Learning Innovations in Higher Education*, pp. 323–337. Oxfordshire, UK: Libri Publishing Ltd.

Goobie, B. (2013). *Jason's why*. Markham, ON: Red Deer Press.

Gregory, K. E. & Vessey, J. A. (2004). Bibliotherapy: A strategy to help students with bullying. *The Journal of School Nursing*, 20(3), pp. 127–133.

Khong, L. (2021). Facilitating active student learning using innovative approaches in pre-service teacher education. In Enomoto, K., Warner, R. & Nygaard, C. (Eds.), *Teaching and Learning Innovations in Higher Education*, pp. 301–321. Oxfordshire, UK: Libri Publishing Ltd.

Kogan, B. A. (1970). *Health: Man in a changing environment*. New York, NY: Harcourt, Brace & World, Inc.

Land, R., Rattray, J. & Vivian, P. (2014). Learning in the liminal space: A semiotic approach to threshold concepts. *Higher Education*, 67(2), pp. 199–217.

Leavitt, M. (2015). *Calvin*. Toronto, ON: House of Anansi Press.

McLeod, S. (2020). *Maslow's hierarchy of needs*. Retrieved March 20, 2020, from https://www.simplypsychology.org/maslow.html#classroom

Mental Health Commission of Canada (2019). Retrieved June 15, 2020, from https://www.mentalhealthcommission.ca

Mezirow, J. (2000). *Learning as transformation: Critical perspectives on a theory in progress*. San Francisco, CA: Jossey-Bass.

Perry, B. & Szalavitz, M. (2017). *The boy who was raised as a dog*. New York, NY: Basic Books.

Prater, M. A., Johnstun, M. L., Dyches, T. T. & Johnstun, M. R. (2006). Using children's books as bibliotherapy for at-risk students: A guide for teachers. *Preventing School Failure: Alternative Education for Children and Youth*, 50(4), pp. 5–10.

Raphael, D. (Ed.). (2016). *Social determinants of health: Canadian perspectives* (3rd ed.). Toronto, ON: Canadian Scholars' Press.

Ratcliff, J. D. (1982). *I am Joe's body*. New York, NY: Berkley Publishing, Co.

Rosenblatt, L. (1978). *The reader, the text, the poem: The transactional theory of the literary work*. Carbondale, IL: Southern Illinois UP.

Rosenblatt, L. M. (1982). The literary transaction: Evocation and response. *Children's Literature*, 21(4), pp. 268–277.

Rowley, J. (2021). Discovering professional identity through reflective narrative writing: a case study of pedagogic proficiency. In Enomoto, K., Warner, R. & Nygaard, C. (Eds.), *Teaching and Learning Innovations in Higher Education*, pp. 357–373. Oxfordshire, UK: Libri Publishing Ltd.

Rozalski, M., Stewart, A. & Miller, J. (2010). Bibliotherapy: Helping children cope with life's challenges. *Kappa Delta Pi Record, 47*(1), pp. 33–37.

Saskatchewan Ministry of Education (2010). Curriculum.gov.sk.ca

Schooling, D. (2021). Teaching from the Native American circle: an innovative teaching framework. In Enomoto, K., Warner, R. & Nygaard, C. (Eds.), *Teaching and Learning Innovations in Higher Education*, pp. 339–356. Oxfordshire, UK: Libri Publishing Ltd.

Socha, T. & Cameron, E. (2019). A sociocultural perspective on teaching health and physical literacy. In Barret, J. & Scaini, C. (Eds.) *Physical and Health Education in Canada: Integrated approaches for elementary teachers.* Champaign, IL: Human Kinetics.

Slavich, G. & Zimbardo, P. (2012). Transformational teaching: Theoretical underpinnings, basic principles and core methods. *Educational Psychology Review, 24*, pp. 569–608.

Vygotsky, L. S., (1978). Interaction between learning and development. In M. Cole, V. John-Steiner, S. Scribner & E. Souberman (Eds.), *Mind in society: The development of higher psychological processes*, pp. 79–91. Cambridge: Harvard University Press.

Wason Ellam, L. (1987). *Sharing stories with children: Reading aloud and storytelling.* Calgary, AB: Warren West.

Chapter 19

Collaborative Enquiry-based Learning in an Oral Health Program

Hanna Olson

Introduction

With my chapter, I contribute to this book, *Teaching and Learning Innovations in Higher Education*, by demonstrating how collaborative enquiry-based learning is used as an innovative method to engage students in student-directed learning (SDL) and self-reflection. This innovative method was implemented for final year undergraduate students in Oral Health as part of a semester-long course in *Community Oral Health & Oral Health Promotion* at the University of Otago, New Zealand. In the module, students use the innovative method of enquiry-based learning as they develop a project plan guided by SMART principles for goal setting (Doran, 1981). The innovation, I present, is a process innovation as it is an equitable method for student engagement, including reflection on practice for undergraduate students and academic staff. This is important because, upon graduation, students can register with the Dental Council of New Zealand and practice as Oral Health Therapists.

In this chapter, I elaborate and discuss enquiry-based learning containing elements of collaborative practice and SDL for oral health students. Referring to the learning-centred five-tier model of innovation in higher education (Dobozy & Nygaard, 2021, Chapter 2 in this book), my process innovation draws on a constructivist perception of learning. Perceiving learning as a constructivist, I primarily see my process innovation as a means to engagement through collaboration and reflection. The innovation is underpinned by the guiding principles of experiential learning theory (Kolb, 1984). Implementing such a process innovation in curriculum development can bring about positive outcomes for both students and teachers, which I describe in Section 3.

Reading this chapter, you will gain the following three insights:
1. learn how to outline an enquiry-based learning approach in planning an oral health promotion program;
2. gain insight into staff/student reflections on adding a component of collaborative practice and sessions of SDL;
3. reveal teaching strategies to replicate this module as part of curriculum development for future student collaboration projects and group assignments.

Overview of main sections

This chapter has four main sections. Section 1 provides a rationale for enquiry-based learning and why it became part of students' curriculum. In Section 2, the intervention is explained in more detail, with an elaboration on essential attributes such as collaborative practice, student-directed learning and reflection on practice. Section 3 includes a description of both student and staff perceptions of the module after being involved in the innovative practice. In the final section, a discussion takes place on how the intervention can be replicated to be part of curriculum development and incorporated in other settings and programs to provide students with the important skill of life-long learning.

Section 1: The background

Collaborative engagement methods of learning have been shown to increase student engagement and increased learning, and improving both conceptual understanding and class attendance when compared to the employment of traditional lecturing (Slavich & Zimbardo, 2012). Transformational praxes, such as communities of scholarship and practice, are enacted in support of transformational pedagogy and student-directed engagement (Adams & Bell, 2016). A collaborative approach to structured reflection on teaching and learning may lead to such transformational praxes (Ossa Parra et al., 2014). Already in 1978, Vygotsky argued that through collaborative experiences and social interactions, students could learn to manage their emotions. Furthermore, he suggested that within the right learning environment, it would be possible for students to master concepts and ideas that they cannot understand on their own (Vygotsky, 1978).

Experiential learning has been described in a variety of terms, such as problem-based learning, project-based learning, transformational learning, reflective learning and student-directed learning (Transformational learning is further explored by Jaunzems-Fernuk *et al.*, 2021, Chapter 20 in this book). Kolb, the best-known proponent of experiential learning, in his early work, described the experiential learning cycle as a process of experiences, including observation and reflection that forms new knowledge to apply in new situations (Kolb, 1984). Following on from this earlier work, he eventually concluded that experiential education might be a useful framework for educational innovations such as curriculum development and life-long learning (Kolb, 2014; Kolb's theory of experiential learning is further explored by Swann, 2021, Chapter 22 in this book). Learning, that is enquiry-based, has similarities with the teaching-learning cyclical model, described earlier by Warner & Enomoto (2021, Chapter 10 in this book), as aspects of enquiry-based learning are recognisable in each of the four categories; 1. reflection and observation; 2. abstract & conceptualisation; 3. active experimentation; and 4. concrete experience (Kolb, 1984). The learning and teaching innovation in this chapter, however, takes a collaborative student-learning approach and was a result of reflections on student evaluation outcomes from course content in previous years.

As an early career researcher and lecturer in oral health, I set up a primary goal for my teaching. The goal is to provide students with skills applicable for lifelong professional learning, enabling them to provide excellent patient care through collaborative practice within their profession as well as interprofessional education (a collaborative approach to cross-disciplinary learning is further explored by Willcocks & Lange (2021, Chapter 21 in this book). However, the theory does not always align with what is manageable in practice or indeed acceptable to other professional stakeholders.

The issue of acceptability had also been raised by students in previous cohorts of *Community Oral Health & Oral Health Promotion*. They opined that it was a somewhat boring course, with no relevance to clinical practice, which they just wanted to complete as soon as possible (correlating to what is further discussed by Jaunzems-Fernuk *et al.*, 2021, Chapter 20 in this book). Some of the students argued that there was no connection between theory and practice, and did not see the link nor the relevance of this course to their future work as oral health professionals. For the most of the course, during sessions of didactic teaching, students would sit quietly, appearing unengaged. At the University of Otago, attending lectures is not a compulsory component of a course or a program, although highly recommended. The drop-out rate for attending lectures in this particular course was high, with barely one-third of students attending the lectures provided in this particular course.

The latest University of Otago Undergraduate programs evaluation report was conducted by the Dental Council of New Zealand (DCNZ, 2020), as a result of their visit to the Faculty of Dentistry in September 2019. The report suggested that co-design and collaborative planning of treatment and delivery of care were important factors when preparing oral health students for collaborative team care. For example, enhanced collaborative approaches across services and the patient journey pathways were made as suggestions to assure public safety. To foster a collaborative dental team approach to care, joint patient management opportunities were expected to be reinstated within the Faculty. Furthermore, joint management of patients outside of the dental team should also be explored (DCNZ, 2020). These collaborative approaches, also embedded in learning theories from an experiential educational perspective, gave rise to enquiry for principles of interprofessional learning and collaborative practice to be implemented and explored in the forthcoming curriculum.

Peacock & Cowan (2018) concluded that student abilities to increase their level of cognitive and interpersonal development such as critical thinking are associated with a learning-centred approach, supported by SDL. Already in the 1960s, Rogers had the idea of what might become of education, when offering students the freedom to learn (Rogers, 1969). Other factors, such as shifting the conceptualisation of role and relationship between student and staff (Healey *et al.*, 2015), along with empowering students into peer-learning (Nygaard *et al.*, 2009), are some influencing factors for the expansion and increased use of SDL in higher education. From an enquiry-based learning perspective, students should achieve outcomes such as critical thinking, independent inquiry, intellectual growth and maturity as well as responsibility for own learning

– all which would prepare them for valuable life-long learning (Lee et al., 2004). Over one decade ago, Spronken-Smith (2008:8) concluded that *"Inquiry-based learning, if carefully constructed and implemented, provides an excellent avenue for the development of deep approaches to learning."*

All of the attributes mentioned above, coupled with recommendations from the DCNZ (2020), were taken into consideration when planning the innovative shift from teacher-led to student-directed learning. This was undertaken as part of the curriculum development of a course module addressing oral health promotion.

Section 2: The practice

The module discussed in this chapter, forms part of a practical component of an oral health promotion course for undergraduate students, with an innovation centred around collaboration and teamwork. In the third and final year of the bachelor program, students are given a group assignment with the instructions to develop an oral health promotion project plan using the SMART model for goal setting. The expectations are that all group members will contribute to the assignment and finalise the project together. This innovative, collaborative approach is a step forward towards enhancing deeper learning through sessions of SDL. Along with the project plan, students will also hand in an individual statement reflecting their experience working as members of a team. With the increased demand for collaborative approaches stemming from the oral health workforce, the intention was to incorporate a module on collaborative practice and SDL into the curriculum and to prepare students for this essential skill of life-long learning, already during their time of undergraduate health professional studies. In delivering the module, it was important for me to explicitly explain both the structure of the module and the expectations of the students. Thus, as the course coordinator and lecturer for this module, I explained to the students that the module would comprise a combination of lectures and SDL tutorials. Students would be expected to work on a group assignment that involved the creation of an oral health promotion project plan.

In the first session, students were divided into small groups and assigned a specific topic area related to oral health. Within their group, students were expected to collectively plan the project, with the final outcome of a written group assignment. Along with the group project plan, each student would also submit an individual reflective statement on both their perceptions of how well the group worked together, along with specifying their personal contribution.

The theoretical knowledge students needed, to plan their project accordingly, was provided through a series of lectures in health promotion. In the second year, students were taught a generic course in health promotion. This year, within the course *Community Oral Health & Oral Health Promotion*, students expanded on their previous health promotion knowledge by studying oral health promotion in particular, including the process of planning and evaluating a community oral health program. This fundamental didactic teaching was taught in the classroom before starting sessions of SDL and collaborative practice.

Due to the widespread Covid-19 outbreak in 2020, students were in lockdown for most of the module, studying remotely away from campus. With short notice, the University of Otago started to prepare for remote online teaching, and all of the patient clinics within the Faculty of Dentistry that were not classified as essential services had to close abruptly. This included the student clinics in which the students treated patients daily.

Students were told to leave campus and advised to travel back home. Those international students, who were unable to travel overseas due to strict border restrictions, or students who did not have a different place to go, in such a short timeline, had to stay put in their current location; having to remain outside of the campus area. Teaching staff and academics were required to go home and prepare for remote teaching as soon as practicable. IT-support was given to both staff and students, including distance-learning support to enable remote teaching and learning for everyone. When the country was forced into lockdown, the web-based platform Zoom was immediately used as a real-time communication tool between staff and students. It was also over this platform that sessions of SDL would take place, in this particular module on 'oral health promotion' within the course *Community Oral Health & Oral Health Promotion*.

Each tutorial was facilitated by a lecturer (the author), who joined students in their group discussions and break-out rooms within the online platform, and answered students' queries. Students were divided into groups, and they agreed on how they would work together in the project. Most groups collaborated on a shared document, via Google Docs or iCloud, to which they could all contribute. Before commencing the project plan, the lecturer commented on the suitability of the target groups, health promotion goals and objectives of each project.

Students were instructed that goals and objectives should align with the acronym SMART (see Figure 1), meaning that the project should be specific, measurable, achievable, relevant and time-bond (Doran, 1981). The entire oral health promotion module comprised sessions of didactic teaching and enquiry-based learning, including collaborations and sessions of SDL. A total number of six sessions of SDL was scheduled over four weeks.

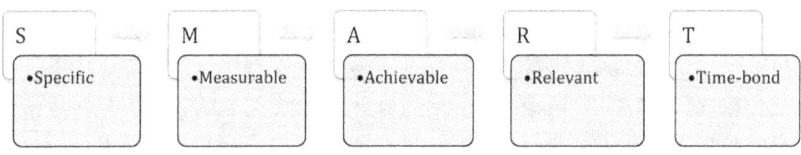

Figure 1: SMART Principles for setting goals, adopted from Doran (1981).

2a: A brief overview of the curriculum

The learning and teaching intervention in this particular course is structured to integrate all knowledge learnt within the program, with key aspects of understanding the public health approach. This course in community oral health and oral health promotion comprises one theoretical and one practical component, with equal contribution to students' final mark. The oral health promotion project contributed with 40% towards the practical component of the course.

According to the module objectives, students would learn about health promotion principles, the Ottawa Charter for health promotion, health behaviour models and different strategies available to improve oral health of communities. In particular, within the New Zealand context, students learn the principle of the Treaty of Waitangi in relation to oral health promotion targeted at Māori oral health and well-being (Health Promotion Forum of New Zealand, 2002; Durie, 1998). Indeed, there is a range of literature that addresses the issue of oral health- with particular emphasis on the New Zealand population and context, which form part of the recommended course reading (Signal & Ratima, 2015; Ministry of Health, 2008; Health Promotion Forum of New Zealand, 2002; Durie, 1998). Included in the text-books are real-life examples which were discussed during the lectures of didactic teaching. Among health promotion books and other publications (Daly et al., 2013; Green et al., 2015; Ministry of Health, 2008; WHO, 2004; Talbot & Verinder, 2018), students were given insight in how to plan and evaluate health promotion programs.

Students were also exposed to a step-by-step guide (checklist) on how to plan a health promotion project. The Western Australian Centre had prepared this checklist for Health Promotion Research at Curtin University of Technology (Curtin University, 2020) This checklist included important components for students to remember such as needs assessment (*What does the community need?*), program planning including examples of SMART goals and objectives (Doran, 1981), risk factors and protective factors for oral health (Sheiham & Watt, 2000), the Ottawa Charter for health promotion (WHO, 1986), along with resources for implementation and evaluation of the program when conducting such a project (Hawe et al., 1995). The checklist comprised all important and essential information students would need to include while following the required content (Table 1) when submitting their complete outline of a group project plan for oral health promotion.

In addition to paying attention to the learning objectives specifically addressed in this module, the main focus of this innovative practice was to help students realise how all the different elements of learning adequately align together, including more diverse courses with overlapping themes. With this holistic view, students would then be able to apply skills and knowledge learnt during their three years of study when collaboratively preparing this oral health promotion plan, as part of an SDL team approach.

2b: An introduction to the innovative practice

The innovation of this oral health promotion module was to create a collaborative team-effort within small student groups, which would be crucial to complete a group assignment of this calibre, comprising all aspects of being SMART (Figure 1). It is a significant task for students to be both innovative and to create such a massive project plan, considering all the elements included in oral health promotion. However, with task appropriate preparation materials, and facilitation skills, we anticipated a positive student-learning outcome. Bearing these twin issues of appropriate task materials and facilitation skills in mind, we gave an introduction to different health promotion projects. We demonstrated examples of how people engage and interact with each other to reach a common goal. This was actioned as a means to enrich and enhance students' process of learning and served as a starting point for the planning of their oral health projects.

A class of 40 students, in this mandatory course for students enrolled in the program, were divided into groups of either three or four and allocated one out of two broad topic areas. Those areas were 'early childhood caries' and 'older people's oral health care'. In their allocated group, students were expected to work collaboratively, while preparing their project plan outlining suitable SMART goals and objectives (Doran, 1981) to their specific topic.

Examples of SMART objectives for the two given topics:

1. To reduce early childhood caries among Māori children under age 5, in the Gisborne area, by 25% in 5 years.

2. To improve the oral health of older adults (aged 65+) living in an aged-care facility in South Dunedin, by 30% within 2 years.

Students were expected to set rules on how they would work together on the project. It was emphasized that students would need to agree on an oral health promotion goal within their group, suitable for their allocated topic/target area, and to use an appropriate health promotion planning model to guide the development of their plan. To highlight the importance of working towards a collaborative approach with other groups of health professionals, when carrying out such a project, students were reminded of the importance of a focus on the population level rather than on individual treatment needs. The outline of the project plan was introduced to the students and included as part of the required content (Table 1) in the course plan. In addition to the oral health promotion plan, each student was instructed to submit a 100–200-word reflective statement on their group's performance and their personal contribution.

	Required Content
Background and Rationale	Key issues and contributing risk factors
Priority and Target Groups	Describe the groups who experience this issue the most, specifically the group you are intending to target
Goal	Clearly state your health promotion goal
Objectives	Clearly state your objectives
Strategies	Describe the key strategies to achieve your objectives
Evaluation plan	Outline your plan for conducting a process, impact and outcome evaluation of your health promotion goal
Supporting evidence	Refer to recent, relevant research to support your discussion, including research on similar interventions and their outcomes
Reference list	Include a formal reference list
Individual reflective statement	Each student to submit a reflective statement on how the group worked together, including their own personal contribution

Table 1: Required content for students' oral health promotion group assignment.

2c: Organisation of the innovative practice

Prior learning, about health promotion and oral health promotion, in particular, served as a starting point for discussion within the student groups. It was hoped that the students would start to think of a suitable context and explore different arenas for their project to take place and collaboratively discuss this with each other.

The intention with these SDL sessions was to create a learning space, in which students could come and work on their project plan together with members of their allocated group. The lecturer would also be present to answer any questions and guide students in an appropriate direction using facilitating skills. For example, questions initiated by students would be reflected upon, sometimes with a contra question, allowing students to broaden their perspective, looking at a problem from different angles, to understand the complexity of health promotion. This process helps students to realise and eventually reach the conclusion that there might be more than just one adequate answer to their question, especially since there are many different ways of planning and conducting a health promotion intervention. It was hoped that through this enquiry approach, which started by defining their own goals and objectives for their project plan, would aid in students' development of deeper learning. Another positive aspect of this exercise was to allow students to be particularly creative and use their imagination when planning the oral health promotion project. This involved consideration of what has previously worked well, and for whom, in similar situations, in particular by defining the appropriate support and resources needed.

As previously mentioned, in response to lockdown, the collaborative practice within each SDL group had to take place virtually. Instead of booking rooms at campus, Zoom sessions, with break-out rooms for student groups to meet and discuss their projects, were organised for them. As the course coordinator and lecturer in oral health promotion, I attended these SDL sessions to answer any student queries, alongside guiding the learners in an appropriate direction (if they needed my guidance). The main focus for these sessions was strictly enquiry-based learning with an SDL teamwork approach.

A total number of six SDL-sessions were planned, however, due to different circumstances, including a more collaborative approach of working together, and no patient clinics to attend, students managed to finish and submit their project plan before the deadline, resulting in the cancellation of the last two SDL-sessions. Students were assured that they could email questions any time up until the submission deadline.

2d: Preparation of the innovation

The innovative practice in this chapter is best referred to as enquiry-based learning, with the emphasis on collaborative practice and an SDL approach. It was originally planned that sessions of SDL would take place in a seminar room on campus, open for students to come and work in their allocated groups. Due to Covid-19, the SDL group work of the module operated entirely outside of the physical classroom, now with synchronous group meetings and discussion via zoom.

When struggling to develop assignments, incorporation of SDL was something Gibson (2011) found helpful to inspire, motivate and engage her students. She used SDL as an engagement exercise, thus building on previous knowledge. Likewise, in preparation for this innovative practice of SDL collaboration, it was important to build on students' previous knowledge. Last year (in Year 2), students were introduced to a course in health promotion, so they were already somewhat familiar with the terminology used and steps to take when conducting a health promotion project. In that same year, although not being formally assessed, students were introduced to the concept of SDL during sessions of small-group SDL tutorials; each with a topic related to their clinical practice, which they presented in a lecture theatre in front of an audience of teachers and classmates.

To put previous knowledge into action, general health promotion principles from Year 2 were interwoven within this course (*Community Oral Health & Oral Health Promotion*) in Year 3. By building on knowledge from previous coursework and clinical relevance, instead of learning new facts, students were now able to concentrate on the innovative practice, refining and mastering their skillset of enquiry-based learning with a collaborative approach through sessions of SDL.

Section 3: The outcome

This innovative teaching and learning component had different outcomes. Student learning outcomes were centred around students' behaviour towards one another, within the group in which they worked. It was found that students worked better together if they started early on to get to know each other well, to sit down and discuss team roles, and when and where to meet. These groups seemed to be able to evolve, and students learnt to appreciate one another in a friendly and collegial manner. However, in groups with a later start, and where no one took charge, or in groups where students decided to divide their work among themselves, writing about one or two specific topics all alone, there was a resonance of dissatisfaction among the team members.

The primary student learning outcomes in terms of collaboration were exceptionally well managed in groups with high satisfaction of collaborative practice and teamwork, with all students contributing to all sections of the oral health promotion plan. Likewise, in groups where team-effort was high on students' agenda for completing the task, the module objectives were met well above the level of expectations. When comparing the absence rate of this cohort of students with previous cohorts, classes with an SDL component had fewer absences. In conclusion, all of the students passed the course, with an average mark significantly higher in the oral health promotion module, compared to previous cohorts of students attending this course in the past five years.

Students are now in their last and final semester of the program; some have already applied for jobs, and have managed to secure an interview. When deciding on a candidate's employability, some of the important questions that are being raised by future employers are the ability to share knowledge and working to achieve common goals as part of a team. Such questions align well with the theory of collaborative practice guided by the DCNZ to become competent in their professional role as oral health therapists.

3a: Student perspective

Thanks to the written self-reflecting statement from each individual student on their experience working together in the group along with their own personal contribution, we now have a reliable source of reflection from each student involved in this module. The majority of the students enjoyed the teamwork within their SDL groups, and the reflective statements showed proof of everyone's participation. In rare circumstances, where one or two students in a group did not participate to the same extent compared to their fellow group members, this was reflected upon by the student themselves as well as commented on by other students within the same group.

Student outcomes in this specific module compared to the previous year's activity of more didactic teaching showed a distinct difference in terms of student satisfaction which was also reflected upon in their individual statements. In previous years, a student evaluation questionnaire had been distributed, with questions focusing on students' view of the teachers' ability to stimulate their interest in the subject. It did not specifically confirm students' ability to learn or engage, whether it be in class discussions, SDL or other means of interaction. This time, by having students reflecting on their own practice, the learning outcomes and student engagement were adequately addressed, which consequently improved their ability to learn. For example, in their reflection, students expressed that group work was an effective way of learning health promotion skills. The fact that students were not able to meet in person came across as a challenge for some. However, this was overcome in other groups by having everyone on board from an early start, giving room for all students to work as important members of the team, working together and discussing every part of the assignment. Other students commented that they felt proud over their input and their group's SDL project. Overall, the incorporation of a mandatory self-reflection exercise appears to have improved student learning outcomes as well as course satisfaction.

3b: Teacher perspective – my reflections

For me, as a lecturer in this oral health promotion module, it was extremely satisfying to see how oral health students, who in previous years had shown very little interest in the taught subject, suddenly felt engaged. At the same time, they collaboratively worked together on their given assignment, to make this task worthwhile.

The take-home message was clear; give students little but clear instructions, working backwards by design; by highlighting the generic outcome and factors for students to consider, and giving them the necessary tools and resources to complete the task, and they can surprise the teacher and find meaning in any given assignment. Teaching is really about the student learning experience, their engagement and effort of collaboration, and appears to have little correlation with how well the teacher presents or discusses a given topic.

Through the lens of this new innovative practice, it is now clearer than ever that my role as a lecturer has shifted from the traditional view of being an educator-as-performance to becoming a facilitator deeply engaged in student learning activities. I have developed from being 'a sage on the stage to being a guide on the side'. This is a powerful transformation and enlightenment for me as an educator. In contrast to being a traditional teacher, I find myself readily comfortable in the role of a facilitator, guiding and challenging students in their process of learning, preparing them for life-long learning as oral health professionals that goes well beyond University studies.

If I were to do this again, I would replicate the process from start to finish. There would be one exception though, that is placing more emphasis on the effort and joy it brings for everyone involved to include team-spirit, to have an open mind for different views, and to celebrate diversity within the group while being involved in collaborative practice and SDL activity. It was affirming to realise that the student-learning outcomes from the module in oral health promotion were demonstrably highly achieved, which was shown not only in students' well-developed oral health promotion project plans, but it was also reflected upon from a student's perspective in their individual reflective statements. When reflecting on the format of online delivery, which turned out to be a real success, especially for SDL, and staff facilitation, it would be most appropriate to continue with this means of interaction within this particular module for years to come.

Section 4: Moving forward

After this recent curriculum development of enquiry-based learning, through collaborative practice with sessions of SDL and self-reflection, it is evident that the student-learning outcomes were well achieved. Engaging in teamwork has challenged students to develop critical thinking strategies while working as members of a project team. Although, the interruption of face-to-face teaching due to Covid-19 was not part of a strategic plan for curriculum change, hindsight, the movement towards online teaching aid particularly well for enquiry-based learning through sessions of SDL and teamwork. Therefore, this will be incorporated as part of the new normal in this oral health promotion module in the course *Community Oral Health and Oral Health Promotion*.

This innovative practice could well be adapted and incorporated as part of curriculum development, not only for oral health students but for any other student as part of a module or entire course in higher education. Although the theory of enquiry-based learning is not a new approach, there is a paucity of literature exploring activities for learners to engage in enquiry approaches (Spronken-Smith, 2008). With the addition of including sessions of SDL and self-reflection, it would be possible to explore not only if students have gained a deeper understanding of the learning process, but also, more specifically, how they perceived to be involved in this innovation.

When choosing this approach, the workload for students may seem to be higher, teachers may need to 're-think' their style of teaching, and in contrast to being the front person delivering knowledge for students to remember, take a step back, to portray themselves as equal partners to the students.

Conclusion

Through collaborative practice and SDL teamwork, students from the Bachelor of Oral Health Program at the University of Otago, New Zealand, have raised their knowledge and skills by collaborating in a group project resulting in a written assignment by creating an oral health promotion project plan. Provided by a broad topic, students were elaborating in small SDL groups to set SMART goals and objectives for their project plan. By allowing students to discuss and implement oral health promotion that is of particular interest for them, they expanded their learning through engagement and critical thinking. This cohort of students had an overall higher mark than previous cohorts. Organising online sessions of SDL, teaching facilitation and team-effort, was contributed partly to this success. Considering the constructivist theory of learning, students had gained experience by building on and making connections on already existing knowledge. They were involved in working together in small groups through collaborative practice and had become active, self-directed learners. The previous problem addressed with unmotivated students, and lack of interest has turned around. They are now able to see the relevance of what they are learning, and the usefulness of this module when seeking questions to resolve challenges within oral health promotion. Students are now well equipped for their future workforce and are better prepared to work collegially as members of a healthcare team.

About the Author

Hanna Olson is a lecturer, Deputy Convenor of the Bachelor of Oral Health Program in the Faculty of Dentistry, and Program Interprofessional Education (IPE) Convenor in the Department of Oral Sciences, at the University of Otago, New Zealand. She can be contacted at this e-mail: hanna.olson@otago.ac.nz

Bibliography

Adams, M. & Bell, L. A. (2016). *Teaching for diversity and social justice.* New York, NY: Routledge.

Curtin University (2020). *Checklist for Planning and Evaluating Health Promotion Programs.* Retrieved October 16, 2020 from: http://ceriph.curtin.edu.au

Daly, B., Batchelor, P., Treasure, E. & Watt, R. (2013). *Essential dental public health.* Oxford: OUP.

DCNZ (2020) Dental Council (New Zealand). Available from: www.dcnz.org

Dobozy, E. & Nygaard, C. (2021). A learning-centred five-tier model of innovation in higher education. In Enomoto, K., Warner, R. & Nygaard, C. (Eds.), *Teaching and Learning Innovations in Higher Education,* pp. 19–46. Oxfordshire, UK: Libri Publishing Ltd.

Doran, G.T. (1981). There's a S.M.A.R.T way to write managements' goals and objectives. *Management Review,* 70, pp. 35–36.

Durie, M. (1998). *Whaiora: Māori Health Development* (2nd ed.) Auckland: Oxford University Press.

Gibson, L. (2011). Student-directed learning: An exercise in student engagement. *College Teaching,* 59(3), pp. 95–101.

Green, J., Tones, K., Cross, R. & Woodall, J. (2015). *Health promotion: Planning and strategies,* Sage Publications Ltd.

Hawe P. & Shiell A. (1995). Preserving innovation under increasing accountability pressures: the health promotion investment portfolio approach. *Health Promotion Journal Australia* (5), pp. 4–9.

Healey, M., Bovill, C. & Jenkins, A. (2015). Students as partners in learning: In Lea, J. (Ed.) *Enhancing Learning and Teaching in Higher Education: Engaging with the Dimension of Practice,* pp. 141–172. Open University Press: Milton Keynes.

Health Promotion Forum of New Zealand – Runanga Whakapiki ake i te Hauora a Aotearoa. (2002). *THUA-NZ. A Treaty Understanding of Hauora in Aoteaora-New Zealand.*

Jaunzems-Fernuk, J., Kalyn, B. & Martin, S. (2021). Transformative inquiry through the Human Curriculum. In Enomoto, K., Warner, R. & Nygaard, C. (Eds.), *Teaching and Learning Innovations in Higher Education,* pp. 425–449. Oxfordshire, UK: Libri Publishing Ltd.

Kolb, D. A. (1984). *Experiential learning: experience as the source of learning and development.* Englewood Cliffs, NZ: Prentice-Hall.

Kolb, D. A. (2014). *Experiential learning: Experience as the source of learning and development* (2nd ed.). Upper Saddle River, NJ: Pearson.

Lee, V. S., Greene, D. B., Odom, J., Schechter, E. & Slatta, R. W. (2004). What is inquiry-guided learning? In V. S. Lee (Ed.), *Teaching and Learning Through Inquiry: A Guidebook for Institutions and Instructors*, pp. 3–16. Stirling, Virginia: Stylus.

Ministry of Health (2008). *Promoting Oral Health: A toolkit to assist the development, planning, implementation and evaluation of oral health promotion in New Zealand*. Wellington: Ministry of Health.

Nygaard, C., Holtham, C. & Courtney, N. (2009). Learning outcomes, politics, religion or improvement? In Nygaard, C., Holtham, C. & Courtney, N. (Eds.), *Improving Students' Learning Outcomes*. Copenhagen, Denmark: Copenhagen Business School Press.

Ossa Parra, M., Guitierrez, R. & Aldana, M. F. (2014). Engaging in critically reflective teaching: From theory to practice in pursuit of transformative learning. *Reflective Practice*, 16, pp. 16–30.

Peacock, S. & Cowan, J. (2018). Towards online student-directed communities of inquiry. *Journal of Further and Higher Education*, 42(5), pp. 678–693.

Rogers, C. (1969). *Freedom to Learn: A View of What Education Might Become*. Columbus, Ohio: Charles E Merrill Publishing Co.

Sheiham, A. & Watt, R. G. (2000). The Common Risk Factor Approach: a rational basis for promoting oral health. *Community Dental Oral Epidemiology*, 28, pp. 399–406.

Signal, L. & Ratima, M. M. (2015). *Promoting Health in Aotearoa New Zealand*. Dunedin, NZ: Otago University Press.

Slavich, G. M. & Zimbardo, P. G. (2012). Transformational teaching: Theoretical underpinnings, basic principles, and core methods. *Educational Psychology Review*, 24, pp. 569–608.

Spronken-Smith, R. (2008). Experiencing the process of knowledge creation: The nature and use of inquiry-based learning in higher education. In report published from *International Colloquium on Practices for Academic Inquiry*. University of Otago, New Zealand, pp. 1–17.

Swann, S. (2021). Building employability skills through collaborative group work. In Enomoto, K., Warner, R. & Nygaard, C. (Eds.), *Teaching and Learning Innovations in Higher Education*, pp. 475–506. Oxfordshire, UK: Libri Publishing Ltd.

Talbot, L. & Verinder, G. (2018). *Promoting Health. The Primary Health Care Approach*. 6th Ed. NSW, Australia: Elsevier.

Vygotsky, L. (1978). *Mind in Society*. Cambridge, MA: Harvard University Press.

Warner, R. & Enomoto, K. (2021). An innovative assessment method to evaluate independent learning and academic writing skills. In Enomoto, K., Warner, R. & Nygaard, C. (Eds.), *Teaching and Learning Innovations in Higher Education*, pp. 209–231. Oxfordshire, UK: Libri Publishing Ltd.

Willcocks., J. & Lange., S. (2021). Using Cross-disciplinary Object-based Learning to Create Collaborative Learning Environments. In Enomoto, K., Warner, R. & Nygaard, C. (Eds.), *Teaching and Learning Innovations in Higher Education*, pp. 451–473. Oxfordshire, UK: Libri Publishing Ltd.

World Health Organization (1986). *Ottawa charter for health promotion*. Health promotion, 1, iii-v.

Chapter 20
Transformative Inquiry through the Human Curriculum

Judy Jaunzems-Fernuk, Stephanie Martin and Brenda Kalyn

Introduction

With our chapter, we contribute to this book, *Teaching and Learning Innovations in Higher Education* as we showcase a fourth-year undergraduate course that introduced 'The Human Curriculum' to a cohort of forty students, in a College of Education. At the forefront of our innovation was a process innovation that was constructivist in nature. Our innovation provided an opportunity for teacher candidates (TCs) to learn through 'the human curriculum', a model focused on the humanistic and relational elements of teaching and learning. As TCs staged through the content (knowledge), application of the content (skills), and consideration of the applicability of skills to the classroom (attitudes), they strengthened confidence and competence in their practice through personal development with the goal of transference of skill to the classroom.

This innovation took place in a course titled, *Inquiry Project and Learning Experience: Surviving & Thriving as a 21st Century Educator*. The course was available as an elective option to fourth year, Bachelor of Education students, at the University of Saskatchewan, Canada. Referring to the learning-centred five-tier model of innovation in higher education (Dobozy & Nygaard, 2021, Chapter 2 in this book) our process innovation draws on a constructivist perception of learning by perceiving learning as a process of knowledge construction through relational engagements with content, as it applies to self and others (a cycle of experiential learning applied as active learning in Khong, 2021, Chapter 14 in this book). We see our innovation as a means by which to invite TCs to engage in a process of personal and professional development to build strength for their role in a demanding caregiving profession. The process starts with educator-activities, guiding TCs as they collaborate and reflect on personal goals and values, and asks TCs to consider how the practices may transition to work and life. This process is referred to by Scott-Webber *et al.* (2021, Chapter 3 in this book) as a 'learning continuum' within which students, in our case as future educators themselves, set their own goals and measure engagement.

In our example, as TCs engaged in transformational inquiry, they were tasked with participating in a cycle of introspective analysis, acquiring skills of self-awareness through a process of learning focused on personal and professional growth, to assess transference to the profession. This growth orientation challenges TCs to consider what elements might support their strengths and facilitate their remaining in the profession, despite the currently high rates of burnout and attrition. Implementing and using a constructivist process within this innovation has implications for both students and teachers, as the learning transforms from a focus on building TC strengths to supporting student success.

The Human Curriculum is a model founded on five themes that were devised as a result of the first listed author's doctoral research (Jaunzems-Fernuk, 2020). The themes are known herein, as the Five Ms: mindset, meaning, mental health, mentorship, and management. Each theme provides a means by which philosophies, perspectives, and psychological foundations are drawn from the work of various scholars and disciplines. The innovation was designed to support teacher capacity to thrive in what can be a demanding profession, with increasing rates of burnout, often leading to attrition (Karsenti & Collin, 2013). The Five Ms serve as principles in support of skill development in four areas: resilience, relational capacity, resourcefulness, and routines (Four Rs). Course activities focused on cultivating reflexive processes and practices in teacher candidates (TCs), in support of self-growth and action through lectures led by the instructor and the use of 'non-traditional texts', also seen in Kalyn *et al.* (2021, Chapter 18 in this book). The learning experience required TCs to apply content to themselves first and then others, through group collaboration and self-study. Through post-course surveys, TCs reflected on how a curriculum focused on personal or professional growth helped to build their capacity to thrive as individuals and eventual leaders in education.

A unique feature of this course was that TCs chose resources (texts and experiences) to fulfill personal learning goals. Learning was then applied to the TCs' lives and experiences and served as a tool to teach others. The learning was unique to each TC and focused on what individuals could gain either personally or professionally. The curriculum honored the needs and interests of the people at the heart of the work, strengthening them from within through relational pedagogy. Thus, our innovation is defined in this chapter through a curriculum model that applies humanistic psychology in an undergraduate educational setting to support TCs to be able to apply concepts to self. This is then followed by inquiry that assesses their growth to influence wellness in practice. Content is applied to foster a holistic understanding of the nature of teaching with the hope that the experiential and person-focused aspects translate to students and strengthened classroom practice.

Reading this chapter, you will gain the following three insights:

1. how personal and professional growth through the Five Ms of the human curriculum can enhance pedagogical and practical skill development to support thriving in one's personal and professional life;

2. how the Four R areas can be supported through the human curriculum with a focus on self-study and transformative inquiry; and

3. how transformational learning can be utilized to guide personal and professional growth and strengthen teacher capacity to thrive.

Overview of main sections

This chapter has four main sections. In Section 1, we outline background for the innovation, including relevant literature. Section 2 describes the course and practices used, which unfolded in three phases of inquiry through the human curriculum. At the end of the course, an optional brief qualitative survey designed to understand the TCs' learning experience in more depth, was introduced (approved by the institutional ethics review board). In Section 3, we describe TCs' reflections on using the innovation and the educators' reflections upon teaching this course. Based on the outcomes of our innovation, Section 4 provides ideas for future applications.

Section 1: Background

Research from around the globe cites teaching as one of the most stressful of all occupations (Johnson et al., 2005). With as many as one third to one-half of educators considering leaving the profession, due to stress or burnout within the first five years (Kutsyuruba et al., 2019), the human curriculum contributes to the profession by strengthening personal and professional practices from within. In Saskatchewan, a 2012 study found, in a review of over 700 teachers, that over 30% had sought medical care for migraines, 25% had sought support for depression or other mood-related disorders, and 78% reported difficulty sleeping. The majority of the participants in the 2012 study indicated that *"the demands of their work as teachers had a negative impact on their ability to pursue personal interests (78%); disrupted their family lives (69%); their relationships with their spouses/partners (64%); and friends (55%)"* (Martin et al., 2012:20). Though many factors can contribute to burnout, the stress of meeting the needs of an increasingly diverse student population has been identified as a key factor impacting teacher well-being (Oliver & Reschly, 2007). Globally, inclusive education practices and increasing mental health concerns have contributed to the complex nature of school dynamics, and all that teachers have to manage (Darling-Hammond & Baratz-Snowden, 2007).

Teachers are required to support a variety of physical, social, emotional, mental, cognitive, and cultural needs (Specht & Young, 2010). Estimates of the number of students in K – 12 environments receiving special education or health-related services in general education settings range anywhere from 9% to 50% (Canadian Council on Learning, 2009). By adding mental health, emotional-behavioral, or trauma-related concerns to the range of students requiring unique classroom accommodations, as many as 30% to 90% of students can require differentiation and informed-care practices to support their learning (American Psychological Association, 2008; Perry & Szalavitz, 2007). Teachers report that they lack the skills and strategies to support many of their student's needs, struggling to manage their well-being given the demands of this context as well (Stough et al., 2015).

This is why our innovation, developed with the stressful nature of the teaching profession borne in mind, was an experience of the human curriculum. Transformative inquiry *"as a way of taking time and space to draw on personal passions to put that energy to use within a relational framework to address burning issues"* (in this case, teacher burnout and attrition) was the foundation for the course (Tanaka et al., 2014:153). The course also utilized transformational learning theory (Mezirow, 2000), which aims to: 1) teach, by elaborating on themes and frames of reference; 2) support engagement in active reflexive learning, and 3) transform habits of mind and points of view. An inquiry cycle (Stripling, 2013) along with human-centered pedagogy and practices informed by the disciplines of education, psychology, and mental health provided content in the Five M areas to impact the development of Four Rs (Figure 1).

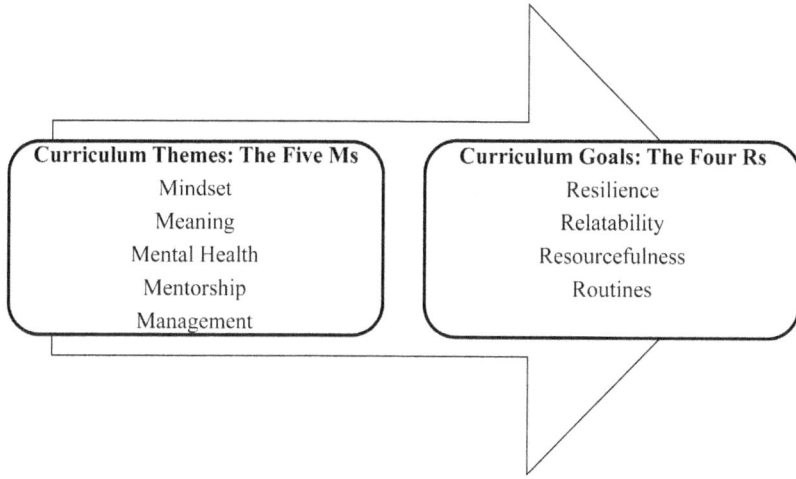

Figure 1: Overview of the human curriculum.

Recent literature highlights the need to support teachers to address the many demands of the classroom (Darling-Hammond & Baratz-Snowden, 2007). As an experienced educator, the instructor for this course spent years providing workshops, mentorship, and classroom-focused action research projects to support teachers in their work (Jaunzems-Fernuk & Kalyn, 2018). Teachers often communicated challenges with behavioral supports, social-emotional learning, mental health, and classroom management. A desire for holistic support to help manage stress and support well-being fueled the dissertation research of the first author, who completed a qualitative thematic analysis of thriving early career teachers (ECTs). The Five M and Four R areas (Figure 1) were the result of that qualitative study as they were disseminated by the first author and formed into 'the human curriculum' a process-oriented innovation aimed to strengthen TCs by implementing this knowledge from the field. The human curriculum was designed to develop and refine skills in self that could be transferred to the classroom to support thriving, over barely surviving, in one's career through a focus on teacher inquiry and well-being.

Humanistic psychology (needs-focused, developmental, attachment-based, neuro-sequential, relational) formed the basis for much of the content of the human curriculum, which offered opportunities for TCs *"to look deeply within the self, with the knowledge that self-awareness is requisite for self-growth"* (Clark, 2016:2). Transformative inquiry guided the process through three phases of inquiry. TCs chose Five M areas to anchor personal and professional growth, and corresponding assignments guided them to investigate areas of interest within the curriculum (Assignment 1). Reflexive opportunities and collegial discussions provided opportunities for practical applications of the learning (Assignment 2), and this experience culminated in a large inquiry through self-study (passion project, Assignment 3). The phases evolved from instructor-led to instructor-guided, and then to student-led, from which activities and action pushed TCs into challenging learning experiences. Collaboration and connection through individual and group reflection were key. The innovation of utilizing the Five Ms as themes to guide course work encouraged reflexive practice and skill development in the Four R areas.

Section 2: The Practice

Transformative inquiry (Tanaka et al., 2014) and transformational learning theory (Mezirow, 2000) provided the structure for the course as TCs participated in a journey through human-centered content. The goal was an active immersion in readings and experiences that could transform the TCs through self-study. The course was designed so that the learning could be applied in the TCs future classrooms to complete the transformative cycle in support of student well-being. Pedagogically the course was structured around relational and reflective practices known to strengthen those impacted by stress or burnout (Johnson et al., 2005).

The Five Ms were guiding themes connecting the TCs interests and passions to capacity building in the Four Rs. The inquiry cycle (Stripling, 2013) was scaffolded throughout, providing steps that went from questioning and planning to action and reflection. TCs participated in self-evaluation and reflection around learning and practice throughout. An introduction to core concepts (Five Ms) via lecture, reflexive activities, and group work supported skill development and practical applications of the work. Two books served as anchoring texts, and they covered themes and content related to skills being developed (Southwick & Charney, 2018; Steele, 2017). An early activity introduced the TCs to themes and goals by requiring them to rate their capacity in each of the Four R areas. They next reflected on questions pertaining to the Five Ms, subsequently setting goals and planning projects through group and self-study:

1. Mindset: Am I growth-oriented and mindful in my practice and relationships with self and others?

2. Meaning: Am I guided by a sense of purpose; do my work and play have significance?

3. Mental Health: Do I understand the role of stress and emotions? Do I have suicide or mental health first aid training? Do I practice self-care? Do I understand the impact of trauma and trauma-informed care? Do I know how to foster resilience in self and others? Do I understand the role of self-regulation in learning? Can I utilize basic reframing strategies to influence my own and others' well-being?

4. Mentorship: Do I see the importance of relationship, collaboration, and camaraderie? Do I seek and support others?

5. Management: Do I know about and practice effective classroom management routines that promote self-discipline? Do I have effective communication skills? Am I confident in the face of conflict? Do I have courageous conversations?

2a: An introduction to the innovative practice

The course progressed over 12 weeks, with weekly sessions lasting approximately three hours. During the first four weeks, TCs participated in classes with lecture and activities combining individual reflection and group collaboration. Then, TCs spent the subsequent two weeks collaborating to work on a group assignment, followed by TC and guest presentations for another two weeks. The final four weeks were allocated for self-study and presenting the outcomes of each TCs' learning. As TCs learned about and developed those social-emotional capacities required for reflexive action and problem-solving, they connected their learning to on-going personal or professional challenges. Avenues for problem-solving in the Five M areas provided opportunities for personal and collegial conversations around the demands of the profession and an individual's capacity to face adversity. The reflective and collaborative nature of this work encouraged mindful and purposeful group work and supported and encouraged inquiry. TCs learned strategies that honored the importance of balance in guided learning and inquiry as they made choices and even mistakes throughout the process.

2b: A brief overview of the curriculum

This course was designed to facilitate inquiry-based learning opportunities for students that were both guided and self-directed. Any student who had completed their first three years of their education degree could opt to take this fourth-year elective course. Throughout the course, students actively engaged in the construction of knowledge, supporting resilience, relational capacity, resourcefulness, and routines, as 21st-century educators through engagement with: assigned readings; analysis and critique of primary and secondary source material; interactions with each other and the educator; and by completing personal and interpersonal inquiries (passion projects). Topics related to the changing dynamic that is the 21st-century classroom were explored as they related to building teacher confidence and competence as lifelong learners and educators: mindset, meaning, mental health, mentorship, and management, as each relates to teacher growth and thriving in the profession guided project-based learning. Students developed a sense of self, through the process of transformative inquiry, as they worked to understand and assess their limits, responsibilities, and strengths while combining their learning with presenting concerns in education today.

The course is structured through three phases with increasing TC responsibility throughout. Each phase introduced TCs to various resources, aligned with a corresponding assignment to support the process of inquiry (Table 1). In Phase 1, TCs completed a review of literature from primary source material on teacher involved action research, in one of the five M areas (Assignment 1 of 3). TCs sought out literature on their own and rationalized choices for approval by the educator. In Phase 2, TCs engaged with research-based curriculum supplements (e.g. teenmentalhealth.org) or other professional publications (e.g. Perry, 2007) of their choice, as they explored areas of interest for collaborative inquiry (Assignment 2 of 3). Following the completion of the first half of the course, in Phase 3, time was allocated for the final assignment (Assignment 3 of 3). Throughout this latter portion, students read professional publications, attended workshops, or completed volunteer work while reflecting on readings, content, and their experiential learning as a passion project. Journaling and other reflective practices (documenting through pictures and anecdotes) were expected throughout. Students then selected a medium of their choice (e.g. Blog, Vlog, Scrapbook) through which they shared their experience with peers.

Phases of Inquiry	Corresponding Assignments
Phase 1: What is Inquiry? (instructor-led)	**Assignment 1** • teaching, learning, and reflecting on concepts as they apply to self and then to teaching practice; • a review of primary research on a topic of TCs choosing through Assignment 1; • aligned with instructor-led lectures and workshops on the Five M areas.
Phase 2: Cultivating Community & Collaborative Learning & Inquiry (instructor-guided)	**Assignment 2** • teaching, learning, and reflecting on concepts as they apply in collaboration with others; • educator guided, student-led Assignment 2; • collaborative inquiry rooted in one of the Five M's.

Phase 3: In-Depth Personal Inquiry, Passion Projects (student-led)	Assignment 3 • experiential learning opportunity with imbedded application and reflection on concepts through a personal or professional lens; • an evaluation of the learning as it could be applied to career; student-led, Assignment 3; • presentation of passion project and written narrative describing the process (what I learned, how I learned, how I will use knowledge and share ideas with others).

Table 1: Phases of inquiry and corresponding assignments.

Outcomes were linked to Teacher Education Classification and Certification (TECC) competency goals in the province of Saskatchewan (education.usask.ca) and were achieved through engagement with course content. Educator, group-, and individual-led activities supported TCs to be able to complete the following:

- demonstrate how the nature of inquiry helps to strengthen teacher identity and build resilience resourcefulness, routines, and relationship through reflective practice;
- demonstrate curiosity and respect for collegial learning through the inquiry process and recognize and honor unique and diverse approaches to learning (socially, emotionally, cognitively, physically, spiritually, culturally, or other);
- employ an inquiry approach to the construction of personal and professional knowledge, particularly related to one of the Five Ms; and
- explain or demonstrate a process of inquiry and its relevance to one of the Five Ms and share this learning with colleagues, participating in a reciprocal process of providing constructive feedback.

2c: Organization of the innovation

The three phases of this innovation exposed TCs to relational, student-centered, needs-based, and cultural pedagogies that could be applied in the classroom (e.g. Brokenleg & Van Bockern, 2003; Glasser, 1990; Gossen, 1998; Maslow, 1970; Rogers, 2009). Theoretical, instructional, and content choices provided understanding and experience in building trust, reciprocity, and a working alliance amongst the group, as TCs were staged through reflective and collaborative activities. TCs were invited to consider how the knowledge, skills, attitudes, and strategies may support their future classrooms.

Phase I – Assignment I

TCs chose an area of focus (M) for skill development (R), based on interest and completed a review of one piece of academic literature. TCs were informed that their topics could fit diverse themes, as the Five Ms are flexible areas for professional exploration. Topics, inquiry questions, and plans were presented in stages throughout and this process supported later less structured explorations. Some examples were: mindfulness-based stress reduction strategies for the classroom; supporting LGBTQ students and colleagues through spiritual and wellness practices; and successful mentorship and induction programs. In keeping with a student-centered philosophy, all queries and ideas for potential topics were allowed if the TC could rationalize a fit to the course themes and their interests.

Upon completion, TCs participated in a 'Think-Pair-Share' (TPS) strategy (Lyman, 1981) to reflect on and share relevant aspects of their literature reviews. The TPS strategy encourages thoughtful discussion as it allows time for students to think about responses, sharing them with one or two others, before bringing ideas to a larger group. Sharing opportunities allowed each TC to become more expert in their topic areas and to practise mentoring others on the applicability of their topics. TCs were then grouped by area of interest (M) for in-class discussions about applications to personal growth and professional learning. A significant amount of time was given for these guided discussions. The educator modelled how to encourage reflection and discussion, through strategies such as TPS and through the process of an ongoing feedback loop.

An important aspect of this course was the notion of classroom management, which was expanded as a concept of overall self-management. Self-care and self-regulation skills were highlighted as key skills needed by leaders who must help to socially and emotionally regulate others (Oberle & Schonert-Reichl, 2016). Group expectations and norms were pre-established in a collaborative and co-constructive manner to show how this type of management style can be effective. Based on Gossen's (1998) work, TCs were invited to consider values and reflect on connections to one another, through TPS activities that challenged them to consider an ideal classroom (Glasser's Quality World) as they co-constructed group norms and created belief statements to guide their work. This model has been used in schools to influence the discussion, group unity, and an ability to face challenges constructively.

With group norms established, expectations for discussions were clear; the educator served as a moderator while students learned from one another. In small groups, leadership was encouraged, as students were challenged to ask and answer questions amongst themselves, using their strengths, with little educator intervention. TCs shared personal insights and queries to keep conversations on-task. If challenges or differences arose, students were encouraged to refer back to their personal beliefs and to problem-solve. Reflexive questions were posed, and in each case the TCs might have slightly different perspectives, depending on the role they were training for in a school (e.g. general education, secondary education, special education). Working through these questions early on supported foci for inquiry:

- What does the 21st-century classroom look like?
- What are the demands of my role?
- Am I prepared for my role?
- What have I done to prepare myself mentally, emotionally, socially, physically, or spiritually to face diverse needs within my future classrooms?
- Who am I as an individual, teacher, colleague within my role?

Phase 2 – Assignment 2

In phase two, the course became centered on cultivating a collaborative inquiry team (CIT) of approximately eight TCs. Based on a framework for professional development (DuFour & Eaker, 2008), groups focused on understanding the nature of group collaboration and growth throughout the process. The context of collegial learning was supported throughout, as the foundations for learning had been established in phase one. The human curriculum was delivered in two parts during this phase (Table 2) and addressed the development of each of the Five Ms, through various resources in support of refining skills in Four R areas.

Part 1: Calm Classrooms, Mental Health & Human Informed Care (Regulation & Co-Regulation)	• physiology of stress and the stress response system (brain, mind, body) and systems that perpetuate or mitigate stress; • self-regulation (stress & emotions); • preventative classroom management practices rooted in restitution, choice theory, and attachment-based philosophies; • mindset and meaningful interactions/relations.
Part 2: Psychology & Human Development	• cognitive reframing; thought distortion; mind over mood; • developmental Psychology; Interpersonal Neurobiology; Neuro-sequential Model; • needs-based and community-oriented classrooms; understanding the importance of relationship, culture and diversity in leading/learning.

Table 2: Topics and design of the human curriculum.

Phase 2 of the course relied on foundations of wellness, relationship, and inter-personal responsibility. TCs were challenged to consider, and work through, self-care, self-management, self-improvement, and self-discipline to ready for the challenges of their future roles as leaders. TCs considered their strengths and embraced the notion of community. The sequence of *aware* (work to support self), *care* (change behaviors and actions to align with learning and beliefs), and *cope* (transfer that learning to teach and support others) (ACC) was used to support the sequence of the learning through the human curriculum (Figure 2).

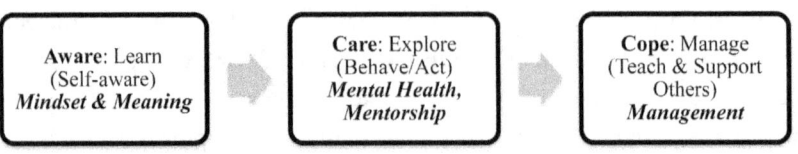

Figure 2: *Aware care cope; sequence of learning through the human curriculum (Jaunzems-Fernuk, 2020).*

This approach empowered TCs to consider preventative aspects of their role over consequence-focused routines in management. TCs learned that management is a group responsibility and from facing challenges oneself, skills and strategies can be learned. The relational aspects of managing emotions, (self and co-regulation), and the role of the stress response system was shared and valued as learning tools. It was stressed that a relationship and commitment to self could support well-being in others and calm in the classroom. Cognitive behavioral therapies (CBT) and mindful based approaches were used to help TCs reframe conflict and see opportunity and lessons from adversity. An overview of the different psychological and physiological systems (see Table 2) provided a framework that emphasized the development of these practices as they relate to all. Transference of these practices from self-care to student-care was discussed. The human curriculum taught the *what* (content), through analysis of the *who* (we are) and the *how* (we do things).

Throughout this phase, groups selected a resource of either a professional publication, curriculum supplement, or workshop in the area of their theme (Five Ms). TCs reflected on the process of learning, group interaction, and application to thriving in their profession. Presentations shared applicable content knowledge, TCs diverse perspectives, and the process of collaboration through inquiry. Following the group presentations, TCs received two guest lectures to prepare them for the individualized inquiry (passion projects). One presentation was from a mental health practitioner, who led students through a mindful-based stress-awareness and stress-reduction activity; the second was a visit from an elder to provide Indigenous and cultural connections to holistic wellness practices, learning, and leadership. TCs were then set out on their own, for three weeks, to complete their passion projects.

Phase 3, Assignment 3

In the final phase, TCs were given three weeks to complete their passion projects based on their chosen resources: a) attendance at a workshop or reading of a professional publication; or, b) completion of volunteer work or an analysis of a leadership experience. Some resources utilized by TCs to complete passion projects were: Mindset, Limitless Mind (Boaler, 2019); Meaning, The Science of Well-being (Yale; Coursera, 2020); Mental Health, various workshops or curriculum guides (Kutcher, 2016); Mentorship, University Peer Mentorship Programs or volunteer work (Experiential Leadership); Management, Teachability Factor (Neufeld, 2012).

Reflection and on-going self-evaluation (active-reflexive process) throughout, required TCs to analyze the development and growth of self and the potential to utilize their knowledge to support others. TCs were expected to track their engagement through the inquiry process by collecting pictures, reflections, activities, videos, or other anecdotes and artifacts to share. The culmination of this process was presented by developing an online platform for sharing their learning, such as a blog or vlog; creating a visual presentation depicting their journey (e.g. power-point); or through the creation of a physical portfolio or scrapbook with collected writings and artifacts. TCs uploaded their progress to a collective discussion board and ended the full cycle of inquiry by sharing and responding to the work of their peers. TCs also submitted a 1500-word descriptive-narrative essay, describing the process of inquiry and their learning journey throughout the course, reflecting on the pedagogical and practical use of this experience.

2d: Preparation of the innovation

First, themes from current literature along with professional publications, as they relate to the Five Ms, were selected and presented by the course instructor. These resources could vary as long as they supported thriving through a relation to personal or professional development in the Five M areas. TCs were responsible for their learning throughout the course and were expected to be self-motivated and disciplined.

The early stages of inquiry aided TCs to question and then explore areas of interest and passion, by connecting personal and professional development to areas of growth. TCs were motivated and engaged to fulfill their learning goals, and the objectives of the course, as the transference of the skills to their own classrooms was evident. For anyone replicating this innovation, it would be important to note, this model is flexible, as long as the fundamental principles of the human curriculum (Five Ms) are used to help develop skills and practices to increase capacity in the Four Rs. The inquiry approach means that no two courses would be alike, as each person in the space brings a unique background, experiences, and interests to the transformative process of self-study. TCs were invited to complete a post-course qualitative survey (Williams, 2014) to assess their learning in each area, as it pertained to personal growth and professional practices.

Section 3: The Outcome

A total of forty students were enrolled in the course. However, with the changes to campus settings, upon the declaration of a worldwide pandemic, it made the collection of this end of course survey data more difficult. Students were emailed surveys and asked to return them voluntarily to a colleague who collected them, removed identifiable information, and passed them on to the instructor. With this method, fifteen surveys were returned, of which 100% of responses were positive. Whilst there must be a recognition that 25 out of 40 students did not respond and that there is a possibility that only the positive ones were willing to spend the time to respond, we were able to field valuable data about the student experience. Student survey data has been widely used to support an understanding of the student experience in higher education (Williams, 2014). In this case, the returned surveys conveyed a remarkable connection to course content and themes as they pertained to the student experience.

Students were enthusiastic about inquiry and exploring the Five Ms to develop skills in the Four R areas. One student shared: "*There are so many different methods and strategies to the inquiry process! Curriculum can be focused on so much more than just academic content.*" TCs also came to understand collaborative work as more than just "group work" and that thoughtful and purposeful group cohesion, connection, and camaraderie could be fostered by navigating working together in proactive and positive ways. It was apparent this learning transferred to TCs personal lives as well: *"when this semester began, I did not take this class seriously I then realized how what I had already learned in the course affected me outside of the classroom, and I noticed that I started sharing my new knowledge."*

As a result of this course, TCs expressed that they would be more open to learning from conflict and mistakes, and many realized they could embrace difficulties or challenges by learning about and strengthening self before supporting others: *"I feel more prepared than I did prior to this course. I never took the time to consider what skills and practices I must develop within myself as a person and teacher, in order to be thriving in my profession."*

An alignment between educator and TCs, and between TCs and their peers, was also key. Co-constructing group norms helped align goals, roles, and responsibilities based on everyone's needs (Gossen, 1998). A working alliance (Rogers, 2009) meant educator and TCs were encouraged to be united around goals and practices. Learning how to address conflict and have difficult conversations was an inherent aspect of achieving group cohesion. One student reflected on the impact of this personal and relational learning:

- *"In order to be a resilient educator, you do not have to be the best at everything, you just have to be open to change and monitor yourself constantly, reflecting on your beliefs, wellness, needs. I now realize that reaching out to others is one of the best ways to gain knowledge and support in the profession."*

We have learnt that preparing TCs to be resilient involves theoretical and practical content, but more important, gentle guidance through experience and action just outside of their comfort zone (Vygotsky, 1978). Preparing educators to be active in this process can be difficult, as it involves handing over much of the process to the learner- who must face challenges and apply social-emotional skills on their own, to support self and others in active learning. The practice took time and patience, yet the TCs emerged as strong colleagues and leaders. Establishing group norms upfront helped TCs see the importance of proactive leadership and alignment amongst learners in groups. Moreover, determining the group expectations based on one another's values and beliefs prepared TCs for their roles in monitoring each other's progress. One groups' written belief statement showed this collegiality and compassion as it transferred from self (TC) to supporting others (colleagues):

- *"In our group, we believe in supporting each other by being inclusive, accountable, optimistic, and open-minded as we work collaboratively with one common goal in mind: understanding and promoting a meaningful and mindful educational journey."*

3a: Student perspective

This course was offered for students in their fourth year of a Bachelor of Education program. The majority of the TCs were post-internship, meaning they had already completed the final student-teaching phase of their four-year degree program. Though TCs were anxious to complete their classes and move on to professional roles, students began to disclose trepidations as the course unfolded. The TCs main concerns revolved around classroom management and mental health, referring both to their needs, as well as their students':

- *"Prior to the course I was burnt-out from my internship and was simply trying to get through my degree…but I know that I am more equipped to either handle stress or figure out who can help me handle stress. This class primarily taught me that everyone faces stress, and it's not a sign of weakness."*

TCs shared that their awareness about the impact of stress and the need for self-care were immeasurable outcomes of the human curriculum:

- *"I have changed my life drastically because of this course. I have implemented reflection into my daily life…I also started opening up more with those around me about my levels of stress and where my mood was at today because of how the instructor modelled this."*

- *"Within my internship, I was told many times that the sign that you were doing things right and that you are a good teacher was burnout. After this class, I really don't think that is true."*

Facing these fears with a focus on the power of mindset and meaning in one's work helped TCs to realize the importance of attention to personal needs, as they play a large, often unforeseen role, in their ability to thrive. TCs began to make a shift from seeing the Five Ms as external topics to learn about concerning students as they internalized concepts as important to their well-being:

- *"A course like this makes teachers more aware of the importance of these implicit practices (health, self-care, resilience, management). This course set the stage for the ongoing inquiry needed in teaching and learning and the importance of the psychological aspects that build teacher resilience."*

Others commented about an increased awareness through attention to self and how meaningful that was for them as emerging educators: *"I feel that I will be a more aware practitioner who is able to support my students and myself holistically."*

3b: Teacher perspective – my reflections

The Five Ms have been important aspects of my personal experience and research. I learned, from the TCs in this course, that the topics explored were more important and necessary in teacher development than I had initially realized. Many TCs expressed, at the outset of the course, that they just wanted to get the course over with; they felt anxious to complete their degrees and begin their careers as educators. I almost second-guessed the need for a course such as this, and what I could offer them as a wellness educator. However, what we all learned was that as far as the TCs needs and interests were concerned, this was a highly relevant and timely course in their teacher education program. By focusing on self-study and personal connections to the learning, the TCs felt an internal connectedness to the importance of the work through self-awareness and reflective practices.

Section 4: Moving Forward

This course provided the time and guidance to refine essential personal and professional skills. It supported authenticity, trust, openness, and a willingness to support and collaborate through purposeful attention to self. From this experience, we also learned that it was necessary to pay attention to an implied sixth M: *metacognition*. Schraw (1998) notes that traditional models of teaching and learning require students to *prove self* through knowledge acquisition, competing against content and others in the process of learning. In a course like this, the attention to the process of learning was a means by which TCs focused on *improving self*, as goals were self-directed and self-enacted. Schraw's distinction could be key in subsequent deliveries of this course, where the realities of educator-led assessment could impact authentic opportunities for growth. Tying assessment pieces to metacognitive processes of a course such as this might be achieved through combined educator and self- assessment, or by handing assessment completely over to the TCs. Involving students in the assessment and analysis of personalized growth could influence further, an emotionally safe space for authentic and meaningful learning.

In future courses, the final assignment (as it carried 50% of the courses final mark) should include some portion of student self-assessment. As the nature of the course content encouraged TCs to be vulnerable and compassionate, student-centered assessment could further promote growth by attending to the distinction between cognitive growth and metacognitive insights during growth experiences. As Schraw (1998:113) states: *"cognition [prove self] and metacognition [improve self] differ in that cognitive skills are necessary to perform a task, while metacognition is necessary to understand how the task was performed"*. This distinction aligns well with the nature of our inquiry and self-study.

Conclusion

As many of the TCs expressed that the notion of *barely surviving* over *thriving* was the picture being painted of the profession, this course served to increase morale and motivation. Future offerings -with increased attention to the connections and conversations that link learning and assessment to metacognitive insights- may translate to more meaningful experiences for teachers and students in K – 12 environments. This awareness could be attended to in classrooms, as a means by which students and educators continue to improve their overall well-being though self-improvement practices conducive to thriving. By attending to areas of growth for self and others in the learning environment, this innovation provided a space for personal and professional development, through aligned and personalized goals, novel experiences for many of the TCs:

- *"I found that after this course, my mental state of worry and fear of the unknown had subsided. I do believe that working through this type of learning prior to starting as a teacher is incredibly beneficial – I feel prepared in knowing what I need to balance my own life."*

A sense of community was cultivated, and shared beliefs and values helped TCs pursue inquiry and self-study with authentic connections to areas of practice as future teachers. This work helped TCs to find ways to meet one another's needs, and each predicted how various skills and strategies could be applied in their classrooms. Many survey respondents noted the meaningful nature of this work and the potential for it to transfer to any discipline where people are at heart:

- *"I would recommend this course to other teacher candidates . . . it is one of the few undergraduate courses I have taken that directly addresses these issues (mental health, classroom management)."*

The most influential aspect of this course was the TCs experiences within the Five Ms, as they increased their capacity to understand self through personal and professional development. We learned that as educators, we cannot underestimate the need for social-emotional learning through the development of management skills and perspectives in areas of well-being at the pre-service level, especially as the world is changing and becoming more unpredictable. Strong teachers, with a capacity to problem solve, and who thrive in their work, are key. As TCs experienced this innovation, through transformative inquiry and transformational learning, they experienced the human curriculum, strengthening their resilience, resourcefulness, relationships, and routines as thriving 21st-century educators. This capacity for self-awareness, reflection, and action directly translates to work that can continue once they enter the classroom, thus completing the cycle of learning for both teacher and student.

Chapter 20

About the Authors

Judy Jaunzems-Fernuk, PhD, is a sessional Lecturer at the University of Saskatchewan and a Registered, Master Therapeutic Counsellor. She can be contacted at this e-mail: judy.fernuk@usask.ca

Stephanie Martin is a Professor and Registered Doctoral Psychologist in the Department of Educational Psychology and Special Education, College of Education, University of Saskatchewan. She can be contacted at this e-mail: stephanie.martin@usask.ca

Brenda Kalyn is an Associate Professor in the Department of Curriculum Studies, College of Education, University of Saskatchewan. She can be contacted at this e-mail: brenda.kalyn@usask.ca

Bibliography

American Psychological Association. (2008). *Children and trauma: Update for mental health professionals*. https://apa.org/pi/families/resources/update.pdf

Beck. J. S. (2011). *Cognitive behavioural therapy: basics and beyond 2nd ed*. New York, NY: Guilford Press.

Boaler, J. (2019). *Limitless mind: learn, lead, and live without barriers*. Sydney, Australia: HarperCollins.

Brokenleg, M. & Van Bockern, S. (2003). The science of raising courageous kids. *Reclaiming Children and Youth*, 12(1), pp. 22–26.

Canadian Council on Learning. (2009). *Does placement matter? Comparing the academic performance of students with special needs in inclusive and separate settings. Lessons in learning*. https://eric.ed.gov/?id=ED519296

Clark, C. S. (2016). Watson's human caring theory: Pertinent transpersonal and humanities concepts for educators. *Humanities*, 5(2), pp. 1–12.

Darling-Hammond, L. & Baratz-Snowden, J. (2007). A good teacher in every classroom: Preparing the highly qualified teachers our children deserve. *Educational Horizons*, 85(2), pp. 111–132.

Dobozy, E. & Nygaard, C. (2021). A learning-centred five-tier model of innovation in higher education. In Enomoto, K., Warner, R. & Nygaard, C. (Eds.), *Teaching and Learning Innovations in Higher Education*, pp. 19–46. Oxfordshire, UK: Libri Publishing Ltd.

DuFour, R. & Eaker, R. (2008). *Professional learning communities at work: best practices for enhancing students achievement.* Bloomington, IN: Solution Tree Press.

Dweck, C. S. (2008). *Mindset: The new psychology of success.* New York, NY: Random House Digital, Inc.

Glasser, W. (1990). *The quality school: Managing students without coercion.* New York, NY: Harper and Row Publishers, Inc.

Gossen, D. C. (1992). *Restitution: Restructuring school discipline.* Chappel Hill, NC: New View Publications.

Gossen, D. (1998). Restitution: restructuring school discipline. *Educational Horizons,* 76(4), pp. 182–88.

Jaunzems-Fernuk J. L. & Kalyn B. (2018). *Calm classrooms: Teacher behaviors that promote healthy, calm, learning environments.* Hawaii International Conference on Education. Honolulu, HI, January 6, 2018.

Jaunzems-Fernuk, J. (2020). *Exploring the Knowledge, Skills, and Attitudes of Four Thriving Early Career Teachers in Saskatchewan* [Doctoral Dissertation University of Saskatchewan]. Retrieved from: https://harvest.usask.ca/handle/10388/381

Johnson, S., Cooper, C., Cartwright, S., Donald, I., Taylor, P. & Millet, C. (2005). The experience of work-related stress across occupations. *Journal of Managerial Psychology.* 20(2), pp. 178–187.

Karsenti, T. & Collin, S. (2013). Why are new teachers leaving the profession? Results of a Canada-wide survey. *Education,* 3(3), pp. 141–149.

Kaylyn, B., Brenna, B. & Jaunzems-Fernuk, J. (2021). Using fiction and non-fiction literature to teach sensitive health issues in teacher education. In Enomoto, K., Warner, R. & Nygaard, C. (Eds.), *Teaching and Learning Innovations in Higher Education,* pp. 375–403. Oxfordshire, UK: Libri Publishing Ltd.

Khong, L. (2021). Facilitating active student learning using innovative approaches in pre-service teacher education. In Enomoto, K., Warner, R. & Nygaard, C. (Eds.), *Teaching and Learning Innovations in Higher Education,* pp. 301–321. Oxfordshire, UK: Libri Publishing Ltd.

Kutcher, S., Wei, Y. & Coniglio, C. (2016a). Mental health literacy: past, present, and future. *The Canadian Journal of Psychiatry,* 61(3), pp. 154–158.

Kutsyuruba, B., Walker, K., Stasel, R. S. & Al Makhamreh, M. (2019). Developing resilience and promoting well-being in early career teaching: Advice from the Canadian beginning teachers. *Canadian Journal of Education/Revue Canadienne de l'éducation,* 42(1), pp. 285–321.

Linehan, M. M. (2015). *DBT skill training manual.* New York: Guilford Press.

Lyman, F. (1981). The responsive classroom discussion. In Anderson, A. S. (Ed.), *Mainstreaming Digest.* College Park, MD: University of Maryland College of Education.

Martin, R. R., Dolmage, W. R. & Sharpe, D. (2012). *Seeking wellness: Descriptive findings from the survey of the wwork-life and health of teachers in Regina and Saskatoon.* Saskatchewan Health Research Foundation, University of Regina. Retrieved from: https://www.stf.sk.ca/sites/default/files/seeking_wellness.pdf

Maslow, A. H., Frager, R. & Fadiman, J. (1970). *Motivation and personality (Vol. 2).* New York: Harper & Row.

McCrimmon, A. W. (2015). Inclusive education in Canada: Issues in teacher preparation. *Intervention in School and Clinic, 50*(4), pp. 234–237.

Mezirow, J. (2000). *Learning as transformation: Critical perspectives on a theory in progress.* San Francisco, CA: Jossey-Bass.

Neufeld, G., Mediamax Interactive Productions (Producers). (2012). Teachability Factor: An 8-hour course on why teaching is getting harder and what can be done about it [DVD]. Retrieved from www.NeufeldInstitute.com

Oberle, E. & Schonert-Reichl, K. A. (2016). Stress contagion in the classroom? The link between classroom teacher burnout and morning cortisol in elementary school students. *Social Science & Medicine, 159,* pp. 30–37.

Oliver, R. M. & Reschly, D. J. (2007). *Effective classroom management: Teacher preparation and professional development.* (TQ Connection Issue Paper on Improving Student Outcomes in General and Special Education). National Comprehensive Center for Teacher Quality. Retrieved from: https://files.eric.ed.gov/fulltext/ED543769.pdf

Perry, B. D. & Szalavitz, M. (2007). *The boy who was raised as a dog: And other stories from a child psychiatrist's notebook- What traumatized children can teach us about loss, love and healing.* New York: Basic Books.

Perry, B. S. M. (2013, November). Introduction to the neurosequential model of therapeutics. [Conference presentation]. Meeting of the Psychology Association of Saskatchewan, Saskatoon, SK.

Rogers, D. (2009). The Working Alliance in Teaching and Learning: Theoretical Clarity And Research Implications. *International Journal for the Scholarship of Teaching & Learning, 3*(2), Article 28.

Schraw, G. (1998). Promoting general metacognitive awareness. *Instructional science, 26*(1–2), pp. 113–125.

Scott-Webber, L., Loeffelman, P., Denison, M. & Runyan, D. (2021). Is higher education ready for the transformed learner coming from 9–12? A Case Study. In Enomoto, K., Warner, R. & Nygaard, C. (Eds.), *Teaching and Learning Innovations in Higher Education*, pp. 47–82. Oxfordshire, UK: Libri Publishing Ltd.

Siegel, D. J. (2020). *The developing mind: How relationships and the brain interact to shape who we are.* New York: Guilford Press.

Southwick, S. M. & Charney, D. S. (2018). *Resilience: The science of mastering life's greatest challenges.* Cambridge, UK: Cambridge University Press.

Specht, J. A. & G. Young. (2010). How administrators build schools as inclusive communities. In A. Edmunds & R. Macmillan (Eds.), *Leadership for inclusion: A practical guide*, pp. 65–72. Rotterdam: Sense Publishers.

Steele, W. (2017). Teacher resilience, sustained effectiveness and self-care. In Steele, W. (Ed.). *Optimizing Learning Outcomes: Proven Brain-centric, Trauma-sensitive Practices.* pp. 111–134. New York: Routledge.

Stough, L. M., Montague, M. L., Landmark, L. J. & Williams-Diehm, K. (2015). Persistent classroom management training needs of experienced teachers. *Journal of the Scholarship of Teaching and Learning*, 15(5), pp. 36–48.

Stripling, B. (2013). Inquiry in the digital age. In Harada, V. H. & Coatney, S. (Eds.). *Inquiry and the Common Core: Librarians and Teachers Designing Teaching for Learning*, pp. 93–108. Santa Barbara, CA, USA: Libraries Unlimited.

Tanaka, M., Stranger, N., Tse, V. & Parish, M. (2014). *Transformative inquiry.* AppleiBooks. The Transformative Inquiry Research Team. University of Victoria, British Columbia. Retrieved from: www.transformativeinquiry.ca.

Williams, J. (2014). Student feedback on the experience of higher education: a significant component of institutional research data. In *Using Data to Improve Higher Education*, pp. 65–80. Rotterdam: Sense Publishers.

Vygotsky, L. S. (1978). Interaction between learning and development. In M. Cole, V. John-Steiner, S. Scribner & E. Souberman (Eds.), *Mind in society: The development of higher psychological processes*, pp. 79–91. Cambridge, MA: Harvard University Press.

Chapter 21

Using Cross-disciplinary Object-based Learning to Create Collaborative Learning Environments

Judy Willcocks and Silke Lange

Introduction

With our chapter, we contribute to this book, *Teaching and Learning Innovations in Higher Education,* by presenting a process innovation we have implemented in the discipline of museological teaching in higher education. Our process innovation draws on pedagogy and curriculum development and explores object-based learning in a collaborative learning environment fostering cross-disciplinary exploration and exchange. The chapter asks '*how can working with objects in a collaborative cross-disciplinary environment introduce students to new ideas and new ways of working and thinking in an art and design setting?*'

Our chapter describes a collaboration between curriculum development staff and the Museum & Study Collection at Central Saint Martins (CSM), one of the six colleges that comprise the University of the Arts London (UAL). Together we developed an innovative object-based learning and teaching intervention (described throughout as an 'event'). The 'event' was implemented in the *Bigger Picture*, a four-week collaborative Unit for second-year BA students that explores the University's values in relation to questions of design theory and practice through cross-disciplinary and intercultural interaction. Our ambition was to introduce a new methodology to be used with and by students in cross-disciplinary groupings to teach them the value of engaging with a wide variety of disciplines, knowledge bases and cultures.

We focus on three integrated concepts: 1) object-based learning, 2) collaborative learning environments, 3) cross-disciplinary exploration and exchange. The concept of object-based learning in a museum context was first introduced by Paris (2002). It has subsequently become an academic approach pursued by many university museums in the UK and beyond. We define object-based learning as a pedagogic framework which encourages transactions between objects and students to stimulate curiosity and allow *"meaning construction"* to take place (Paris, 2002:xvi). We understand collaborative learning environments as discursive spaces that encourage cross-disciplinary exploration and exchange of practices and approaches. Such spaces simulate the cross-disciplinary environments students may enter after graduation and foster learning around how to work as a diverse team, negotiating everyone's contribution and utilising the skill sets available in a cross-disciplinary team. Referring to the learning-centred five-tier model of innovation in higher education (Dobozy & Nygaard, 2021, Chapter 2 in this book) our process innovation is underpinned by a constructivist approach to learning which understands learning as a human-centred process. Such a process places the student centre-stage and helps them to develop a rich portfolio of transferable skills.

Working across disciplines offers the opportunity for this kind of human-centred or social learning (Freire, 1968; Vygotsky, 1978) where students focus on developing skills in areas such as self-direction, confidence, interpersonal relationships, curiosity, and perseverance, rather than focussing on the content of a particular discipline. Object-based learning also offers opportunities for human-centred learning, from exploring the collaborative meaning-making experience (Hooper-Greenhill, 2002) to developing a greater knowledge of personal learning habits, cultural capital (Bordieu & Passeron, 1977) and disciplinary lenses (Barton & Willcocks, 2017). Both practices locate the student at the heart of the learning experience and emphasise the value of multiple viewpoints. As such, these practices also have a role to play in contributing to the increasingly important decolonial agenda, combating structural inequalities in higher education and making arts education more inclusive (Hatton, 2015).

Iterations of the object-based teaching and learning 'event' have been run over two successive years, for between 270 and 350 students. Data on how the students and their facilitators responded to the 'event' has been gathered through evaluations, reflective essays, teaching observations and facilitator feedback, enabling us to analyse the impact of the workshops on students' knowledge, understanding and practice. This chapter will focus on the most recent 'event', which benefited from many small improvements made in response to student feedback, and which we called *Objects and Identity*.

Reading this chapter, you will gain the following three insights:

1. the potential for object-based collaborative practice to establish empathetic engagement and respect for a range of cultures, identities and disciplines;

2. the power of objects as mediators for students working across disciplines and on collaborative projects;

3. the potential for mobilising object-based learning on a large scale.

Overview of main sections

The chapter is divided into three sections. In Section 1, we describe the genesis of the collaboration and how it resulted in the development of the *Objects and Identity* teaching intervention. In Section 2, we explain the intervention in more detail and offer up suggestions for how it might be emulated or replicated in other educational settings. We also acknowledge some of the challenges inherent in working with large groups of students in this context. In Section 3, we describe the impact of the intervention, through our reflections as educational practitioners and as evidenced through feedback from students and teaching staff involved in the intervention. Here we explore the range of skills and competencies that can be gained from working with objects in cross-disciplinary settings and share insights from the student experience.

Section I: The background

The collaboration arose from a combination of motivations. In 2015 a new Associate Dean of Learning, Teaching and Enhancement (AD:LTE) was appointed at CSM. Their portfolio included developing more participatory, collaborative and interdisciplinary practices across the College. At the same time, the College's Museum & Study Collection was thinking strategically about how to use its collections to better support learning and teaching across the university and working to develop its understanding and practice around the discipline of object-based learning. Both, cross-disciplinary collaboration and object-based learning are described as areas for development in the UAL Learning, Teaching and Enhancement Strategy 2015–2022. In 2016 the Museum & Study Collection was brought under the management of the AD:LTE, creating new opportunities for developing innovative learning and teaching activities, as well as setting up structures that enable students to develop skills transferable to future employment.

The key focus for the development of collaborative practice at Central Saint Martins is a cross-disciplinary Unit, currently known as the *Bigger Picture*, which brings together undergraduate students from BA Architecture, Ceramic Design, Graphic Communication Design and Product Design to work together for one month in their second year. When the activity described in this chapter was initiated, the Unit was undergoing substantial revision in response to student feedback. At the same time, the Museum had been building a reputation for action-based research into the role of objects in supporting teaching and learning in higher education (Chatterjee & Hannan, 2015), building a solid evidence base for the potential of object-based learning to help students address troublesome knowledge and develop a wide range of transferable skills including research, analysis, communication and team-building (Willcocks, 2015). Later research would explore the role of the object as mediator (Engeström, 1999) and as a means of encouraging self-reflection and self-knowledge in students (Barton & Willcocks, 2017).

The Museum & Study Collection worked with curriculum development staff to create an object-based learning and teaching 'event' that would contribute to the *Bigger Picture* by promoting respect for a range of cultures, identities, and disciplines and acting as a catalyst for positive intercultural transformation. The 'event' was informed by recent Museum efforts to address colonial history through material culture, co-curated exhibitions and research initiatives. It began with self-led museum visits, culminating in a half-day workshop that included talks and an object analysis session. In addition, associated teaching activities would variously explore representation, meaning-making, identity and the power of objects to inspire intercultural conversations, leading to the acquisition of new skills, and ways of seeing and understanding.

Section 2: The practice

2a: An introduction to the innovative practice

The *Bigger Picture* learning experience breaks from subject-specific teaching traditions, providing space for second-year art and design students to work across disciplines, making new connections and exploring new ways of being and thinking. Cross-disciplinarity has had a long history at Central Saint Martins, reaching back to the 1950s and William Johnston's introduction of Basic Design principles (such as colour theory, form, line and geometry) which underpinned all subjects taught in the college (Westley & Williamson, 2015). The College's move to a new building in 2011, with huge communal spaces and shared studios, built on this legacy, facilitating the erosion of boundaries between different courses and encouraging collaborative practice.

The *Bigger Picture* goes a step further in that it requires students to work in multi-disciplinary teams to engage with a range of evolving themes, topics and ideas. Instead of knowledge transmission via lectures, large-scale 'events' that promote social learning are designed and facilitated. Teaching is thematic and based around a framework informed by the University's values and behaviours. These include social justice and sustainability, respect and diversity and creativity for positive social change. The 'events' are designed to encourage students to interact and ask questions. Students are split into groups of around thirty (working closely with one facilitator) and further broken down into teams of five or six, with a range of students deliberately drawn from across the cohort of courses. Each small team develops a project which is presented to the larger group at the end of the Unit. As part of the assessment, each student produces a reflective essay, addressing the Unit's themes and the process of working collaboratively based on their own experience.

The Unit is based on three of these 'events', all of which involve talks by practitioners followed by interactive workshops. The *Objects and Identity* 'event' kept to the same pattern with talks by three curators or makers with links to museum practice, preceding a mass object-handling session focused on individual and collaborative meaning-making, identity, representation and respect for difference. The inclusion of the *Objects and Identity* 'event' is testament to UAL's position as an innovator in the field of object-based learning within the wider context of object-based learning in UK universities. Object-based learning as an academic approach has been gaining traction in the UK in the last decade, driven by academic staff at University College London (Duhs, 2010; Chatterjee & Hannan, 2015) and later embraced by other higher education institutions, such as Bournemouth University (Hardie, 2015) and the University of Brighton.

Willcocks (2015) has suggested the unique ability of art and design pedagogy to contribute to debates around object-based learning because many related teaching practices are shaped by embodied experiences or analysis of existing objects and artworks. Hence, object-based practices are well embedded in art schools, and teaching staff have often developed complex ways of conceptualising the use of objects in curriculum design. The inclusion of object-based learning in UAL's Learning, Teaching and Enhancement Strategy 2015–2022 and several university-wide initiatives (including conferences and events and the instigation of an object-based learning Community of Practice) have resulted in a number of object-based teaching innovations. These include object-led self-reflection (Barton & Willcocks, 2017) where objects are used as a basis for exploring student's emotional and extra-rational responses, and ludic practice (Campbell, 2019) where structured game playing with objects generates new ideas and new ways of seeing. A special *Libraries, Archives and Special Collections* edition of *Spark*, the UAL's online journal, details the wider UAL landscape (2019).

One of the things that distinguishes object-based learning in the art school is that it has evolved to support the development of skills and competencies specific to art and design pedagogies, including emotional intelligence, adaptability and resourcefulness (Shreeve et al., 2009). The ability to negotiate ambiguity (Shreeve et al., 2010) and the importance of the emotions (Spendlove, 2007) have also been noted as key components of art and design education. It was this focus on emotional or extra-rational responses to objects that formed the basis of the *Objects and Identity* intervention, which sought to challenge the student's assumed positions and unconscious biases.

The CSM Museum & Study Collection usually runs object handling workshops for small numbers of students (between 15 to 20). Offering a handling session as part of the *Bigger Picture* required significant scaling up, as the workshops involved up to 350 students. In order to achieve this safely, a great deal of forward planning was required to ensure the selection of robust but meaningful objects (between 55–70) and handling instructions for each piece. In spite of recruiting volunteers from other university collections, there were not enough professional curatorial staff to monitor each of the tutor groups. Therefore, a training workshop was offered to all of the facilitators on the *Bigger Picture* to ensure that they were able to look after the objects and lead discussions around them. Alongside introductory training in curatorial practice and object-based learning, facilitators were invited to attend a workshop on facilitating students' learning. The purpose of the workshop was to collectively develop approaches to setting up spaces for students to collaborate, connect and relate to each other throughout the Unit. Furthermore, with a common approach, it was hoped to achieve some form of parity in the student experience across the tutorial groups.

Learning and teaching at CSM is underpinned by a concern with social justice, diversity and the expansion of the curriculum to reflect our diverse student body (Jabbar & Mirza, 2019). It was, therefore, important to ensure that the team of facilitators was drawn from diverse backgrounds in terms of ethnicity and disciplines and that they received appropriate training to help them understand their position, not just as teaching staff, but as agents for supporting positive intercultural and interdisciplinary exchange (Brockbank & McGill, 2007).

2b: A brief overview of the curriculum

The *Bigger Picture* 'events' are not intended to be subject-specific, traditional lectures for the transmission of knowledge; instead, they invite students to interact, ask questions and engage with a range of ideas. The 'events' offer a variety of perspectives and present various ways for students to develop a set of approaches to collaboration – something they can draw from, not only during the Unit but long after it has finished. This notion of collaborative practice is a common theme of the chapters shared in this section of this book (Jaunzems-Fernuk *et al.* in Chapter 20; Olson in Chapter 19; Swann in Chapter 22), with each author drawing attention to the fact that, in the face of rapid change, successful learning depends on agility in responding to uncertain contexts. Therefore, the content for *Bigger Picture*, rather than being fixed, is open to change and evolves each year, depending on the speakers and facilitators who are invited to contribute, as well as students' responses to and interpretations of the material included.

In order to complete the *Bigger Picture* successfully, students are required to evidence their achievement of the Unit's learning outcomes in two pieces of work. The first is a collaboratively produced group project communicated in the form of an eight-minute presentation. The second is an individually produced reflective essay of 2,000 words that considers the Bigger Picture's themes, topics and the process of working collaboratively. The group project and reflective essay are assessed using holistic assessment (Sadler, 2009), which requires teaching staff to respond to the student's work as a whole before mapping the quality of the work onto a notional grade scale. This allows for the recognition of personal challenges and growth and an array of skills from the integration of complex knowledge, through problem-solving to innovation and creative thinking. Holistic assessment also helps to address what Gourlay (2015) describes as the 'tyranny of participation', where Western education systems tend to privilege a particular model of student engagement, typified by active and observable participation. Holistic assessment offers opportunities to reward fewer public forms of engagement, and because of the uncertainty of working across disciplines on an open-ended and collaborative project, assessors pay close attention to the depth and quality of the collaborative process, as much as the end result.

2c: Organisation of the innovation

The *Objects and Identity* 'event' began with self-led visits to museums and galleries across London. All of the suggested locations were selected because of their engagement with issues of identity, and all were free to enter. Examples include the *London, Sugar and Slavery* gallery at the Museum of London, the *Being Human* exhibition at the Wellcome collection, *A Queer Walk through British Art* at Tate Britain and *Fons Americanus*, Kara Walker's Hyundai Commission at Tate Modern. Students were asked to critique the way the institutions facilitated public engagement with objects. Areas for discussion included how objects were displayed, and whether curatorial narratives embraced a variety of cultures or allowed space for individual meaning-making.

Following the self-led museum and gallery visits, the students attended a half-day workshop, which began with three short presentations from creative or curatorial practitioners who addressed racial, cultural, sexual or gender identity in their work. Students then split into small, cross-disciplinary groups to carry out an exercise in object analysis, led by their group facilitators (Figure 1). The object analysis required the students to engage with both individual meaning-making (achieved through a silent, contemplative, structured response to an object) and collaborative meaning-making (achieved through a group 'reading' of the same object.) Worksheets (see Appendix) were provided to help structure the object handling sessions.

Figure 1: Students conducting an object analysis led by their group facilitator. © Silke Lange 2019.

During the individual 'reading' of the object, students were encouraged to explore their unique viewpoint, and how their past experiences influenced their emotional or extra-rational responses to the object. During the collaborative 'reading' (Figure 2), students were asked to share what the object meant to them personally, before stitching together new narratives about the object from multiple viewpoints. Time was provided at the end of the session for facilitators to discuss with their groups how much of themselves they put into their work, whether they consider how other people will encounter what they make and how issues of identity link to their practice or their *Bigger Picture* project.

Figure 2: CSM Museum & Study Collection object handling session. © *Judy Willcocks 2016.*

2d: Preparation of the innovation

The object handing element of this teaching and learning activity was delivered using materials from an on-site teaching collection. The presence of this collection, and of the expert curatorial staff who look after it, allows for the curation of a thematic workshop, with the capacity to change year on year. Students were allocated one object per group of five students, which necessitated the selection and preparation of up to 70

Museum objects for the workshops. In keeping with the *Objects and Identity* theme, all of the objects chosen for the activity had the capacity to promote discussion around race, gender, sexuality or cultural difference. Examples include prints by the feminist printmaker Barbara Hanrahan, textiles celebrating gay culture by the textile designer John Drummond, woodcuts produced by school children in Cyrene in North Africa in the 1950s and garments made by the Thai-born designer, Teerabul Songvich. It was important to balance the requirements of the workshop against the need to ensure the safety of the Museum objects which did limit the kind of objects that could be selected, and therefore, the depth of discussions that ensued.

The question has been asked whether this kind of workshop could be delivered using 'any old objects' – not just the kind of objects that are found in a museum. The answer is that it would be possible, but that the impact of the activity would be different. There is an assumed preciousness around museum objects – what Walter Benjamin (1999) describes as their 'aura' – that generates a greater level of reverence, engagement and interest. The presence of a relatively large collection also allows for subtler curatorial choices (such as the selection of a large number of artefacts that specifically address issues of identity). However, it is not necessary to have a special collection to deliver this kind of activity.

Section 3: The outcome

3a: Student perspective

We gathered data on how students responded to the *Objects and Identity* 'event' via student evaluations (179 surveys were completed) and reflective essays submitted on completion of the group project. We analysed a sample of 50 essays; 15 students mentioned the *Object and Identity* 'event'. Group facilitators were asked to provide feedback on their experience of supporting the *Objects and Identity* 'event' and identify potential areas of impact for their students. During the object handling workshop, we made observational drawings, photographs and notes. Appropriate permissions were sought from all parties for the use of the data. This process (which was approved by the university's ethics committee) included giving all students the option of opting out of having their data from the end of the

Unit evaluation included in the research and gaining informed consent from each student whose essay we refer to in the chapter.

Student feedback on the *Bigger Picture* in general (as evidenced in the end of the unit evaluation and student reports) focussed on the benefits of working in a multi-disciplinary team and learning how other disciplines approach a question or problem. As one student explained: the *Bigger Picture* "*enabled me to gain a fresh perspective on elements of my day-to-day practice; from questioning my core values and interest as a designer to considering how 'socially engaged' I feel my work should be.*" A number of students noted the benefits of being able to work and socialise with those from other design disciplines, as there were surprisingly few platforms to support this outside the *Bigger Picture*. Many of the student reports reflected on the experience of group work, from challenging their own reluctance to speak up to negotiating the complexities of group dynamics. There was a general acknowledgement that this way of collaborative working more closely reflects the realities of the professional design process than working alone or within a single discipline. This chimes with the suggestion that group work offers opportunities for learning experiences that feel authentic and relevant to the world beyond formal education. (Stein *et al.*, 2004).

The student perception of the object-led 'event' was highly positive, with 75% of responses to the survey noting that the 'event' had led them to new understandings and insights. The responses were grouped thematically, with by far the largest group (25%) saying that the 'event' helped them to understand the importance of multiple perspectives. Moreover, 10% of respondents said they had an increased understanding of the relationship between objects, individuals and society, while 10% expressed an increased understanding of the importance of keeping an open mind and engaging in analysis and critical thinking. Interestingly, 8% noted the power of objects to generate ideas and conversations while a final group described objects as a focal point for reflection, listening and collaboration.

The end of unit evaluations proved highly useful in providing a broad evidence base for the efficacy of the *Objects and Identity* 'event'. It proved that the intervention did have an impact and that many of the students benefited from taking part. The negative responses (for example, a number of students noted how noisy and chaotic the object handling session felt) will also help us to modify and improve the 'event' for future iterations. However, it was through a close analysis of a sample of student essays that the real richness of the learning experience became apparent.

Students talked about the impact of the *Objects and Identity* 'event' on their thinking, their approach to group work, and their understanding of their discipline. A key theme was the capacity of shared experiences around objects to invigorate and change group dynamics. It was through the object analysis that many students came to have an increased respect for other group members as their cultural, geographic, disciplinary or ethnic backgrounds brought fresh insights and revealed differences in perspectives and skills. Some had continued to use the methodological frameworks shared during the *Objects and Identity* 'event', both to understand the work of other designers and to better understand the multiple contexts of their own work. A number of students also cited the impact of the experience on their work as designers:

- *"At a base level, I think this activity emphasises a necessity within my own practice as an Architect to interpret and critically analyse my work from the perspective of the other parties involved – particularly those who will use the space or have an existing relationship with the site."*

- *"The event made me think about myself as a designer and how meaningless looking objects actually are significant and have a lot of meaning behind them. I was taught to think more than just the surface of design."*

- *"Analysing the object has influenced how I thought throughout the design process. I realised that any decision we make as a group, either if that's adding a button in our app, or adjusting pixilation levels of the faces, has some level of influence in society and that I am accountable and responsible for it."*

A number of students identified the *Objects and Identity* 'event' as a transformational experience in terms of their thinking or the shaping of their group project. One student recounted: *"...the thematic and contextual links that we began to construct as a group during this time directly formed the basis of our design approach and as such had very strong links to our final outcome."*

Feedback from the facilitators leading the object analysis element of the workshop was that it enabled students from varying disciplines and cultural backgrounds to verbalise their experiences of engaging with objects and find common (as well as different) perspectives to objects and their relationships with them. The potential for object analysis to bridge the gap between disciplines and generate intercultural conversations was also noted. As one facilitator put it: "*Some groups ran really well with their object and used it as a catalyst to generate multidisciplinary or cross-disciplinary insights.*"

There was also an emphasis on how the 'event' led to the enhancement of observational and imaginative skills, and the development of new skills, such as being open-minded in response to an object, which were, according to another facilitator: "*evidenced in most of their final proposals.*" Finally, it was felt that the skills and competencies gained through the *Objects and Identity* workshop would help prepare the students to design for uncertain futures, where designers would increasingly need to be, in the words of a facilitator: "*empathetic practitioners who can actively listen, anticipate and cater for diverse needs of diverse groups and communities.*"

Less positive responses from both students and facilitators related mainly to logistics and relevance to the assignment:

- "*The object handling session felt chaotic, and it was hard at the start of the project to see how the events were going to feed into the group project.*"

- "*Some groups struggled maintaining attention and keeping with the pace of the session, trying to move faster through the task. I think the physical setting…and the group size did affect this.*"

One facilitator commented on the importance of the choice of object to encourage a meaningful exchange between the students:

- "*One less successful item was a black and white photo depicting students and staff using a printing press, possibly in the 40s or 50s. The group seemed to quickly exhaust the conversation and struggled. Whether this was the object, group dynamic or combination of both, is difficult to say. Due to the literal depiction in the photograph (and a relative absence of 'action') perhaps there was less space for interpretation and that students were more aware of getting the answer wrong or right, in response to the prompts. I think this means some objects work more effectively and had greater 'depth' than others in mediating students' cross-disciplinary discussions.*"

3b: Teacher perspective

The *Bigger Picture* Unit is an educational and social idea that encourages students and staff from different parts of the College to interact and collaborate, thereby enriching theory and practice by sharing and negotiating a range of cultural and disciplinary viewpoints. Meeting and working with new colleagues and ideas requires developing qualities of openness, empathy and teamwork, all of which are vital for graduate designers working in the world today. Throughout the Unit, we explore different methods and techniques for learning from and with each other, creating an environment of discovery. The object-based learning activity is one example of creating discursive spaces, inviting students to view objects, material and ideas from different disciplinary perspectives.

When observing the object-based learning activity, we witnessed a fuelled sense of curiosity and motivation, referred to by Jackson and Shaw (2006:97): *"the great engine of academic creativity is intellectual curiosity… the desire to find out, understand, explain, prove or disprove something or simply to imagine something different."* The role of the facilitator is crucial in creating and nurturing such learning environments, requiring them to listen, engage and support the student learning, so that learning becomes a collaborative process where the knowledge is generated in an interconnected way rather than being isolated to a top-down process.

This approach to teaching, which begins with the student's experience, tallies with Vygotsky's suggestion that the teacher ought to construct the learning environment so that the students teach themselves: *"Education should be structured so that it is not the student that is educated, but that the student educates himself… The real secret of education lies in not teaching."* (Vygotsky (1986) cited in Neary 2010:6). For a detailed analysis of this notion of constructivism, revisit the learning-centred five-tier model of innovation in higher education in Chapter 2 in this book (Dobozy & Nygaard, 2021).

Working on the *Bigger Picture* gave the Museum an opportunity to be involved in a large-scale learning and teaching activity that purposefully challenged disciplinary boundaries and required students to realise a project in a cross-disciplinary group. This was the largest managed handling session ever delivered by the Museum & Study Collection and naturally prompted fears, not just for the safety of the objects, but for how the object analysis workshop would play out when led by teaching staff with limited experience of working with Museum collections. However, this experiment has proven that it is possible to replicate the kind of experiences students report in smaller, more closely managed object handling workshops for vastly bigger class sizes.

That said, there were some issues arising from the sheer size of the activity. Negative responses from the student evaluations were largely centred on the difficulty of managing an object handling session for such a large group of students, from the acoustics of the space to the limited choice of objects. Facilitators also expressed frustration that they were not better prepared in terms of knowing which objects they would be working with before the workshop took place. These are ongoing challenges for consideration, particularly as the *Bigger Picture* Unit will be expanding to more than 500 students in subsequent years. It is hoped that further forward planning, a different venue, hybrid delivery and improved training for facilitators will go some way to ironing out these issues.

Section 4: Moving Forward

There is an increasing move among Higher Education Institutions to acknowledge their position as one of privilege and power. Universities are spaces of agency, which seek to have an impact on the way people think and behave, and they expect their students to shape the world when they graduate.

The development of this object-based exploration of identity, meaning-making and collaborative practice was rooted in notions of ethics, social justice and representation, with the emphasis placed on the student voice and the student experience. The project has proven the potential for objects and object analysis to contribute to the curriculum developments that seek to liberate or decolonise the curriculum, enabling conversations around self-knowledge, cultural capital and identity (Hatton, 2015).

Moving forward, we will seek to further develop object-led practices to support institutional efforts to enhance cross-disciplinary practice and become more student-centred. In the light of the positive feedback for the *Objects and Identity* 'event' we plan to develop and enhance the object-based 'event' at the *Bigger Picture*, which in coming years will expand to encompass the Fine Art programme, as well as additional design-based subjects.

However, we acknowledge that not all feedback received from staff and students participating in the *Objects and Identity* 'event' was positive, and in the light of more challenging comments, we have planned a number of changes to the way the 'event' is introduced and managed. A key development for the next iteration of the 'event' will be financial provision for additional curatorial support to select and prepare objects to be used in the physical handling session and to provide enhanced information about them, which can be shared with *Bigger Picture* facilitators before the 'event' takes place. It is anticipated that this will further cultivate their ability to lead rich discussions around the objects.

A second development (resulting from lessons learned during the Covid-19 pandemic) will be the mobilisation of virtual learning environments in support of the physical elements of the 'event'. Building on our experience of delivering what might be considered 'haptic' content online during the period of enforced physical distancing, students will be required to engage with a range of simple object-based activities, introduced via the virtual learning environment prior to the 'event' taking place. Thus, we anticipate that both academic staff and students will enter the object handling session with an improved understanding of what to expect and experience richer learning outcomes.

Conclusion

This chapter has explored how object-based learning can be mobilised in cross-disciplinary and collaborative settings and asked whether, in that context, working with objects could introduce students to new ideas and new ways of working and thinking in an art and design environment. Feedback from students and those facilitating the object-led activity discussed in this chapter indicates that our process innovation can be applied as a means to motivate and engage curiosity through interconnected and collaborative practices. It suggests that working with objects does provide new perspectives, encourages respect for others, acts as a focal point for listening and collaborating, and helps to unify cross-disciplinary groups as they develop their collaborative practice. On the basis of these findings, we will continue to develop object-based learning and teaching activities for the *Bigger Picture* Unit and other initiatives that seek to diversify the curriculum and support student-centred learning. It is hoped that the evidence cited in this chapter will also encourage colleagues in other higher education institutions to mobilise their special collections to facilitate cross-disciplinary and intercultural learning.

About the Authors

Judy Willcocks is Head of Museum & Study Collections and Senior Research Fellow at Central Saint Martins, University of the Arts London, UK. She can be contacted at this e-mail: j.willcocks@csm.arts.ac.uk

Silke Lange is Associate Dean of Learning, Teaching and Enhancement at Central Saint Martins, University of the Arts London, UK. She can be contacted at this e-mail: s.lange@csm.arts.ac.uk

Appendix

Forensic reading of an object

Below are some useful questions to bear in mind when you are doing a detailed or forensic reading of an object. The questions are based on a methodology outlined by Jules Prown in the 1980s. Prown believed that objects were the raw data for the study of material culture and suggested approaching the object in three stages – description, deduction and hypothesis – to help prevent errors of judgement or conclusions driven by emotional or extra-rational responses. You should begin the process by switching off your emotional responses, your likes and dislikes. Treat the object merely as a lump of stuff. This is not a definitive list of questions, but it should provide a helpful framework for your own questioning. Don't panic if you can't answer all of them. In the first instance, it can be helpful to list what you can see.

Theme	General area of questioning	Specific questions you can think about asking (not all of these will be relevant)	Notes
Description – what you can directly see and feel	Look and feel	How big is it? What is its colour? Shape? Smell? Is it complete, or has it been worn or damaged?	
	Identifying markings	Does it have a serial number or date mark? Does it have a maker's mark or hallmark?	
	Materials	What is it made of? Is it made of a single material or multiple materials?	
	Construction	How was it made? Was it made by hand or by machine? Has it been altered or adapted?	
Deduction – what can you work out by close study of the object?	Purpose and function	What was it used for? Does it have one use or several uses? Has its use changed over time?	
	Context and history	Where and when was it made? Who made it? And who owned or used it? Where was it found?	
	Spiritual and artistic significance	Does the object have spiritual significance? Was it intended to be a work of art? How is it decorated, and what does it tell you about the technical skills of the maker?	
	How was the object valued	Did the object have a value for the person who made it or the person who used/owned it? Has the object's meaning or value changed over time?	
Hypothesis – now you can move away from the object and allow yourself some educated guesses	Context and history	What can this object tell you about when it was made? What can you guess about the person who made it? Or the people who used it? What can it tell you about society or culture?	

Chapter 21

Theme	General area of questioning	Specific questions you can think about asking (not all of these will be relevant)	Notes
	Artistic background	What can the object tell you about how artists were working when it was made? What techniques were they using? Were they new techniques?	
	Materials	Can you think of ways the materials and techniques in this object could be used elsewhere? Or in your own work?	

Emotional or extra-rational reading of an object

"*From ancient to modern times, theories of aesthetics have emphasised the role of art in evoking, shaping and modifying human feelings*" (Silvia, 2005:342). Below are some useful questions to bear in mind when you are doing an emotional or extra-rational reading of an object. The emotional or extra-rational reading focuses on how an individual's disciplinary training, cultural background and life experience can drive their response to an object. This exercise requires the reader to be self-aware, explore their inner world and question their habituated responses to objects. Those facilitating an emotional or extra-rational object reading should look out for objects causing a negative response – perhaps touching a raw nerve or recalling a painful memory. It can also be useful to watch for the physical gestures made when viewers discuss the object – sometimes gestures can be more revealing than words.

Theme	General area of questioning	Specific questions you can think about asking (not all of these will be relevant)	Notes
Personal responses	Emotional response	What is your immediate reaction to this object? Do you like it? Dislike it? Does it make you feel uncomfortable in any way? Or does it make you happy?	

Theme	General area of questioning	Specific questions you can think about asking (not all of these will be relevant)	Notes
	Physical response	Do you feel stimulated or aroused by your experience of engaging with this object? Can you explore what is going on in your body? Do you feel calm? Or is your heart rate increasing? What about your breathing?	
Relationship to previous experience	Memory	What does this object remind you of? What else does it make you think of?	
	Cultural and social	Can you relate this object to yourself or your life?	
	Unconscious bias and habituated responses	If you have had a strong reaction to the object, what do you think is driving those responses?	
Empathy for objects	Imagination	Imagination is an important part of experience. What are you imagining when you see and feel this object?	
	Feeling and meaning	What does it mean to you to be able to touch and hold this object? Are you making a connection with the maker or those who have used or viewed the object? What are you feeling?	

Bibliography

Barton, G. & Willcocks, J. (2017). Object-based self-enquiry: A multi- and transdisciplinary pedagogy for transformational learning. *Spark: UAL Creative Teaching and Learning Journal*, 2(17), pp. 229–245.

Benjamin, W. (1999). *Illuminations*. London: Pimlico.

Bourdieu, P. & Passeron, J-C. (1977). Cultural reproduction and social reproduction. In Karabel, J. & Halsey, A. (Eds.), *Power and Ideology in Education*, pp. 487–511. New York: Oxford University Press.

Brockbank, A. & McGill, I. (2007). *Facilitating Reflective Learning in Higher Education*. Maidenhead, UK: Society for Research into Higher Education and Open University Press.

Campbell, S. (2019). Ludic practice: the case for play in university museums in *Spark: UAL Creative Teaching and Learning Journal*, 4(1), pp. 59–70.

Chatterjee, H. & Hannan, L. (Eds.) (2015). *Engaging the Senses: Object-Based Learning in Higher Education*. Farnham, UK: Ashgate Publishing.

Dobozy, E. & Nygaard, C. (2021). A learning-centred five-tier model of innovation in higher education. In Enomoto, K., Warner, R. & Nygaard, C. (Eds.), *Teaching and Learning Innovations in Higher Education*, pp. 19–46. Oxfordshire, UK: Libri Publishing Ltd.

Duhs, R. (2010). *Learning from university museums and collections in Higher Education: University College London* (UMAC Journal 3 2010, Putting University Collections to Work in Teaching and Research: Proceedings of the 9th Conference of the ICOM for University Museums and Collections).

Engeström, Y. (1999). Activity theory and individual and social transformation. In Engeström, Y., Miettinen, R. & Punamäki, R.-L. (Eds.), *Perspectives on Activity Theory*, pp. 19–38. Cambridge, UK: Cambridge University Press.

Freire, P. (1968). *Pedagogy of the Oppressed*. New York: Seabury Press.

Gourlay, L. (2015). Student engagement and the tyranny of participation, *Teaching in Higher Education*, 20(4), pp. 402–411.

Hardie, K. (2015). *Wow: the power of objects in object-based learning and teaching*. Innovation Pedagogies Series, York, UK: Higher Education Academy.

Hatton, K. (2015). *Towards an Inclusive Arts Education*. UCL London: Trentham Books.

Hooper Greenhill, E. (2002.) *Museums and the Interpretation of Visual Culture*. New York: Routledge.

Jabbar, A. & Mirza, M. (2019). Managing diversity: academic's perspective on culture and teaching, *Race Ethnicity and Education*, 22(5), pp. 569–588.

Jackson, N. J. & Shaw, M. (2006). Developing subject perspectives on creativity in higher Education. pp. 89 –108. In *Developing Creativity in Higher Education: An Imaginative Curriculum*, pp. 89–108. Abingdon: Routledge.

Jaunzems-Fernuk, J., Kalyn, B. & Martin, S. (2021). Transformative inquiry through the Human Curriculum. In Enomoto, K., Warner, R. & Nygaard, C. (Eds.), *Teaching and Learning Innovations in Higher Education*, pp. 425–449. Oxfordshire, UK: Libri Publishing Ltd.

Olson, H. (2021). Collaborative enquiry-based learning in an oral health program. In Enomoto, K., Warner, R. & Nygaard, C. (Eds.), *Teaching and Learning Innovations in Higher Education*, pp. 405–423. Oxfordshire, UK: Libri Publishing Ltd.

Paris, S. G. (2002). *Perspectives on Object-Centred Learning in Museums.* Mahwah, N.J.: Routledge.

Sadler, D. R. (2009). Transforming holistic assessment and grading into a vehicle for complex learning. In Joughin, G. (Ed.), *Assessment, Learning and Judgement in Higher Education,* pp. 45–63. Netherlands: Springer.

Shreeve, A., Sims, E. & Trowler, P. (2010). "A kind of exchange": learning from art and design teaching. *Higher Education Research and Development, 29*(2), pp. 125–138.

Shreeve, A., Waring, S. & Drew, L. (2009). Key aspects of teaching and learning in the visual arts. In Fry, H., Ketteridge, S. & Marshall, S. A. (Eds.), *A Handbook for Teaching and Learning in Higher Education: Enhancing Academic Practice,* pp. 345–362. Abingdon: Routledge.

Silvia, P. J. (2005). Emotional Responses to Art: From Collation and Arousal to Cognition and Emotion. *Review of General Psychology, 9,* pp. 342- 357.

Spendlove, D. (2007). A Conceptualisation of Emotion within Art and Design Education: A Creative, Learning and Product-Orientated Triadic Schema. *International Journal of Art and Design Education, 26*(2), pp. 155–156.

Stein, S. J., Isaacs, G. & Andrews, T. (2004). Incorporating authentic learning experiences within a university course. *Higher Education, 29*(2), pp. 239–258.

Swann, S. (2021). Building employability skills through collaborative Group Work. In Enomoto, K., Warner, R. & Nygaard, C. (Eds.), *Teaching and Learning Innovations in Higher Education,* pp. 475–506. Oxfordshire, UK: Libri Publishing Ltd.

Vygotsky, L. S. (1978). *Mind in Society,* Cambridge, Mass.: Harvard University Press.

Vygotsky, L.S. (1986) cited in Neary, M. (2010). Student as Producer: A Pedagogy for the Avant-Garde? *Learning Exchange (1)* 1, Retrieved from: http://sprints.lincoln.ac.uk/4186/

Westley, H. & Williamson, B. (2015). William Johnstone: International and interdisciplinary art education. In N. Llewellyn & B. Williamson (Eds.), *The London Art Schools: Reforming the Art World, 1960 to Now,* pp. 25–36. London, UK: Tate Enterprises.

Willcocks, J. (2015). The power of concrete experience: museum collections, touch and meaning-making in art and design pedagogy. In Chatterjee, H. & Hannan, L. (Eds.) *Engaging the Senses: Object-Based Learning in Higher Education,* pp. 43–56. Farnham, UK: Ashgate Publishing.

Chapter 22

Building Employability Skills through Collaborative Group Work

Sarah Swann

Introduction

With my chapter, I contribute to this book, *Teaching and Learning Innovations in Higher Education*, by showing how we, at Leeds Beckett University, have implemented collaborative group work to build students' employability skills. The collaborative group work is a process innovation, referred to as The Legacy Projects, which are implemented in a year 2-module, *The Professional Self* on the BA (Hons) Childhood Studies degree. Collaborative group work has three integrated purposes: 1) to make University education more relevant and meaningful for undergraduates; 2) to equip students with the experience, skills and attributes employers look for; and 3) to meet the needs and demands of the 'real world' such as accountability, taking responsibility, and problem-solving. Innovation is defined as active agency and students as the innovators are positioned as agents of change.

Referring to the learning-centred five-tier model of innovation in higher education (Dobozy & Nygaard, 2021, Chapter 2 in this book), our process innovation of collaborative group work draws on a constructivist perception of learning. Implementing a constructivist model of learning places emphasis on students' active participation in meaning-making. Learning is a process and many of the innovations described in this book are innovative in the sense of building experimentation, intellectual enquiry, imaginative thought, personal development and self-actualisation. The content and tools to deliver this are both stimulating and motivating and provide outcomes which might never have materialised in the conventional classroom context. Similarly, Willcocks and Lange (2021, Chapter 21 in this book) explored how collaborative group work in a cross-disciplinary environment enabled students to explore and integrate knowledge from different disciplines which is seen as an approach to unlock the otherwise hidden potential of students.

The Legacy Projects present a new way to think about delivering graduates with high employability skills to the job market. In this sense, the concept of innovation is fused to the massification and commodification of UK higher education. In the context of Childhood Studies, finding ways to foster innovation potentially generates solutions to 'real-world' social problems. This innovation came seven years after the UK Government's austerity measures which resulted in rising child poverty (Cooper & Whyte, 2017) affecting the professional practices of all spheres involving children, young people and families. Through their Legacy Projects, students became part of a professional field impacted by child poverty and we later discuss some of the impactful career pathways resulting from this work.

Reading my chapter, you will gain the following three insights:
1. observe two worked examples of how different Legacy Projects connect and meaningfully synthesise theory to 'real world' practices;
2. reflect how Legacy Projects as a socially accountable pedagogy supports specific skills and knowledge development in a safe, supportive environment which promotes active learning and student ownership of assessment and learning outcomes; and
3. understand how students applied specific skills, knowledge and experience from the Legacy Projects for postgraduate training or employment applications at a later stage.

Overview of main sections

The chapter is divided into four sections. Section 1 sets the scene, identifying the 'undergraduate student experience' as the contextual backdrop, which inspired the Legacy Project as a process innovation. Section 2 introduces the new core spine of double-weighted 'employability' modules which ran on the BA (Hons) Childhood Studies, for the first time in 2018–19. Whilst the Legacy Project is a pedagogical approach that cuts across all three years, the specific focus of the chapter is on the year-2

Legacy Project, which students complete as a team. Section 3 describes the outcome. I focus firstly on the overall deliverables for the students themselves in terms of their final graduate outcomes, before I outline the different kinds of student learning evidence on two of the Legacy Projects. Finally, Section 4 describes our future aspirations for the Legacy Project before the conclusion.

Section 1: The Background

I became course director in October 2018 and was set with the task of 'turning around' the fortunes of the BA (Hons) Childhood Studies degree in a large and diverse School of Education. Our school seeks to redefine the education and professional development of the children and young people's workforce through distinctive and creative programmes responsive to the changes taking place in society and focusing on the diverse skills required of modern professionals. This is a large, interdisciplinary course with approximately 85 students in each year group. Most students entering our degree do not have a firm career destination in mind so part of the role of our degree is to develop content to support and enable a range of career trajectories.

Two factors inspired the Legacy Projects. First were external drivers (and institutional reputation) and the second was civic duty. The performance of the BA (Hons) Childhood Studies degree was poor as defined through the downward trend in both the course's Destination of Leavers of Higher Education (DLHE); and, the National Student Survey (NSS) statistics. These metrics, to a large extent, reflect the purposes of Higher Education in the UK now. Launched in 2005, the NSS is an annual survey composed of 28 questions scored on a Likert scale (*Definitely agree; Mostly agree; Neither agree nor disagree; Mostly disagree; Definitely disagree; Not applicable*) which collects the opinions of final year undergraduate students' opinions of the quality of their degree course. The NSS survey has been widely criticised as a clumsy tool to measure course quality since it positions "...*the student: not as a Newman scholar, learner or inquirer but as a consumer*" (Dean & Gibbs, 2015:5) which means the university comes to operate under forces of marketisation which limits academics to a service provider.

The DLHE survey ascertained what UK graduates are doing in terms of employment or study six months after graduation. However, since 2018, this was replaced by the Graduate Outcomes Survey, which graduates are asked to complete 15 months after graduating. In 2018, employment indicators suggested only about 25% of students graduating from a BA (Hons) Childhood Studies degree progressed to Highly Skilled Employment or Further Study. Employability is a key performance indicator when demonstrating institutional success. In this respect, our Legacy Projects can be viewed instrumentally as *'recognising and playing the game'* (Bathmaker et al., 2013). As this chapter unfolds, we do see how Legacy Projects shape and contribute to an upward trend in this area. This was also an ethical matter since UK undergraduate tuition fees are now £9,250 per year for 'home' students and £10,500 for international students, most students understandably want to see a long-term labour market return on this investment.

The second driver, I label as civic duty is captured in the University's Strategic Planning Framework (2020:np) in ensuring *"we use our knowledge and resources to make a positive and decisive difference to people, communities and organisations"*. The key phrase was *"decisive action"* as it denotes action, impact and results. Hence, the course team needed to reflect on how to design assessments for positive *"decisive action"* on 'real' children and families in the 'real world'. The Childhood Studies degree was revalidated; now having a core of double-weighted 'employability' modules running across the three years (*The Academic Self*; *The Professional Self*; and, *The Graduate Self*). In these modules, students undertake a placement of 180 hours, so upon graduation, students have accumulated 540 hours of practical work experience, which aim to instil those graduate-level skills and attributes that appeal to employers. The Legacy Project assessment has a problem-solving remit where students set for themselves clear and precise objectives and are held accountable to these. This was an important reconceptualisation since accountability is an important characteristic of the twenty-first-century workplace.

As a new form of teaching, learning and assessment, students work in groups to identify a need in their placement setting. They then design, plan and execute a Legacy Project with the broad purpose of adding something positive (either directly or indirectly) to the lives of children, young people and families in a specific setting. Unlike the traditional work placements which had come before, students are now held accountable for the outcomes of their work with children, young people or families on placement, and they present this in a final group presentation for their assessment.

Section 2: The Practice

2a: An introduction to the innovative practice

The new core spine of double-weighted 'employability' modules first ran in 2018–2019 and as a pedagogical approach which cuts across all three years, the Legacy Project is inherently social, with an emphasis on students as active participants 'owning' the project and being the driving force behind their innovation. In designing, planning and executing a Legacy Project, innovation means autonomy, experimentation, creativity and learning. When unexpected problems arise, students must be flexible and adaptable, show initiative in the way they work and apply disciplinary knowledge and concepts to create practical solutions.

As an assessment, students are held accountable rather than responsible for the outcomes of their Legacy Project. Accountability provides a structure which allows students to take ownership of their progress. The rationale here is that by learning how to respond to accountability – even in failure – students gain a deeper level of understanding of the impact of their decisions and are importantly learning how to work in an emotionally intelligent team. Although there is a rich literature on the value of group work in Higher Education, there was no easy way to hold students individually accountable for a group Legacy Project. An individually-graded portfolio of evidence which supports the group presentation seemed to provide the fairest method of evaluation. This included amongst other artefacts of evidence, each student's activity log which documented how, where and when each student spent their 180 hours; a timesheet and placement report completed and signed off by the placement host; and, 'before' and 'after' photographs to evidence impact. Cumulatively, this formed a robust record of each student's recorded participation and engagement.

In the second-year module *The Professional Self*, the Legacy Project works as a collaborative group project. Working as a team of 8–10 students alongside paid professionals within a professional organisation, students (depending on the project) gain experience of careful planning and preparation as a team, running a project to a schedule, identifying problems and implementing solutions, budget management, communication and so on. This is an authentic vehicle for students to develop graduate skills in an applied manner.

We wanted the placement to give students an insight into their career sectors of interest, so we firstly captured data on students' intended career choices at the end of year-1. Only a small minority of students had a concrete career goal in mind at this point. Using the information we had, we approached a broad range of organisations, representing the following breadth of professional sectors: teaching; special needs provision; charities/not for profit; youth work/criminal justice; counselling and healthcare. The major challenge for the year-2 placement was to find placements that would accommodate 8–10 students. Therefore, we contacted organisations directly, followed up suitable prospects with an e-mail and hosted an information event to explain more about what would be involved. Preparing the placement partnerships demanded a significant investment of time. Still, we committed to engage productively with local organisations to create long-term collaborations and we hope to continue working with them in the years to come. We emphasised the value we were expecting students to provide to the placement-provider and the following examples were used to highlight what a 'typical' Legacy Project might look like- both to the placement providers, and later to the students themselves:

- *Building a sensory garden for a specialist SEN school.* Pupils and teachers within the school might have identified the need for a stimulating space for learning which our students would turn into their Legacy Project. They would be responsible for researching the resources needed – choosing the right plants and materials – they would think about selecting plants and to evoke the five senses. They might then raise money, buy the materials, build the garden with the children, and assess its success using a model of their choosing.

- *Starting a Film Club at a Sure Start Children's Centre.* One of the workers at Sure Start notes that they have a lot of single mothers who come in for support- many feel lonely and lack confidence.

Students working in this setting might therefore set up a Film Club as a fun, open way to engage with these mothers and build trust- screening films based on the theme of mothering and design questions/activities to start conversations. To understand the barriers and create an intervention, they might draw on Bourdieu's (1977) concepts of habitus, capital and field and will then assess its success using a model of their choosing.

After this, we worked in conjunction with each placement provider to write an entry for the placement booklet. Information was organised with consistent headings, outlining the nature of the work within each setting, a suggested academic focus and a Person Specification describing the attributes students would need to possess to secure that placement. Some of the placement partners had a clear idea of what they thought would work in their settings, so they described 1–3 Legacy Projects students might work on, which we also included in the booklet. The last thing we wanted was for students' Legacy Projects to be 'botched' and amateurish, and the Placement Booklet had an important function in establishing a culture of accountability from the start by describing something of the demands of each workplace and the competencies students should demonstrate. Preparing the placement partners for the risk that the student Legacy Projects might fail to deliver the intended result was another important component at the planning stage. Here, the Placement Booklet and the weekly placement timesheet (documenting students' activities on placement) later helped to hold students to account if things did not go to plan, which inevitably often proved to be the case.

The students first interact with the group Legacy Project in the first lecture of *The Professional Self* module where they are presented with the Placement Book and the choice of nine professional pathways. Rather than simply allocate students to a professional pathway based on their preference alone, students are given two weeks to *'submit an application for consideration'*, and are then sorted and sifted on the 'match' of the skills, experiences and knowledge their application communicates. Thus, we are mimicking the reality of job applications in the 'real world'. As well as a 'sorting' tool, the application thus works usefully as a formative assessment tool (to identify skills which need building) and also, allows us to measure the 'distance travelled' throughout University and ultimately, the value we add as a Course Team. From the resulting applications, we determined we needed to build in specific employment literacies to yield positive outcomes when students prepare applications for jobs or postgraduate training in their final year of study.

The sort and shift of students into professional pathways based on their applications resulted in unfamiliar student teams. Students worked with students they did not yet know, so building teamwork and collaboration skills were vital to each team's success. Each team is allocated an academic advisor who provides the team support throughout the academic year. Rather than the outdated image of a 'sage on the stage' the academic advisor in this context acts as a coach – she listens, guides, questions, and challenges. The first component of the academic advisor's role is helping students define and focus the parameters of their group's Legacy Project. This covers all aspects of the Legacy Project cycle such as team building, identifying a need, goal setting, identifying and resolving issues and evaluating the end result. The second part of the academic advisor's role is to help students translate theoretical knowledge into practical skills to manage 'real-world' problems. The academic advisor -in both senses- is positioned as the More Knowledgeable Other (Vygotsky, 1978) who provides structure and support to her team of students through ongoing scaffolding to ensure each Legacy Project becomes a rich and stimulating mode of experiential learning (Kolb, 1984). As part of the wider learning strategy of experiential learning, this scaffolding is removed in the final year for *The Graduate Self* module when students themselves set the agenda for their tutorials together with their academic advisors.

Resourcing this adequately is key to success as academic advisors with appropriate expertise must be found to oversee each project. Fortunately, the BA (Hons) Childhood Studies degree is a large degree and benefits from a large academic team of lecturers coming from diverse professional backgrounds- each holding specialist subject knowledge and academic expertise. We cover two Case Studies in detail under Outcomes which shows some of this in practice, but below is a summary of the nine resulting Legacy Projects year-2 students designed and worked on 2018–19 to show how this played out in different places in several different ways. One of the goals was to enhance learning by integrating theory into practice at a deep, authentic level, so we include in brackets a synopsis of each theory employed in each:

- *Legacy Project 1: 'Showing' rather than 'telling' on the Knife Crime Intervention Project with West Yorkshire Police* (Bourdieu's, 1977, concepts of habitus and social capital).

- *Legacy Project 2: Helping children make good progress throughout different phases of education* (Vygotsky's, 1978, zone of proximal development).

- *Legacy Project 3: Supporting Leeds families who are living in poverty at Leeds Babybank* (Bronfenbrenner's, 2005, bioecological model of 'nested structures').

- *Legacy Project 4: Youth Work with Community Action for Hope In Harehills (CATCH)* (broad concepts of community and youth work).

- *Legacy Project 5: Promoting social connectivity through a new communal outdoor space at an outdoor activity centre used by children* (research on the benefits of outdoor environments).

- *Legacy Project 6: Fundraising £1600 for a new Childline Counsellor* (concepts of safeguarding and Child Protection).

- *Legacy Project 7: Engagement Project for Parents with Children with Complex and Multiple Needs* (framed around theorising and challenging the concepts of disablism/ ableism as per the work of Goodley, 2016).

- *Legacy Project 8: Designing a 'Fascination Zone' for Children across the Autistic Spectrum* (Kaplan & Kaplan's, 1989 1995/2005, theory of attention restoration coupled with the Japanese philosophy of 'Shinrin Yoku').

- *Legacy Project 9: A wellbeing project to support children with social, emotional and mental health needs* (the concept of positive regard as in Farber & Doolin, 2011).

2b: A brief overview of the curriculum

Table 1 below shows an overview of the BA (Hons) Childhood Studies curriculum which is interdisciplinary and designed for breadth and depth. Students undertake eleven compulsory core modules, covering the basic disciplines, and a choice of three elective modules to give students agency to focus on specialist areas relevant to career goals or interests. Students intending to become Social Workers would choose the *Working with Vulnerable Families* module, whereas a student interested in a career in counselling would choose the *Children's Counselling, Coaching and Mentoring* module. Each module has a role in fulfilling the University's three Graduate Attributes: digital literacy; holding a global outlook; and, to be enterprising.

To foster digital literacy students are encouraged to embrace digital technologies to facilitate both individual and group engagement. All materials and information needed for study are stored on the university's Virtual Learning Environment (VLE). This includes a range of learning, teaching and assessment resources such as module handbooks, e-books, journal articles, directed tasks and workbooks.

	TEACHING BLOCK 1	TEACHING BLOCK 2	TEACHING BLOCK 3
Y1	Core Modules: • Developmental Psychology • The Sociology of Childhood	Core Modules: • Children and Young People's Rights & Entitlements • Diverse Childhoods	Double-weighted core 'employability' module: • The Academic Self

	TEACHING BLOCK 1	TEACHING BLOCK 2	TEACHING BLOCK 3
Y2	Core Modules: • Social Inequality and Social Policy • Philosophy & Childhood	Core Module: Researching Childhood A choice of one elective module: • Child Wellbeing and Family Support • Issues in Early Childhood • Visual and Literary Perspectives on Childhood • Young People and Society	Double-weighted core 'employability' module: • The Professional Self
Y3	A choice of two elective modules: • Autism: The Needs of Children and Families • Black/white mixed-race lives: identity, childhood and schooling • Children's Counselling, Coaching and Mentoring • Children Crime and Social Justice • Health Promotion for Children and Families • Perspectives on Play • Working with Vulnerable Families	Double-weighted core module: • Major Independent Study	Double-weighted core 'employability' module: • The Graduate Self

Table 1: An overview of modules on the BA (Hons) Childhood Studies degree.

Students are also supported in developing a high level of competence, making informed judgements regarding the reliability and validity of different sources of information. For example, in year-1, *The Academic Self* module introduces students to online journal searching to locate complex literature and make quality judgements about the material. In the year-2 module, *The Professional Self* module, students foster community and collaboration by virtually collaborating on documents in teams and in *Philosophy and Childhood* students participate in online seminars to wrestle with challenging concepts. In year-3, the *Major Independent Study* module further augments these skills by supporting students to use a variety of digital means to plan and execute a research project, grounded in academic literature sourced and critiqued using online searching.

In terms of having a global outlook of childhood and children's lives, three key areas are represented in the curriculum: inter-cultural awareness, international perspectives, and application in practice. Students are encouraged to critically analyse the traditions, policies and practices in the UK and the 'west' to make the familiar unfamiliar, and by discovering the nature of childhood in diverse cultures, to make the unfamiliar familiar in new and different ways. In the year-1 core module, *Diverse Childhoods*, for instance, students observe the first year of a baby's life in diverse locations such as Tokyo, Namibia, Mongolia and San Francisco. In year-2 module, *Visual and Literary Representations of Childhood*, students explore the telling of fairy tales in different cultures and in *Philosophy and Childhood*, students use the Sapir-Whorf hypothesis (Carroll, 1956) to understand the connection between a child's language, thought and meaning and explore how language shapes the way a child thinks about the world.

In the employment module spine, 'being enterprising' broadly means activating skills, seizing opportunities, adapting to challenges and integrating academic knowledge into authentic problem-solving on 'real world' Legacy Projects. In the first year, students work closely with our placement team to arrange their own placement which is an important component of tailoring the Childhood Studies degree to specific interests or career goals, and here we encourage students to challenge themselves. This might mean becoming a volunteer counsellor for Childline, or applying to be a magistrate hearing cases in the Family Court. In year-2, as we have seen, students apply for a professional pathway. As they progress to *The Graduate Self* module a year later, students undertake their final placement and prepare to submit postgraduation applications for employment or training in a diverse range of fields including teaching, social work, nursing, counselling, occupational therapy, and graduate leadership programs. Through the 'being enterprising' curriculum strand, we also seek to enhance students' sense of worth and self-esteem as they gain confidence and resilience in tackling obstacles and attempting new ideas and practices.

2c: Organisation of the innovative practice

There is much backstage and off-stage work to do for the year-2 group Legacy Projects which does require time commitment in the planning stage, so here I distil the information presented in the following section about the practice into an easy step-by-step guide for any practitioners thinking of using this approach:

Step 1: Capture information about students' intended career destinations through a quick poll administered in the lecture theatre. Use this to identify high-quality placements which connect to these destinations. Consider the geographic spread of placement partners- some students will need to travel longer than others.

Step 2: Identify and secure a range of placements in the sectors students want to work in. Finding placement partners who will take 10 students is the most time-consuming part, it is worth investing time in sharing the benefits of working with a university.

Step 3: Once the placement partners have been secured; academic advisors are then asked to match themselves to a pathway based on their own areas of experience and expertise. Later, all academic advisors will be part of the 'sort and sift' of students into the different professional pathways and will then oversee their group's progress over the course of the year.

Step 4: The Course Director, year-2 level leader and academic advisors draft up a robust entry for each placement in the student placement handbook. This should be done in close conjunction with the placement provider. This is important as it provides an explicit statement of what the students and placement providers can expect. It serves as a document which the academic advisor can use if tensions arise during the Legacy Project.

Step 5: In the first lecture of the year, students are introduced to the group Legacy Project and are presented with a Placement Book, which gives a menu choice of professional pathways. Students have two weeks to '*submit an application for consideration*', and they list their top three placement choices on their application. We emphasise to students that it is crucial to comply with the deadline since it represents the cut-off date for the course team to consider all the applications – late applications cannot be considered, and students who do not submit by the deadline will be allocated a placement where there are spaces after the main 'sort and sift'.

Step 6: On the deadline date, the course team meets for a full afternoon to shortlist and match each student to a pathway based on the strength of their skills, experiences and knowledge communicated in their applications. In this year group, we were able to match all students to one of the three placements they had listed as a favourite on their application. The final student groupings for each Legacy Project and the academic advisor overseeing each pathway is communicated to students later this day.

Step 7: Expect at this point to receive complaints from a small minority of students who are dissatisfied at not receiving their first-choice pathway and have a procedure in place to manage this quickly and efficiently. In this case, the Course Director received two complaints which she addressed directly with the students concerned by giving individualised feedback on their application. As a target, and in the spirit of learning from experience, these students were asked to reflect on how they would use this advice when preparing their postgraduate applications in the following year.

Step 8: The academic advisors arrange to meet their own group of students later this week and are briefed on the nature of the placement itself as well, the learning outcomes they are expected to fulfil in their work, and what distinguishes a Legacy Project from a traditional placement. We are mindful of how language communicates intent and consciously employ language which encourages students to take responsibility and ownership of the group's decisions and actions from the start. Active, the second-person talk was typically used such as: "*Each team member has been given 180 hours, and as a group of 10, you are collectively responsible for how you use your 1800 hours*".

Step 9: The whole year group now receives fortnightly lectures on the broad nature of professionalism in *The Professional Self* module. The content of lectures included: 1) Understanding the dynamics of your team,

2) Using theory to shape practice, 3) Emotional labour, 4) Analysing the use of professional discourse in the workplace and 5) The role of professional standards in work with children and families. Students also receive a half-day training course in safeguarding and Child Protection. This work is contextualised in individual teams through directed tasks and regular tutorials with their academic advisor to discuss the progress of their Legacy Project. We ask students to maintain timesheets to log their experiences which makes it easy for each academic advisor to scrutinise the activity and outputs of their group of students.

Step 10: At the end of the academic year, students present their work and their finished Legacy Projects in a formal 30-minute group presentation which is delivered in a lecture theatre to the whole year group. Although this is a formal University assessment, the assessment day itself is pitched as a celebratory way to mark the end of the placement and also mark the end of the academic year. All the academic advisors, as well as the placement-partners, are invited to sit in on these assessments. For the students, this day provides another structured learning process as they provide feedback and critique to the other teams on the work presented. It helps to demystify the assignment itself, but also helps students share their own knowledge and learn from other students.

2d: Preparation of the innovative practice

An important distinction with *The Professional Self* module is that students must apply for a professional pathway rather than source their own placement, as they do in the first and final years of the degree. This is the first step of preparing students for placement but also for a competitive graduate employment field. The application itself is composed of three parts. The first is a CV which presents relevant skills and accomplishment, telling the story of each student's professional experience to date. The second part is an academic reflection which tells us how each student believes the concepts and theories learnt in year-1 modules will connect to the main activities and goals of their first-choice placement. This reflection forms the real starting point of students taking control of their own learning process. Thinking about what they already knew and determining which theory can be used to extend their understanding helps the application become an expression of the students' interests. Strategically, it also equips the course team with starting points from which academic advisors can help students to acquire academic and intellectual capital. At the start of year-2, students' perceptions of the placements and attempts to articulate the usefulness of module learning to these specific contexts were stated in indefinite terms such as:

- *"[Sociology] helped me learn about the unequal power distributions between people [on the basis of] social class, gender and race…This links in with my first choice…it is important that I respect and support everyone."* (Student applying for CATCH Placement Pathway).

- *"[The Development Psychology module] connects with Babybank as we looked directly at how children are affected developmentally by poverty and what can/ could be done…I will be researching the long-term effects on children brought up in this…"* (Student applying for Leeds Babybank Placement Pathway).

The final part of the application is the Personal Statement. In applying for postgraduate employment or training, students will be shortlisted according to their response to the essential and desirable criteria as detailed in a Person Specification. To write a strong personal statement, students need to study the job description and articulate their skills, knowledge and experience accordingly. Here we wanted to see how students identified the specific skills and qualities developed during their degree. We again found there was a tendency to overuse vague and generic phrases, such as:

- *"As a current Childhood Studies student, I have an in-depth knowledge of the development of children."*

- *"I am a highly motivated and reliable individual with a hard work ethic…"*

- *"One of the most rewarding aspects in life is seeing a young person grow in confidence, and having the opportunity to be part of that process is such a positive feeling."*

A year later, students would need to showcase specific knowledge, skills and attitudes developed on the degree as assets to present to employers, tailored to the context within which they seek to work. As well as a 'sorting' tool, the application works usefully as a formative assessment tool to identify skills which need building in this area and allow us as a course team to measure something of the 'distance travelled' throughout

University. From this exercise, we identified the need to build in specific application literacies which would hopefully enable students to navigate transitions into graduate employment or postgraduate training. Legacy Projects, though diverse in design, had the common aim of developing our students into employable, trainable graduates so graduate destinations will be the focus of our outcome in Section 3.

Section 3: The outcome

We are unable to document the outcomes from all 85 students from their work on the Legacy, so our focus is on two case studies. In the teacher perspective, we first draw on more general evidence of quality assurance from the External Examiner reports before exploring some of the challenges, constraints and assumptions the course team encountered. Undergirding the whole discussion are Kolb's (1984:25–38) six assumptions of experiential learning which provide a useful framework to take stock of what the work of the Legacy Projects achieved overall:

1. Learning is a 'holistic and adaptive process' rather than an outcome.
2. Learning is driven from experience which provides the basis for observation and reflection.
3. Learning requires the learner to resolve conflicts through dialogue.
4. Learning takes place through a holistic and integrative perspective that allows a role for consciousness and subjective experience.
5. Learning requires the dynamic interaction of the individual within her environment.
6. Learning is the process of creating knowledge.

3a: Student perspective

An overview of the graduate outcomes of this student cohort
As an active constructivist process, the Legacy Project assessment was devised as a new way of enabling students to think and practise in Childhood Studies with the long-term aim that the pay-off would come in the form of improved graduate outcomes. This aim was fulfilled. We

opened the chapter by describing the poor outcomes inherited on the BA (Hons) Childhood Studies degree, but 15 months after completing the group Legacy Projects and a month after completing their final year, 51% students of on the BA (Hons) Childhood Studies degree have now secured either graduate employment or places on postgraduate education courses and 12% still have applications pending. The remaining 37% of students are leaving university for jobs which are ambiguous in terms of the 'highly skilled or professional roles' graduate outcome- typically as a Pupil Support Worker, Teaching Assistant, or Family Support Worker. A small minority of students within this cohort are leaving university with an intention to undertake volunteering opportunities or unemployment.

Although we have yet to make 100% on the Graduate Outcomes Survey, the bulk of students in this cohort secured careers in the education, healthcare, criminal justice and social work sectors. The fact that students were leaving the degree for ethical professions undergirded by common values of empathy, compassionate care and equality perhaps points to something of a moral purpose to this mode of experiential learning which we had not anticipated. The course director had a very clear idea about what Childhood Studies students would become in the long term and it was not the cold, bureaucratic indifference which we see in the ambiguously titled 'Health Care Professional' in Ken Loach's (2016) social realist film *I, Daniel Blake*. The roles students did secure and the optimistic, positive attitudes expressed are the opposite end of the spectrum to this:

- *"Yesterday I had my nursing interview, and today they have sent me an e-mail and given me the place!!!...I am so excited, and I cannot put into words how grateful I am...I'm super excited to become a nurse, and I cannot wait..."*

- *"...I've been offered a place on the teacher training course! :) They seemed very eager to grab me up from the experiences I have had in school and the amount of acquired knowledge that I have about childhood as a whole."*

- *"I secured my first graduate job as a Pupil Support Worker!!! It was my very first interview, and I was successful!...so excited to finally be able to do what I love and really make a difference to young people's lives."*

To show how experiential learning on the Legacy Projects played out in different ways, we now turn to two that the year-2 students designed and worked on in *The Professional Self* module in 2018–19.

Spotlight on Legacy Project 1: 'Showing' rather than 'telling' on the Knife Crime Intervention Project with West Yorkshire Police
According to data from the National Audit Office and the Office for National Statistics, West Yorkshire had the highest rate of knife and 'sharp incident' crime outside London in 2018, and 18% involved children and young people aged 10–17. Under the mentorship of an experienced Police Constable at West Yorkshire Police, these students worked as the Blue Light Champions in preparing the groundwork for their Legacy Project, therefore, learnt about current anti-knife crime legislation, and what it means when a young person is cautioned, reprimanded or convicted. Academic input for this pathway was provided by an academic advisor who had worked as a Senior Analyst in the Force Intelligence Unit for West Yorkshire Police and has also co-edited two editions of a popular safeguarding textbook. Discussions in their group tutorials focused on the wider context of knife crime. By framing knife crime as a problem arising from issues of poverty, inequality and social deprivation, students generated a theoretical model based on Bourdieu's (1977) concepts of habitus and social capital to challenge the knife crime phenomenon. This informed the design of their Legacy Project as students sought to 'disrupt' social capital by transforming experience into knowledge.

The Blue Light Champions worked with 20 teenagers who were aged between 14 and 17. Sixteen young people in this group said that they would carry a knife for protection, so it was clear that simply making knowledge 'deposits' (Freire, 2018:76) about the dangers of carrying a knife was going to be ineffectual. Students felt it important to design a practical activity which directed young people towards a kind of 'experiential expertise', so they gave each young person a white t-shirt to wear and a red Bingo dabber pen. In a confined space, the young people had 15 seconds to try and put as many dots and lines on each other's t-shirts whilst avoiding being marked themselves. The students then placed each t-shirt over a life-sized body organs poster for the group to analyse the shirt as artefacts of knife crime. Students also planned a questioning strategy which fed in key facts: "*We can see multiple puncture wounds here,* but which vital organs would the knife have hit? Would this be a fatal wound? Actually, if you don't get to an ambulance within 30 seconds, you would die." This was a powerful intervention since, after the activity, 16 young people said they would not carry a knife, although the students themselves were surprised that 4 young people reported that they would still carry a knife.

This Legacy Project allowed students to communicate specific areas of expertise to suit the needs of the diverse sectors students chose to pursue in their postgraduate applications. The following examples showcase some of this:

- *"…Under the mentorship of an experienced Police Constable at West Yorkshire Police, we learnt about the wounds and injuries which is relevant since nurses now have a new legal duty to spot warning signs of knife violence."* (Student 1's application for MSc. Paediatric Nursing).

- *"Working in a team of 10 students with West Yorkshire Police on a knife crime intervention project will help me as a Social Worker since some of the young people came from families with histories of violence or neglect."* (Student 2's application for MA Social Work).

- *"During this placement, working constructively as a team was the only way to achieve success. We initially delegated job roles to each member of the team using Belbin's Team Role Theory."* (Student 3's application for the Leeds City Council Graduate program).

Each extract conveys a high level of professional legitimacy and importantly also avoids the vague and generic statements of learning showcased in Section 2a that the students had submitted only 15 months earlier. To further contextualise the third example, this student was drawn most to working in the Children and Families Directorate which consists of multidisciplinary teams delivering a range of services including services to support children with learning difficulties and disabilities.

Spotlight on Legacy Project 2: Helping children make good progress throughout different phases of education.

Students who successfully applied for the Education pathway had expressed a strong interest in postgraduate teacher-training in their applications. Some students were at the time working in after school clubs while others had not spent any time in a school since being a pupil. In this respect, the placement needed to be an effective testing ground. Rather than simply volunteering in schools though, students were encouraged to apply for paid work with Education Recruitment Agencies where they would gain experience in nurseries, primary, secondary, SEND (special educational needs and disabilities) schools and Pupil Referral Units. They would work as Supply Teachers, Cover Supervisors, Teaching Assistants and Teaching Support Staff which would allow each student to excavate something of the realities, dynamics and nuances to teaching and ultimately determine whether teacher-training was indeed for them. Each person had to complete a total of 180 hours but could choose from flexible daily supply, a part-time permanent role, or something in between. From this paid work, the rationale was that students would later be able to provide 'provable' references in their applications to postgraduate teacher-training programmes.

The academic advisor overseeing this pathway was experienced in teacher-training, having previously held a strategic leadership role for Initial Teacher Training by driving the Quality Assurance (QA) agenda. Here she oversaw every ITE student's progress for Teaching Standard 7 over eight-degree courses when behaviour-management was an OFSTED national priority area, an integral part of the framework of core content for Initial Teacher Training and one of the quality criteria that is used to determine the future allocation of training places.

Students chose to focus their final Legacy Project on their impacts on children's learning in the classroom. Close attention was paid to the DfE's (2012) Teaching Standard 2: *Promote good progress and outcomes by pupils*, and cumulatively, the group focused on the child's journey through the education system from EYFS to KS2. Focusing on specific outcomes set by the EYFS and National Curriculum for children to meet at each stage contextualised the 'expected' incremental growth of skills and knowledge. In the 'real world' of the classroom, students gained experience of using different methods to respond to the diverse strengths and needs of all children, including those with special educational needs; those of higher ability; and, those learning English as an additional language. Vygotsky's (1973) zone of proximal development was used as a theoretical foundation for the complexities of this work, and students applied Vygotsky's ideas to specific challenges within the classroom. Authentic classroom experiences, coupled with regular group tutorials with the academic advisor generally worked to enhance self-awareness and reflection on this Legacy Project. This skill set proved to be a useful resource later when students applied for and were interviewed for a place on postgraduate teacher-training courses, as they were able to draw on experiences which bypassed the clichéd two-dimensional 'I am passionate about becoming a teacher' responses.

One encouraging outcome to this placement pathway was how the placement itself enabled students to find their professional 'fit'. All teacher-training applicants on this pathway successfully secured offers to qualify to teach at all ages and stages with a range of teacher-training routes such as Red-Kite, School-centred initial teacher training (SCITT) program as well as the traditional postgraduate certificate in education (PGCE) route. Analysis of student testimonials reveal something of the specialist training and socialisation inherent in this Legacy Project as a constructivist process:

- "I completed 180 hours…, which has been graded as OFSTED 'outstanding'. I was placed in a year-2 class, …many areas of valuable experience from understanding the function of hands-on classroom experience of teaching and guiding pupils…Seeing the improvement that children made, emphasised for me the sense of accomplishment…" (Student 4's application for the PGCE Primary Education).

- "…I worked in a Reception class…seeing how they developed independence, confidence, resilience and curiosity. I gained experience of the 'Maths Mastery' approach…so they can move on confidently in their learning…" (Student 5's application for the PGCE EYFS Education).

In these two short extracts we see how both students draw heavily on the professional discourse of teachers in the UK: 'OFSTED outstanding'; 'comprehension groups'; 'lower-ability pupils'; 'Reception'; 'Maths Mastery approach'; 'secure knowledge'; 'KS1'. This seems to reveal something significant about the ways the Legacy Project can help to construct a professional identity and the ways in which specific kinds of professional selves are negotiated and enacted. For instance, to the casual observer, 'secure knowledge' may sound a commonplace phrase, but it holds special significance in the UK primary school since 'secure' was the adjective currently being used to describe attainment and progression of children within a primary school. Typically, primary schools were using three categories to document pupil progress as follows:

1. *Emerging*: Yet to be secure in the end of year expectations.

2. *Expected*: Secure in the end of year expectations.

3. *Exceeding*: Secure in almost all, or all, end of year expectations and able to display knowledge and skills confidently.

'Secure knowledge' is also a phrase lifted from the DfE's (2011:np) Teacher's Standards where teachers must *"…have a secure knowledge of the relevant subject(s) and curriculum areas, foster and maintain pupils' interest in the subject, and address misunderstandings."* The academic advisor had focused on exploring the content of the Teacher's Standards in her tutorials since these set the minimum requirements for teachers' practice and conduct.

For two students on this pathway, the reality and demands presented from the placements revealed a mismatch. As demonstrated with students working on other Legacy Projects, sometimes the mismatch revealed a lack of fit between the student's beliefs and perceptions and the requirements of the job and these two students judged that teaching was not the career for them. Like Student 4, our first student had gained much experience of working with small groups of Primary School on guided reading interventions which she enjoyed. This practical experience, coupled with a serendipitous tutorial with the academic advisor, triggered an interest in the psychological aspects of learning. She successfully applied for a place to study an MSc. in Educational Psychology with the ambition of becoming an Educational Psychologist.

The tutorial which was significant was one where the students had been comparing experiences of working with bilingual children. The academic advisor asked students to imagine the worldview of a bilingual child. To demonstrate the concept, the academic advisor discussed how an abstract concept of time in the English language runs on a horizontal continuum, so the past is *behind* us, and the future is *in front* of us. We can move meetings *back* or *forward*. This is something we take for granted, but for the Mandarin speaker, time is also vertical with the past being above us and the future being below, so rather than travelling through time, we drop through it. In the measurement outcomes for year-1 mathematics, children in England are expected to measure and begin to record the time (hours, minutes, seconds) and tell the time *to* the hour and half *past* the hour, which again draws on a notion of time moving horizontally. This was recapping on the Sapir-Whorf hypothesis (Carroll, 1956) which students had covered earlier in the year, and in particular, a close seminar reading of a paper by Boroditsky (2001) but the abstract theory was brought to life when brought to bear upon concrete experiences from placement.

Another student applied for the Education pathway with the original career goal of qualifying to be an Art Teacher in the secondary phase of education where he would work with 11–18-year olds. He was a keen artist who worked to commissions, but his experience of working and interacting in an art department of a Secondary School challenged his mind as he explained in an e-mail:

- *"…I really wanted to be an art teacher at a secondary school or college because …this is where students really will make or break as an artist… The teachers always seemed snowed under with work…the art teachers seemed to be neglected by the higher heads of the school…some students were really rude to me…throwing paints at each other…I didn't really know how to handle this (…) I think working as a teacher everyday just would not be suited to me."*

According to Kolb (1984), experiential learning is a holistic and integrative perspective involving the whole body and, in this account, we see how this student learns not *from* experience but learns *in* experience through emotions, sensations, perception and cognition. Completing the year-2 Legacy Project ultimately propelled this student to take a completely different career direction, and this student went on to successfully apply for a postgraduate Physiotherapy (pre-registration) course.

End reflections from the student perspective:

The role of placement experience on the BA (Hons) Childhood Studies degree should not be underestimated. Where it works best, this constructivist process innovation allowed students to reach informed choices about their career paths. Although most students gained positive results, a note of caution must be drawn in assuming this had a uniformly positive effect, and in the following teacher perspective, we go on to discuss some of the challenges, constraints and assumptions that must be taken into consideration to reach a balanced view.

3b: Teacher perspective- my reflections

Overall, the External Examiner stated of *The Professional Self* module that, "*This assessment task is highly effective in supporting transferable student employability skills including professional liaison, group collaboration and presentation*" and one long term major pay off as we discussed earlier has been the realisation of concrete career goals. Although student motivation and engagement sometimes came later than expected, we are able to see the enthusiasm and personal satisfaction oozing from some of the e-mails documented in the student perspective. The year-2 group Legacy Projects was part of a raft of changes, so it was a relief when the External Examiners reported of the degree as a whole, "*What is in place on the Childhood Studies degree course, across all areas on the teaching and learning, can only be described as best practice. I fully commend the teaching team on their success in delivering a wonderfully multifaceted degree course.*" No actions were set – the External Examiners gave glowing reports of our course which gave both the 'new' course director (9 months in post at the time) and the 'new' course team confidence that we were delivering a rigorous, job-relevant degree. There was however one note of caution in the report: "*… it is imperative that the degree is continued to be effectively resourced and staffed, in order for tutors to maintain the excellent standards outlined in this report.*" We therefore take the time to reflect upon some of the resourcing issues here.

As a method of experiential learning, the Legacy Projects were designed to help students develop the skills required for independent problem-solving. This did, however, assume that students would benefit from autonomy and be motivated by taking ownership. To a large extent, this goal was realised, as students shared this unprompted in their Module Evaluations in comments like: "*I enjoyed being able to have more control over activities in my placement*" and, "[This work] *inspired me and given me the courage to just go out there and get what I want.*" However, designing, carrying out and assessing the Legacy Projects as a pedagogy meant navigating carefully through some political minefields like how best to promote long-term graduate employment and how to mobilise capitals to enhance future social mobility which raised challenges in the ways we shape student expectations and manage their professional learning needs.

First, in the initial stages there was a disconnect between what students perceived they could realistically 'do' for their year-2 group Legacy Project in a real work setting. For instance, on a BA (Hons) Childhood Studies degree, it is never going to be possible to send unqualified year-2 students to deliver unsupervised therapeutic interventions to vulnerable children with social, emotional and mental health needs in the role of an Art Therapist without the necessary qualifications; nor, was it possible to walk into a setting and expect to gain first-hand experiences of Child Protection cases by 'doing' Social Work with vulnerable families living in hardship and poverty. This is obvious and perhaps reflective of students' own naiveites, but in the first year in post, managing student expectations is where the bulk of the academic advisors' time went, so it is important to be aware of the resource implications of this.

There was also a failure to recognise the potential within each placement, which came out in three comments in the module evaluation. For instance, one comment read: *"I feel that the course should have made more connections with organisations working with contemporary issues within childhood, such as mental health."* (Module Evaluation comment). Collectively, the placements offered a context to work with a rich body of contemporary issues within childhood, including poverty, inclusion, teenage knife crime, to name but some; and, there were two opportunities for students to gain specific experience of supporting children and young people's mental health and emotional wellbeing. The first was the SEMH school which contains three explicit references to mental health; and on, the NSPCC pathway at the application stage, students were presented with two options: charity fundraising or applying to be a Childline counsellor where students would gain experience of supporting children with different mental health issues. Despite further promoting this role in lectures and seminars as well as the placement booklet itself, none of the students chose to apply to train as a Childline counsellor, and this student did not express an interest in mental health in her application some months' earlier.

While we could not use comments like these to make concrete adjustments to the placement provision itself, the information collected from the module evaluations was incredibly useful as it highlights something noteworthy about Kolb's (1984:33) notion of knowledge as 'a holistic, adaptive process' rather than an outcome. The process of submitting a module evaluation gives students the opportunity to reflect something of their educational experience, and the words are like icebergs with the meanings lying beneath the surface. As a year-2 student who is just beginning to hone skills in the specific disciplinary ways of thinking from Childhood Studies, the use of jargon unwittingly presents a barrier to effective communication. In this specific feedback comment, we can see that while we are initially lulled into a false sense of security by the use of specialist terminology, this would, without analysis, obscure the need to be attentive to developing students' cognitive abilities as an ongoing professional development need. Although specific lectures are provided on both the needs of each placement before students make their applications, and the nature of professional discourse in the workplace, more space perhaps needs to be given in seminars to interrogate what the language of each placement entry meant to students so they can make informed, carefully-considered judgements on the applications for their first-choice pathways. It also continues to stress the importance of ensuring that students are skilled at identifying the skills, knowledge and experiences they can document in postgraduate applications.

This is a point affirmed in the individual conversations which continued to take place between students and academic advisors in year-3 module, *The Graduate Self*. To show a 'typical' snapshot of this playing out in practice, the following student's ambition was to train as a Psychological Well-being Practitioner, but she could not see the relevancy of the experiences she had accrued so far:

- *"My experience with…wasn't exactly what I was expecting…I am more interested in working with adolescents rather than young children, and I am particularly interested in mental health…it has not really equipped me with the experience I need to enhance my skills towards my future career."* (E-mail correspondence).

The academic advisor's response to this was 100% positive. She reassured her through e-mail that this was all excellent experience which does link to her intended career destination: *"The trick is to pull out the 'right' bits in your future applications"*. To enable her to view the placement experience as relevant, the academic advisor invested time in crafting bespoke prompts for her. These prompts were drawn from a collection of materials including the academic advisor's knowledge of the student's work on the year-2 group project, the student's timesheets, the academic feedback provided at the time; and knowledge of two of the elective modules the student was studying at the time. We include a snippet of the prompts which draws on the latter:

- *"All of the children here have experienced domestic violence, trauma and loss. Some of these children have been forced to leave their home. Can you...reflect on the importance of your role in this setting? You have gained a good understanding of the impact of trauma on children from the Working with Vulnerable Families module. Did you see anything of this expressed in the nursery?(....) How did this understanding motivate you to provide both emotional and practical support for these children and their mothers?"* (extract from academic advisor's notes).

What may be gleaned from the prompts are the meaningful interconnections the academic advisor is able to forge from both the placement and specific elements of module learning. These more informal and spontaneous modes of academic advising have a powerful pedagogical impact; taking the time to do this paid off as can be seen from this student's reply:

- *"It's funny because I went into...after I had read your e-mail and I really started to notice more how it was related to what I'd like to do in the future, it was almost as if I had a completely new perspective on everything...I'm definitely going to start focusing on my application for jobs now I have had your help."* (E-mail correspondence).

Overall, while the Legacy Projects enabled students to gain and construct knowledge by interacting with the relevance of theory to placement, we can, however, see something of the resourcing implications inherent in developing and nurturing students' capacities for this work.

Section 4: Moving forward

Self-reflection is a basic part of teaching and learning and, *"it is not sufficient to have an experience in order to learn. Without reflecting on this experience, it may quickly be forgotten, or its learning potential lost"* (Gibbs,

1988:9). The Legacy Projects started at ground zero with nothing and scaffolding had to be constructed on an as-needed basis which was complicated, time-consuming and involved fire-fighting. Over a year later, though, we are now able to see benefits. The increased personal interaction with students as they prepared postgraduate applications has been transformed into a resource, *The Big Book of Childhood Studies Careers* for students in *The Academic Self*; *The Professional Self*; and *The Graduate Self* modules to enable students to reflect thoughtfully and honestly about their 'possible professional selves' and how to plan their journeys strategically through the degree to secure their long-term career ambitions. Thus, despite increased massification and commodification of UK Higher Education, with this innovation, we hope to continue to show in real terms how universities can be *"the gatekeepers of opportunity"* (Millburn 2012:2). All of this practical intervention work on Graduate Outcomes is crucial at the course level in a discipline such as Childhood Studies which concerns itself with matters of social justice and connects in with the Carnegie School of Education's branding – there is absolutely no point in us talking about social justice and social mobility unless we exercise it in our own practices.

Conclusion

This chapter has introduced Legacy Projects as an effective example of a process innovation which enhances the undergraduate student learning experience in a number of ways. The results, as described, allow for the following conclusions to be drawn.

The major student benefit of Legacy Projects lies in the realisation of concrete career goals a year later, which played a role in raising student satisfaction. The introduction of collaborative group work group in real-world situations enabled students to prepare authentic applications for postgraduate employment and training which drew on concrete knowledge, skills and experiences from their year-2 Legacy Projects which would never have materialised in a conventional classroom context. As a pedagogic approach, the Legacy Projects increased employability skills. Constructivism emphasises student construction of their own understandings and Kolb (1984) places emphasis on creating spaces for dialogue to resolve conflicts. Academic advising is the cornerstone of the learning in Legacy Projects and this role, when done well, results in a better understanding of students' needs and attitudes towards both placement and studies. The skilled academic advisor uses students' needs and attitudes as a starting point to scaffold learning.

At the student level, however, it also necessitates a close examination of the relationship between higher education and wider structural inequalities, and how to mobilise capital for graduate employment. Attracting, recruiting and retaining students from areas underrepresented in higher education has been positive but in order to adequately support these students into highly skilled graduate employment, a true commitment to the cause and greater investment is needed which has resource implications. The students described herein were the first-year group pushed through this new model and we are now seeing stronger ambition coming through in first and second-year students. This chapter shows something of the work entailed in moving from macro-level down to individual student level to diagnose student needs and develop bespoke interventions. It is unfortunate that the accountability built into UK higher education from tools such as the NSS excludes information on the value of this work; students do not always recognise this as one of the 'extras' we provide.

About the Author

Sarah Swann is Course Director of Childhood Studies at Leeds Beckett University. She can be contacted at this e-mail: s.swann@leedsbeckett.ac.uk.

Bibliography

Bathmaker, A. M., Ingram, N. & Waller, R. (2013). Higher education, social class, and the mobilisation of capitals: recognising and playing the game. *British Journal of Sociology of Education*, 34, pp. 723–743.

Boroditsky, L. (2001). Does Language Shape Thought?: Mandarin and English Speakers' Conceptions of Time. *Cognitive Psychology*, 43, pp. 1–22.

Bourdieu, P. (1977). *Outline of a Theory of Practice*. Cambridge: Cambridge University Press.

Bronfenbrenner, U. (Ed.) (2005). *Making human beings human: Bioecological perspectives on human development.* Sage Publications Ltd.

Carroll, J. B. (Ed.) (1956). *Introduction to Language, Thought and Reality: Selected writings of Benjamin Lee Whorf.* Cambridge, Mass: MIT Press.

Cooper, V. & Whyte, D. (Eds.) (2017). *The Violence of Austerity.* London: Pluto Press.

Dean, A. & Gibbs, P. (2015). Student satisfaction or happiness? *Quality Assurance in Education* 23(1), pp. 5–19.

Department for Education (DfE) (2012). *Teachers' Standards.* Accessed online October 16, 2020: https://www.gov.uk/government/publications/teachers-standards

Department for Work and Pensions. (2011). Healthcare professionals: their role in the provision of DWP benefits and services. London: The Stationery Office.

Dobozy, E. & Nygaard, C. (2021). A learning-centred five-tier model of innovation in higher education. In Enomoto, K., Warner, R. & Nygaard, C. (Eds.), *Teaching and Learning Innovations in Higher Education*, pp. 19–46. Oxfordshire, UK: Libri Publishing Ltd.

Farber, B. A. & Doolin, E. M. (2011). Positive regard. *Psychotherapy*, 48, pp. 58–64.

Farrar, M. (2002). The Northern "Race Riots" of the Summer of 2001 – Were They Riots, Were They Racial? A case study of the events in Harehills, Leeds. *Presentation to Parallel Lives and Polarisation workshop*, British Sociological Association 'Race' Forum, City University, London.

Freire, P. (2018) *Pedagogy of the oppressed.* USA: Bloomsbury Publishing.

Gibbs, G. (1988). *Learning by doing: a guide to teaching and learning methods.* Oxford: Further Education Unit, Oxford Polytechnic.

Goodley, D. (2016). *Disability Studies. An Interdisciplinary Introduction.* London: Sage Publications Limited.

Kaplan, R. & Kaplan, S. (1989). *The Experience of Nature: A Psychological Perspective*, Cambridge, Mass.: Cambridge University Press.

Kaplan, R. & Kaplan, S. (1995). Restorative experience: the healing power of nearby nature. In Francis, M. & Hester, R. (Eds.), *The Meaning of Gardens*, pp. 238–243. Cambridge, Mass.: MIT Press.

Kaplan, R. & Kaplan, S. (2005). Preference, restoration and meaningful action in the context of nearby nature. In Bartlett, P. (Ed.), *Urban Place: reconnecting with the natural world*, pp. 271–299. Cambridge, Mass.: MIT Press.

Kolb, D. (1984). *Experiential Learning: Experience as the source of learning and development.* New Jersey: Prentice-Hall.

Leeds Beckett University. (2020). *Strategic Planning Framework*. Accessed online October 16, 2020: https://www.leedsbeckett.ac.uk

Loach, K. (Dir.) (2016). *I, Daniel Blake*. UK: Sixteen Films.

Milburn, A. (2012). *University Challenge*: How *Higher Education Can Advance Social Mobility a Progress Report* by the *Independent Reviewer* on *Social Mobility* and *Child Poverty*. London: Cabinet Office.

Vygotsky, L. S. (1978). *Mind in society: The development of higher psychological processes*. Cambridge, Mass.: Harvard University Press.

Willcocks, J. & Lange, S. (2021). Using cross-disciplinary object-based learning to create collaborative learning environments. In Enomoto, K., Warner, R. & Nygaard, C. (Eds.), *Teaching and Learning Innovations in Higher Education*, pp. 451–473. Oxfordshire, UK: Libri Publishing Ltd.

www.ingramcontent.com/pod-product-compliance
Lightning Source LLC
Chambersburg PA
CBHW071723080526
44588CB00013B/1880